W9-AZS-591

ANNUAL EDITIONS

Sociology

07/08

Thirty-sixth Edition

Editor

Kurt Finsterbusch
University of Maryland, College Park

Kurt Finsterbusch received a bachelor's degree in history from Princeton University in 1957 and a bachelor of divinity degree from Grace Theological Seminary in 1960. His Ph.D. in sociology, from Columbia University, was conferred in 1969. Dr. Finsterbusch is the author of several books, including *Understanding Social Impacts* (Sage Publications, 1980), *Social Research for Policy Decisions* (Wadsworth Publishing, 1980, with Annabelle Bender Motz), and *Organizational Change as a Development Strategy* (Lynne Rienner Publishers, 1987, with Jerald Hage). He is currently teaching at the University of Maryland, College Park, and, in addition to serving as editor for *Annual Editions: Sociology,* he is also editor of *Annual Editions: Social Problems,* and McGraw-Hill/Dushkin's *Taking Sides: Clashing Views on Controversial Social Issues.*

 **Contemporary Learning Series**

2460 Kerper Blvd., Dubuque, IA 52001

Visit us on the Internet
http://www.mhcls.com

Credits

1. **Culture**
   Unit photo—Getty Images/Monica Lau
2. **Socialization and Social Control**
   Unit photo—Royalty-Free/CORBIS
3. **Groups and Roles in Transition**
   Unit photo—Big Cheese Photo/Jupiter Images
4. **Stratification and Social Inequalities**
   Unit photo—Eric Audras/Photo Alto/Picture Quest
5. **Social Institutions: Issues, Crises, and Changes**
   Unit photo—Royalty-Free/CORBIS
6. **Social Change and the Future**
   Unit photo—Photo Alto

Copyright

Cataloging in Publication Data
Main entry under title: Annual Editions: Sociology. 2007/2008.
1. Sociology—Periodicals. Kurt Finsterbusch. Title: Sociology.
ISBN: 978–0–07–339733–7   MHID: 0–07–339733–4   658'.05   ISSN 0277–9315

Thirty-sixth Edition

Cover image © Brand X Pictures/PunchStock and F64/Getty Images
Compositor: Laserwords Private Limited

Editors/Advisory Board

Members of the Advisory Board are instrumental in the final selection of articles for each edition of ANNUAL EDITIONS. Th of articles for content, level, currentness, and appropriateness provides critical direction to the editor and staff. We think that y find their careful consideration well reflected in this volume.

EDITOR

Kurt Finsterbusch
University of Maryland, College Park

ADVISORY BOARD

Peter K. Angstadt
Wesley College

Jason L. Blank
Rhode Island College

Gail Bonnell
Jefferson Community and Technical College

Kenneth Colburn
Butler University

William F. Daddio
Georgetown University

Brenda Forster
Elmhurst College

Gary Heath
Ashford University

Anna Karpathakis
Kingsborough Community College

Joseph A. McFalls
Villanova University

Kathy K. Miller
Concordia University

Larry Rosenberg
Millersville University

Rita P. Sakitt
Suffolk Community College

Margaret A. Terry
North Carolina State University

Lisa Grey Whitaker
Arizona State University

Joseph D. Yenerall
Duquesne University

Staff

Preface

In publishing ANNUAL EDITIONS we recognize the enormous role played by the magazines, newspapers, and journals of the public press in providing current, first-rate educational information in a broad spectrum of interest areas. Many of these articles are appropriate for students, researchers, and professionals seeking accurate, current material to help bridge the gap between principles and theories and the real world. These articles, however, become more useful for study when those of lasting value are carefully collected, organized, indexed, and reproduced in a low-cost format, which provides easy and permanent access when the material is needed. That is the role played by ANNUAL EDITIONS.

The new millennium has arrived with difficult new issues such as how to deal with new levels of terrorism, while many of the old issues remain unresolved. There is much uncertainty. Almost all institutions are under stress. The political system is held in low regard because it seems to accomplish so little, to cost so much, and to focus on special interests more than the public good. The economy has recovered from the recession but the debt is huge. In the long term it suffers from foreign competition, trade deficits, economic uncertainties, and a worrisome concentration of economic power in the hands of relatively few multinational corporations. Complaints about the education system continue, because grades K–12 do not teach basic skills well and college costs are too high. Health care is too expensive, many Americans lack health care coverage, and some diseases are becoming resistant to our medicines. The entertainment industry is booming, but many people worry about its impact on values and behavior.

News media standards seem to be set by the tabloids. Furthermore, the dynamics of technology, globalization, and identity groups are creating crises, changes, and challenges. Crime rates have declined somewhat, but they are still at high levels. The public is demanding more police, more jails, and tougher sentences, but less government spending. Government social policies seem to create almost as many problems as they solve. The use of toxic chemicals has been blamed for increases in cancer, sterility, and other diseases. Marriage and the family have been transformed, in part by the women's movement and in part by the stress that current conditions create for women who try to combine family and careers. Schools, television, and corporations are commonly vilified. Many claim that morality has declined to shameful levels. Add to all this the worldwide problems of ozone depletion, global warming, deforestation, soil loss, desertification, and species loss and it is easy to be pessimistic. Nevertheless, crises and problems also create opportunities.

The present generation may determine the course of history for the next 200 years. Great changes are taking place, and new solutions are being sought where old answers no longer work. The issues that the current generation faces are complex and must be interpreted within a sophisticated framework. The sociological perspective provides such a framework. It expects people to act in terms of their positions in the social structure, within the political, economic, and social forces operating on them, and in the norms that govern the situation.

Annual Editions: Sociology 07/08 should help you to develop the sociological perspective that will enable you to determine how the issues of the day relate to the way that society is structured. The articles provide not only information but also models of interpretation and analysis that will guide you as you form your own views. In addition, both the Topic Guide and the Internet References can be used to further explore the book's topics.

This thirty-sixth edition of *Annual Editions: Sociology* emphasizes social change, institutional crises, and prospects for the future. It provides intellectual preparation for acting for the betterment of humanity in times of crucial change. The sociological perspective is needed more than ever as humankind tries to find a way to peace, prosperity, health, and well-being that can be maintained for generations in an improving environment. The numerous obstacles that lie in the path of these important goals require sophisticated responses. The goals of this edition are to communicate to students the excitement and importance of the study of the social world, and to provoke interest in and enthusiasm for the study of sociology.

Annual Editions: Sociology depends upon reader response in order to develop and change. You are encouraged to return the postage-paid article rating form at the back of the book with your opinions about existing articles, recommendations of articles you think have sociological merit for subsequent editions, and advice on how the anthology can be made more useful as a teaching and learning tool.

Kurt Finsterbusch

Kurt Finsterbusch,
Editor
Dedicated to young people who are
willing to work to improve the world.

Contents

UNIT 1
Culture

The concepts in bold italics are developed in the article. For further expansion, please refer to the Topic Guide and the Index.

UNIT 2
Socialization and Social Control

UNIT 3
Groups and Roles in Transition

The concepts in bold italics are developed in the article. For further expansion, please refer to the Topic Guide and the Index.

UNIT 4
Stratification and Social Inequalities

The concepts in bold italics are developed in the article. For further expansion, please refer to the Topic Guide and the Index.

UNIT 5
Social Institutions: Issues, Crises, and Changes

The concepts in bold italics are developed in the article. For further expansion, please refer to the Topic Guide and the Index.

UNIT 6
Social Change and the Future

The concepts in bold italics are developed in the article. For further expansion, please refer to the Topic Guide and the Index.

The concepts in bold italics are developed in the article. For further expansion, please refer to the Topic Guide and the Index.

The concepts in bold italics are developed in the article. For further expansion, please refer to the Topic Guide and the Index.

Topic Guide

This topic guide suggests how the selections in this book relate to the subjects covered in your course. You may want to use the topics listed on these pages to search the Web more easily.

On the following pages a number of Web sites have been gathered specifically for this book. They are arranged to reflect the units of this *Annual Edition*. You can link to these sites by going to the student online support site at *http://www.mhcls.com/online/*.

ALL THE ARTICLES THAT RELATE TO EACH TOPIC ARE LISTED BELOW THE BOLD-FACED TERM.

Internet References

The following Internet sites have been carefully researched and selected to support the articles found in this reader. The easiest way to access these selected sites is to go to our student online support site at *http://www.mhcls.com/online/.*

Annual Editions: Sociology 07/08

The following sites were available at the time of publication. Visit our Web site—we update our student online support site regularly to reflect any changes.

General Sources

Library of Congress
http://www.loc.gov

Examine this extensive Web site to learn about resource tools, library services/resources, exhibitions, and databases in many different subfields of sociology.

Intute: Social Sciences
http://sosig.esrc.bris.ac.uk

Formerly SOSIG, this online catalog of Internet resources is relevant to social science education and research. Resources are selected by librarians or subject specialists.

Sociological Tour Through Cyberspace
http://www.trinity.edu/~mkearl/index.html

Prepared by Michael Kearl at Trinity University, this extensive site provides essays, commentaries, data analyses, and links on death and dying, family, the sociology of time, social gerontology, social psychology, and more.

Unit 1: Culture

New American Studies Web
http://www.georgetown.edu/crossroads/asw/

This eclectic site provides links to a wealth of resources on the Web related to American studies: gender studies, environment, race, and more. It is of great help when doing research in demography, genealogy, and population studies.

Anthropology Resources Page
http://www.usd.edu/anth/

Many cultural topics can be accessed at this site from the University of South Dakota. Click on the links to find information about differences and similarities in values and lifestyles among the world's peoples.

Human Rights and Humanitarian Affairs
http://www.etown.edu/vl/humrts.html

Through this part of the World Wide Web Virtual Library, you can conduct research into a number of human-rights topics in order to gain a greater understanding of issues affecting indigenous peoples in the modern era. The site also provides links to many other subjects related to sociology.

Unit 2: Socialization and Social Control

Center for Leadership Studies
http://www.situational.com

The Center for Leadership Studies (CLS) is organized for the research and development of the full range of leadership in individuals, teams, organizations, and communities.

Crime Times
http://www.crime-times.org

This interesting site lists research reviews and other information regarding causes of criminal, violent, and psychopathic behavior. It is provided by the Wacker Foundation, publishers of *Crime Times.*

Ethics Updates/Lawrence Hinman
http://ethics.sandiego.edu/

This site provides both simple concept definition and complex analysis of ethics, original treatises, and sophisticated search-engine capability. Subject matter covers the gamut, from ethical theory to applied ethical venues. There are many opportunities for user input.

National Institute on Drug Abuse (NIDA)
http://www.nida.nih.gov/

Use this site index of the National Institute on Drug Abuse for access to NIDA publications and communications, information on drugs of abuse, and links to other related Web sites.

Unit 3: Groups and Roles in Transition

The Gallup Organization
http://www.gallup.com

Links to an extensive archive of public opinion poll results and special reports on a huge variety of topics related to American society are available on this Gallup Organization home page.

Marriage and Family Therapy
http://www.aamft.org/index_nm.asp

This site has links to numerous marriage and family therapy topics. Online directories, books and articles are also available.

The North-South Institute
http://www.nsi-ins.ca/english/default.asp

Searching this site of the North-South Institute—which works to strengthen international development cooperation and enhance gender and social equity—will help you find information on a variety of issues related to social transitions.

PsychNet/American Psychological Association
http://www.apa.org/topics/homepage.html

By exploring this site, you will be able to find links to an abundance of articles and other resources related to interpersonal relationships throughout the life span.

SocioSite: Feminism and Woman Issues
http://www.pscw.uva.nl/sociosite/TOPICS/Women.html

Open this enormous sociology site of the University of Amsterdam's Sociological Institute to gain insights into a number of issues that affect both men and women. It provides biographies of women through history, an international network for women in the workplace, links to gay studies, affirmative action, family and children's issues, and much more. Return to the site's home page for many other sociological links.

Unit 4: Stratification and Social Inequalities

Americans With Disabilities Act Document Center
http://www.jan.wvu.edu/links/adalinks.htm

This Web site, the Job Accommodation Network, contains copies of the Americans With Disabilities Act of 1990 (ADA) and ADA regulations. This Web site also provides you with links to other Internet sources of information concerning disability issues.

American Scientist
http://www.amsci.org/amsci/amsci.html

Investigating this Web site of the *American Scientist* will help students of sociology to access a variety of articles and to explore issues and concepts related to race and gender.

Give Five
http://www.independentsector.org/give5/givefive.html

The Give Five Web site is a project of Independent Sector, a national coalition of foundations, voluntary organizations, and corporate giving programs working to encourage giving, volunteering, not-for-profit initiatives, and citizen action.

Joint Center for Poverty Research
http://www.jcpr.org

Finding research information related to poverty is possible at this site. It provides working papers, answers to FAQs, and facts about who is poor in America. Welfare reform is also addressed.

NAACP Online: National Association for the Advancement of Colored People
http://www.naacp.org

The principal objective of the NAACP is to ensure the political, educational, social, and economic equality of minority group citizens in the United States.

Unit 5: Social Institutions: Issues, Crises, and Changes

Center for the Study of Group Processes
http://www.uiowa.edu/~grpproc/

The mission of the Center for the Study of Group Processes includes promoting basic research in the field of group processes and enhancing the professional development of faculty and students in the field of group processes.

International Labour Organization (ILO)
http://www.ilo.org

ILO's home page leads to links that describe the goals of the organization and summarizes international labor standards and human rights. Its official UN Web site locator can point to many other useful resources.

IRIS Center
http://www.iris.umd.edu

The project on Institutional Reform and the Informal Sector (IRIS) aims to understand transitional and developing economies. Examine this site to learn about research into government institutions and policies that helps to promote successful economic change in the global age.

National Center for Policy Analysis
http://www.ncpa.org

Through this site, you can reach links that provide discussions of an array of topics that are of major interest in the study of American politics and government from a sociological perspective, including regulatory policy, affirmative action, and income.

National Institutes of Health (NIH)
http://www.nih.gov

Consult this site for links to extensive health information and scientific resources of interest to sociologists from the NIH, one of eight health agencies of the Public Health Service.

Unit 6: Social Change and the Future

Human Rights and Humanitarian Affairs
http://www.etown.edu/vl/humrts.html

Through this part of the World Wide Web Virtual Library, you can conduct research into a number of human-rights concerns around the world. The site also provides links to many other subjects related to important social issues.

The Hunger Project
http://www.thp.org

Browse through this nonprofit organization's site to explore how it tries to achieve its goal: the end to global hunger through leadership at all levels of society. The Hunger Project contends that the persistence of hunger is at the heart of the major security issues threatening our planet.

Terrorism Research Center
http://www.terrorism.com/index.shtml

The Terrorism Research Center features definitions and original research on terrorism, counterterrorism documents, a comprehensive list of Web links, and monthly profiles of terrorist and counterterrorist groups.

United Nations Environment Program (UNEP)
http://www.unep.ch

Consult this home page of UNEP for links to environmental topics of critical concern to sociologists. The site will direct you to useful databases and global resource information.

William Davidson Institute
http://www.wdi.bus.umich.edu

The William Davidson Institute at the University of Michigan Business School is dedicated to the understanding and promotion of economic transition. Consult this site for discussion of topics related to the changing global economy and the effects of globalization in general.

We highly recommend that you review our Web site for expanded information and our other product lines. We are continually updating and adding links to our Web site in order to offer you the most usable and useful information that will support and expand the value of your Annual Editions. You can reach us at: *http://www.mhcls.com/annualeditions/*.

UNIT 1
Culture

Unit Selections

1. **The Islamists' Other Weapon,** Paul Marshall
2. **The Atrophy of Social Life,** D. Stanley Eitzen
3. **Two Cheers for Hypocrisy,** P. J. O'Rourke
4. **Diversity within Unity: A New Approach to Immigrants and Minorities,** *The Commutarian Reader: Beyond the Essentials*
5. **The Dubious Value of Value-Neutrality,** Stephen H. Balch

Key Points to Consider

• To what extent does Islamic culture today conflict with Western culture?

• What do you think are the core values in American society?

• What are the strengths and weaknesses of cultures that emphasize either cooperation or individualism?

• What is the relationship between culture and identity?

• What might a visitor from a primitive tribe describe as shocking and barbaric about American society?

• What are you most proud about American culture and why?

Student Web Site
www.mhcls.com/online

Internet References
Further information regarding these Web sites may be found in this book's preface or online.

New American Studies Web
http://www.georgetown.edu/crossroads/asw/
Anthropology Resources Page
http://www.usd.edu/anth/
Human Rights and Humanitarian Affairs
http://www.etown.edu/vl/humrts.html

The ordinary, everyday objects of living and the daily routines of life provide a structure to social life that is regularly punctuated by festivals, celebrations, and other special events (both happy and sad). These routine, and special times are the stuff of culture, for culture is the sum total of all the elements of one's social inheritance. Culture includes language, tools, values, habits, science, religion, literature, and art.

It is easy to take one's own culture for granted, so it is useful to pause and reflect on the shared beliefs and practices that form the foundations for our social life. Students share beliefs

1

and practices, and thus, have a student culture. Obviously the faculty has one also. Students, faculty, and administrators share a university culture. At the national level, Americans share an American culture. These cultures change through the decades and especially between generations. As a result, there is much variety among cultures across time and across nations, tribes, and groups. It is fascinating to study these differences and to compare the dominant values and signature patterns of different groups.

The article in the first subsection deals with some of the variety among cultures. Paul Marshall describes the beliefs and objectives of Islamic extremists; to spread Islam and to establish many Islamist states governed by Sharia law.

In the next subsection, two authors focus on some peculiarities of American culture. Stanley Eitzen raises concerns about the increasing isolation of individuals in America. Since social interaction "is the basic building block of intimate relationships, small groups, formal organizations, communities, and societies . . . [he] believes we should be concerned by some disturbing trends in our society that hinder or even eliminate social interaction and that indicate a growing isolation as individuals become increasingly separated from their neighbors, their co-workers, and even their family members." Among the factors that contribute to this isolation are changing residences, changing jobs, divorce, new technologies, less visiting with neighbors, both parents working, TV viewing patterns, consumerism, and time pressures. Then, P. J. O'Rourke humorously analyzes the current youth culture relying mainly on surveys, though he suspects that teenagers lie to survey interviewers like he did. He notes a general lack of questioning and little passion for change but also "a strong moralistic streak."

The third subsection delves into some cultural issues. The first article tries to work out a satisfactory solution to the perplexing problem of honoring diversity of cultures within a national unity. It is the platform statement focusing on the problems of legal and illegal immigration and created and signed by 150 members of a communitarian conference. They suggest that unbounded multiculturalism fragments society to a harmful degree, but unity that oppresses separate cultures is also harmful. The second value issue raised in this subsection is the issue of values in the college classroom. Science should be value-neutral, so the university should be value-neutral. This sounds right, but we do not actually believe it. We want young people to be exposed to values as long as they are the right values, and all discussions are open to criticism and opposing views. This leads to criticism of established order and established ideas, and that will upset some people, but the university can not thrive without it.

The Islamists' Other Weapon

PAUL MARSHALL

Islamists are among the most garrulous of enemies: in a plethora of videotapes, audiotapes, declarations, books, letters, *fatwas,* magazines, and websites, they have explained their actions repeatedly and at length. Each bombing or other atrocity seems to be accompanied by the equivalent of a press kit, attempting to justify the action in terms of Islamic teaching and history. The goal of these extremists, as they have announced again and again, is nothing less than to restore a unified Muslim *ummah* (community), one ruled by a new caliphate, organized to wage jihad against the rest of the world, and, above all, governed by what they regard as the immutable divine law declared by God to Muhammad—the *shari'a.*

Indeed, nothing has been more central to the rhetoric of Osama bin Laden and his followers than denunciations of democracy, legislatures, and "man-made law." The great crime of the rulers of Saudi Arabia, bin Laden declared, is "ruling by laws other than those which Allah has revealed," and thereby making it "incumbent on [their] subjects, by Allah's command, to rebel." To Iraqis contemplating participation in the January 30 elections, he warned that their constitution was *jahiliyya* (pre-Islamic) and that Muslims are allowed only to elect a leader for whom "Islam is the only source of the rulings and laws." The terrorist group Ansar al-Sunnah seconded this notion, telling Iraqis not to vote—and threatening bloodshed if they did—because "democracy is a Greek word meaning the rule of the people ... This concept is apostasy." Abu Musab al-Zarqawi, the head of al Qaeda's Iraq affiliate, declared "a fierce war on this evil principle of democracy."

Despite these repeated challenges to Western notions of law and political legitimacy, American policy-makers have shown remarkably little interest in Islamist ideology, and seem content to treat it as simple fanaticism. This is a disabling mistake, comparable to trying to fight Communism without bothering to learn about Marxism. If we are to defeat the jihadists and radical Islam, especially on the battleground of ideas, it is important that we better understand their far-reaching ideological ambitions.

The Problem of Definition

Islamic "law" is how *shari'a* is usually rendered, but this definition is not expansive enough. Although *shari'a* covers matters of crime and judicial procedure, it provides guidelines for a range of other activities as well, from marriage and economics to spiritual and moral issues like prayer, pilgrimage, and ritual cleansing.

The original sense of the term is "the path" or "the way," so it is better compared with the traditional Jewish understanding of biblical and rabbinic law than with a Western legal code. To believing Muslims of every variety, criticism of *shari'a* as such often sounds strange because, much as they might disagree with stoning adulterous women or cutting off the hands of thieves, the word is roughly synonymous with "justice" or "goodness."

There are several different schools of *shari'a,* all of them efforts to synthesize material from the Qur'an, the sayings of Muhammad (*hadith*), and accounts of his life into a systematic body of guidance. The most influential approach among Sunnis is the Hanafi school; among the Shiites it is the Jafari school. Historically, however, *shari'a* has seldom been the sole source of legitimacy in Islamic polities. Muslim governments have freely adopted local and customary law and, in recent centuries, have borrowed also from Western legal codes.

Most Muslims still live in communities governed by their own distinctive combination of Islamic law and local traditions. When given the choice—as in Muslim-majority democracies like Indonesia, Malaysia, Bangladesh, and Turkey—they have consistently rejected extreme versions of *shari'a.* Algeria's Islamic Salvation Front might have instituted such an extreme version had the army allowed it to win the election there in 1992, but its campaigning downplayed this part of its program. Similar parties in Malaysia, Pakistan, and Nigeria have managed to win elections only at the provincial and state level.

Despite this lack of popular support, however, radical interpretations of Islamic law have spread dramatically during the past quarter-century, thanks in large part to the aggressive tactics of Islamists and their state patrons. Worse, in a growing number of Muslim countries, those who have taken a stand against extreme versions of *shari'a* have been vilified, imprisoned, beaten, and even killed.

Agitation for extreme versions of *shari'a* is nothing new in the Islamic world. It has been central to the agendas of Egypt's Muslim Brotherhood and the Deobandi movement in Pakistan and India for some 80 years. Over the past quarter-century, however, the cause has received an unprecedented boost from two rather different sources.

Saudi Arabia

The first of these is Saudi Arabia. The Saudis have long maintained that their own literalist Wahhabi school of *shari'a* is the only valid one within the Sunni tradition (leaving aside the still more outrageous heresies, as they see it, of Shiite Muslims). Since the early 1980's, the Saudis have spent billions of dollars to build mosques and *madrassas* (religious schools) in every corner of the Muslim world for propagating their intolerant creed. Though Osama bin Laden has condemned the House of Saud for its supposed infidelity—and himself hopes to displace the royal family—these institutions have trained vast numbers of actual and would-be jihadists.

Even now, in the wake of 9/11 and while facing a serious domestic threat from al Qaeda, the Saudi regime rejects any law or legislation outside its own narrow tradition as an "infidel" accretion to the pristine teachings of Islam. As Crown Prince Abdullah stressed in a statement late last year, the Saudis are willing to consider any number of political and social reforms—just as long as the centrality of Islamic law is not open to debate. In Saudi Arabia, as in regimes and movements influenced by its example, questioning the government can be regarded as tantamount to questioning God; political opposition can be seen as apostasy or blasphemy, and punishable as such.

Another main source for the spread of an extremist version of *shari'a* has been Iran, where the Ayatollah Khomeini introduced an unprecedented form of Islamic rule after overthrowing the shah in 1979. By contrast with traditional Shiite practice, wherein spiritual leaders have taken a "prophetic" role in challenging public authorities, Khomeini declared himself head of the government and claimed almost divine powers; his own words, regardless of their relation to sacred texts, would define the boundaries of Islam.

The Iranian fundamental law issued in Khomeini's name bars from political office non-Muslims or Muslims who do not demonstrate allegiance to the mullah's rule, which is referred to as the "guardian-ship of the jurist." The law allows political participation—the formation of parties, rights of assembly, a free press—but only on condition of its "compatibility with standards of *shari'a*," a restriction that has allowed the authorities to suppress almost every meaningful expression of democratic opposition.

The penal side of Iranian law is equally harsh. For an unmarried perpetrator, the punishment for adultery is 100 lashes; for a married one, death by stoning. It is a crime to listen to certain forms of music or to watch certain movies, and employment is restricted to those who believe in the "guardianship of the jurist." The penalty for killing a woman or a non-Muslim is less than that for killing a Muslim man, and there is no penalty at all for killing "apostates" or members of unrecognized religious minorities like the Bahais.

Despite their strong mutual animosity, Wahhabism and Khomeinism have exerted a revolutionary influence on the Muslim world over the past generation. In country after country, and often in the face of long-standing traditions of moderation, these imported ideologies have provided support and encouragement to local extremists, giving rise to an enormously destructive view of Islam's demands.

The effects of this process may be seen in a brief survey of the landscape.

Pakistan

Pakistan was established in 1947 as a Muslim-majority state but not as an Islamic one. As the independence leader Muhammad Ali Jinnah emphasized, "You may belong to any religion or caste or creed—that has nothing to do with the business of the state." Indeed, the first temporary president of Pakistan's constituent assembly was a Hindu "untouchable."

By 1973, however, a new constitution had been established, renaming the country the Islamic Republic of Pakistan and declaring Islam the state religion. All existing laws, it was declared, "shall be brought in conformity with the injunctions of Islam as laid down in the holy Qu'ran and Sunnah." Though Prime Minister Zulfiqar Ali Bhutto's plans to implement *shari'a* were stopped in 1977 when General Zia Ul-Haq overthrew him, Zia himself introduced ordinances based on *hudud* (Islamic criminal law) two years later, including punishments like amputation and stoning. In the 1980's, blasphemy laws were introduced, subjecting those who "defiled" the name of the prophet to the death penalty. More recent legislation makes it possible to imprison for three years any member of the minority Ahmadi sect who calls himself a Muslim or does anything that "outrages the religious feelings of Muslims."

Under Pakistan's influence (and with considerable support from Saudi Arabia), the Taliban regime in Afghanistan began in 1994 to institute its own uncompromising version of *shari'a*. No formal legislation was involved. Instead, judges or others claiming Taliban authority simply enforced what they believed Islam to require. Women were forbidden to go to school, work outside the home, or travel without a male relative. Apostates and homosexuals were killed, and music was banned.

Even now, under Afghanistan's American-supported democratic government, many of these measures remain in place. The current head of the supreme court, Fazul Hadi Shinwari, has declared that, under his jurisdiction, adulterers will be stoned, thieves will have their hands amputated, and those in possession of alcohol will receive 80 lashes. A non-Muslim, as he told National Public Radio, should be invited to accept Islam; if he does not convert, he must obey Islam; if he refuses such accommodations, the only option, Shinwari said, is to "behead him."

Sudan

In Sudan, the long-time ruler General Jafaar al-Numeiri introduced radical *shari'a* in 1983, partly to win the support of the Islamic Charter Front, an offshoot of Egypt's Muslim Brotherhood. In one especially theatrical show of piety, thousands of bottles of whiskey were immediately dumped into the Nile. More gruesome measures soon followed. In just the first year of the new laws, 58 public amputations were carried out in Khartoum province alone, including twelve "cross-limb" procedures in which a hand and a foot were cut from opposite sides of the offender's body. Public floggings were broadcast daily on national television, and public hangings, followed by crucifixion, were carried out at sites built especially for the purpose. In 1985, seventy-six-year-old Mahmoud Mohamed Taha, perhaps the country's leading religious scholar, was hanged, having been convicted of apostasy for criticizing the new laws. Opposition to these barbaric practices—which were inflicted for the most part on poor Christians from southern Sudan—renewed a rebellion that, until the recent peace agreement, claimed more than two million lives.

In Nigeria, *shari'a* personal-status law has been a part of the legal system for decades, but in 1999 Alhaji Ahmed Sani, the governor of the state of Zamfara in the northwest, announced that he would institute a more comprehensive system of *shari'a* and assign responsibility for enforcement to the *hizbah* (religious police). Eleven other northern and central states quickly followed suit, closing churches and non-Muslim schools and mandating "Islamic" dress. In 2002, Sani took the additional step of requiring all residents of Zamfara to use Arabic, a language few speak. In the last five years, tens of thousands of people have died in *shari'a*-related violence in Nigeria. The governor of Yobe state has said that he will defend the new laws even at the cost of civil war, and Sani has urged the advocates of *shari'a* to form their own armies to defend Muslims and promote Islam.

Militant versions of *shari'a* have also made inroads in the more moderate corners of the Islamic world. In Malaysia, the Parti Islam SeMalaysia (PAS) came into power in the northern state of Kelantan in 1990, promptly prohibiting the sale of alcohol to Muslims and banning gambling, discotheques, and unisex hair salons. Three years later, the state introduced a *shari'a*-based criminal code, though it was quickly overturned by the central government. More recently, PAS has experienced several electoral setbacks at the state level, but it remains the only viable opposition in the national legislature and, should the current secular coalition stumble, would stand a chance of forming a government.

Indonesia

Indonesia, too, has experienced only mixed success in resisting Islamist influence. Lawmakers have roundly defeated efforts to incorporate *shari'a* into the constitution, and the terrorist group Jemaah Islamiah, which carried out the October 2002 bombing in Bali and other attacks, has largely been discredited. But Islamic radicals have managed to advance their agenda through intimidation and piecemeal legislation, especially at the local level. In Sulawesi, Sumatra, eastern Java, Banten, Flores, Sumba, and the Bandung area, they have forced women to wear *hijabs,* attacked nightclubs, and forcibly closed shops at prayer

times. Though lacking in enforcement authority, southern Sulawesi has even enacted Islamic criminal laws.

Indeed, almost everywhere one looks in the Muslim world, Islamists have grown more assertive and violent in advancing their program. In Kenya, the chairman of the country's council of imams and preachers has warned that unless their demands for *shari'a*-based laws are met, Muslims in the northeastern provinces will break away. In Tanzania, Islamic radicals have bombed bars and attacked women whom they consider immodestly dressed. Chechnyan rebels have adopted *shari'a* law from Sudan. The draft Palestinian constitution, in a bow to Hamas and Islamic jihad, declares that the "principles of the Islamic *shari'a* are a main source for legislation." And so on.

Western attention to the widening influence of extreme versions of *shari'a* has been, at best, intermittent. News coverage has tended to focus on sensational cases involving the status of women or the imposition of inhuman punishments, as when provincial courts in Nigeria have sentenced women guilty of adultery to death by stoning. Such publicity is vital—it has saved the lives of a number of victimized women—but its effect has been to make *shari'a* seem a less formidable threat, an unfortunate recrudescence of medieval penology rather than a comprehensive ideological challenge.

As applied to an increasing number of countries, however, extreme *shari'a* does far more than mete out cruel punishments. With its untrained judges, vague and haphazard standards, nonjudicial decrees, and extrajudicial enforcement, it undermines all efforts at establishing the rule of law. By treating women and non-Muslims as second-class citizens or nonpersons, it systematically deprives Islamic societies of the full benefit of their human resources. Worst of all, perhaps, by turning political dissent and debate into crimes against God, the *shari'a* of the Islamists closes off any possibility of genuine democratic and religious reform.

Extreme versions of *shari'a* may thus be the most serious obstacle to the political and religious reform in Muslim societies—and Arab ones in particular—that is needed if democracy is to be established and they are to stop serving as incubators for martyrdom-minded jihadists. For the security of the West, to say nothing of the cause of human rights, reversing the legal and social advances of the Islamists is every bit as important as defeating their armies on the field of battle.

PAUL MARSHALL is a senior fellow at Freedom House's Center for Religious Freedom.

The Atrophy of Social Life

D. STANLEY EITZEN

Harvard political scientist Robert Putnam has written a provocative book entitled *Bowling Alone,* in which he argues that we Americans are becoming increasingly disengaged from each other. That is, we are less likely than Americans of a generation or two ago to belong to voluntary associations such as the Rotary Club, to play bridge on a regular basis to participate in a bowling league, to belong to the P.T.A., or to vote. In short, Putnam maintains that in the past 50 years or so social life has changed dramatically throughout the United States as various social trends isolate us more and more from each other. The effect, he suggests, is that the bonds of civic cement are disintegrating as we become increasing separated from each other, from our communities and from society. Consequently, the social glue that once held communities together and gave meaning to individual lives is now brittle, as people have become more and more isolated.

I am a sociologist. We sociologists focus on things social the most fundamental of which is social interaction. This is the basic building block of intimate relationships, small groups, formal organizations, communities, and societies. I am concerned and I believe we should all be concerned by some disturbing trends in our society that hinder or even eliminate social interaction, and that indicate a growing isolation as individuals become increasingly separated from their neighbors, their co-workers, and even their family members.

Moving Away

Ours is a mobile society. We move, on average about every five years. We change jobs (14 percent of workers in a typical year leave their jobs voluntarily) or we lose jobs involuntarily (a recent survey indicated that 36 percent of Americans answered "yes" to the question: "Has anyone in your immediate family lost a job in the last three years?"). It's important to note here that the bond between workers and employers is badly frayed as employees are no longer loyal to our employers and employers are clearly not loyal, to their employees as they downsize locally and outsource their jobs and operations to low-wage economies.

We are also moving away from intimate relationships. With 1.25 million divorces occurring annually in the U.S. 2.5 million move away from their spouses. Immigration has the same consequence, creating transnational families, where families are separated with some members living in the U.S. and one or more members back home in another country.

When we move out of relationships or to new geographical areas, or to new kinds of work, we leave behind our relationships with former neighbors. co-workers, and friends. If we anticipate moving, we act like temporary residents, not making the effort to join local organizations, to become acquainted with our neighbors, and invest our time and money to improve the community.

Living Alone

In 1930, 2 percent of the U.S. population lived alone. In 2000, some 10 percent (27.2 million) of the nation's 105 million households were occupied by single people without children, roommates, or other people. People are living longer and the elderly, especially older women, are most likely to live alone. Divorce, by definition, initiates living alone, with 2.5 million former spouses annually moving into separate living arrangements. Another source for living alone is the phenomenon of commuter marriage—an arrangement where wives and husbands maintain separate households as a way of solving the dilemmas of dual-career marriages.

Technology and Isolation

Modern technology often encourages isolation. Consider the isolating consequences of air conditioning, certainly a welcome and necessary technology in many places. Before air conditioning, people spent leisure time outside increasing the likelihood of interaction with neighbors and friends. Now they are inside their homes with doors and windows shut enjoying the cool air, but isolating themselves from their neighbors. Television, too, along with VCRs, DVDs, and video games entice us to stay in our homes more and more.

Before refrigerators, shopping was done every day. This meant that people would see the same shop proprietors and their fellow shoppers daily. This created a daily rhythm, a set of interactions, and the sharing of information, gossip, and mutual concerns. Thus, refrigerators, while reducing the spoilage of food and the necessity of going to the store every day, changed interaction patterns.

Because of computers and telecommunications there is a growing trend for workers to work at home. At last count 28 million Americans worked out of their homes, using computers or telephony instead of face-to-face interaction. While home-based work allows flexibility and independence not found in most jobs, these workers are separated from the rich social networks that often give rise to numerous friendships and make working life enjoyable or at least tolerable.

With the new communications technology, you don't even have to go to a funeral to pay your respects. A new company is now broadcasting funerals on the Internet and you can even sign an electronic guest book and e-mail condolences to the family. Similarly, one can take college courses without attending classes, just using the Internet to communicate with their instructors. Missing, of course, is the face-to-face interaction with fellow students and professors.

Paradoxically, the current communications revolution increases interaction while reducing intimacy. Curt Suplee, science and technology writer for the *Washington Post,* says that we have seen tenfold increases in "communication" by electronic means, and tenfold reductions in person-to-person contact. The more time people spend online, the less they can spare for real-life relationships with family and friends. In effect, as we are increasingly alone before a computer screen, we risk what former U.S. Secretary State Warren Christopher has called "social malnutrition." John L. Locke, a professor of communications, makes a convincing argument in his book, *The De-Voicing of Society,* that e-mail, voice mail, fax machines, beepers, and Internet chat rooms are robbing us of ordinary social talking. Talking, he says, like the grooming of apes and monkeys, is the way we build and maintain social relationships. In his view, it is only through intimate conversation that we can know others well enough to trust them and work with them harmoniously. Most face-to-face communication is nonverbal. Phone communication reduces the nonverbal clues, and e-mail eliminates them entirely. So the new information technologies only create the illusion of communication and intimacy. The result, according to Locke, is that we are becoming an autistic society, communicating messages electronically but without really connecting. In short, these incredible communication devices that combine to network us in so many dazzling ways also separate us increasingly from intimate relationships. Sometimes we even use the technology to avoid the live interaction for whatever reason. Jeffrey Kagan, a telecom industry analyst, sums up the problem: "We are becoming a society that finds it easier, and even preferable to hide behind our computer screens and chat with a raceless, nameless stream of words from across the country or across the globe rather than deal with people face to face and all the complexities, good and bad, of the human relationship."

Geography and Isolation

There is a strong pattern of social homogeneity by place. Cities are arranged into neighborhoods by social class and race. This occurs because of choice, economic means, and the discriminatory behaviors by neighbors, realtors, and lending institutions.

Among multiracial societies, only South Africa exceeds our rate of segregation—a problem that concentrates poverty, social disorder, and dysfunctional schools as well as diminishing social cohesion. The degree of racial/ethnic segregation by neighborhood is higher now than in 1990. A Harvard University study found that about 2.3 million African American and Latino children attend "apartheid" schools, where virtually all students are minorities. Similarly, some neighborhoods are segregated by age. Some retirement communities, for example, limit their inhabitants to persons over 55 and those without minor children. Some 6 million households are in neighborhoods that have controlled-entry systems with guards and electric gates. These gated communities wall the residents off physically and socially from "others." Regarding this exclusiveness, sociologist Philip Slater said that we need heterogeneous neighborhoods: "A community that does not have old people and children, white-collar and blue-collar, eccentric and conventional, and so on, is not a community at all, but [a] kind of truncated and deformed monstrosity . . ."

Even in non-gated communities, we isolate ourselves. One in three Americans has never spent an evening with a neighbor. The affluent often belong to exclusive clubs and send their children to private schools. Two million children are home schooled, which isolates them from their peers. Some people exercise on motorized treadmills and use other home exercise equipment instead of running through their neighborhoods or working out with others.

The suburbs are especially isolating. Rather than walking to the corner grocery or nearby shop and visiting with the clerks and their neighbors, suburbanites drive somewhere away from their immediate neighborhood to shop among strangers. Or they may not leave their home at all, working, shopping, banking, and paying their bills by computer. For suburban teenagers and children almost everything is away—practice fields, music lessons, friends, jobs, schools, and the malls. Thus, a disconnect from those nearby. Suburban neighborhoods in particular are devoid of meeting places. The lack of community and common meeting places in our cities and especially in the suburbs compounds the isolation of those who have experienced a divorce or the death of a spouse.

Isolation within Families

An especially disturbing trend is the separation of family members from each other. Many spouses are either absent or too self-absorbed to pay very much attention to their children or each other. A recent cover story in Newsweek noted that many dual-income couples no longer or rarely have sex because they are too exhausted and too stressed. On average, parents today spend 22 fewer hours a week with their children than parents did in the 1960s. Part of this is because both parents are working outside the home. But it also results from children being overscheduled with outside-the-home activities. These children have little time for play with other children and their activities replace parent-child interaction. To amplify the last point, American children spend more than half of their waking hours in supervised, child-centered environments. This causes economist Ellen Frank to ask: "What happens to parents, to children, and to the rest of us when children are stored out of sight?"

Although living in the same house, parents and children may tune each other out emotionally, or by using earphones, or by engaging in other solitary activities. A survey by the Kaiser Family Foundation found that the average child spends five and one-half hours a day alone watching television, on the Internet, playing video games, or reading. Some 30 percent of children under 3 have a television in their bedroom. Some older children even have their own rooms equipped with a telephone, television, VCR, microwave, refrigerator, and computer, which while convenient, isolates them from other family members. Many families rarely eat together in an actual sit-down meal. Family members are often too busy and too involved with their individual schedules to spend quality time together as a family. These homes may be full of people but they are really empty.

The Architecture of Isolation

Another contemporary trend—the increased number of mega-houses in the suburbs—results in what we might call the architecture of isolation. These huge houses, built, ironically, at the very time that family size is declining, tend to isolate their inhabitants from outsiders and from other family members. They provide all of the necessities for comfort and recreation, thus glorifying the private sphere over public places. Moreover, the number and size of the rooms encourages each family member to have their own space rather than shared spaces. Thus, the inverse correlation between house size and family interaction.

Contemporary house and landscape design focuses interaction in the backyard, surrounded by privacy fences, some of which make our homes and lots to resemble medieval fortresses. Back yards are inviting with grass and flowerbeds, barbeque pits, swimming pools, jungle gyms, and trampolines. The front of the house no longer has a porch. In the past, families spent time on the porch, relaxing and visiting with neighbors. The front yard, too, is less inviting than the back, often with rock instead of grass. It is important to note that the more affluent we are, the more likely our homes and consumer goods promote social isolation.

Consumerism and Isolation

Sociologist George Ritzer in his recent book, *The Globalization of Nothing,* argues that the social world, particularly in the realm of consumption, is increasingly characterized by "nothing," which he defines as a social form that is generally centrally conceived and controlled and comparatively devoid of distinctive substance. The "something" that is lost is more than likely, an indigenous custom or product, a local store, a familiar gathering place, or simply personalized interaction. Corporations provide standardized, mass-produced products for us to consume and become like other consumers in what we wear, what we eat, and what we desire. We purchase goods in chain stores and restaurants (Dillard's, McDonalds) that are efficient but devoid of distinctive content. A mall in one part of the world may be structured much the same in another location. We bank at ATMs anywhere in the world, but without social interaction. The same is true with shopping on the Internet.

Increasingly, Ritzer says, adults go through their daily routines without sharing stories, gossip, and analyses of events with friends on a regular basis at work, at a coffee shop, neighborhood tavern, or at the local grain elevator. These places of conversation with friends have been replaced by huge stores (Wal-Mart, Home Depot) where we don't know the clerks and other shoppers. The locally owned café has been replaced by chain restaurants. In the process we lose the intimacy of local stores, cafes, and hardware stores, which give their steady customers sense of community and the comfort of meaningful connections with others. Sociologist Philip Slater said that "community life exists when one can go daily to a given location at a given time and see many of the people one knows."

Implications for Society

There are several important implications of increasing social isolation for society. First, the disengaged do not participant in elections, leaving a minority to elect our leaders as occurred in the 2000 presidential election when George Bush was elected with 24 percent of the votes of those eligible. This means that, the voices of outsiders will be faint if heard at all while the voices of the affluent and their money arc heard all the more. All of these consequences support the conservative agenda, as sociologist Paul Starr notes: "These trends could hardly please anyone who cares about the republic, but they have been particularly disturbing to liberals. The most intense periods of liberal reform during the past century—the Progressive era, the New Deal, and the 1960s—were all times when the public was actively engaged, and new forms of civic action and participation emerged. Reforms in that tradition are unlikely to succeed again without the same heightened public arousal, which not only elects candidates but also forces them to pay attention once they are in office."

Second, the breakdown in social connections shows up in everyday sociability, with pernicious effects for social relations as people are less and less civil in schools, at work, in traffic, and in public places.

Third, when people focus only on themselves and people like themselves, they insulate themselves from "others" and from their problems. Thus, we favor dismantling the welfare state and safely net for the less fortunate. We oppose, for example, equity in school funding, allowing rich districts to have superior schools while the disadvantaged have inferior schools. We allow this unraveling of community bonds at our peril, as the walls become thicker between the "haves" and the "have-nots," crime will increase and hostility and fear will reign.

Implications for Individuals

As for individuals, the consequences of this accelerating social isolation are dire. More and more Americans are lonely, bitter, alienated, anomic, and disconnected. This situation is conducive to alcohol and drug abuse, depression, anxiety, and violence. The lonely and disaffected are ripe candidates for membership in cults, gangs, and militias where they find a sense of belonging and a cause to believe in, but in the process they may become more paranoid and, perhaps, even become willing terrorists or mass murderers as were the two alienated adolescents who perpetrated the massacre at Columbine High School in a Denver suburb. At a less extreme level, the alienated will disengage further from society by shunning voluntary associations, by home schooling their children, and by voting against higher taxes for the public good. In short, they will become increasingly self-absorbed, caring only about themselves and ignoring the needs of their neighbors and communities. This translates into the substitution of accumulating things rather than cultivating relationships. In this regard, we should take seriously, the admonition by David Wann the coauthor of *Afluenza: The All-Consuming Epidemic,* who says "We need to acknowledge—as individuals and as a culture—that the best things in life really aren't things. The best things are bonus with people . . ."

What to Do?

I am not a Luddite. I appreciate the wonders of technology. I welcome change. There are good reasons to move and to change careers and to live in nice houses. But we must recognize the unintended consequences of societal trends that deprive us of our shared humanity. Once we have identified the downside of these trends and our complicity in them, what can we do to reverse their negative effects? I don't have all the answers, but I believe that a few structural changes will help to reduce their negative consequences. As a start, we need to rethink urban design. We must reverse urban sprawl, increasing urban density so that people live near their work, near their neighbors, and within walking distance of stores and recreation. Second, as a society we need to invest in the infrastructure that facilitate public activities such as neighborhood schools, walking and biking trails, parks, the arts, libraries, and community recreation centers. Third, communities need to provide activities that bring people together such as public concerts, fairs, recreational sports for people of all ages, and art festivals. And, fourth, since U.S. society is becoming more diverse, we need to break down the structural barriers that isolate us from "others." We need to affirm affirmative action in legislation and deed, eliminate predatory lending practices and other forms of discrimination, and improve our schools so that equality of educational opportunity

actually occurs rather than the present arrangement whereby school systems are rigged in favor of the already privileged. You will note that these proposals are opposite from current policy at the community, state, and federal levels, resulting in a descending spiral toward social atomization. We allow this to occur at our own peril.

At a personal level, we need to recognize what is happening to us and our families and work to counteract these isolating trends. Each of us can think of changes in our lives that will enhance human connections. To those changes, may I suggest the following: Engage in public activities. Have meaningful face-to-face conversations with friends on a regular basis. Get to know your neighbors, co-workers, and the people, who provide services for you. Join with others who share a common interest. Work to improve your community. Become an activist, joining with others to bring about social change. And, most of all, we need to moderate our celebration of individualism and our tendency toward self-absorption and develop instead a moral obligation to others, to our neighbors (broadly defined) and their children, to those unlike us as well as those similar to us, and to future generations. If not, then our humanity is compromised and our quality of life diminished.

Suggested Further Readings

Kane, Hal. 2001. *Triumph of the Mundane: The Unseen Trends that Shape Our Lives and Environment.* Washington, D. C.: Island Press.

Locke, John L. 1998. *The De-Voicing of Society: Why We Don't Talk to Each Other.* New York: Simon and Schuster.

Oldenburg, Ray. 1997. *The Great Good Place: Cafes, Coffee Shops, Community Centers, Beauty Parlors, General Stores Bars, Hangouts, and How They Get You Through the Day.* New York: Marlowe.

Putnam, Robert D. 2000. *Bowling Alone: The Collapse and Revival of American Community.* New York: Simon and Schuster.

Ritzer, George. 2004. *The Globalization of Nothing.* Thousand Oaks. CA: Pine Forge Press.

Slater, Philip. 1970. *The Pursuit, of Loneliness: American Culture at the Breaking Point.* Boston: Beacon Press.

D. STANLEY EITZEN is a Professor Emeritus in sociology, Colorado State University. He is the author or co-author of nineteen books on various social problems, crime, and sport. This article is a revised version of a speech delivered at Angelo State University, San Angelo, Texas (October 16, 2003). This speech was reprinted in Vital Speeches of the Day (December 15, 2003).

Two Cheers for Hypocrisy

**As the Gallup Organization has discovered, the young
are another country—and one day it's going to be ours**

P. J. O'ROURKE

What is on the mind of American youth? Well, of course—but youth must spend a little time thinking about something besides *that*. Youth has its opinions, ideas, and ideals. And youth will inherit the nation. Although by the time the Baby Boom, that entrenched Court of Chancery, is done with its *Jarndyce v. Jarndyce* national patrimony, youth won't be very young. Yet presumably the formative years produce values that endure. (Would that the bodily forms of the formative years endured so well.)

One way to find out what young people are thinking is to ask them. From time to time the Gallup Organization does this, querying groups of approximately 500 to 1000 youngsters aged thirteen to seventeen. The teens are chosen randomly, but with an organized randomness, which is the mystery of opinion polling. This allows Gallup to assert that it has "95% confidence that the maximum error attributable to sampling and other random effects is $+/-5$ percentage points." Gallup does, however, add a caveat: "Question wording and practical difficulties in conducting surveys can introduce error or bias into the findings." So the following informal ion, drawn from a baker's dozen of teen opinion polls, is, on average, reliable—as reliable, that is, as adolescents, on average, are.

Gallup tells us that the political values of young people are startlingly unstartling. Seventy-one percent say their views on politics are "about the same" as those of their parents. This from kids all born since 1988, who have never known a towering national leader, let alone a noble one. Consider the electoral flora among which teens have grown up: scrubby Bushes; weedy, tangled Dukakis; overripe Dole; deadwood Core; and Kerry full of prickles and thorns. Nothing large or impressive has grown in this political jungle except an egotistically bloated and morally obese couple of Clintons and a Gingrich. That's what their parents voted in, and young people say it's fine by them.

The kids could be lying to the pollsters. In 1970, when I was a kid (or anyway still acting like one), a census form was delivered to a disreputable pad where I was crashed. To this day in the U.S. Census Bureau files there is record of a three-room apartment in Columbus, Ohio, occupied by 240 Native Americans and the Gautama Buddha.

But "I'm just like my mom and dad" is such a tepid fib. Perhaps lukewarm is to teens today what shit-hot or cool as a cucumber was to teens of yore. A full 56 percent of contemporary adolescents say their politics are "moderate," while a total of just 13 percent call themselves either "very conservative" or "very liberal." And among that 13 percent the difference is split in a happy medium almost down the middle. Never mind that only 38 percent of adults call themselves moderates, despite all the dull throes of moderation that adulthood entails.

According to Gallup, 30 percent of teenagers identify themselves as Republicans, 37 percent as Democrats, and 27 percent as independents—a statistical distribution that could have been produced without the bother of polling, by a reasonably honest three-card monte dealer.

I'd have expected more left-wingers among the young. This is not because of the Long March through the educational institutions that the lefties of my generation supposedly took. In my experience, teachers" opinions don't affect students. Admittedly, I went to high school in the era of the dinosaurs. Mr. Jarokowski, the phys-ed instructor, comes to mind. But if pupils were influenced by pedagogues, Woodstock would have featured Patti Page. No, it's that being young is a socialist experience. Children live in the only successful Marxist state ever created: the family. "From each according to his ability, to each according to his need" is the family's practice as well as its theory. Even with today's scattershot patterns of marriage and parenting, a family is collectivist to a more than North Korean degree. And—again according to Callup—kids do not consider this communism to be oppressive. Seventy-three percent of teens say the family provides them freedom. Eighteen percent go so far as to say they're too free. As a simple matter of social continuity, kids should be out knocking on doors for Ralph Nader or Dennis Kucinich.

On the other hand, I'd also have expected more right-wingers among the young—at least if I'm to believe what else Gallup tells me. Forty-four percent of the teens who attended church or synagogue in the week before the political-ID poll was taken planned to vote Republican. Mosque, let us note, was not mentioned. Even so, the implication is that religious teens are more conservative than their fellows. And information from two additional Gallup polls, whose subjects are "The Word of God" and "The Origin of Species," indicates that teens are every bit as religious as their constant pronouncements of "ohmigod" would indicate.

Eighty-five percent of teenagers believe that the Bible is the actual or the inspired word of God. Eighty-one percent believe that evolution either was guided by God or just plain never happened. Teens apparently believe God even more than they believe their parents. And (I say this as a practicing Christian) on slimmer evidence, given adolescent knowledge of theology and science versus adolescent knowledge of Mom and Dad.

Thirty-eight percent of teenagers claim they subscribe to the following statement: "'God created humans pretty much in their present form within the last 10,000 years or so." This sounds like hard-shell boobocracy even to those of us who think "survival of the fittest" has a faintly tautological whiff. There are 20,000-year-old cave paintings in the Dordogne aesthetically superior to the stained glass in most churches. But we should not necessarily assume an upsurge in teen fundamentalism or future membership in the COP. When I was in high school, I was one of at least 38 percent of students who subscribed to the statement "2b ÷ $(x^2 - y^2)$ = I couldn't care less." And listening to teens or reading their text messages shows that 100 percent of them couldn't care less about grammar.

The young are adept at learning but even more adept at avoiding it. For example, Gallup maintains that 39 percent of teens think the Bible is the "actual word of God" (presumably in English, just as Jesus spoke it). And nearly a quarter of those who do not identify themselves as born-again Christians still say this. Forty-six percent of teens think the Bible is the "inspired word of God." Another 14 percent think it's an "ancient book of fables, legends, history, and moral precepts recorded by man." Many middle- and secondary-school students may read the Bible (or tell Gallup pollsters that they do). But it is also my understanding that many students read (or need to say that they have read) *The Color Purple,* by Alice Walker. I'd guess that a similar poll about the latter work would generate similar answers concerning whether Ms. Walker's words are "actual," "inspired," or "ancient." with similar bored confusion as to what adults mean by the terms. (And before we dismiss teenagers as complete chowderheads, consideration should be given to Gallup's statement that 45 percent of American adults believe man was plopped down on earth sometime since 8000 B.C., just like he is today, in Dockers and Nikes, the spitting image of God.)

L et's admit that we aren't interested in teen political and religious values. The kids can't vote until they're eighteen and don't vote much once they are. Plus, God is well known as an old softy when it comes to kids; privately even predestinarians and sticklers for infant baptism think so. What we really want to know is what teenagers are doing in the back seats of cars. Although given the modern subcompact "tuner"-style cars favored by teens, and given their modern parents, who stay at work until six or eight in the evening, it's probably been

a long time since anything other than the stashing of beer cans and bongs has been done in the back seats of cars.

I have not seen a Gallup poll asking the questions that every parent (and prig and lecher) wants to ask. And it may be just as well if Gallup doesn't bother. Gallup does ask. "What Are Teens Doing After School?" Forty-four percent say homework. Only 12 percent admit to "playing video games." A paltry five percent concede that they "talk on the phone." I say, "LOL" ("laughing out loud"), as the 11 percent who confess to being "on the computer" would put it.

Fifty-six percent of teens say "young people should abstain from sex until marriage." Sixty-four percent of teenage girls say so. What kind of abstention they say they're favoring, however, is open to interpretation. Gallup, in its analysis of this poll finding, brings in a professed expert on the subject, a "clinician and health educator" at a "teen sexual health center in suburban New Jersey." The expert avers, "Oral sex has become a popular way to postpone intercourse. Teens don't think of it as having sex." For another poll, titled "Teens' Marriage Views Reflect Changing Norms," Gallup brings in additional experts, from something called the National Marriage Project, at Rutgers University. (As long as Gallup is being New Jersey-centric, maybe Bruce Springsteen should have been questioned too.) The Rutgers people declare that 65 percent of young people have sex before they finish high school.

Put expert testimony together with a supposition that a few teens continue to use the ten-cent birth-control device advocated by parochial school nuns: a dime between your knees. Then add the observable fact that a fair portion of high school boys are still collecting Star Wars figurines and don't need a Yoda mask to go to a Halloween party. The conclusion is that regular teens are going at it like the Navy in port.

Our adolescents are hypocrites. And let's not forget that there are worse values than hypocrisy. A hypocrite knows good from bad, and maybe even right from wrong. This is more, it seems, than can be said for a certain former majority leader of the House of Representatives or several former reporters from CBS and *The New York Times.*

Whether or not teenagers act on their morals, they have a strong moralistic streak. Ninety-five percent consider "married men and women having an affair" to be morally unacceptable. Lively teen imaginations may be at work here, with mental pictures of icky grown-up bodies doing the deed. Still, the kids are within a +/−5 percentage-point sampling error of total condemnation.

If what these teens say is factual, they are so different from the adolescents of my heyday that they may be the spawn of alien invaders.

In the matter of abortion, 72 percent of teens consider it morally wrong, and 32 percent would make it illegal in all circumstances (compared with 17 percent of adults who take this absolutist view). And if we inspect the poll numbers on what might be called "Right to Life Lite." we find that 55 percent of teens believe medical testing on animals is immoral as well.

Perhaps logic is not to be expected from moralists, let alone very young ones. While nearly three quarters of kids think abortion is morally wrong, only 42 percent think having a baby outside of marriage is morally acceptable. What's a girl to do? And though practically all adolescents condemn adultery, two thirds of them condone divorce. Maybe this is credulity, and the kids really believe that their parents are divorcing "for the sake of the children" and not for the sake of the pool boy or the twenty-six-year-old executive assistant. Divorce famously imposes more hardships on women than on men, but 74 percent of teenage girls countenance splitups, versus only 58 percent of boys. That confirms a suspicion that divorced dads take their sons to sporting events on alternate weekends, while divorced moms complain about divorced dads to their daughters nonstop.

Although fewer than half of teenagers think it's all right to have sex before marriage, 62 percent think "young people are responsible enough to be sexually active" at age eighteen or younger. Meanwhile, only 41 percent think they are responsible enough to drink alcohol before they're twenty-one. Kids are apparently unfazed by the idea that they can be old enough to vote, join the Army, get married, make babies, be tried as adults and executed by lethal injection, but as for having a beer . . .

Such conundrums east more doubt, not so much on the values of youth as on the value of polling teens. Gallup itself provides the strongest case for skepticism. In a poll on alcohol use an improbable 17 percent of teens say they have "occasion to use alcoholic beverages." Only nine percent say they've been a passenger in a car driven by a teen under the influence of alcohol. And seven percent (the few, the defiant) admit to having been that driver. If the preceding numbers are even remotely factual, we are dealing with adolescents so different from those of my heyday that they may be the spawn of intergalactic alien invaders. Either that or we really *do* have a horrific drug problem in this country. Kids have abandoned knocking back brewskis and

have taken up imbibing godawful substances we've probably never heard of. (I have a fuzzy recollection that this has happened before.)

Kids will find some way to alter their painfully acute and frustratingly inchoate little consciousnesses. For a sample of teen consciousness I give you the following from a Gallup poll titled "What Frightens America's Youth?" As would be expected in a generation for whom 9/11 is the most shocking event in the history of mankind, the most common fear is terrorism. But what is the fear that comes in only one percentage point behind terrorism? Spiders.

The kids are yanking our chain. They have taken to heart the W. H. Auden poem "Under Which Lyre," which cheers the eternal war that young, playful, mischievous Hermes wages against mature, pompous, government-approved and corporate-sponsored Apollo. I doubt the kids have taken the poem to heart literally, or know of Auden or of Hermes, except as a brand of bling. But in their own thoughtless way they're thinking.

> *Thou shale not answer questionnaires*
> *Or quizzes upon World-Affairs,*
> *Nor with compliance*
> *Take any test. Thou shalt not sit*
> *With statisticians nor commit*
> *A social science.*

As to what values youth in fact has, time will tell. But time will not tell us much, because we'll be senile or dead. Meanwhile, the path to greater wisdom is not charted by the interrogation of teenagers—or, probably, by the interrogation of anyone, whether in a Gallup poll, at Guantánamo Bay, or in anonymously sourced deep-think interviews for important periodicals. We'd be better off heeding the Dian Fossey lesson: We know as much as we do about gorillas because they cannot speak.

P. J. O'ROURKE is a correspondent for *The Atlantic*. His most recent book is *Peace Kills*.

Diversity within Unity: A New Approach to Immigrants and Minorities

The following platform is the product of a meeting of scholars and elected officials from eleven countries. The meeting was held in Brussels in November of 2001 and was organized by the Communication Network. The platform has been endorsed by over 150 scholars elected officials, and other public leaders from over 20 countries.

We, the endorsers of this statement, have come together from many different social backgrounds, countries, and viewpoints to address our fellow citizens about the place of immigrants, and more generally minorities, in our diversifying societies.

Our Basic Orientation

We note with growing concern that very large segments of the people of free societies sense that they are threatened by massive immigration and by the growing minorities within their borders that hail from different cultures, follow different practices, and have separate institutions and loyalties. We are troubled by street violence, verbal outbursts of hate, and growing support for various extremist parties. These are unwholesome reactions to threats people feel to their sense of identity, self-determination, and culture, which come on top of concerns evoked by globalization, new communications technologies, and a gradual loss of national sovereignty. To throw the feelings of many millions of people in their faces, calling them "discriminatory," "exclusionary," "hypocritical," and worse, is an easy politics, but not one truly committed to resolution. People's anxieties and concerns should not be dismissed out of hand, nor can they be effectively treated by labeling them racist or xenophobic. Furthermore, telling people that they "need" immigrants because of economic reasons or demographic shortfalls makes a valid and useful argument, but does not address their profoundest misgivings. The challenge before us is to find legitimate and empirically sound ways to constructively address these concerns. At the same time, we should ensure that these sentiments do not find antisocial, hateful, let alone violent expressions.

Two approaches are to be avoided: promoting assimilation and unbounded multiculturalism. Assimilation—which entails requiring minorities to abandon all of their distinct institutions, cultures, values, habits, and connections to other societies in order to fully mesh into the prevailing culture—is sociologically difficult to achieve and unnecessary for dealing with the issues at hand, as we shall see. It is morally unjustified because of our respect for some normative differences, such as to which gods we pray.

Unbounded multiculturalism—which entails giving up the concept of shared values, loyalties, and identity in order to privilege ethnic and religious differences, presuming that nations can be replaced by a large number of diverse minorities—is also unnecessary. It is likely to evoke undemocratic backlashes, ranging from support for extremist, right-wing parties and populist leaders to anti-minority policies. It is normatively unjustified because it fails to recognize the values and institutions undergirded by the society at large, such as those that protect women's and gay rights.

The basic approach we favor is diversity within unity. It presumes that all members of a given society will fully respect and adhere to those basic values and institutions that are considered part of the basic shared framework of the society. At the same time, every group in society is free to maintain its distinct subculture—those policies, habits, and institutions that do not conflict with the shared core—and a strong measure of loyalty to its country of origin, as long as this does not trump loyalty to the society in which it lives if these loyalties come into conflict. Respect for the whole and respect for all is at the essence of our position.

We observe that such diversity within unity enriches rather than threatens the society at large and its culture, as is evident in matters ranging from music to cuisine, and most notably it greatly enhances the realm of ideas to which we are exposed and expands our understanding of the diverse world around us. We further note that, in each society, the basic shared core of identity and culture has changed over time and will continue to do so in the future. Hence minorities that hold that this core does not reflect values dear to them are free to act to seek to change it—via the democratic and social processes available for this purpose in all free societies.

The unity of which we speak is not one imposed by government orders or regulations, not to mention by police agents, but one that grows out of civic education, commitment to the common good, the nation's history, shared values, common experiences, robust public institutions, and dialogues about the commonalities and requirements of a people living together and facing the same challenges in the same corner of the earth.

Such diversity within unity allows one to fully respect basic rights, the democratic way of life, and core values, as well as those minority values that do not conflict with it.

Which elements belong in which category—the realm of unity or of diversity—is a matter that can be readily decided about many key items. Basic rights must be respected by one and all. For instance, discrimination against women cannot be tolerated, whatever a group's cultural or religious values. Respect for law and order is essential. Democratic institutions are not one option among several. No one who seeks citizenship in a given country, and membership in a given society, can buy out of the collective responsibilities that society has for its past actions and toward other societies, assumed by treaty or otherwise.

At the same time, little deliberation is required to recognize that there is no reason to object if minorities are keen to maintain their language as a second one, close ties with another country (as long as they do not trump loyalty to the current country, as already indicated), and special knowledge and practice of their culture. All of this is not to deny that much deliberation and public dialogue are called for on contested issues such as how "law and order" is to be interpreted and how strong and how deep down liberal-democratic approval should go. Deliberation and public dialogue are also crucial before one can conclude whether certain other items belong in the realm of unity or diversity, as is explored below.

In short, we ought not to sacrifice unity or diversity to the other part of the equation, but ought to recognize that we can learn both to live with more diversity and to protect well legitimate unity.

Issues and Policies

The Law: Variances, Basic Rights, and Compelling Public Interest

Assimilationist models favor maintaining universal laws—those that apply to all citizens and other people within a given jurisdiction. They tolerate some variations and exemptions, but those are to be based on individual needs (e.g., mental illness) or demographic categories (e.g., minors), not on ethnic or racial groupings. Group rights are not recognized.

Unbounded diversity favors allowing each community to follow its traditions, even if they conflict with prevailing laws (for instance, allowing for forced marriages and female circumcision), although most pro-diversity approaches recognize that some universal laws must be observed. According to this approach, ethnic and racial groups should be granted a great measure of autonomy to set and enforce their own laws, either by being accorded considerable territorial autonomy or community-based autonomy—for instance by religious authorities such as imams or rabbis. Also, by this approach, people are viewed as imbued with strong rights just by being members of a protected group, such as native Canadians or Americans.

The diversity-within-unity (DWU) model favors a *bifocal approach:* it sharply distinguishes between those laws that all must abide by and those for which various group-based variances and exemptions are to be provided. Although there is room for disagreement on what falls within these two categories, several criteria suggest themselves as principled guides to which laws and policies must be universal, and which can be group-particular.

Leading the universal category are *basic human rights,* as defined by the country's constitution, basic laws, the laws of regional communities such as the European Union, and the United Nations Universal Declaration of Human Rights. Thus no one can be legally bought and sold, detained without due process, refused the right to vote, and so on, by any member group of any society. Leading feminists are correctly opposed to several group variances because they fear that these would entail "losing whatever we gained in terms of gender equality."

Compelling public interest provides another universal criterion. If carrying guns is considered a major safety hazard, no group should be exempted from this rule. The same holds for violations of public health, such as a refusal to immunize children. (Many states in the United States, and other countries such as the Netherlands, exempt parents who claim religious objections from this requirement, a policy that deeply troubles public health officials.)

Whatever is not encompassed in such policies should be considered legitimate subjects for variation. These might well include variances regarding laws, such as those concerning closing days (e.g., laws might require shops to be closed one day a week, but not necessarily Sunday) and those concerning animal rights (to allow ritual slaughter); variances on zoning regulations (e.g., to allow building Mosques); exemptions to allow the use of controlled substances during religious services; and some limited exemptions from various occupational safety, food preparation, and related regulations to help newly established ethnic businesses. (Some of these variances might be limited to a transition period and combined with helping immigrants and minorities in general to adapt to the prevailing laws.)

Arguments that territorial groups or the home-born have a higher level of rights than immigrants are incompatible with the DWU model. Indeed, groups that are territorially concentrated are more inclined than others to push diversity to the point that it may endanger unity, as we witness with groups that are concentrated in one given area, which are much more likely to secede than dispersed groups. Some minority groups may have legitimate reasons to seek to secede, but this constitutes the death knell of unity. While in the past struggles for self-determination were usually involved in the break-up of empires and hence as a rule enhanced democratic representation, regions that now break away from democratic societies are unlikely to enhance self-government and may well weaken it.

Our focus is on practices, not on speech. Thus, it is acceptable for a given group to advocate illiberal practices, but until the laws or constitution are changed, the group should not be allowed to practice them, and surely not impose them on others. Extreme followers of one religion or another may argue that banning some of their practices undermines their whole distinct culture; however, being a member of a free society entails avoiding practices that treat any members in ways that violate their basic rights.

There are no reasons to oppose compromises—if they meet the criteria just articulated. Thus, if Sikhs are willing to wear their daggers but modify them so they cannot be unsheathed, that might bridge the difference between subculture and basic laws.

Whatever position one holds regarding economic equality and social rights, we assume that everyone has the same moral worth bestowed upon them just by being human, whether or not they are citizens, and that discrimination based on race, ethnicity, religion, or gender is illegal. (Whether this applies to private organizations, such as social clubs that receive no public support or tax exemptions, is an open question.)

Rights carry with them corollary responsibilities. This principle can be fully applied to member groups. Thus if a nation is engaged in war with another nation, minority members who have historical and cultural ties to that other nation must serve in the army of the new homeland, like other citizens. If fight we must, no one is exempt on the basis of being a member of a specific racial or ethnic group. (People who are conscientious objectors on religious or secular ethical grounds, assuming their commitments are verified and they are willing to engage in alternative national service, may well be exempt.) The same holds for attending to one's children, paying taxes, Good Samaritan acts, and so on.

State and Religion

Most of the states here under discussion have historically had (or still have) one religion they formally recognize as their only one—Christianity in many of them (including a specific version of it, such as Lutheranism in Sweden). In addition, these states provide extensive financial support directly and indirectly to the institutions of the official state religion, mainly for clergy and places of worship. (France and the United States are the exceptions in this regard as, in the commonly used phrase, they have no established religion.) Almost all of these nations now face massive immigration and growing numbers of minorities that believe in different religions, especially Islam.

Where might one go from here? One option is to maintain the official church. Although often the official religions have placed relatively few demands on people (whether members of minorities or the majority), supporters of assimilation in effect expect considerable stripping of the beliefs held by minorities, who often have strong religious commitments. Importantly, under this approach, minority children are expected to attend public schools in which the values of the governing religion are taught; minority residents and citizens are required to participate in public events in which the prayers are those of another religion; and public lite is studded with symbols of the governing religion and laws reflecting it. This is a maximal challenge to diversity.

A second option is to lift all religions to the same status as the official one. This would entail not only fully supporting the clergy and places of worship (and social services) provided by all religions, but also opening official events with multiple prayers, displaying in public buildings and schools religious symbols of all groups on an egalitarian basis, and so on and on. Such a move would likely be perceived as a direct assault on the historical and cultural identity of a nation, and would be apt to lead to a high level of contention. It would undermine unity considerably.

A third option is for the official standing of the prevailing religion to gradually lapse (as it did in Sweden). Under this model, no new religion would be recognized as the official religion of the state, but financial support for the clergy and places of worship of all religions would be provided. The amount would be determined by the number of people who indicate, annually, that a given religion is theirs. (This would get the state out of the business of determining who is entitled to get support.) This is especially an issue for countries that rely heavily on voluntary associations and social groups to administer social services paid for by the public, as is common in parts of Europe. If religious groups are not included, this amounts to discrimination against those whose primary social affiliation is religious. At the same time, no such support should be available to groups that promote values, whether religious or secular, that are illiberal.

This third model is most compatible with the DWU approach because removing formal recognition of any state religion puts all religions on more equal footing (at least in legal terms and financially) without directly challenging history and identity. Although such a move constitutes a step away from tradition, it does not replace it with any new official requirements. It allows the majority to retain a sense of the centrality of its values (which is not fully satisfactory to minorities). At the same time, it allows the minorities to recognize that the majority has accommodated them in a major way (which leaves some of those who hail from the majority less than fully content). This model allows for diversity without explicitly undermining unity. (It finds a precedent in the way shops were once required to be closed on Sundays, for religious purposes, but are now allowed to have a closing day suiting any religion—say, Friday or Saturday—without officially demoting Sunday.) The sensibilities of the majority are also to be respected.

DWU Schooling

Schooling should neither be used to suppress all cultural differences and distinctions nor to reinforce the segregation and ghettoization of minorities.

The assimilationist model assumes that immigrants and minority members of society will be taught in public schools, that they will be taught basically the same material as other members of the society and more or less the same material as was previously provided. An unbounded diversity model calls for setting up separate schools—publicly supported—and distinct curricula for various ethnic groups from kindergarten to grade 12, such as, for instance, separate Muslim or Jewish schools, not merely as "Sunday" schools but as full-time schools.

A DWU approach, based on the concept of neighborhood schools, suggests that:

(a) a major proportion of the curriculum—say, 85 percent or more—should remain universal (i.e., part of the processes that foster unity). The commonalities of sharing 85 percent or so of the curriculum are intended not merely to ensure that all members of the next generation are exposed to a considerable measure of the same teaching materials, narratives, and normative content, but also that they will mix socially. Hence, teaching the same material but in ethnically segregated schools is incompatible with our approach. (Granted that the segregating effects of such schooling can largely be mitigated if they teach a considerable amount of the "universal" material and endeavor to provide for social mixing, if not in their own confines, elsewhere.) Although teachers of all backgrounds should be welcomed, insisting that children must be taught by teachers who are members of their ethnic group is not compatible with the DWU model.

(b) Minorities should have major input concerning 15 percent or so of the curriculum; this could be in the form of electives or alternative classes in which students particularly interested in one subject or history or tradition could gain enriched education in that area.

(c) The universal, unity-related content of the curriculum should be recast to some extent to include, for instance, more learning about minority cultures and histories. Bilingual education might be used, but only during a transition phase before mainstreaming begins and not as a continuous mode of teaching that is, in effect, segregated along ethnic lines. (Reference is to education that is conducted in the languages of immigrants and not to educational policies in a country that has historically embraced two or more languages.)

Of particular concern is the teaching of values. This issue is highlighted by the fact that many of the most contentious issues in schools, ranging from displacing crucifixes to requiring Muslim girls to wear swimsuits to banning Sikhs' traditional turbans, relate to religion.

One may start with the observation that schools must help develop character and teach basic values rather than merely being institutions for learning "academics." One may also assume that the classes that all pupils will be required to attend (the unity sector of 85 percent-plus) will include classes in which basic civic values will be taught, such as respect for the constitution or basic laws, human rights, the merit of democracy, and the value of mutual respect among different subcultures. (These are to include civic practicums, such as playacting as parliament or civil court or doing community service.) But such education may well not suffice to provide the needed character education and is unlikely by itself to provide a sufficient substitute for the substantive values taught in the past by religions. Given that schools are in the character education "business," the question must be faced, what substantive values are they to instill beyond narrowly crafted civic virtues?

Providing public school classes for each religion (in line with the notion of equal official recognition of all religions) and allowing students to choose which to attend (including classes in secular, humanist ethics) helps diversity, but does little for unity. One way to improve on this approach is for public schools to work with the various religious groups to ensure that the teachers selected for religious teaching (and the teaching materials they use) refrain from advocating or implementing illiberal religious practices. (Although we previously stated that we do not object to illiberal advocacy as distinct from practices, children, whose hearts ands minds have not yet been formed, require extra protection.) It might be said that a democracy should tolerate the teaching of anti-democratic values so long as those who hold them are not seriously challenging the democratic system. However, not all the societies at issue have long-established and well-grounded democratic polities, and hence straining them is not called for. Above all, without leaving fundamentalism out of classrooms, no sufficient sharing of values may be found.

Many of us hold that only public schools can provide an environment in which children are exposed to a rich core of shared values, are protected from fundamentalism, and mix socially with children from different social and religious backgrounds. Some hold that the same may be achieved in private schools, even if controlled by one ethnic or religious group or another, as long as the state ensures that all schools teach a strong core of shared values. In either case, the same essential criteria must be met if schools are to provide effective opportunities to move toward a DWU model in contrast to a homogenous, assimilationist model or a segregated, unbounded multiculturalist one: a core of shared values and social mixing.

Citizenship for Qualifying, Legal Immigrants

Debates over immigration and citizenship policy have often been characterized by wild swings between emotionally fraught, divisive positions and radical proposals for assimilation or unbounded diversity: either we end all immigration or we open our borders to virtually anyone; either immigrants are a burden on taxpayers and responsibility for integration rests solely with newcomers or all newcomers should be given substantial public assistance and helped to maintain their cultures, languages, and identities; either all illegal immigrants should be deported immediately or there should be no distinction between legal and illegal immigrants.

A diversity within unity approach emphasizes that societies are best served if those who are legal immigrants, and have met educational requirements, are allowed to become full citizens rather than treated as guest workers, which is often a term that conceals their true status as permanent, but second class, residents. The key to a democratically defensible and economically viable approach to immigration is to make decisions up front about the scope and nature of immigration that the nation favors. Then the government can provide permanent status for those admitted and facilitate their access to citizenship. This approach offers a more sensible way to staff the labor market, unite families, and allow citizens to assess the way immigration is shaping the national economy and culture.

Cultural preferences—for example, for Spain to prefer immigrants from Spanish-speaking countries—are acceptable because they help sustain unity, so long as they do not prevent immigration for family reunification or refugee purposes and are based on culture rather than race or blood. Public support for immigration also requires that enforcement policies are carried out. Hence, better border control, employer sanctions, perhaps even a national identity card for all legal residents, are best included in any approach that aims to create an effective, publicly defensible system. (These measures do not apply to true political asylum seekers.) More serious efforts to enforce immigration laws that are coupled with sound and transparent criteria for admission will also provide a way of dealing with the ongoing reality of illegal immigration in ways that are consistent with core democratic values. As such a system is introduced, a society can reorient its citizenship away from representing only a bundle of rights and toward an emphasis on civic participation and responsibility.

For legal immigrants, democratic nation-states must provide fair and objective procedures for admission, including reasonable application costs. Linguistic and educational requirements may well be set higher than the current ones, to ensure that citizens-to-be have acquired familiarity not only with the workings of democratic government but also with the unifying elements of the given society. Consideration may be given that immigrants who have not yet completed their citizenship processes could nevertheless be accorded the right to vote in local elections and to serve in civil service as ways to help them acquire the civic practice that makes for good citizens and to help create a civil service that is better equipped to deal with minorities.

Dual citizenship could be allowed or even encouraged so long as appropriate principles and practices for reconciling conflicts among loyalties can be established—notably the principle that the nation of permanent residence takes priority.

All in all: citizenship constitutes a critical way a person becomes a responsible and accepted member of a community. Hence it should not be awarded without proper preparation nor denied to those who have completed the required measure of acculturation.

Throughout this section we assume that citizenship is not based on blood-lines or racial membership but is based on becoming a part of a historical community with its own culture and identity. To join this community is to come to share in that history, culture, and identity—up to a point, as characterized by the difference between elements of unity and diversity previously discussed. To reiterate, history does not stop, and culture and identity continue to be recast, in part under the influence of the new members.

Citizenship should not be a free good, but a communal undertaking, a status and identity that constitutes both rights and social responsibilities. This holds for those who seek to become citizens as it does for those who are already so endowed.

Language: An Inescapable Element of Unity?

The assimilationist model tends to stress that all must acquire the prevailing language (sometimes, as in Belgium, at least one of them), that it should be considered the official language, and that the use of other languages should be banned in official business, courts, ballots, and street signs. Unbounded diversity opposes the recognition of any one language as the official one and seeks to provide a coequal status in courts, documents, etc., to several languages, sometimes a rather large number.

A DWU approach recognizes the strong advantages of having one shared language (two if necessary) and teaching it to all immigrants, minority members, and people whose education is lagging for other reasons. However, the state should provide ample translators and translated documents for those who have not yet acquired the shared language, even if this results in some lowering of the motivation for immigrants to learn the prevailing language.

Neighborhoods should be free to *add* signs in any language, but *not to replace* those in one (or two) of the shared ones. The state may well also encourage keeping the languages of immigrants as second languages and the teaching of second languages in general.

Core Substance, Symbols, National History, Holidays, and Rituals

In numerous situations, differences arise concerning matters that are relatively limited in importance in their own right but acquire great symbolic meaning regarding the rejection, or partial or full acceptance, of people of diverse cultures. These include dress codes (e.g., regarding girls wearing head-scarves), boys and girls swimming together, the display of ethnic versus national flags, areas in which ethnic celebrations can take place, noise levels tolerated, and so on. In effect, practically any issue can be turned into a highly charged symbolic one, although some issues (such as flags) tend more readily to become such.

It is important to recognize that trying to deal with these issues one by one, or by focusing on the surface arguments, will often not lead to consensual resolution, as the matters at hand typically stand for deeper issues. The contested symbols serve as hooks on which people hang their resentment of those of different cultures (including the dominant one) and of the need to adapt to a different world. These symbols serve as expressions of people's sense that their culture, identity, national unity, and self-determination are all being challenged. Only as these deeper issues are addressed might societies be able to work out satisfactory resolutions of the symbolic issues.

Attacking deeply felt and deeply ingrained sentiments, denying that immigrants or minorities are different, and so on—especially labeling all such sentiments as "racist" or "xenophobic" prejudices and demanding that people drop them or be subject to reeducation if not rehabilitation—is as unfair as it is counterproductive.

A DWU position indicates that we understand why people feel the way they do, but also assures them that the cultural changes that they must learn to cope with will not violate their basic values, will not destroy their identity, nor end their ability to control their lives. Indeed, it is the prime merit of the DWU approach that it allows such a framing of the issue, not as a public relations posture or a political formula, but as a worked-out model of laws, policies, and normative concepts that gives substance to such assurances.

Once this basic position is established, we note that adhering to old patriotism, which demands an unquestioning embrace of a nation's past, is just as inappropriate as calling for the dismantling of national identity in order to accommodate diversity. Thus, to expect immigrants from previously colonized countries to see great glory in the imperial past is not compatible with the DWU model any more than is calling on a nation to give up its shared values, symbols, and meanings and to become merely a thin and formal affiliation. Arguments to "rethink what it means to be British" (or French, etc.) are welcome if they mean to redefine commonalities and to point to legitimate differences, but not if they are code words for abandoning shared substantive meanings and values. Nor should one assume that even in a full-fledged European federation national identities and cultures will vanish in the foreseeable future, thus dissolving the deeper issues at hand.

The assimilationist model favors stressing the nation's shared fate and glorious achievements in textbooks (especially those concerning history), national holidays, and rituals. Some champions of unbounded diversity call for redefining history as long periods of lessons in national disgrace (for example, one scholar suggested that American history be taught as a series of abuses of minorities, beginning with Native Americans, turning to slaves, then to Japanese Americans during World War II, and so on). Others favor separate ethnic and religious holidays, such as Christmas, Hanukkah, and Kwanza, to replace rather than supplement shared national holidays.

The DWU position on these issues remains to be worked out. As far as the teaching of history is concerned, surely many would agree that to the extent that textbooks and other teaching materials contain statements that are truly offensive to minorities, they should be removed or corrected, and that recognition of minorities' contributions to the society should be added. In addition, history of parts of the world other than one's own should occupy an important part in any curriculum. Still, the teaching of history is a major way that shared meanings and values are transmitted and it should neither be "particularized" nor become a source of attack on the realm of unity.

As far as holidays are concerned, a combination of shared holidays (such as Unification Day in Germany) with separate ethnic and religious ones may be quite compatible with a DWU model. In effect, the existence of some ethnic holidays (such as Cinco de Mayo) enriches rather than diminishes the shared culture.

We focus here on shared and divergent values in a society that is a community of communities rather than a mindless, over-homogenized blend. This focus is in no way meant to distract attention from the need to be concerned with economic interests and their articulation and matters dealing with the distribution of power. However, given that these issues have been often explored, our focus has been on values (and related institutions), a core part of any society that is able to sustain itself and change peacefully at the same time.

The most challenging issue of them all is to consider, beyond changes in symbolic expressions and even in laws and policies, what would be encompassed in a modified but unified core of shared substantive values? Commitment to a bill of rights, the democratic way of life, respect for basic laws (or, more broadly, a constitutional faith or civic religion), and mutual tolerance come (at least relatively) easily. So do the communitarian concepts that rights entail responsibilities, that working differences out is to be preferred to conflict, and that society is to be considered a community of communities (rather than merely a state that contains millions of individuals). However, as important as these are and as much as they move us forward, these relatively thin conceptions of unity (and those limited to points of commonality—overlapping areas of consensus—among diverse cultures) constitute an insufficient core of shared values to sustain unity among diversity.

The challenge for the DWU model is to ask how the realm of unity, however restated, can be thick enough without violating the legitimate place of diversity. The answer may be found in part in secular humanist values and ethics (including respect for individual dignity and autonomy) and thicker communitarian values that spell out our obligations to one another. It may encompass a commitment to building still more encompassing communities (such as the European Union), to assisting those in need in the "have-not" countries, and to upholding the United Nations Universal Declaration of Human Rights. Still, the question stands as to what will provide a source of shared commitments to define and promote what is right versus wrong, and what will provide an answer to transcendental questions of life, as far as they concern public life, if it will not be based on religious doctrines, nor be sheerly relativistic or based on the beliefs of particularistic groups.

The DWU approach is a work in progress. It does not claim to have all or even most of the answers needed to bridge the schisms that have opened up between many immigrants and the majorities in the free societies in which they live. It does offer, we state, a basic orientation that respects both the history, culture, and identity of a society and the rights of members of the society to differ on those issues that do not involve the core of basic values and universally established rights and obligations.

Endorsers are of one mind on the broad thrust of this platform and the necessity of this intervention into the current dialogue, without necessarily agreeing with every single, specific statement. We look forward to future discussions of how this platform applies to other problems that arise and to various different societies.

Note

To allow for productive deliberations, we limit this initial examination to well-established nations and those with democratic governments, including those in Western Europe, North America, Japan, and Australia. We do not deal with immigration and identity issues in countries that are in the nation-building stage (and hence might need to first build a shared identity and shared institutions before they face the question of how these might be protected or changed) or in those that rely on a non-democratic government to deal with the issues at hand. The discussion covers both immigrant and minority groups of citizens within a country.

For a history and overview of the Diversity Within Unity project and a list of endorsers, plus German, Italian, and Spanish translations, please visit www.communitariannetwork.org.

The Dubious Value of Value-Neutrality

STEPHEN H. BALCH

Legislative hearings into allegations of political bias against conservative students at Pennsylvania's universities have yielded a steady stream of news. Most reports have focused on whether charges that individual students have been victims of classroom bias can be substantiated. What is getting lost is a more fundamental issue raised in the hearings: Does academe's claim to "value-neutrality" mask the imposition of leftist values?

What would it take to be genuinely value-neutral?

The Web site of the University of Pittsburgh's School of Social Work proclaims that it is "committed to promoting the values of social and economic justice." Pitt's women's-studies program lists "activism/advocacy" as one of its purposes, declaring that it serves "as a clearinghouse by helping to connect activist groups with the university community." Pitt's cultural-studies program announces that the discipline "tends to be inclined toward left-inflected social change."

Presented with the last of those self-definitions during one of the hearings, Pitt's provost, James V. Maher, at first responded with embarrassed surprise: "And that's the description of the program by the people who are in the program?" But steadying himself, he sought to put the facts into the reassuring context that "we're institutionally value-neutral, which allows us to be a meeting ground for all the different viewpoints that are characterized in the human condition. Individuals within the university and small groups of professors can describe themselves in one way or another as long as they, when they're dealing with our students, obey our rules about treating those students correctly."

Some legislators may have thereby inferred that a crawl through Pitt's Web pages would disclose parallel programs with declared commitments to "social and economic liberty," or that are "right-inflected," or that serve as clearinghouses for anti-abortion groups. Happily for Mr. Maher, that hypothesis was not immediately testable. Still more fortunate, no one called attention to his office's own "faculty diversity seminars," which seek to "restructure courses to reflect diverse perspectives." Most proponents of the traditional liberal arts would be unlikely to find that multicultural push value-neutral.

Pitt's unusual way of observing value-neutrality is, of course, hardly unique. Just about everywhere in academe, value-neutrality is most conspicuously honored in the breach. Programs in social work, education, women's studies, sociology, etc., commonly wear ideological affiliations proudly on their sleeves, and hardly a college lacks an office devoted to the celebration of multicultural ideals. In fact, they go further. At Rhode Island College, a conservative student in a social-work program was told he could receive a failing grade for refusing to lobby for legislation he opposed. At Washington State University, a Christian student was nearly run out of an education program because his understanding of topics like "race, power, gender, class, sexual orientation, and privilege in American society" was at variance with the views of his professors.

But American higher education's deficiencies in value-neutrality may not be entirely its own fault. The norm itself has some severe shortcomings.

Historically, education has rarely been value-neutral. Few have ever wanted it to be. At the lower grades, the inculcation of shared ideals of personal conduct, group allegiance, and political philosophy has long been expected. And the rejection of value-neutrality has been nearly as complete at education's higher levels. European universities were traditionally religion-centered, a fact of massive consequence for defining instruction, acceptable scholarly discourse, student admissions, and faculty appointments. Until the Civil War, religious purposes initiated the overwhelming majority of academic foundings in the United States as well.

Value-neutrality has been rejected for good philosophical reason. It's impossible to frame a program of education without making suppositions about its larger purposes or the type of society it is meant to sustain. In some educational domains, objectives can be merely technical: how to do this or that. But curricula in humane studies are appealing largely to the extent that they address problems that are thought morally, as well as intellectually, significant. The very term "liberal education" denotes a course of study preparing one for the obligations and opportunities of free citizenship—considered to be a fundamental good.

Just about everywhere in academe, value-neutrality is most conspicuously honored in the breach.

What subjects are worth emphasizing, and what are not, is a question necessarily fraught with moral significance. That doesn't mean that an education need be "relevant" in any day-to-day sense. To identify questions as "great," "transcendent," or "universal" is also a value-laden act. But unless anchored in moral judgment, education loses coherence.

Descending from the philosophical to the sociological, education's normative entanglements remain no less binding. Universities have a number of distinguishing characteristics. They are intimate communities, with inhabitants often living at close quarters. They are voluntary associations, with members able to withdraw if unhappy about the quality of life. And they are devoted to rigorous discourse, requiring due care that emotion doesn't overwhelm intellect. Can such fragile assemblages survive without base-line norms governing colloquy? Are the dictates of reason likely to be upheld in an environment of chronic vituperation and abuse? Serious deliberation requires some effort at maintaining a shared sense of moral community.

Contemporary university leadership is more than a little obsessed with the need to keep campus speech "sensitive" and "non-offending." If by that administrators mean that their institutions cannot function in a constant tumult of hatred and derision, they're no doubt correct. The problem is not with the principle they urge that reasoned discourse without some mutual respect ceases to be reasoned—but in the way they have disingenuously applied it.

Through speech codes and other devices, they have regularly hijacked the principle for crudely partisan purpose, applying a most accommodating standard of acceptable acrimony to arguments they favor, and another, severe and capricious, to those they oppose. Compared to such rank unfairness, value-neutrality appears, quite reasonably, the superior alternative, and efforts to enforce it under the aegis of First Amendment jurisprudence have given flagrant abuses some highly salutary checks. But viewed as an academic principle of systemic application, value-neutrality is a chimera, its allure largely the consequence of frustration and despair.

To be sure, strict value-neutrality does have its proper academic place, and that is in scientific research. Research agendas reflect normative as well as intellectual commitments, but research methods, and the interpretation of research data, must be free of wishful thinking to yield useful results. Universities are, of course, crucial sites of scientific investigation and must protect the honesty of research. But to say that doesn't mean that they need embrace value-neutrality in any more global sense.

So Provost Maher doubly misspoke. His institution isn't value-neutral, *and* it shouldn't have to be. What, then, should it be? Let me coin a new formulation. Our universities shouldn't embody value-neutrality but "value-liberality," a term I hope captures a two-part meaning.

I ts first part recommends that our universities embrace values supportive of those broad confines of personal and civil liberty that a system of representative constitutional government affords. That is not, obviously, a value-neutral conception of education's role; it embodies fidelity to a particular form of social and political organization—liberalism traditionally understood. But it is one that the great majority

of Americans are likely to see as legitimate and that is entirely consistent with cultivating critical powers of mind and a broad spectrum of reasoned discourse. Universities should not be reluctant to say that they believe in republican government, or that they work to strengthen its frameworks and practices.

The second component advises a counterpart organization of academic life that exposes scholars and students to the full contest of serious moral and theoretic persuasions. The governing principle here is an openness to all points of view able to make their case at a level of logical cogency and evidentiary support commensurate with appropriate disciplinary standards, and willing to give an attentive hearing when similarly credentialed persuasions reply in kind. That doesn't exclude perspectives that challenge liberal traditions in education or elsewhere, or views that question established conceptions of any kind, but it does exclude opinion poorly informed, cranky, intemperate, dogmatic, or menacing, however protected or popular it may be in the larger public square. (Needless to say, those strictures should be applied far more firmly to faculty members operating in professional settings than to students engaged in extracurricular debate.)

In general, value-liberality demands that universities give extended, continuing, and probably institutionalized consideration to how reasonable and intellectually pluralistic environments can be effectively sustained—something they rarely now attempt.

T he absence of value-liberality constitutes the gravest intellectual failure of contemporary academic life. In its stead, we have a "value-partisanship" that gives privileged place to a narrow, leftward segment of the intellectual spectrum. The academy has wandered into that dead end partly because, in kidding itself about its vaunted value-neutrality, it has not provided the organizational underpinnings necessary to sustain an environment of disparate opinion and robust, multisided debate. It has been especially remiss in the realms of humane learning, where factional passions have always been strong. The outcome has been the creation of a closed intellectual shop.

I have previously suggested that we establish "intellectually diverse" programs of an autonomy sufficient to afford a measure of professional security to the philosophical factions lodged within them, but simultaneously required to participate in a broader system of rational disputation defined by common rules of intellectual rigor, fairness, and professional respect. That kind of niched, academically distinct programming is, in fact, spreading at an accelerating pace—a process in which the National Association of Scholars has played a quiet but considerable role for more than a decade.

Viewed as an academic principle of systemic application, value-neutrality is a chimera, its allure the result of frustration and despair.

Although the children of the 1960s provided something of a model in the various specialty "studies" they used as wedges into university life, the new movement differs greatly from theirs in philosophy and strategic conception, aiming at pluralism, not capturing the curriculum; education, not activism; and eschewing disruptive tactics. The NAS's role has involved recruiting program architects from within its faculty networks; sponsoring workshops, retreats, and conferences; sharing proven program designs; advising inexperienced grant seekers; helping to draw additional groups into a collective effort; and working with them to enlist alumni, donors, and public officials.

To be sure, none of this has been rocket science, and a goodly number of academics have been able to launch very successful programs on their own. The idea is simply in the air, awaiting only the final blessing of the establishment.

New programs have already been created at institutions as diverse as Brown, Clemson, Colgate, Duke, and Princeton Universities; the City University of New York (based at Bernard Baruch College, but operating systemwide); the Universities of Alaska at Fairbanks, Colorado at Boulder, and Wisconsin at Milwaukee; and City Colleges of Chicago's Wilbur Wright College, among others. Virtually all of them focus on subject matter unfashionable in the "progressive," postmodern, dead-white-male-averse academy. Specific themes include political theory (the Political Theory Project at Brown, "especially interested in market-based approaches to social problems" and the investigation of ideals of "freedom and social accountability"); the intersection of politics, economics, and the humanities (the Gerst program at Duke, stressing an "understanding of the central importance of freedom for democratic government, moral responsibility, and economic and cultural life"); Western civilization as a comprehensive and integrating theme (the Center for Freedom and Western Civilization at Colgate and the Center for Western Civilization at Colorado); the Great Books (programs at Wisconsin and Wilbur Wright); free institutions (the CUNY Free Institutions Initiative, based at Baruch College's School of Public Affairs and Alaska's Democracy Forum); capitalism and freedom (the Clemson Institute for the Study of Capitalism); and American ideals and institutions (the James Madison program in American ideals and institutions at Princeton). Perhaps even more important, they are intensely earnest about fostering the civil, reasoned engagement with scholars of different views often lacking elsewhere. As the director of one prominent program says, "We practice what they preach."

Most of these programs are still small, but also growing, raising money, attracting students, and, most vital for the long term, enlisting private and public donors. Just last year, the program on religion in American public life at the University of Notre Dame and the Gerst program at Duke received large National Endowment for the Humanities challenge grants to help build their endowments. The majority of programs, however, rely almost completely on private donors, frequently drawn from alumni looking to broaden the perspectives to which students are exposed. The budget of the Madison program at Princeton has now risen to about $1.3-million per year and that of Brown's Political Theory Project to about $500,000 annually, and several other programs are moving into the multiple-six-figure range.

Nearly all these programs sponsor lectures and symposia or promote research—but many are also creating curricula. And where programs sponsor concentrations or individual courses (as at Brown, Duke, and Wisconsin), opportunities to influence departmental hires have been developing. Restoring intellectual pluralism to university faculties is an indispensable measure if value-liberality is to be made real. Only the clash of opposing faculty minds will make the university's commitment to freedom and open discourse convincing.

Value-neutrality has a deceptive allure. It suggests that higher education can avoid making philosophic choices, standing above controversy in some unsullied realm of austere fact. In truth, those choices are impossible to avoid, even if different institutions may wish to make them in different ways. The problem is that they have almost always made them in the very same way, with value-neutrality serving as no more than a public-relations cover. The values overwhelmingly chosen have been narrowly factional and adversarial, embodying a radical critique of traditional American practices. Such choices are not long likely to be tenable, particularly within the taxpayer-supported sector of American higher education. Nor will they lead to good education: Their constriction of argument ensures stultification. Better to elect an outlook that fortifies academic purpose, allows a breadth of discourse both orthodox and heterodox, and embraces the ideals of openness, freedom, and honest civility, cherished by the majority of Americans.

STEPHEN H. BALCH is president of the National Association of Scholars.

From *Chronicle of Higher Education*, Vol. 52, no. 41, June 16, 2006, pp. B15–B16. Copyright © 2006 by Stephen Balch. Reproduced with permission of the author.

UNIT 2

Socialization and Social Control

Unit Selections

Key Points to Consider

- What are the major natural differences between males and females, and how are they socialized differently?

- How can the ways in which children are socialized in America be improved?

- What are the principal factors that make people what they are?

- Why has crime declined in the United States in the past two decades?

- What are the differences between street crime and white collar crime? Which has more harmful effects? What are the differences in the severity of the punishments for the two types of criminals? Explain these differences.

- What are the most effective ways to deal with crime?

Student Web Site

www.mhcls.com/online

Internet References

Further information regarding these Web sites may be found in this book's preface or online.

Center for Leadership Studies
http://www.situational.com
Crime Times
http://www.crime-times.org
Ethics Updates/Lawrence Hinman
http://ethics.sandiego.edu/
National Institute on Drug Abuse (NIDA)
http://www.nida.nih.gov/

Why do we behave the way we do? Three forces are at work: biology, socialization, and the human will or internal decision maker. The focus in sociology is on socialization, which is the conscious and unconscious process whereby we learn the norms and behavior patterns that enable us to function appropriately in our social environment. Socialization is based on the need to belong, because the desire for acceptance is the major motivation for internalizing the socially approved attitudes and behaviors. Fear of punishment is another motivation. It is utilized by parents and institutionalized in the law enforcement system. The language we use, the concepts we apply in thinking, the images we have of ourselves, our gender roles, and our masculine and feminine ideals are all learned through socialization. Socialization may take place in many contexts. The most basic socialization takes place in the family, but churches, schools, communities, the media, and workplaces also play major roles in the process.

The first subsection deals with issues concerning the basic influences on the development of our character and behavior patterns. Matt Ridley reviews the latest science on the nature versus nurture debate. It is clear that both are important, and now we are learning that there is an interaction between genes and the environment. Ridley explains that "genes are not static blueprints that dictate our destiny. How they are expressed— where and when they are turned on or off and for how long—is affected by changes in the womb, by the environment, and by other factors." In the next article, Hara Estroff Marano reviews the literature on the genetic differences between men and women, including mental, sexual, health, emotional, and psychological differences. For example, did you know that women have more gray brain matter and men have more white brain matter? Gray matter provides concentrated processing power and more thought linking capability. White matter helps spatial reasoning and allows for single-mindedness. Marano also explains many other differences.

The following subsection deals with crime, law enforcement, and social control—major concerns today because crime and violence seem to be out of control. In the first article in this subsection, John Donohue applies economic cost-benefit analysis to many aspects of crime control and makes recommendations based on these analyses, including that we should abolish the death penalty, legalize drugs, pass sensible hand gun laws, and stop building new prisons. On the other hand, we should expand police forces. In the subsequent piece, Jennifer Roback Morse argues that "for some people, prisons are a substitute for parents . . . [for] without parents—two of them, married to each other, working together as a team—a child is more likely to end up in the criminal justice system." A key role of parents is to help a child develop a conscience and self-control, and two loving married parents do this job the best. Morse shows that dealing with criminals is very costly for society, and indirectly the failure of many marriages contributes substantially to these costs. In the final article, David Anderson tries to put into monetary terms the impacts of various types of crimes in the United States. The results produce some surprises. First, when he includes many costs that are seldom taken into account—such as the costs of law enforcement, security measures, and lost time at work—the total bill is over $1 trillion, or over $4,000 per person. Another surprise is the relative costs of white-collar crime versus street crime. Fraud and cheating on taxes costs Americans over 20 times the costs of theft, burglary, and robbery.

Ambition: Why Some People Are Most Likely to Succeed

**A fire in the belly doesn't light itself. Does the spark of ambition lie
in genes, family, culture—or even in your own hands? Science has answers**

JEFFREY KLUGER

You don't get as successful as Gregg and Drew Shipp by accident. Shake hands with the 36-year-old fraternal twins who co-own the sprawling Hi Fi Personal Fitness club in Chicago, and it's clear you're in the presence of people who thrive on their drive. But that wasn't always the case. The twins' father founded the Jovan perfume company, a glamorous business that spun off the kinds of glamorous profits that made it possible for the Shipps to amble through high school, coast into college and never much worry about getting the rent paid or keeping the fridge filled. But before they graduated, their sense of drift began to trouble them. At about the same time, their father sold off the company, and with it went the cozy billets in adult life that had always served as an emotional backstop for the boys.

That did it. By the time they got out of school, both Shipps had entirely transformed themselves, changing from boys who might have grown up to live off the family's wealth to men consumed with going out and creating their own. "At this point," says Gregg, "I consider myself to be almost maniacally ambitious."

It shows. In 1998 the brothers went into the gym trade. They spotted a modest health club doing a modest business, bought out the owner and transformed the place into a luxury facility where private trainers could reserve space for top-dollar clients. In the years since, the company has outgrown one building, then another, and the brothers are about to move a third time. Gregg, a communications major at college, manages the club's clients, while Drew, a business major, oversees the more hardheaded chore of finance and expansion. "We're not sitting still," Drew says. "Even now that we're doing twice the business we did at our old place, there's a thirst that needs to be quenched."

Why is that? Why are some people born with a fire in the belly, while others—like the Shipps—need something to get their pilot light lit? And why do others never get the flame of ambition going? Is there a family anywhere that doesn't have its overachievers and underachievers—its Jimmy Carters and Billy Carters, its Jeb Bushes and Neil Bushes—and find itself wondering how they all could have come splashing out of exactly the same gene pool?

Of all the impulses in humanity's behavioral portfolio, ambition—that need to grab an ever bigger piece of the resource pie before someone else gets it—ought to be one of the most democratically distributed. Nature is a zero-sum game, after all. Every buffalo you kill for your family is one less for somebody else's; every acre of land you occupy elbows out somebody else. Given that, the need to get ahead ought to be hard-wired into all of us equally.

> **"For me, ambition has become a dirty word. I prefer hunger."**
> **—Johnny Depp**

And yet it's not. For every person consumed with the need to achieve, there's someone content to accept whatever life brings. For everyone who chooses the 80-hour workweek, there's someone punching out at 5. Men and women—so it's said—express ambition differently; so do Americans and Europeans, baby boomers and Gen Xers, the middle class and the well-to-do. Even among the manifestly motivated, there are degrees of ambition.

Steve Wozniak co-founded Apple Computer and then left the company in 1985 as a 34-year-old multimillionaire. His partner, Steve Jobs, is still innovating at Apple and moonlighting at his second blockbuster company, Pixar Animation Studios.

Not only do we struggle to understand why some people seem to have more ambition than others, but we can't even agree on just what ambition is. "Ambition is an evolutionary product," says anthropologist Edward Lowe at Soka University of America, in Aliso Viejo, Calif. "No matter how social status is defined, there are certain people in every community who aggressively pursue it and others who aren't so aggressive."

Dean Simonton, a psychologist at the University of California, Davis, who studies genius, creativity and eccentricity, believes it's more complicated than that. "Ambition is energy and determination," he says. "But it calls for goals too. People with goals but no energy are the ones who wind up sitting on the couch saying 'One day I'm going to build a better mousetrap.' People with energy but no clear goals just dissipate themselves in one desultory project after the next."

"Ambition is like love, impatient both of delays and rivals."

—Buddah

Assuming you've got drive, dreams and skill, is all ambition equal? Is the overworked lawyer on the partner track any more ambitious than the overworked parent on the mommy track? Is the successful musician to whom melody comes naturally more driven than the unsuccessful one who sweats out every note? We may listen to Mozart, but should we applaud Salieri?

Most troubling of all, what about when enough ambition becomes way too much? Grand dreams unmoored from morals are the stuff of tyrants—or at least of Enron. The 16-hour workday filled with high stress and at-the-desk meals is the stuff of burnout and heart attacks. Even among kids, too much ambition quickly starts to do real harm. In a just completed study, anthropologist Peter Demerath of Ohio State University surveyed 600 students at a high-achieving high school where most of the kids are triple-booked with advanced-placement courses, sports and after-school jobs. About 70% of them reported that they were starting to feel stress some or all of the time. "I asked one boy how his parents react to his workload, and he answered, 'I don't really get home that often,'" says Demerath. "Then he handed me his business card from the video store where he works."

Anthropologists, psychologists and others have begun looking more closely at these issues, seeking the roots of ambition in family, culture, gender, genes and more. They have by no means thrown the curtain all the way back, but they have begun to part it. "It's fundamentally human to be prestige conscious," says Soka's Lowe. "It's not enough just to be fed and housed. People want more."

If humans are an ambitious species, it's clear we're not the only one. Many animals are known to signal their ambitious tendencies almost from birth. Even before wolf pups are weaned, they begin sorting themselves out into alphas and all the others. The alphas are quicker, more curious, greedier for space, milk, Mom—and they stay that way for life. Alpha wolves wander widely, breed annually and may live to a geriatric 10 or 11 years old. Lower-ranking wolves enjoy none of these benefits—staying close to home, breeding rarely and usually dying before they're 4.

Humans often report the same kind of temperamental determinism. Families are full of stories of the inexhaustible infant who grew up to be an entrepreneur, the phlegmatic child who never really showed much go. But if it's genes that run the show, what accounts for the Shipps, who didn't bestir themselves until the cusp of adulthood? And what, more tellingly, explains identical twins—precise genetic templates of each other who ought to be temperamentally identical but often exhibit profound differences in the octane of their ambition?

Ongoing studies of identical twins have measured achievement motivation—lab language for ambition—in identical siblings separated at birth, and found that each twin's profile overlaps 30% to 50% of the other's. In genetic terms, that's an awful lot—"a benchmark for heritability," says geneticist Dean Hamer of the National Cancer Institute. But that still leaves a great deal that can be determined by experiences in infancy, subsequent upbringing and countless other imponderables.

Some of those variables may be found by studying the function of the brain. At Washington University, researchers have been conducting brain imaging to investigate a trait they call persistence—the ability to stay focused on a task until it's completed just so—which they consider one of the critical engines driving ambition.

The researchers recruited a sample group of students and gave each a questionnaire designed to measure persistence level. Then they presented the students with a task—identifying sets of pictures as either pleasant or unpleasant and taken either indoors or outdoors—while conducting magnetic resonance imaging of their brains. The nature of the task was unimportant, but how strongly the subjects felt about performing it well—and where in the brain that feeling was processed—could say a lot. In general, the researchers found that students who scored highest in persistence had the greatest activity in the limbic region, the area of the brain related to emotions and habits. "The correlation was .8 [or 80%]," says professor of psychiatry Robert Cloninger, one of the investigators. "That's as good as you can get."

It's impossible to say whether innate differences in the brain were driving the ambitious behavior or whether learned behavior was causing the limbic to light up. But a number of researchers believe it's possible for the non-ambitious to jump-start their drive, provided the right jolt comes along. "Energy level may be genetic," says psychologist Simonton, "but a lot of times it's just" Simonton and others often cite the case of Franklin D. Roosevelt, who might not have been the same President he became—or even become President at all—had his disabling polio not taught him valuable lessons about patience and tenacity.

I s such an epiphany possible for all of us, or are some people immune to this kind of lightning? Are there individuals or whole groups for whom the amplitude of ambition is simply lower than it is for others? It's a question—sometimes a charge—that hangs at the edges of all discussions about gender and work, about whether women really have the meat-eating temperament to survive in the professional world. Both research findings and everyday experience suggest that women's ambitions express themselves differently from men's. The meaning of that difference is the hinge on which the arguments turn.

"Ambition makes you look pretty ugly."
—Radiohead

Economists Lise Vesterlund of the University of Pittsburgh and Muriel Niederle of Stanford University conducted a study in which they assembled 40 men and 40 women, gave them five minutes to add up as many two-digit numbers as they could, and paid them 50¢ for each correct answer. The subjects were not competing against one another but simply playing against the house. Later, the game was changed to a tournament in which the subjects were divided into teams of two men or two women each. Winning teams got $2 per computation; losers got nothing. Men and women performed equally in both tests, but on the third round, when asked to choose which of the two ways they wanted to play, only 35% of the women opted for the tournament format; 75% of the men did.

"Men and women just differ in their appetite for competition," says Vesterlund. "There seems to be a dislike for it among women and a preference among men."

"Ambition, old mankind, the immemorial weakness of the strong."
—Vita Sackville-West

To old-line employers of the old-boy school, this sounds like just one more reason to keep the glass ceiling polished. But other behavioral experts think Vesterlund's conclusions go too far. They say it's not that women aren't ambitious enough to compete for what they want; it's that they're more selective about when they engage in competition; they're willing to get ahead at high cost but not at any cost. "Primate-wide, males are more directly competitive than females, and that makes sense," says Sarah Blaffer Hrdy, emeritus professor of anthropology at the University of California, Davis. "But that's not the same as saying women aren't innately competitive too."

As with so much viewed through the lens of anthropology, the roots of these differences lie in animal and human mating strategies. Males are built to go for quick, competitive reproductive hits and move on. Women are built for the it-takes-a-village life, in which they provide long-term care to a very few young and must sail them safely into an often hostile world. Among some of our evolutionary kin—baboons, macaques and other old-world monkeys—this can be especially tricky since young females inherit their mother's social rank. The mothers must thus operate the levers of society deftly so as to raise both their own position and, eventually, their daughters'. If you think that kind of ambition-by-proxy doesn't translate to humans, Hrdy argues, think again. "Just read an Edith Wharton novel about women in old New York competing for marriage potential for their daughters," she says.

Import such tendencies into the 21st century workplace, and you get women who are plenty able to compete ferociously but are inclined to do it in teams and to split the difference if they don't get everything they want. And mothers who appear to be unwilling to strive and quit the workplace altogether to go raise their kids? Hrdy believes they're competing for the most enduring stakes of all, putting aside their near-term goals to ensure the long-term success of their line. Robin Parker, 46, a campaign organizer who in 1980 was already on the presidential stump with Senator Edward Kennedy, was precisely the kind of lifetime pol who one day finds herself in the West Wing. But in 1992, at the very moment a President of her party was returning to the White House and she might have snagged a plum Washington job, she decamped from the capital, moved to Boston with her family and became a full-time mom to her two sons.

"Being out in the world became a lot less important to me," she says. "I used to worry about getting Presidents elected, and I'm still an incredibly ambitious person. But

Donald Trump

Achievements

Before he ever uttered the words "You're fired," Trump developed more than 18 million sq. ft. of Manhattan real estate, naming most of it after himself.

Early Signs Of Ambition

While in college, Donald read federal foreclosure listings for fun. It paid off: he bought his first housing project before he graduated.

Bill Clinton

Achievements

Former U.S. President, current global celebrity.

Early Signs Of Ambition

At 16, he beat out some 1,000 other boys to win a mock state senate seat and a trip to Washington, where he knew "the action was." Once in the capital, he got himself into position to shake hands with his idol, President John F. Kennedy.

Oprah Winfrey

Achievements

Her $1 billion media empire includes movies, a magazine and her talk show, now in its 20th year.

Early Signs Of Ambition

She could read at 2, and although she was just 5 when she started school, she insisted on being put in first grade. Her teacher relented. The next year young Oprah was skipped to third grade.

Tiger Woods

Achievements

At 21, he was the youngest golfer ever ranked No. 1 in the world. Now 29, he holds the record for most prize money won in a career—$56 million and counting.

Early Signs Of Ambition

At 6, he listened to motivational tapes—"I will make my own destiny"—while practicing his swing in the mirror.

Martha Stewart

Achievements

The lifestyle guru rules an empire that includes one magazine, two TV shows, a satellite-radio deal, a shelf full of best sellers and a home-furnishings line at Kmart.

Early Signs Of Ambition

As a grade-schooler, she organized and catered neighborhood birthday parties because, she says, the going rate of 50 an hr. for babysitting "wasn't quite enough money."

Vera Wang

Achievements

She turned one-of-a-kind wedding gowns into a $300 million fashion business.

Early Signs Of Ambition

Although from a wealthy family, she spent her high school summers working as a sales clerk in a Manhattan boutique.

After college, she landed a job at *Vogue* magazine, where she put in seven-day workweeks, rose quickly and became a senior editor at 23.

Condoleezza Rice

Achievements

The current Secretary of State and former National Security Adviser was 38 when she became Stanford University's youngest, and first female, provost.

Early Signs Of Ambition

A gifted child pianist who began studying at the Birmingham Conservatory at 10, the straight-A student became a competitive ice skater, rising at 4:30 a.m. to spend two hours at the rink before school and piano lessons.

Sean Combs

Achievements

Diddy, as he's now known, is a Grammy-winning performer and producer and a millionaire businessman with a restaurant, a clothing line and a marketing and ad agency.

Early Signs Of Ambition

During his days at Howard University, he learned about business by doing: he sold term papers and tickets to dance parties he hosted.

Jennifer Lopez

Achievements

The former Fly Girl dancer has sold 40 million records, is the highest-paid Latina actress in Hollywood and has launched fashion and perfume lines.

Early Signs Of Ambition

When she signed with Sony Music, she insisted on dealing with its chief, Tommy Mottola. She told him she wanted "the A treatment. I want everything top of the line."

Britney Spears

Achievements

Her first single and first four albums made their debut at No. 1. Since then she has sold 76 million records and amassed a $150 million fortune.

Early Signs Of Ambition

Spears used to lock herself in the bathroom and sing to her dolls. After each number, she practiced smiling and blowing kisses to her toy audience.

Tom Cruise

Achievements

He's a movie superstar who gets $25 million a film, an accomplished actor with three Oscar nods and a gossip staple who has sold a zillion magazines.

Early Signs Of Ambition

After his first role in a high school musical, he asked his family to give him 10 years to make it in show business. Within four, he was starring in the surprise hit film *Risky Business*.

what I want to succeed at now is managing my family, raising my boys, helping my husband and the community. In 10 years, when the boys are launched, who knows what I'll be doing? But for now, I have my world."

But even if something as primal as the reproductive impulse wires you one way, it's possible for other things to rewire you completely. Two of the biggest influences on your level of ambition are the family that produced you and the culture that produced your family.

There are no hard rules for the kinds of families that turn out the highest achievers. Most psychologists agree that parents who set tough but realistic challenges, applaud successes and go easy on failures produce kids with the greatest self-confidence.

What's harder for parents to control but has perhaps as great an effect is the level of privilege into which their kids are born. Just how wealth or poverty influences drive is difficult to predict. Grow up in a rich family, and you can inherit either the tools to achieve (think both Presidents Bush) or the indolence of the aristocrat. Grow up poor, and you can come away with either the motivation to strive (think Bill Clinton) or the inertia of the hopeless. On the whole, studies suggest it's the upper middle class that produces the greatest proportion of ambitious people—mostly because it also produces the greatest proportion of anxious people.

When measuring ambition, anthropologists divide families into four categories: poor, struggling but getting by, upper middle class, and rich. For members of the first two groups, who are fighting just to keep the electricity on and the phone bill paid, ambition is often a luxury. For the rich, it's often unnecessary. It's members of the upper middle class, reasonably safe economically but not so safe that a bad break couldn't spell catastrophe, who are most driven to improve their lot. "It's called status anxiety," says anthropologist Lowe, "and whether you're born to be concerned about it or not, you do develop it."

"Ambition is so powerful a passion in the human breast that however high we reach, we are never satisfied."

—Niccolo Machiavelli

But some societies make you more anxious than others. The U.S. has always been a me-first culture, as befits a nation that grew from a scattering of people on a fat saddle of continent where land was often given away. That have-it-all ethos persists today, even though the resource freebies are long since gone. Other countries—where the acreage is smaller and the pickings are slimmer—came of age differently, with the need to cooperate getting etched into the cultural DNA. The American model has produced wealth, but it has come at a price—with ambition sometimes turning back on the ambitious and consuming them whole.

The study of high-achieving high school students conducted by Ohio State's Demerath was noteworthy for more than the stress he found the students were suffering. It also revealed the lengths to which the kids and their parents were willing to go to gain an advantage over other suffering students. Cheating was common, and most students shrugged it off as only a minor problem. A number of parents—some of whose children carried a 4.0 average—sought to have their kids classified as special-education students, which would entitle them to extra time on standardized tests. "Kids develop their own moral code," says Demerath. "They have a keen sense of competing with others and are developing identities geared to that."

Demerath got very different results when he conducted research in a very different place—Papua, New Guinea. In the mid-1990s, he spent a year in a small village there, observing how the children learned. Usually, he found, they saw school as a noncompetitive place where it was important to succeed collectively and then move on. Succeeding at the expense of others was seen as a form of vanity that the New Guineans call "acting extra." Says Demerath: "This is an odd thing for them."

That makes tactical sense. In a country based on farming and fishing, you need to know that if you get sick and can't work your field or cast your net, someone else will do it for you. Putting on airs in the classroom is not the way to ensure that will happen.

Of course, once a collectivist not always a collectivist. Marcelo Suárez-Orozco, a professor of globalization and education at New York University, has been following 400 families that immigrated to the U.S. from Asia, Latin America and the Caribbean. Many hailed from villages where the American culture of competition is alien, but once they got here, they changed fast.

As a group, the immigrant children in his study are outperforming their U.S.-born peers. What's more, the adults are dramatically outperforming the immigrant families that came before them. "One hundred years ago, it took people two to three generations to achieve a middle-class standard of living," says Suárez-Orozco. "Today they're getting there within a generation."

So this is a good thing, right? Striving people come here to succeed—and do. While there are plenty of benefits that undeniably come with learning the ways of ambition, there are plenty of perils too—many a lot uglier than high school students cheating on the trig final.

Human history has always been writ in the blood of broken alliances, palace purges and strong people or nations beating up on weak ones—all in the service of someone's hunger for power. There's a point at which you find an interesting kind of nerve circuitry between optimism and hubris," says Warren Bennis, a professor of business administration at the University of Southern California and the author of three books on leadership. "It becomes an arrogance or conceit, an inability to live without power."

While most ambitious people keep their secret Caesar tucked safely away, it can emerge surprisingly, even suddenly. Says Frans de Waal, a primatologist at the Yerkes Primate Center in Atlanta and the author of a new book, Our Inner Ape: "You can have a male chimp that is the most laid-back character, but one day he sees the chance to overthrow the leader and becomes a totally different male. I would say 90% of people would behave this way too. On an island with three people, they might become a little dictator."

But a yearning for supremacy can create its own set of problems. Heart attacks, ulcers and other stress-related ills are more common among high achievers—and that includes nonhuman achievers. The blood of alpha wolves routinely shows elevated levels of cortisol, the same stress hormone that is found in anxious humans. Alpha chimps even suffer ulcers and occasional heart attacks.

For these reasons, people and animals who have an appetite for becoming an alpha often settle contentedly into life as a beta. "The desire to be in a high position is universal," says de Waal. "But that trait has co-evolved with another skill—the skill to make the best of lower positions."

Humans not only make peace with their beta roles but they also make money from them. Among corporations, an increasingly well-rewarded portion of the workforce is made up of B players, managers and professionals somewhere below the top tier. They don't do the power lunching and ribbon cutting but instead perform the highly skilled, everyday work of making the company run. As skeptical shareholders look ever more askance at overpaid corporate A-listers, the B players are becoming more highly valued. It's an adaptation that serves the needs of both the corporation and the culture around it. "Everyone has ambition," says Lowe. "Societies have to provide alternative ways for people to achieve."

Ultimately, it's that very flexibility—that multiplicity of possible rewards—that makes dreaming big dreams and pursuing big goals worth all the bother. Ambition is an expensive impulse, one that requires an enormous investment of emotional capital. Like any investment, it can pay off in countless different kinds of coin. The trick, as any good speculator will tell you, is recognizing the riches when they come your way.

What Makes You Who You Are

Which is stronger—nature or nurture? The latest science says genes and your experience interact for your whole life

MATT RIDLEY

The perennial debate about nature and nurture—which is the more potent shaper of the human essence?—is perennially rekindled. It flared up again in the London *Observer* of Feb. 11, 2001. REVEALED: THE SECRET OF HUMAN BEHAVIOR, read the banner headline. ENVIRONMENT, NOT GENES, KEY TO OUR ACTS. The source of the story was Craig Venter, the self-made man of genes who had built a private company to read the full sequence of the human genome in competition with an international consortium funded by taxes and charities. That sequence—a string of 3 billion letters, composed in a four-letter alphabet, containing the complete recipe for building and running a human body—was to be published the very next day (the competition ended in an arranged tie). The first analysis of it had revealed that there were just 30,000 genes in it, not the 100,000 that many had been estimating until a few months before.

Details had already been circulated to journalists under embargo. But Venter, by speaking to a reporter at a biotechnology conference in France on Feb. 9, had effectively broken the embargo. Not for the first time in the increasingly bitter rivalry over the genome project, Venter's version of the story would hit the headlines before his rivals'. "We simply do not have enough genes for this idea of biological determinism to be right," Venter told the *Observer.* "The wonderful diversity of the human species is not hard-wired in our genetic code. Our environments are critical."

In truth, the number of human genes changed nothing. Venter's remarks concealed two whopping nonsequiturs: that fewer genes implied more environmental influences and that 30,000 genes were too few to explain human nature, whereas 100,000 would have been enough. As one scientist put it to me a few weeks later, just 33 genes, each coming in two varieties (on or off), would be enough to make every human being in the world unique. There are more than 10 billion combinations that could come from flipping a coin 33 times, so 30,000 does not seem such a small number after all. Besides, if fewer genes meant more free will, fruit flies would be freer than we are, bacteria freer still and viruses the John Stuart Mill of biology.

Fortunately, there was no need to reassure the population with such sophisticated calculations. People did not weep at the humiliating news that our genome has only about twice as many genes as a worm's. Nothing had been hung on the number 100,000, which was just a bad guess.

But the human genome project—and the decades of research that preceded it—did force a much more nuanced understanding of how genes work. In the early days, scientists detailed how genes encode the various proteins that make up the cells in our bodies. Their more sophisticated and ultimately more satisfying discovery—that gene expression can be modified by experience—has been gradually emerging since the 1980s. Only now is it dawning on scientists what a big and general idea it implies: that learning itself consists of nothing more than switching genes on and off. The more we lift the lid on the genome, the more vulnerable to experience genes appear to be.

This is not some namby-pamby, middle-of-the-road compromise. This is a new understanding of the fundamental building blocks of life based on the discovery that genes are not immutable things handed down from our parents like Moses' stone tablets but are active participants in our lives, designed to take their cues from everything that happens to us from the moment of our conception.

Early Puberty
Girls raised in fatherless households experience puberty earlier. Apparently the change in timing is the reaction of a STILL MYSTERIOUS set of genes to their ENVIRONMENT. Scientists don't know how many SETS OF GENES act this way

For the time being, this new awareness has taken its strongest hold among scientists, changing how they think about everything from the way bodies develop in the womb to how new species emerge to the inevitability of homosexuality in some people. (More on all this later.) But eventually, as the general population becomes more attuned to this interdependent view, changes may well occur in areas as diverse as education, medicine, law and religion. Dieters may learn precisely which combination of fats, carbohydrates and proteins has the greatest effect on their individual waistlines. Theologians may develop a whole new theory of free will based on the observation that learning expands our capacity to choose our own path. As was true of Copernicus's observation 500 years ago that the earth orbits the sun, there is no telling how far the repercussions of this new scientific paradigm may extend.

To appreciate what has happened, you will have to abandon cherished notions and open your mind. You will have to enter a world in which your genes are not puppet masters pulling the strings of your behavior but puppets at the mercy of your behavior, in which instinct is not the opposite of learning, environmental influences are often less reversible than genetic ones, and nature is designed for nurture.

Fear of snakes, for instance, is the most common human phobia, and it makes good evolutionary sense for it to be instinctive. Learning to fear snakes the hard way would be dangerous. Yet experiments with monkeys reveal that their fear of snakes (and probably ours) must still be acquired by watching another individual react with fear to a snake. It turns out that it is easy to teach monkeys to fear snakes but very difficult to teach them to fear flowers. What we inherit is not a fear of snakes but a predisposition to learn a fear of snakes—a nature for a certain kind of nurture.

Before we dive into some of the other scientific discoveries that have so thoroughly transformed the debate, it helps to understand how deeply entrenched in our intellectual history the false dichotomy of nature vs. nurture became. Whether human nature is born or made is an ancient conundrum discussed by Plato and Aristotle. Empiricist philosophers such as John Locke and David Hume argued that the human mind was formed by experience; nativists like Jean-Jacques Rousseau and Immanuel Kant held that there was such a thing as immutable human nature.

Homosexuality
GAY MEN are more likely to have OLDER BROTHERS than either gay women or heterosexual men. It may be that a FIRST MALE FETUS triggers an immune reaction in the mother, ALTERING THE EXPRESSION of key gender genes

It was Charles Darwin's eccentric mathematician cousin Francis Galton who in 1874 ignited the nature-nurture controversy in its present form and coined the very phrase (borrowing the alliteration from Shakespeare, who had lifted it from an Elizabethan schoolmaster named Richard Mulcaster). Galton asserted that human personalities were born, not made by experience. At the same time, the philosopher William James argued that human beings have more instincts than animals, not fewer.

In the first decades of the 20th century, nature held sway over nurture in most fields. In the wake of World War I, however, three men recaptured the social sciences for nurture: John B. Watson, who set out to show how the conditioned reflex, discovered by Ivan Pavlov, could explain human learning; Sigmund Freud, who sought to explain the influence of parents and early experiences on young minds; and Franz Boas, who argued that the origin of ethnic differences lay with history, experience and circumstance, not physiology and psychology.

Galton's insistence on innate explanations of human abilities had led him to espouse eugenics, a term he coined. Eugenics was enthusiastically adopted by the Nazis to justify their campaign of mass murder against the disabled and the Jews. Tainted by this association, the idea of innate behavior was in full retreat for most of the middle years of the century. In 1958, however, two men began the counterattack on behalf of nature. Noam Chomsky, in his review of a book by the behaviorist B.F. Skinner, argued that it was impossible to learn human language by trial and error alone; human beings must come already equipped with an innate grammatical skill. Harry Harlow did a simple experiment that showed that a baby monkey prefers a soft, cloth model of a mother to a hard, wire-frame mother, even if the wire-frame mother provides it with all its milk; some preferences are innate.

Fast-forward to the 1980s and one of the most stunning surprises to greet scientists when they first opened up animal genomes: fly geneticists found a small group of genes called the hox genes that seemed to set out the body plan of the fly during its early development—telling it roughly where to put the head, legs, wings and so on. But then colleagues studying mice found the same hox genes, in the same order, doing the same job in Mickey's world—telling the mouse where to put its various parts. And when scientists looked in our genome, they found hox genes there too.

Hox genes, like all genes, are switched on and off in different parts of the body at different times. In this way, genes can have subtly different effects, depending on where, when and how they are switched on. The switches that control this process—stretches of DNA upstream of genes—are known as promoters.

Small changes in the promoter can have profound effects on the expression of a hox gene. For example, mice have short necks and long bodies; chickens have long necks and short bodies. If you count the vertebrae in the necks and thoraxes of mice and chickens, you will find that a mouse has seven neck and 13 thoracic vertebrae, a chicken 14 and seven, respectively. The source of this difference lies in the promoter attached to HoxC8, a hox gene that helps shape the thorax of the body. The promoter is a 200-letter paragraph of DNA, and in the two species it differs by just a handful of letters. The effect is to alter the expression of the HoxC8 gene in the development of the chicken embryo. This means the chicken makes thoracic vertebrae in a different part of the body than the mouse. In the python, HoxC8 is expressed right from the head and goes on being expressed for most of the body. So pythons are one long thorax; they have ribs all down the body.

To make grand changes in the body plan of animals, there is no need to invent new genes, just as there's no need to invent new words to write an original novel (unless your name is Joyce). All you need do is switch the same ones on and off in different patterns. Suddenly, here is a mechanism for creating large and small evolutionary changes from small genetic differences. Merely by adjusting the sequence of a promoter or adding a new one, you could alter the expression of a gene.

Divorce

If a FRATERNAL TWIN gets divorced, there's a 30% CHANCE that his or her twin will get divorced as well. If the twins are IDENTICAL, however, one sibling's divorce BOOSTS THE ODDS to 45% that the other will split

In one sense, this is a bit depressing. It means that until scientists know how to find gene promoters in the vast text of the genome, they will not learn how the recipe for a chimpanzee differs from that for a person. But in another sense, it is also uplifting, for it reminds us more forcefully than ever of a simple truth that is all too often forgotten: bodies are not made, they grow. The genome is not a blueprint for constructing a body. It is a recipe for baking a body. You could say the chicken embryo is marinated for a shorter time in the HoxC8 sauce than the mouse embryo is. Likewise, the development of a certain human behavior takes a certain time and occurs in a certain order, just as the cooking of a perfect souffle requires not just the right ingredients but also the right amount of cooking and the right order of events.

How does this new view of genes alter our understanding of human nature? Take a look at four examples.

Language Human beings differ from chimpanzees in having complex, grammatical language. But language does not spring fully formed from the brain; it must be learned from other language-speaking human beings. This capacity to learn is written into the human brain by genes that open and close a critical window during which learning takes place. One of those genes, FoxP2, has recently been discovered on human chromosome 7 by Anthony Monaco and his colleagues at the Wellcome Trust Centre for Human Genetics in Oxford. Just having the

FoxP2 gene, though, is not enough. If a child is not exposed to a lot of spoken language during the critical learning period, he or she will always struggle with speech.

Crime Families

GENES may influence the way people respond to a "crimogenic" ENVIRONMENT. How else to explain why the BIOLOGICAL children of criminal parents are more likely than their ADOPTED children to break the law?

Love Some species of rodents, such as the prairie vole, form long pair bonds with their mates, as human beings do. Others, such as the montane vole, have only transitory liaisons, as do chimpanzees. The difference, according to Tom Insel and Larry Young at Emory University in Atlanta, lies in the promoter upstream of the oxytocin-and vasopressin-receptor genes. The insertion of an extra chunk of DNA text, usually about 460 letters long, into the promoter makes the animal more likely to bond with its mate. The extra text does not create love, but perhaps it creates the possibility of falling in love after the right experience.

Antisocial Behavior It has often been suggested that childhood maltreatment can create an antisocial adult. New research by Terrie Moffitt of London's Kings College on a group of 442 New Zealand men who have been followed since birth suggests that this is true only for a genetic minority. Again, the difference lies in a promoter that alters the activity of a gene. Those with high-active monoamine oxidase A genes were virtually immune to the effects of mistreatment. Those with low-active genes were much more antisocial if maltreated, yet—if anything—slightly less antisocial if not maltreated. The low-active, mistreated men were responsible for four times their share of rapes, robberies and assaults. In other words, maltreatment is not enough; you must also have the low-active gene.

Ancient Quarrel

How much of who we are is learned or innate is an argument with a fruitful but fractious pedigree

Nature We may be destined to be bald, mourn our dead, seek mates, fear the dark
IMMANUEL KANT
His philosophy sought a native morality in the mind
FRANCIS GALTON
Math geek saw mental and physical traits as innate
KONRAD LORENZ
Studied patterns of instinctive behavior in animals
NOAM CHOMSKY
Argued that human beings are born with a capacity for grammar

Nurture But we can also learn to love tea, hate polkas, invent alphabets and tell lies
JOHN LOCKE
Considered the mind of an infant to be a tabula rasa, or blank slate
IVAN PAVLOV
Trained dogs to salivate at the sound of the dinner bell
SIGMUND FREUD
Felt we are formed by mothers, fathers, sex, jokes and dreams
FRANZ BOAS
Believed chance and environs are key to cultural variation

And it is not enough to have the low-active gene; you must also be maltreated.

Homosexuality Ray Blanchard at the University of Toronto has found that gay men are more likely than either lesbians or heterosexual men to have older brothers (but not older sisters). He has since confirmed this observation in 14 samples from many places. Something about occupying a womb that has held other boys occasionally results in reduced birth weight, a larger placenta and a greater probability of homosexuality. That something, Blanchard suspects, is an immune reaction in the mother, primed by the first male fetus, that grows stronger with each male pregnancy. Perhaps the immune response affects the expression of key genes during brain development in a way that boosts a boy's attraction to his own sex. Such an explanation would not hold true for all gay men, but it might provide important clues into the origins of both homosexuality and heterosexuality.

To be sure, earlier scientific discoveries had hinted at the importance of this kind of interplay between heredity and environment. The most striking example is Pavlovian conditioning. When Pavlov announced his famous experiment a century ago this year, he had apparently discovered how the brain could be changed to acquire new knowledge of the world—in the case of his dogs, knowledge that a bell foretold the arrival of food. But now we know how the brain changes: by the real-time expression of 17 genes, known as the CREB genes. They must be switched on and off to alter connections among nerve cells in the brain and thus lay down a new long-term memory. These genes are at the mercy of our behavior, not the other way around. Memory is in the genes in the sense that it uses genes, not in the sense that you inherit memories.

In this new view, genes allow the human mind to learn, remember, imitate, imprint language, absorb culture and express instincts. Genes are not puppet masters or blueprints, nor are they just the carriers of heredity. They are active during life; they switch one another on and off; they respond to the environment. They may direct the construction of the body and brain in the womb, but then almost at once, in response to experience, they set about dismantling and rebuilding what they have made. They are both the cause and the consequence of our actions.

Will this new vision of genes enable us to leave the nature-nurture argument behind, or are we doomed to reinvent it in every generation? Unlike what happened in previous eras, science is explaining in great detail precisely how genes and their environment—be it the womb, the classroom or pop culture—interact. So perhaps the pendulum swings of a now demonstrably false dichotomy may cease.

It may be in our nature, however, to seek simple, linear, cause-and-effect stories and not think in terms of circular causation, in which effects become their own causes. Perhaps the idea of nature via nurture, like the ideas of quantum mechanics and relativity, is just too counterintuitive for human minds. The urge to see ourselves in terms of nature versus nurture, like our instinctual ability to fear snakes, may be encoded in our genes.

MATT RIDLEY is an Oxford-trained zoologist and science writer whose latest book is *Nature via Nurture* (HarperCollins)

The New Sex Scorecard

Talking openly about sex differences is no longer an exercise in political incorrectness; it is a necessity in fighting disease and forging successful relationships. At 109 and counting, *PT* examines the tally.

HARA ESTROFF MARANO

Get out the spittoon. Men produce twice as much saliva as women. Women, for their part, learn to speak earlier, know more words, recall them better, pause less and glide through tongue twisters.

Put aside Simone de Beauvoir's famous dictum, "One is not born a woman but rather becomes one." Science suggests otherwise, and it's driving a whole new view of who and what we are. Males and females, it turns out, are different from the moment of conception, and the difference shows itself in every system of body and brain.

It's safe to talk about sex differences again. Of course, it's the oldest story in the world. And the newest. But for a while it was also the most treacherous. Now it may be the most urgent. The next stage of progress against disorders as disabling as depression and heart disease rests on cracking the binary code of biology. Most common conditions are marked by pronounced gender differences in incidence or appearance.

Although sex differences in brain and body take their inspiration from the central agenda of reproduction, they don't end there. "We've practiced medicine as though only a woman's breasts, uterus and ovaries made her unique—and as though her heart, brain and every other part of her body were identical to those of a man," says Marianne J. Legato, M.D., a cardiologist at Columbia University who spearheads the new push on gender differences. Legato notes that women live longer but break down more.

Do we need to explain that difference doesn't imply superiority or inferiority? Although sex differences may provide ammunition for David Letterman or the Simpsons, they unfold in the most private recesses of our lives, surreptitiously molding our responses to everything from stress to space to speech. Yet there are some ways the sexes are becoming more alike—they are now both engaging in the same kind of infidelity, one that is equally threatening to their marriages.

Everyone gains from the new imperative to explore sex differences. When we know why depression favors women two to one, or why the symptoms of heart disease literally hit women in the gut, it will change our understanding of how our bodies and our minds work.

The Gene Scene

Whatever sets men and women apart, it all starts with a single chromosome: the male-making Y, a puny thread bearing a paltry 25 genes, compared with the lavish female X, studded with 1,000 to 1,500 genes. But the Y guy trumps. He has a gene dubbed Sry, which, if all goes well, instigates an Olympic relay of development. It commands primitive fetal tissue to become testes, and they then spread word of masculinity out to the provinces via their chief product, testosterone. The circulating hormone not only masculinizes the body but affects the developing brain, influencing the size of specific structures and the wiring of nerve cells.

25% of females experience daytime sleepiness, versus 18% of males

---

But sex genes themselves don't cede everything to hormones. Over the past few years, scientists have come to believe that they too play ongoing roles in gender-flavoring the brain and behavior.

Females, it turns out, appear to have backup genes that protect their brains from big trouble. To level the genetic playing field between men and women, nature normally shuts off one of the two X chromosomes in every cell in females. But about 19 percent of genes escape inactivation; cells get a double dose of some X genes. Having fall-back genes may explain why females are far less subject than males to mental disorders from autism to schizophrenia.

What's more, which X gene of a pair is inactivated makes a difference in the way female and male brains respond to things, says neurophysiologist Arthur P. Arnold, Ph.D., of the University of California at Los Angeles. In some cases, the X gene donated by Dad is nullified; in other cases it's the X from Mom. The parent from whom a woman gets her working genes determines how robust her genes are. Paternal genes ramp up the genetic volume, maternal genes tune it down. This is known as genomic imprinting of the chromosome.

For many functions, it doesn't matter which sex genes you have or from whom you get them. But the Y chromosome itself spurs the brain to grow extra dopamine neurons, Arnold says. These nerve cells are involved in reward and motivation, and dopamine release underlies the pleasure of addiction and novelty seeking. Dopamine neurons also affect motor skills and go awry in Parkinson's disease, a disorder that afflicts twice as many males as females.

XY makeup also boosts the density of vasopressin fibers in the brain. Vasopressin is a hormone that both abets and minimizes sex differences; in some circuits it fosters parental behavior in males; in others it may spur aggression.

Sex on the Brain

Ruben Gur, Ph.D., always wanted to do the kind of psychological research that when he found something new, no one could say his grandmother already knew it. Well, "My grandmother couldn't tell you that women have a higher percentage of gray matter in their brains," he says. Nor could she explain how that discovery resolves a long-standing puzzle.

99% of girls play with dolls at age 6, versus 17% of boys

Gur's discovery that females have about 15 to 20 percent more gray matter than males suddenly made sense of another major sex difference: Men, overall, have larger brains than women (their heads and bodies are larger), but the sexes score equally well on tests of intelligence.

Gray matter, made up of the bodies of nerve cells and their connecting dendrites, is where the brain's heavy lifting is done. The female brain is more densely packed with neurons and dendrites, providing concentrated processing power—and more thought-linking capability.

The larger male cranium is filled with more white matter and cerebrospinal fluid. "That fluid is probably helpful," says Gur, director of the Brain Behavior Laboratory at the University of Pennsylvania. "It cushions the brain, and men are more likely to get their heads banged about."

White matter, made of the long arms of neurons encased in a protective film of fat, helps distribute processing throughout the brain. It gives males superiority at spatial reasoning. White matter also carries fibers that inhibit "information spread" in the cortex. That allows a single-mindedness that spatial problems require, especially difficult ones. The harder a spatial task, Gur finds, the more circumscribed the right-sided brain activation in males, but not in females. The white matter advantage of males, he believes, suppresses activation of areas that could interfere with work.

The white matter in women's brains is concentrated in the corpus callosum, which links the brain's hemispheres, and enables the right side of the brain to pitch in on language tasks. The more difficult the verbal task, the more global the neural participation required—a response that's stronger in females.

Women have another heady advantage—faster blood flow to the brain, which offsets the cognitive effects of aging. Men lose more brain tissue with age, especially in the left frontal cortex, the part of the brain that thinks about consequences and provides self-control.

"You can see the tissue loss by age 45, and that may explain why midlife crisis is harder on men," says Gur. "Men have the same impulses but they lose the ability to consider long-term consequences." Now, there's a fact someone's grandmother may have figured out already.

Minds of Their Own

The difference between the sexes may boil down to this: dividing the tasks of processing experience. Male and female minds are innately drawn to different aspects of the world around them. And there's new evidence that testosterone may be calling some surprising shots.

Women's perceptual skills are oriented to quick—call it intuitive—people reading. Females are gifted at detecting the feelings and thoughts of others, inferring intentions, absorbing contextual clues and responding in emotionally appropriate ways. They empathize. Tuned to others, they more readily see alternate sides of an argument. Such empathy fosters communication and primes females for attachment.

Women, in other words, seem to be hard-wired for a top-down, big-picture take. Men might be programmed to look at things from the bottom up (no surprise there).

Men focus first on minute detail, and operate most easily with a certain detachment. They construct rules-based analyses of the natural world, inanimate objects and events. In the coinage of Cambridge University psychologist Simon Baron-Cohen, Ph.D., they systemize.

The superiority of males at spatial cognition and females' talent for language probably subserve the more basic difference of systemizing versus empathizing. The two mental styles manifest in the toys kids prefer (humanlike dolls versus mechanical trucks); verbal impatience in males (ordering rather than negotiating); and navigation (women personalize space by finding landmarks; men see a geometric system, taking directional cues in the layout of routes).

26% of males say they have extramarital sex without being emotionally involved, versus 3% of females

Almost everyone has some mix of both types of skills, although males and females differ in the degree to which one set predominates, contends Baron-Cohen. In his work as director of Cambridge's Autism Research Centre, he finds that children and adults with autism, and its less severe variant Asperger syndrome, are unusual in both dimensions of perception. Its victims are "mindblind," unable to recognize people's feelings. They also have a peculiar talent for systemizing, obsessively focusing on, say, light switches or sink faucets.

Autism overwhelmingly strikes males; the ratio is ten to one for Asperger. In his new book, *The Essential Difference: The Truth About the Male and Female Brain,* Baron-Cohen argues that autism is a magnifying mirror of maleness.

The brain basis of empathizing and systemizing is not well understood, although there seems to be a "social brain," nerve circuitry dedicated to person perception. Its key components lie on the left side of the brain, along with language centers generally more developed in females.

Baron-Cohen's work supports a view that neuroscientists have flirted with for years: Early in development, the male hormone testosterone slows the growth of the brain's left hemisphere and accelerates growth of the right.

Testosterone may even have a profound influence on eye contact. Baron-Cohen's team filmed year-old children at play and measured the amount of eye contact they made with their mothers, all of whom had undergone amniocentesis during pregnancy. The researchers looked at various social factors—birth order, parental education, among others—as well as the level of testosterone the child had been exposed to in fetal life.

Baron-Cohen was "bowled over" by the results. The more testosterone the children had been exposed to in the womb, the less able they were to make eye contact at 1 year of age. "Who would have thought that a behavior like eye contact, which is so intrinsically social, could be in part shaped by a biological factor?" he asks. What's more, the testosterone level during fetal life also influenced language skills. The higher the prenatal testosterone level, the smaller a child's vocabulary at 18 months and again at 24 months.

Lack of eye contact and poor language aptitude are early hallmarks of autism. "Being strongly attracted to systems, together with a lack of empathy, may be the core characteristics of individuals on the autistic spectrum," says Baron-Cohen. "Maybe testosterone does more than affect spatial ability and language. Maybe it also affects social ability." And perhaps autism represents an "extreme form" of the male brain.

Depression: Pink—and Blue, Blue, Blue

This year, 19 million Americans will suffer a serious depression. Two out of three will be female. Over the course of their lives, 21.3 percent of women and 12.7 percent of men experience at least one bout of major depression.

The female preponderance in depression is virtually universal. And it's specific to unipolar depression. Males and females suffer equally from bipolar, or manic, depression. However, once depression occurs, the clinical course is identical in men and women.

The gender difference in susceptibility to depression emerges at 13. Before that age, boys, if anything, are a bit more likely than girls to be depressed. The gender difference seems to wind down four decades later, making depression mostly a disorder of women in the child-bearing years.

As director of the Virginia Institute for Psychiatric and Behavioral Genetics at Virginia Commonwealth University, Kenneth S. Kendler, M.D., presides over "the best natural experiment that God has given us to study gender differences"—thousands of pairs of opposite-sex twins. He finds a significant difference between men and women in their response to low levels of adversity. He says, "Women have the capacity to be precipitated into depressive episodes at lower levels of stress."

Adding injury to insult, women's bodies respond to stress differently than do men's. They pour out higher levels of stress hormones and fail to shut off production readily. The female sex hormone progesterone blocks the normal ability of the stress hormone system to turn itself off. Sustained exposure to stress hormones kills brain cells, especially in the hippocampus, which is crucial to memory.

It's bad enough that females are set up biologically to internally amplify their negative life experiences. They are prone to it psychologically as well, finds University of Michigan psychologist Susan Nolen-Hoeksema, Ph.D.

Women ruminate over upsetting situations, going over and over negative thoughts and feelings, especially if they have to do with relationships. Too often they get caught in downward spirals of hopelessness and despair.

It's entirely possible that women are biologically primed to be highly sensitive to relationships. Eons ago it might have helped alert them to the possibility of abandonment while they were busy raising the children. Today, however, there's a clear downside. Ruminators are unpleasant to be around, with their oversize need for reassurance. Of course, men have their own ways of inadvertently fending off people. As pronounced as the female tilt to depression is the male excess of alcoholism, drug abuse and antisocial behaviors.

The Incredible Shrinking Double Standard

Nothing unites men and women better than sex. Yet nothing divides us more either. Males and females differ most in mating psychology because our minds are shaped by and for our reproductive mandates. That sets up men for sex on the side and a more casual attitude toward it.

Twenty-five percent of wives and 44 percent of husbands have had extramarital intercourse, reports Baltimore psychologist Shirley Glass, Ph.D. Traditionally for men, love is one thing and sex is . . . well, sex.

90% of males and females agree that infidelity is always wrong, 20–25% of all marital fights are about jealousy

In what may be a shift of epic proportions, sexual infidelity is mutating before our very eyes. Increasingly, men as well as women are forming deep emotional attachments before they even slip into an extramarital bed together. It often happens as they work long hours together in the office.

"The sex differences in infidelity are disappearing," says Glass, the doyenne of infidelity research. "In my original 1980 study, there was a high proportion of men who had intercourse with almost no emotional involvement at all—nonrelational sex. Today, more men are getting emotionally involved."

One consequence of the growing parity in affairs is greater devastation of the betrayed spouse. The old-style strictly sexual affair never impacted men's marital satisfaction. "You could be in a good marriage and still cheat," reports Glass.

Liaisons born of the new infidelity are much more disruptive—much more likely to end in divorce. "You can move away from just a sexual relationship but it's very difficult to break an attachment," says Rutgers University anthropologist Helen Fisher, Ph.D. "The betrayed partner can probably provide more exciting sex but not a different kind of friendship."

It's not that today's adulterers start out unhappy or looking for love. Says Glass: "The work relationship becomes so rich and the stuff at home is pressurized and child-centered. People get involved insidiously without planning to betray."

Any way it happens, the combined sexual-emotional affair delivers a fatal blow not just to marriages but to the traditional male code. "The double standard for adultery is disappearing," Fisher emphasizes. "It's been around for 5,000 years and it's changing in our lifetime. It's quite striking. Men used to feel that they had the right. They don't feel that anymore."

Learn More About It:

Eve's Rib: The New Science of Gender-Specific Medicine and How It Can Save Your Life. Marianne J. Legato, M.D. (*Harmony Books, 2002*).

Not "Just Friends": Protect Your Relationship from Infidelity and Heal the Trauma of Betrayal. Shirley P. Glass, Ph.D. (*The Free Press, 2003*).

Male, Female: The Evolution of Human Sex Differences. David C. Geary, Ph.D. (*American Psychological Association, 1998*).

Fighting Crime

An Economist's View

John J. Donohue

O ver the past 40 years, the number of motor vehicle fatalities per mile driven in the United States has dropped an astounding 70 percent. While some of the gains can be attributed to improvements in technology, public policy has made a big difference. The government followed the advice of researchers who had studied auto accidents, improving highway design and instituting a variety of regulations, including mandatory seat belt use and harsher penalties for drunken driving. By contrast, most types of street crime are still above the levels of 40 years ago, despite the impressive drops in the 1990s. A major reason for the difference, I would argue, is that the crime issue has been hijacked by ideologues and special interests, preventing the emergence of a policy consensus driven by research.

Why listen to an economist pontificate on what most people would call criminology? Economists bring a unique perspective to the table—a utilitarian view in which one assumes that behavior can be changed by altering incentives, that the costs of crime can be measured in terms of money and that public policy is best evaluated by comparing costs and benefits. It's hardly the only view, but I would argue that it is a view that provides exceptional insight into limiting the adverse consequences of antisocial behavior.

We know more today than ever how to reduce crime. If we could get past the barriers of ideology and special pleading, we could see reductions in crime rivaling the magnitude of the gains in automobile safety. What follows are a host of measures that would sharply reduce the $400 billion annual toll from street crime in the United States.

Stop the Building Boom in Prisons

Virtually everyone agrees that incarceration must remain a core element of any strategy to fight crime. Locking up more people reduces crime because more criminals are kept off the streets and/ or the prospect of time behind bars deters criminal behavior. But you can have too much of a "good" thing. Between 1933 and 1973, incarceration in the United States varied within a narrow band of roughly 100 to 120 prisoners per 100,000 population. Since then, this rate has been increasing by an average of 5 percent annually. As of June 2003, some two million individuals were imprisoned—a rate of almost 500 per 100,000.

Costs of Prison

To determine whether the current level of incarceration makes sense, one must ask whether the benefits at the margin in terms of less crime exceed the costs to society. On the benefit side, the research suggests that the "elasticity" of crime with respect to incarceration is somewhere between 0.1 and 0.4—that is, increasing the prison population by 10 percent reduces crime by 1 to 4 percent. On the other side of the equation, estimates of the cost of locking up another individual run between $32,000 and $57,000 annually.

The most rigorous study on the relevant elasticity was conducted by William Spelman of the University of Texas. He concluded that "we can be 90 percent confident that the true value is between 0.12 and 0.20, with a best single guess of 0.16." Since Spelman's estimates accounted for the incapacitation effect, but ignore any deterrence effect, I rely conservatively on somewhat larger elasticity of 0.2.

The most carefully constructed and comprehensive study on the costs of incarcerating a criminal was a 1990 report prepared for the National Institute of Justice, which produced the high-end estimate ($57,000 annually, in 2003 dollars). I adjust this figure downward (in part because the study probably overstates prison construction costs and exaggerates the social cost of welfare payments to the dependents of the incarcerated) to arrive at a figure of $46,000 per prisoner per year.

With an elasticity of crime with respect to incarceration of 0.2 and an annual cost of housing a prisoner of $46,000, the "optimal" level of incarceration would require imprisoning 300,000 fewer individuals. This is just a ballpark estimate, of course. But, at the very least, it implies that we cannot expect to get much more crime reduction at reasonable cost by increasing the numbers behind bars. It is time to stop making prison construction the major public works project of our day.

Abolish the Death Penalty

In recent years, the death penalty has been meted out an average of 80 times annually. These executions come at a high tangible cost. For while executing an individual does save the money that would have been used for a lifetime in prison, these savings are dwarfed by the costs of death-penalty trials and appeals. The most scholarly research on the topic, by Philip Cook and Donna Slawson Kuniholm of Duke, found that the State of North Carolina spent $2.16 million per execution more than what would be spent if the maximum penalty were life in prison.

Proponents of the death penalty usually justify these costs by invoking its deterrence effect. But Steve Levitt of the University of Chicago has noted that the risk of execution for those who commit murder is typically small compared with the risk of death that violence-prone criminals willingly face in daily life—and this certainly raises questions about the efficacy of threatening them with the death penalty. Currently, the likelihood of a murderer being executed is less than 1 in 200. By way of comparison, Levitt and his colleague Sudhir Venkatesh find 7 percent of street-level drug sellers die each year. Levitt concludes that "it is hard to believe the fear of execution would be a driving force in a rational criminal's calculus in modern America."

Nor is there direct evidence that the death penalty generates gains for society in terms of murders deterred. In an often-cited paper written in the early 1970s, Isaac Ehrlich (then a graduate student at the University of Chicago) estimated that one execution could save eight lives. But research since has showed that minor changes in the way the figure is estimated eliminate the deterrence effect. Indeed, Levitt, working with Lawrence Katz of Harvard and Ellen Shustorovich of the City University of New York, found that the death penalty might even add to the total number of murders. Thus, abolishing the death penalty would save American taxpayers more than $150 million a year at no apparent cost to society.

Expand the Police Force

In the 1990s, a variety of new policing strategies were introduced in New York City and other localities. New York increased enforcement of statutes on petty crimes like graffiti and marijuana possession and made better use of technology and statistics in identifying crime "hot spots." Boston adopted an innovative multi-agency collaboration that took aim at gang violence. And numerous cities, notably San Diego, introduced "community policing," in which police attempted to work as allies with communities, rather than just antagonists to criminals. The results seem impressive: from 1991 to 1998, the cities that experienced the largest decline in murder rates were San Diego (a 76 percent drop), New York City (71 percent) and Boston (69 percent).

Were better policing strategies responsible for these results, and would cities be wise to adopt or expand such programs? A study of Cincinnati found that a "community service model" of policing, in which cops become more familiar with the neighborhoods they served, did not significantly lower crime. Furthermore, community policing did not seem to affect attitudes toward police.

Two New York Factors

Note, too, that New York's experiments are inconclusive—cities without tough policies on minor crime experienced significant crime drops, too. Moreover, New York's substantial crime declines began before 1993, the year in which Mayor Giuliani took office and initiated the policing changes. Indeed, two other factors seem to explain all of the crime drop in New York City: increases in the total number of police officers and its high abortion rate many years earlier, which Levitt and I found to correlate with subsequent declines in crime because of the reduction in unwanted births of children most at risk of becoming criminals.

Another change in the 1990s—one that received far less press attention than changing policing strategies—was the substantial increase in the size of police forces. From 1994 through 1999, the number of police per capita in the United States grew by almost 10 percent. The expansion was even more pronounced in big cities with high crime rates. Much of this increase can be attributed to the Community Oriented Policing Services (COPS) program, which was signed into law by President Clinton in 1994 and is now in the process of being phased out by President Bush. A report commissioned by the Justice Department credits this program with adding more than 80,000 officers to the streets.

The effects of increases in police, as opposed to changes in policing strategies, have been widely studied, with most studies showing that the benefits have exceeded the costs. The most rigorous studies have found elasticities of crime with respect to police of between 0.30 and 0.79—that is, a 10 percent increase in police reduces crime between 3.0 and 7.9 percent. Using a conservative estimate for this elasticity (0.4) and a rather high estimate of the total annual cost of maintaining an extra police officer ($90,000) while assuming that crime costs $400 billion a year, the United States would have to hire 500,000 additional police officers to reach the optimal policing level. According to the FBI, there are some 665,000 police in the United States. So the optimal level is almost double the number we have today. Thus while adding hundreds of thousands of police officers is hardly a political priority these days, simply restoring financing for the COPS program would be a start.

Adopt Sensible Gun Control

In 2002, there were some 11,000 homicide deaths by firearms. The United States' per capita firearm homicide rate is more than eight times that of Canada, France, Germany, Japan, Spain and Britain. Much could be done to reduce gun-related crime. Most such initiatives are off the table, however, because conservatives have garnered enormous electoral benefits from fighting gun control.

What's more, the highly publicized work of the researcher John Lott has confirmed the views of many conservatives that gun control is already excessive—that allowing citizens to carry concealed handguns would drastically *reduce* violent crime. Lott reasons that the threat of these concealed weapons serves as a deterrent to crime. And his research has been cited by many politicians supporting laws allowing concealed weapons, which have been passed by some 30 states.

There are, however, serious flaws in Lott's research. The best guess based on all the empirical evidence is that these "shall issue" laws actually increase crime, albeit by a relatively modest amount. There are a number of possible explanations for this:

the guns being carried are easier to steal (more than a million guns are stolen each year, which is a major source of supply to criminals), for one, while the threat of being shot in a confrontation may inspire criminals to shoot first. It is worth noting, moreover, that laws allowing for easier access to guns increase the threats of both accidental death and suicide.

One alternative to "shall issue" laws is "may issue" laws, which allow discretion in handing out permits, with an applicant having to prove a need for protection. These laws, which have been passed in 11 states, could have some of the deterrent benefits Lott speaks of without as many of the harmful effects that plague "shall issue" laws if the licensing discretion is used wisely.

Another much-debated gun law was President Clinton's 1994 assault-weapons ban, which was recently allowed to expire. This law prohibited a specific list of semiautomatic guns deemed useful for criminal purposes but unnecessary for sport or self-defense, and banned ammunition feeding devices that accept more than 10 rounds. According to plausible guesstimates, assault weapons were used in about 2 percent of pre-ban murders, and large-capacity magazines were used in about 20 percent. The secondary goal of the assault weapons ban was to reduce the harm from crime by forcing criminals to employ less dangerous weapons. Jeffrey Roth and Christopher Koper of the Urban Institute in Washington found that those murdered by assault weapons had, on average, more wounds than those killed with other guns. They also found that, in mass murders, those involving assault weapons included more victims.

Was the ban effective? Probably not very. The law was rife with loopholes. For one thing, the law grandfathered assault weapons produced before the ban, which led gun manufacturers to increase production before the law took effect. In addition, gun companies could—and did—produce potent legal guns with little change in performance. Admittedly, a true ban on assault weapons would not have a huge effect on homicide since most criminals would simply use less powerful guns if the desired weapons were unavailable. A strong ban on large capacity magazines, however, which are estimated to be used in 20 percent of homicides, could be very helpful.

David Hemenway, an economist and director of the Harvard Injury Control Research Center, has examined the evidence on the potential impact of other gun-related measures and identifies six that have shown some success in lowering crime:

- preventing police from selling confiscated guns.
- instituting one-gun-purchase-per-month laws.
- plugging secondary-market loopholes.
- tracing all guns used in crime.
- producing guns that can be fired only by their owners.
- registering all handguns.

None of these, alas, is an easy political sell in today's America.

Legalize Drugs

The most effective federal crime-fighting public initiative in American history was the lifting of alcohol prohibition in the early 1930s. Homicides fell by 14 percent in the two years after prohibition ended. In all likelihood, similar benefits would emerge if we ended drug prohibition, although obviously other steps would need to be taken to reduce the societal costs associated with drug use.

The logic behind drug legalization as a crime reducer is two-fold. First, a significant number of homicides are caused by drug-related disputes. The FBI has classified about 5 percent of homicides as drug-related. And this number is very conservative since the FBI attributes only one cause to each murder. A fatal dispute about a drug deal may be characterized as an "argument over money" or a "gangland killing" rather than a drug homicide. Paul Goldstein of the University of Illinois at Chicago found that about 9 percent of homicides in New York City were caused by broader "systemic" drug issues.

The major reason so many drug disputes end in violence is the lack of institutional mechanisms to resolve them—buyers and sellers cannot seek redress in court, or complain to the Better Business Bureau. Legalization could also lower crime by freeing crime-fighters for other purposes. About $40 billion is spent annually on the war on drugs.

Decriminalizing drugs would also free space in prisons. Levitt found a substantial "crowding out" effect, meaning that increased incarceration of drug-related criminals decreases incarceration of other criminals. Currently, more than 400,000 individuals are in prison for nonviolent drug crimes, with about 50,000 of them imprisoned for violations involving only marijuana.

Of course, drug legalization is not without risks. Legalization would tend to increase drug consumption, lowering economic productivity and perhaps increasing behavior that is dangerous to nondrug users.

One simple way to restrain drug consumption after legalization would be through taxation. Gary Becker and Kevin Murphy of the University of Chicago along with Michael Grossman of the City University of New York construct a model in which the optimal equilibrium with legalization and taxation can actually lead to higher retail prices—and lower consumption—than the optimal system under prohibition. Such a policy would also raise additional money for the government, which could be used for any number of purposes. It would be substantially easier to enforce a tax on drugs than it is to enforce the current ban on drugs, since most individuals would pay a premium to purchase their drugs legally. Instead of turning the hundreds of thousands of workers in the illegal drug markets (and their customers) into criminals, we could focus law enforcement on the much smaller set of tax evaders to keep consumption no higher than the levels of today.

Given the highly controversial nature of this proposal, a prudent first step might be to adopt this legalization/taxation/demand control scheme for marijuana to illustrate the benefits of shrinking the size of illegal markets while establishing that an increase in drug usage can be avoided. A number of other measures should be adopted to limit demand. Strict age limits could be enforced, advertising could be banned, and some of the money raised by taxes on drugs could be used to market abstinence and treatment of addicts.

Expand Successful Social Programs

In accepting his party's nomination, John Kerry said, "I am determined that we stop being a nation content to spend $50,000 a year to keep a young person in prison for the rest of their life—when we could invest $10,000 to give them Head Start, Early Start, Smart Start, the best possible start in life." He was expressing a belief common on the center-left that early childhood intervention can make children less likely to commit crime and actually save money down the road.

Is this view correct? Studies on Head Start have shown it to have lamentably little effect on participants' outcomes later in life, including their likelihood of committing crimes. Other programs, however, have shown tremendous potential in reducing crime (and enhancing other positive life outcomes), and resources should be shifted away from the unproductive programs toward the few that seem to work.

One of the most notable, the experimental Perry Preschool program, provided preschool classes to a sample of children in Michigan when they were 3 and 4 years old. This program attempted to involve the whole family by having the preschool teacher conduct weekly home visits. By age 19, Perry Preschool graduates were 40 percent less likely to be arrested than a control group, 50 percent less likely to be arrested more than twice, and far less likely to be arrested for major crimes.

While I would not expect a scaled-up program to perform as well as one implemented with a small group, even half the reduction in crime would be cost-effective. Estimates from studies of the program indicate that financial benefits to government, which came in the form of higher taxes from employment, lower welfare utilization and reduced crime, exceeded program costs by as much as seven to one.

Another cost-effective crime-fighting program is the Job Corps, which provides educational and vocational-skills training and counseling to at-risk youths. Each year, Job Corps enrolls some 60,000 kids at a cost of more than $1 billion. Unlike some similar teenage intervention programs, the Job Corps is residential. Like the Perry Preschool Program, Job Corps has proved to pay for itself, generating more revenue in the form of taxes and avoided welfare payments than the costs of training the at-risk teens. Job Corps has also proved effective in lowering crime: a randomized experiment conducted by the research corporation Mathematica estimates that Job Corps participants are 16 percent less likely to be arrested than their peers.

For programs like the Perry Preschool and Job Corps to be successful in lowering crime, they must be targeted at those most likely to commit crimes. Six percent of the population commits more than 50 percent of crimes. While there are moral and legal issues in targeting groups based on race, it should be possible to use such information to expand successful programs so that they cover more high-risk individuals.

Defend Roe v. Wade

One often overlooked variable in crime is the legal status of abortion. Levitt and I found that as much as half of the drop in crime in the 1990s can be explained by the legalization of abortion in the early 1970s. There are two reasons that legalized abortion lowers the crime rate. The first is obvious: more abortions mean fewer children, which in turn can mean fewer criminals when those who would have been born would have reached their high-crime years. The second is more important: abortion reduces the number of unwanted births, and unwanted children are at much greater risk of becoming criminals later on. The five states that legalized abortion before the rest of the country experienced significant drops in crime before other states did. What's more, the higher the rate of abortion in a state in the mid 1970s, the greater the drop in crime in the 1990s.

What would be the impact on crime if *Roe v. Wade* were overturned? If the Supreme Court restored the pre-1973 law allowing states to decide for themselves whether to legalize abortion, I suspect most of the blue states would keep abortion legal. Even in the red states, abortion would not disappear entirely because residents could still find safe, out-of-state abortions. But the number of abortions would fall sharply, particularly for poor women.

Suppose that abortion were outlawed in every state that voted for Bush in 2004 and that the abortion rate dropped by 75 percent in these states but remained the same in blue states. Our research suggests that violent crime would eventually increase by about 12 percent and property crime by about 10 percent over the baseline figure.

Reduce Teen Pregnancy

Keeping abortion legal would prevent crime increases, but we can use the insight from the casual link between abortion and crime reduction to achieve the same ends in a better way: reduce the number of unwanted and teen pregnancies. Take the Children's Aid Society-Carrera program, which aims to reduce births to teenagers by changing their incentives. The three-year after-school program for 13-year-olds includes a work component designed to assist participants to find decent jobs, an academic component including tutoring and homework help, an arts component, an individual sports component, and comprehensive family life and sexual education. Program participants have been 70 percent less likely to give birth in the three years after the program ended than members of a control group.

Again, the success of any social program designed to reduce crime requires targeting, in this case at those most likely to give birth in their teens. The groups with the highest rates of teen births are Hispanics, with a rate of 83 births per 1,000 women 15 to 19 years old, and non-Hispanic blacks, with a rate of 68 per thousand—both well above the national rate of 43. Suppose the program was expanded so that it covered half of all Hispanic and black females ages 13 to 15—some two million girls. With a per-person cost of $4,000, the annual outlay would be roughly $4 billion.

Again, one would not expect a large program to be able to replicate the substantial reductions seen in the smaller program. But an initiative only half as effective in reducing teen births would still lower the birth rates of the 15- to 19-year-old participants by 35 percent. Under these assumptions, the expanded program would lead to about 40,000 fewer teen births a year—a 9 percent reduction.

Recent work by Anindya Sen enables us to quantify the expected reduction in crime from this potential drop in teen births. Sen finds that a 1 percent drop in teen births is associated with a 0.589 percent drop in violent crime years later, when the individuals born to teenagers would have reached their high-crime ages. Thus, the 9 percent reduction in teen births would eventually cut violent crime by 5 percent. Assuming two-thirds of crime costs are attributable to violent crime, this 5 percent reduction would eventually save society more than $14 billion per year. In other words, the benefits would be three times greater than the cost.

Expand the DNA Database

While much of the attention on the use of DNA in criminal justice has focused on its potential for establishing the innocence of the wrongly accused, we have not yet tapped the potential of DNA testing to deter crime. Individuals whose DNA is on file with the government know that leaving even a single hair at the scene of a crime is likely to lead to their arrest and conviction, so a major expansion in the DNA database should generate substantial crime reduction benefits. While some are concerned that the government would get information about a person's medical history, the privacy problem can be minimized. It is possible to take someone's DNA and discard all information except for the unique identifying genetic marker.

Currently, every state requires violent criminals and sex offenders to submit to DNA testing. Most states require testing for all felons and juvenile convicts. If a person is found innocent, his or her DNA sample must be discarded. But the United States' DNA crime-fighting system can be expanded and improved. England tests anyone suspected of a "recordable" offense, with the profile remaining on file even if the person is cleared of the crime. This has allowed Britain to build a DNA database with some two million profiles. England's Forensic Science Service estimates that, in a typical year, matches are found linking suspects to 180 murders, 500 rapes and other sexual offenses, and 30,000 motor vehicle, property and drug crimes. In other words, DNA is used to solve fully 20 percent of murders and a significant fraction of other crimes.

A more drastic—and potentially effective—approach was endorsed by Rudolph Giuliani: recording the DNA of every newborn. One way to lower the costs of the project without eliminating much of the gains would be to test only males, who are far more likely to commit crimes.

To improve the effectiveness of the policy, however, it would be necessary to test every male—not just male babies. This would increase the start-up costs to $15 billion (although thought should be given to the appropriate age cutoff—say age 50—as a plausible cost-reduction measure). In every year thereafter, however, it would be necessary to test only newborns. In 2002, there were a little more than 2 million male births in the United States. So testing every male infant would cost about $200 million annually.

One particular crime-deterrent benefit of having the DNA of every male on file is it would be likely to drastically reduce rapes by strangers. Let's assume (conservatively) that half of all such rapes—half of 56,000 a year—would be deterred by the existence of a complete DNA database. Ted Miller, Mark Cohen and Shelli Rossman added the costs of medical bills, lost productivity, mental health trauma and quality of life changes, to estimate that the average rape costs $90,000. Hence, 28,000 of the rapes by strangers in 2002 cost society about $2.5 billion. While the costs of testing every male—$15 billion in the first year—would exceed the $2.5 billion in benefits in reduced rapes from such a plan, the total benefits from rape reduction alone would exceed the costs in roughly seven years (and perhaps less if the initial testing were limited with a judicious age cutoff). Note, moreover, that stranger rapes are only one of many classes of crimes that would see sharp declines with such expansive DNA testing.

What We Are Losing

Few of these proposals seem likely to be adopted any time soon. Former attorney general John Ashcroft stressed incarceration and the death penalty as principal crime-fighting tools, and President Bush's new attorney general, Alberto Gonzalez, appears wed to an even tougher line. Bush seems intent on shrinking the budget for police and early-intervention social programs. The NRA continues to have success in fighting even the most sensible gun control policies. And few in either political party are willing to discuss the legalization of drugs or a major expansion in the DNA database. The politicians in power thus seem stuck on anti-crime policies that guarantee that crime levels will be far higher than can be justified by any reasonable comparison of costs and benefits—let alone respect for life and property.

Adopting the policies set out above would reduce crime in the neighborhood of 50 percent, saving thousands of lives annually and avoiding crime victimization for millions more. Is anybody in Washington, or the state capitals, listening?

MR. DONOHUE teaches law and economics at the Yale Law School. From "*Fighting Crime: An Economist's View,*" *The Milken Institute Review*, First Quarter 2005, pages 47–58.

Parents or Prisons

JENNIFER ROBACK MORSE

For some people, prisons are a substitute for parents. This apparent overstatement is shorthand for two more precise points. First, without parents—two of them, married to each other, working together as a team—a child is more likely to end up in the criminal justice system at some point in his life. Without parents, prison becomes a greater probability in the child's life. Second, if a child finds himself in the criminal justice system, either in his youth or adulthood, the prison will perform the parental function of supervising and controlling that person's behavior.

Of course, prison is a pathetic substitute for genuine parents. Incarceration provides extreme, tightly controlled supervision that children typically outgrow in their toddler years and does so with none of the love and affection that characterize normal parental care of small children. But that is what is happening: The person has failed to internalize the self-command necessary for living in a reasonably free and open society at the age most people do. Since he cannot control himself, someone else must control him. If he becomes too much for his parents, the criminal justice system takes over.

These necessary societal interventions do not repair the loss the child has sustained by the loss of a relationship with his parents. By the time the penal system steps in, the state is engaged in damage control. A child without a conscience, a child without self-control, is a lifelong problem for the rest of society.

A child without a conscience or self-control is a lifelong problem for the rest of society.

A free society needs people with consciences. The vast majority of people must obey the law voluntarily. If people don't conform themselves to the law, someone will either have to compel them to do so or protect the public when they do not. It costs a great deal of money to catch, convict, and incarcerate lawbreakers—not to mention that the surveillance and monitoring of potential criminals tax everybody's freedom if habitual lawbreakers comprise too large a percentage of the population.

The basic self-control and reciprocity that a free society takes for granted do not develop automatically. Conscience development takes place in childhood. Children need to develop empathy so they will care whether they hurt someone or whether they treat others fairly. They need to develop self-control so they can follow through on these impulses and do the right thing even if it might benefit them to do otherwise.

All this development takes place inside the family. Children attach to the rest of the human race through their first relationships with their parents. They learn reciprocity, trust, and empathy from these primal relationships. Disrupting those foundational relations has a major negative impact on children as well as on the people around them. In particular, children of single parents—or completely absent parents—are more likely to commit crimes.

Without two parents, working together as a team, the child has more difficulty learning the combination of empathy, reciprocity, fairness, and self-command that people ordinarily take for granted. If the child does not learn this at home, society will have to manage his behavior in some other way. He may have to be rehabilitated, incarcerated, or otherwise restrained. In this case, prisons will substitute for parents.

The observation that there are problems for children growing up in a disrupted family may seem to be old news. Ever since Barbara Defoe Whitehead famously pronounced "Dan Quayle Was Right" (*Atlantic Monthly,* April 1993), the public has become more aware that single motherhood is not generally glamorous in the way it is sometimes portrayed on television. David Blankenhorn's *Fatherless America* (Basic Books, 1995) depicted a country that is fragmenting along family lines. Blankenhorn argued, and continues to argue in his work at the Institute for American Values, that the primary determinant of a person's life chances is whether he grew up in a household with his own father.

Since these seminal works, it has become increasingly clear that the choice to become a single parent is not strictly a private choice. The decision to become an unmarried mother or the decision to disrupt an existing family does not meet the economist's definition of "private." These choices regarding family structure have significant spillover effects on other people. We can no longer deny that such admittedly very personal decisions have an impact on people other than the individuals who choose.

There are two parts to my tale. The first concerns the impact of being raised in a single-parent household on the children. The second involves the impact that those children have on the rest of society.

Current Events

The two parts of my story were juxtaposed dramatically on the local page of the *San Diego Union-Tribune* one Wednesday morning at the end of January. "Dangling Foot Was Tip-Off," explained the headline. A security guard caught two teenaged boys attempting to dump their "trash" into the dumpster of the gated community he was responsible for guarding. The guard noticed what looked like a human foot dangling out of the bag. He told the boys he wanted to see what was in it. They refused. As a private security guard, he had no authority to arrest or detain the pair. He took their license plate number and a description of the duo and called authorities.

The "trash" proved to be the dismembered body of the boys' mother. They had strangled her, chopped off her head and hands, and ultimately dumped her body in a ravine in Orange County. The boys were half-brothers. The elder was 20 years old. His father had committed suicide when the boy was an infant. The younger boy was 15. His father had abandoned their mother. As of this writing, the older boy, Jason Bautista, was being held in lieu of $1 million bail. The younger, Matthew Montejo, was being held in juvenile hall.

At first glance, the second news item seems unrelated to the first. On the same page of the newspaper, a headline read, "Mayor Wants 20% Budget Cuts." This particular mayor presides over the city of Oceanside, the same city where the brothers tried to dump their mother's body. In nearby Vista, the mayor's "State of the City Address Warns of Possible Deep Cuts." In Carlsbad, one freeway exit to the south, the city's finances were "Called Good Now, Vulnerable in Future." All these mayors were tightening their cities' belts in response to severe budget cuts proposed by California Governor Gray Davis. The governor expects to reduce virtually every budget category in the state budget except one: the Department of Corrections.

Therein lies the tale: These stories are connected by more than just the date and time of their reportage. The increase in serious crimes by younger and younger offenders is absorbing a greater percentage of state resources, necessarily crowding out other services. The Bautista brothers and others like them do have something to do with the budget woes of state and local governments.

Several other high-profile cases of juvenile crime fit this pattern. Alex and Derek King, aged 12 and 13 respectively, bludgeoned their sleeping father to death with a baseball bat and set fire to the house to hide the evidence. The mother of the King brothers had not lived with them for the seven years prior to the crime. Derek had been in foster care for most of those years until his behavior, including a preoccupation with fire, became too difficult for his foster parents to handle. The murder took place two months after Derek was returned to his father's custody.

John Lee Malvo, the youthful assistant in the Beltway Sniper case, came to the United States with his mother from Jamaica. His biological father has not seen him since 1998. His mother evidently had a relationship with John Allen Mohammed, who informally adopted her son. Mohammed himself, probably the mastermind if not the triggerman in the serial sniper case, was also a fatherless child. According to one of his relatives, Mohammed's mother died when he was young; his grandfather and aunt raised him because his dad was not around.

While these high-profile cases dramatize the issues at stake, excessive focus on individual cases like these can be a distraction. As more information about the Bautista family comes in, for instance, a variety of mitigating or confounding circumstances might emerge to suggest that factors other than living in a single-parent home accounted for the horrible crime. A family history of mental illness, perhaps, or maybe a history of child abuse by the mother toward the children may surface as contributing factors. And indeed, many of the most gruesome crimes are committed not by fatherless children in single-mother households, but by motherless boys, growing up in a father-only household. Some, such as John Lee Malvo, had essentially no household at all. But these confounding factors should not distract us from the overwhelming evidence linking single parents or absent parents to the propensity to commit crimes.

The Statistical Evidence

This result has been found in numerous studies. The National Fatherhood Initiative's *Father Facts,* edited in 2002 by Wade Horn and Tom Sylvester, is the best one-stop shopping place for this kind of evidence. Of the many studies reviewed there, a representative one was reported in the *Journal of Marriage and the Family* in May 1996. Researchers Chris Couglin and Samuel Vuchinich found that being in stepparent or single-parent households more than doubled the risk of delinquency by age 14. Similarly, a massive 1993 analysis of the underclass by M. Anne Hill and June O'Neill, published by Baruch College's Center for the Study of Business and Government, found that the likelihood that a young male will engage in criminal activity increases substantially if he is raised without a father.

These studies, like most in this area, attempted to control for other, confounding factors that might be correlated with living in a single-parent household. If single mothers have less money than married mothers, then perhaps poverty is the fundamental problem for their children. But even taking this possibility into account, the research still shows that boys who grew up outside of intact marriages were, on average, more likely than other boys to end up in jail.

Another set of studies found that the kids who are actually in the juvenile justice system disproportionately come from disrupted families. The Wisconsin Department of Health and Social Services, in a 1994 report entitled "Family Status of Delinquents in Juvenile Correctional Facilities in Wisconsin," found that only 13 percent came from families in which the biological mother and father were married to each other. By contrast, 33 percent had parents who were either divorced or separated, and 44 percent had parents who had never married. The 1987 *Survey of Youth in Custody,* published by the U.S. Bureau of Justice Statistics, found that 70 percent of youth in state reform institutions across the U.S. had grown up in single- or no-parent situations.

Causal Links

There are several plausible links between single parenthood and criminal behavior. The internal dynamic of a one-parent household is likely to be rather different from that of a two-parent household. Two parents can supervise the child's behavior more readily than one. Misbehavior can continue undetected and uncorrected for longer periods of time until it becomes more severe and more difficult to manage.

Likewise, the lowered level of adult input partially accounts for the lowered educational attainments of children of single parents. Such families report parents spending less time supervising homework and children spending less time doing homework. Not surprisingly, kids in these families have inferior grades and drop out of school more frequently. Leaving school increases the likelihood of a young person becoming involved in criminal behavior. It is similarly no surprise that adolescents who are left home alone to supervise themselves after school find more opportunities to get into trouble. Finally, the percentage of single-parent families in a neighborhood is one of the strongest predictors of the neighborhood's crime rate. In fact, Wayne Osgood and Jeff Chambers, in their 2000 article in the journal *Criminology,* find that father absence is more significant than poverty in predicting the crime rate.

These kinds of factors are easy enough to understand. A more subtle connection between the fractured family and criminal behavior is the possibility that the child does not form strong human attachments during infancy. A child obviously cannot attach to an absent parent. If the one remaining parent is overwhelmed or exhausted or preoccupied, the child may not form a proper attachment even to that parent. Full-fledged attachment disorder is often found among children who have spent a substantial fraction of their infancy in institutions or in foster care. (Think of Derek King.)

An attachment-disordered child is the truly dangerous sociopath, the child who doesn't care what anyone thinks, who does whatever he can get away with. Mothers and babies ordinarily build their attachments by being together. When the mother responds to the baby's needs, the baby can relax into her care. The baby learns to trust. He learns that human contact is the great good that ensures his continued existence. He learns to care about other people. He comes to care where his mother is and how she responds to him. Eventually, he will care what his mother thinks of him.

Usually, the parents win the race between the growth of the child's body and that of his conscience.

This process lays the groundwork for the development of the conscience; caring what she thinks of him allows him to internalize her standards of good conduct. As he gets older, bigger, and stronger, his mother can set limits on his behavior without physically picking him up and carrying him out of trouble.

Mother's raised eyebrow from across the room can be a genuine deterrent against misbehavior. As he matures, she doesn't even need to be present. He simply remembers what she wants him to do. Ultimately, he doesn't explicitly think about his parents' instructions. Without even considering punishments or approval, his internal voice reminds him, "We don't do that sort of thing." He has a conscience.

In most families, the parents win the race between the growth of the child's body and that of his conscience. By the time a child is too large and strong to muscle around, he had better have some self-command. If he doesn't, somebody will have to monitor his behavior all the time. He'll lie and steal and sneak. Punishments won't have much impact. He will become more sophisticated at calculating what he wants to try to get away with.

If the parents weren't abusive to begin with, they can become so at this point. They may keep trying to step up the penalties without realizing that the penalties aren't the point. The problem is that the child isn't listening to any inner voice of conscience. The child shouldn't even be thinking about the severity of penalties. The child ought to be thinking, "I am not the kind of person who even considers doing that."

Mental Illness and Genetics

One alternative hypothesis is that a family history of mental illness provides the causal relationship between crime and family structure. People who have a family history of certain kinds of mental illness may also have a higher propensity to become single parents. The same mental instability that contributes to a higher propensity to commit crimes may also make it more difficult for the person to form and sustain long-term relationships such as marriage.

A number of studies examine the relationship between single parenthood and some kinds of mental and emotional problems. A Swedish study by Gunilla Ringback Weitoft, Anders Hjern, Bengt Haglund, and Mans Rosen, released in January 2003 in the British medical journal *Lancet,* considered the impact of single-parent households on adolescents. This study explicitly took account of the family's history of mental illness. The Swedish adolescent children of single-parent households were twice as likely to abuse drugs or alcohol, twice as likely to attempt suicide, and about one and a half times as likely to suffer from a psychiatric illness. Parental history of mental illness accounted for very little of the variation in these various adolescent problems.

An extensive study of British data, reported by Andrew Cherlin and colleagues in the April 1998 issue of the *American Sociological Review,* also establishes a link between living in a single-parent household and some kinds of emotional problems over the child's entire lifetime. These researchers found that having divorced parents increases the likelihood of a wide range of problems, including depression, anxiety, phobias, and obsessions, over the entire lifetime. In addition, these children are more likely to be aggressive and disobedient during childhood.

The increased likelihood of aggressive behavior is confirmed in a variety of American studies, including Michael Workman and John Beer's 1992 study in *Psychological Reports* and

Nancy Vaden-Kiernan's 1995 study in the *Journal of Abnormal Child Psychology*. Not every instance of aggressive behavior is criminal behavior, of course, but it is fair to say that something that increases the likelihood of aggression probably raises the possibility of some kinds of crime.

The Cost of Controlling People

People who do not control themselves have to be controlled by outside forces. This very costly business may, for a while, be hidden from the public eye. The family absorbs the costs. A single mother, for instance, may try to enlist the help of her parents or other extended family members if she has a truly out-of-control child. The family, however it is structured, rearranges itself to protect itself from the child who is disruptive, defiant, or violent. The family has to provide extremely tight supervision or else bear the brunt of the child's behavior.

If the behavior gets serious enough, the criminal justice system will be called into action. People outside the family then have to manage the child's behavior. These people might include some combination of police officers, prison guards, social workers, psychiatrists, judges, and parole officers, depending on the child's age and the seriousness of his crimes. All these people have to be paid, either by the family or by the taxpayers. When the public sector gets involved, the costs become visible to the rest of society.

When the public sector gets involved, the costs become visible to the rest of society.

These costs add up. In California, for instance, the corrections budget has doubled since the 1960s as a percentage of the state's budget. By 2002–03, the prison system accounted for about 6 percent of the state budget, or more than $5.2 billion, an amount greater than what the state spends on transportation. Despite the current California budget crisis forcing cutbacks in most areas, the Department of Corrections is gaining a small boost of $40 million.

Some critics have claimed that these increases are political paybacks: The California Correctional Peace Officers Association has been one of the governor's biggest campaign contributors. This charge has some plausibility, since most of the increases in the department's budget are going to personnel costs. But being a prison guard is not a particularly pleasant job, and somebody, as they say, has to do it. Many of the facilities are in remote, unattractive parts of the state where attracting workers presents a continuing challenge. For instance, the Pelican Bay maximum-security prison in the far north of California is considered, if I may use the term, "godforsaken." The all-male facility recently had to use an ob-gyn as a primary care physician due to the difficulty of attracting an internal medicine doctor there.

While it may be easy for some to conclude that Davis is courting favor with his contributors, the teachers unions are also powerful political players in California, and education faces unprecedented cuts. The Department of Corrections spends $26,700 per adult inmate per year. Nobody seriously wants the governor to empty the prisons to save money.

Other critics claim that California's prison costs have escalated because the system is too tough on criminals. These critics cite the "Three Strikes" law, which requires a lifetime of incarceration for criminals with three offenses, no matter how trivial. Because of the law, an unprecedented number of relatively young people will spend the rest of their lives in prison at taxpayer expense.

Although such a law seems harsh, we should remember why we have a Three Strikes law in the first place: Richard Allen Davis. The sociopathic, unrepentant killer of Polly Klaas had a long history of criminal behavior. He had been recently released from prison when he stole Polly from her own bedroom and killed her. In the courtroom, he not only showed no remorse for his crime, he shouted obscenities at her parents. The people of California were sickened by the thought that a person so obviously dangerous should ever have been released.

As it happens, Richard Allen Davis was part of a disrupted family. His parents divorced when he was nine years old. He had virtually no contact with his mother after that. His father was often absent from the home and would leave his children with his own mother or with his different wives.

Think how much the state would save for every young person who can go on to create a life of his own.

We could pose the question of costs to the taxpayer in this way: Suppose the kids in the juvenile justice system were functioning well enough that they could be a reasonably normal part of society. They could then be in the educational system instead of in the juvenile justice system. Look at the per-person cost of incarceration for a year, compared with the cost of education.

The California Youth Authority is the juvenile branch of California's criminal justice system. The system works with youngsters in a variety of settings, including camps, schools, and residential treatment facilities. According to the state Legislative Analysts Office, the state spends approximately $49,200 per year per person on these programs.

If that same young person could function normally in society, he would cost taxpayers about $8,568 per year while in K–12 education. If he went on to the community college system, he would cost about $4,376—or about a tenth of the cost of a year under the jurisdiction of the Youth Authority. If he went to the prestigious University of California system, he would cost the state $17,392. Think how much the state would save for every young person who can go on to create a life of his own rather than have to have his every move controlled or monitored by someone else.

The educational system represents an investment; the state's expenditures are likely to be repaid over the years by its graduates when they become productive citizens. By contrast, the money spent on incarceration has little prospect of turning the individual into a more productive citizen. These expenditures merely neutralize the negative impact on society of an individual who can't or won't control himself.

Statistics and Probabilities

Some might respond that they personally are acquainted with many wonderful children of single parents. The parents are loving and giving; the children are thriving. But these anecdotal cases are not decisive. For every such story, we could produce a counter-story of a struggling single-parent family that fits the more distressing profile. The mother is a lovely person who did her best, but the boy got out of hand in his teenage years. Or the mother started out as a lovely person, but she became preoccupied with her new boyfriend or her job troubles. Her parents are heartbroken because they can see that their grandchildren are headed for trouble.

Besides, it is important to understand what statistical evidence does and does not prove. To say that a child of a single mother is twice as likely to commit a crime as the child of married parents is not to say that each and every child of every unwed mother will commit crimes or that no child of married parents will ever commit crimes. It is simply to say that growing up with unmarried parents is a significant risk factor.

Nor does saying that single-parent households are a risk factor diminish the possibility that some propensity for criminal activity might be genetically determined. Some individuals may well have a genetic propensity for aggression or for mental instability—or even for sociopathic behavior. These individuals are surely at higher than average risk for criminal activity, whether their parents are married or not. But the claim that some sociopaths are born does not preclude the possibility that some sociopaths are made. It makes sense to minimize the risk factors over which we can exercise a reasonable amount of control.

Some of the causal links between single-parent households and criminal behavior are better established than others. The causal connection between dropping out of school and higher probability of criminal behavior seems pretty straightforward and is well-documented. The link from single-parent households to attachment disorder is a weaker causal connection with a lower probability. But because a lifetime without a conscience is such a serious problem, it makes sense to try to lower the risk.

Look at it this way: When the evidence linking smoking with lung cancer first came to light, many people wanted to minimize that link. People with a serious addiction felt it was impossible for them to give up smoking. They didn't necessarily welcome the arrival of accurate information about a ship that had already sailed. "I know someone who smoked for a lifetime and never had cancer," skeptics replied. And indeed, that could be true. Smokers do not all die of smoking-related illness.

However, looking at the vast sweep of the evidence, enough people do die of smoking-related illnesses that smoking can safely be classified as a serious risk factor. And it is a choice-related risk factor, unlike genetic predispositions toward disease that might increase the likelihood of contracting lung cancer. It makes sense to have public health campaigns to educate the public about the risks associated with smoking, even though people irredeemably addicted to smoking might prefer not to be afflicted with this guilt- and anxiety-provoking information. Similarly, there is now enough evidence about the risks associated with growing up in a single-parent household that people are entitled to accurate information about those risks.

What to Do?

No serious person would claim that the government can or should take over marriage as a matter for "public" regulation and control, even if there are significant externalities to some behaviors. At a minimum, though, the government ought to refrain from counterproductive policies that discourage family formation or encourage family dissolution. The current regime of no-fault divorce, for example, really amounts to unilateral divorce.

Divorce imposes large costs on children. A unilateral divorce also imposes costs on the person who wants to preserve the marriage. Such people are willing to exert effort to stay married, but they don't even have the opportunity to state this case in court. These injured parties, adults and children alike, can never be made fully whole as the law would ordinarily require in a tort. It is a distortion of the idea of freedom to claim that no-fault divorce is the only policy consistent with individual liberty. Even a purely economic theory suggests that the imposition of costs on third parties should not be allowed to occur willy-nilly. Common decency requires that people who impose costs on others at least offer an account of themselves. The law should do no less.

But real policy recommendations have to go well beyond the reach of the law. In matters relating to the family, the dichotomy between "private" and "public," so familiar in policymaking circles, does not really work; these are not mutually exhaustive categories. We need an additional analytical category: "social."

Family matters are first and foremost social matters because a family is a little society. The larger society is built in crucial ways upon the little society of the family. The family is more than a collection of individuals who make quasi-market exchanges with each other. And families are not miniature political institutions. The label of "social" also points us in the right direction for solutions. The most important tools for building up the family are not primarily economic and political, but social and cultural. Accurate information is a necessary educational tool in reversing the culture of despair around the institution of marriage.

A young woman needs to know that the decision to have a child by herself is a decision that exposes her and her child to a lifetime of elevated risks: of poverty, of lower education, of depression, and of prison. Getting and staying married may seem formidable to a young pregnant woman because marriage is filled with a hundred irritations and difficulties. She might think it simpler to strike out alone rather than to put up with the innumerable adjustments and accommodations that are inevitable in married life. And it is easier for us to remain uninvolved in such a decision. But we are not doing the young person any favors by acting as if we are ignorant of the likely consequences of her choices. The time-honored American ethos of "live and let live" has metamorphosed into a categorical imperative to keep our mouths shut.

For years we have heard that single parenthood is an alternative lifestyle choice that doesn't affect anyone but the person who chooses it. We have been instructed that society should loosen the stigma against it in order to promote individual freedom of choice. We have been scolded for being insufficiently sensitive to the plight of single mothers if we utter any criticism of their decisions. At the urging of various activist groups, the government and society at large have been developing a posture of neutrality among family arrangements. There are no better or worse forms of family, we are told. There are no "broken families," only "different families."

The premise behind this official posture of neutrality is false. The decision to become a single parent or to disrupt an existing family does affect people outside the immediate household. These words may seem harsh to adults who have already made crucial life decisions, but it is time to be candid. We need to create a vocabulary for lovingly, but firmly and without apology, telling young people what we know. Surely, telling the truth is no infringement on anyone's liberty. Young people need to have accurate information about the choices they face. For their own sake—and for ours.

Jennifer Roback Morse is a research fellow at the Hoover Institution, Stanford University. She is the author of *Love and Economics: Why the Laissez-Faire Family Doesn't Work* (Spence Publishing, 2001).

From *Policy Review,* August/September 2003, pp. 49–60. Copyright © 2003 by Hoover Institution/Stanford University. Reprinted by permission of Policy Review and Jennifer Roback Morse.

The Aggregate Burden of Crime

DAVID A. ANDERSON

Introduction

Distinct from previous studies that have focused on selected crimes, regions, or outcomes, this study attempts an exhaustively broad estimation of the crime burden. . . .

Overt annual expenditures on crime in the United States include $47 billion for police protection, $36 billion for corrections, and $19 billion for the legal and judicial costs of state and local criminal cases. (Unless otherwise noted, all figures are adjusted to reflect 1997 dollars using the Consumer Price Index.) Crime victims suffer $876 million worth of lost workdays, and guns cost society $25 billion in medical bills and lost productivity in a typical year. Beyond the costs of the legal system, victim losses, and crime prevention agencies, the crime burden includes the costs of deterrence (locks, safety lighting and fencing, alarm systems and munitions), the costs of compliance enforcement (non-gendarme inspectors and regulators), implicit psychic and health costs (fear, agony, and the inability to behave as desired), and the opportunity costs of time spent preventing, carrying out, and serving prison terms for criminal activity.

This study estimates the impact of crime taking a comprehensive list of the repercussions of aberrant behavior into account. While the standard measures of criminal activity count crimes and direct costs, this study measures the impact of crimes and includes indirect costs as well. Further, the available data on which crime cost figures are typically based is imprecise. Problems with crime figures stem from the prevalence of unreported crimes, inconsistencies in recording procedures among law enforcement agencies, policies of recording only the most serious crime in events with multiple offenses, and a lack of distinction between attempted and completed crimes. This research does not eliminate these problems, but it includes critical crime-prevention and opportunity costs that are measured with relative precision, and thus places less emphasis on the imprecise figures used in most other measures of the impact of crime. . . .

Previous Studies

Several studies have estimated the impact of crime; however, none has been thorough in its assessment of the substantial indirect costs of crime and the crucial consideration of private crime prevention expenditures. The FBI Crime Index provides a measure of the level of crime by counting the acts of murder, rape, robbery, aggravated assault, burglary, larceny, motor vehicle theft, and arson each year. The FBI Index is purely a count of crimes and does not attempt to place weights on various criminal acts based on their severity. If the number of acts of burglary, larceny, motor vehicle theft, or arson decreases, society might be better off, but with no measure of the severity of the crimes, such a conclusion is necessarily tentative. From a societal standpoint what matters is the extent of damage inflicted by these crimes, which the FBI Index does not measure.

Over the past three decades, studies of the cost of crime have reported increasing crime burdens, perhaps more as a result of improved understanding and accounting for the broad repercussions of crime than due to the increase in the burden itself. Table 1 summarizes the findings of eight previous studies. . . .

The Effects of Crime

The effects of crime fall into several categories depending on whether they constitute the allocation of resources due to crime that could otherwise be used more productively, the production of ill-favored commodities, transfers from victims to criminals, opportunity costs, or implicit costs associated with risks to life and health. This section examines the meaning and ramifications of each of these categories of crime costs.

Crime-Induced Production

Crime can result in the allocation of resources towards products and activities that do not contribute to society except in their association with crime. Examples include the production of personal protection devices, the trafficking of drugs, and the operation of correctional facilities. In the absence of crime, the time, money, and material resources absorbed by the provision of these goods and services could be used for the creation of benefits rather than the avoidance of harm. The foregone benefits from these alternatives represent a real cost of crime to society. (Twenty dollars spent on a door lock is twenty dollars that cannot be spent on groceries.) Thus, expenditures on crime-related products are treated as a loss to society.

Crimes against property also create unnecessary production due to the destruction and expenditure of resources, and crimes against persons necessitate the use of medical and psychological care resources. In each of these cases, crime-related purchases bid-up prices for the associated items, resulting in higher prices for all consumers of the goods. In the absence of crime, the dollars currently spent to remedy and recover from crime would largely be spent in pursuit of other goals, bidding-up the prices of alternative categories of goods. For this reason, the *net* impact of price effects is assumed to be zero in the present research.

Table 1

Previous Study	Focus	Not Included	$ (billions)
Colins (1994)	General	Opportunity Costs, Miscellaneous Indirect Components	728
Cohen, Miller, and Wiersema (1995)	Victim Costs of Violent and Property Crimes	Prevention, Opportunity, and Indirect Costs	472
U.S. News (1974)	General	Opportunity Costs, Miscellaneous Indirect Components	288
Cohen, Miller, Rossman (1994)	Cost of Rape, Robbery, and Assault	Prevention, Opportunity, and Indirect Costs	183
Zedlewski (1985)	Firearms, Guard Dogs, Victim Losses, Commercial Security	Residential Security, Opportunity Costs, Indirect Costs	160
Cohen (1990)	Cost of Personal and Household Crime to Victims	Prevention, Opportunity, and Indirect Costs	113
President's Commission on Law Enforcement (1967)	General	Opportunity Costs, Miscellaneous Indirect Components	107
Klaus (1994)	National Crime and Victimization Survey Crimes	Prevention, Opportunity, and Indirect Costs	19

Opportunity Costs

As the number of incarcerated individuals increases steadily, society faces the large and growing loss of these potential workers' productivity. . . . Criminals are risk takers and instigators—characteristics that could make them contributors to society if their entrepreneurial talents were not misguided. Crimes also take time to conceive and carry out, and thus involve the opportunity cost of the criminals' time regardless of detection and incarceration. For many, crime is a full-time occupation. Society is deprived of the goods and services a criminal would have produced in the time consumed by crime and the production of "bads" if he or she were on the level. Additional opportunity costs arise due to victims' lost workdays, and time spent securing assets, looking for keys, purchasing and installing crime prevention devices, and patrolling neighborhood-watch areas.

The Value of Risks to Life and Health

The implicit costs of violent crime include the fear of being injured or killed, the anger associated with the inability to behave as desired, and the agony of being a crime victim. Costs associated with life and health risks are perhaps the most difficult to ascertain, although a considerable literature is devoted to their estimation. The implicit values of lost life and injury are included in the list of crime costs below; those not wishing to consider them can simply subtract these estimates from the aggregate figure.

Transfers

One result of fraud and theft is a transfer of assets from victim to criminal. . . .

Numerical Findings

Crime-Induced Production

. . . Crime-induced production accounts for about $400 billion in expenditures annually. Table 2 presents the costs of goods and services that would not have to be produced in the absence of crime. Drug trafficking accounts for an estimated $161 billion in expenditure. With the $28 billion cost of prenatal drug exposure and almost $11 billion worth of federal, state, and local drug control efforts (including drug treatment, education, interdiction, research, and intelligence), the combined cost of drug-related activities is about $200 billion. Findings that over half of the arrestees in 24 cities tested positive for recent drug use and about one-third of offenders reported being under the influence of drugs at the time of their offense suggest that significant portions of the other crime-cost categories may result indirectly from drug use.

About 682,000 police and 17,000 federal, state, special (park, transit, or county) and local police agencies account for $47 billion in expenditures annually. Thirty-six billion dollars is dedicated each year to the 895 federal and state prisons, 3,019 jails, and 1,091 state, county, and local juvenile detention centers. Aside from guards in correctional institutions, private expenditure on guards amounts to more than $18 billion annually. Security guard agencies employ 55 percent of the 867,000 guards in the U.S.; the remainder are employed in-house. While guards are expected and identifiable at banks and military complexes, they have a less conspicuous presence at railroads, ports, golf courses, laboratories, factories, hospitals, retail stores, and other places of business. The figures in this paper do not include receptionists, who often play a duel role of monitoring unlawful entry into a building and providing information and assistance. . . .

Opportunity Costs

In their study of the costs of murder, rape, robbery, and aggravated assault, Cohen, Miller, and Rossman estimate that the average incarcerated offender costs society $5,700 in lost productivity per year. Their estimate was based on the observation that many prisoners did not work in the legal market prior to their offense, and the opportunity cost of those prisoners' time can be considered to be zero. The current study uses a higher estimate of the opportunity cost of incarceration because unlike previous studies, it examines the relative savings from a *crime-free* society.

Table 2

Crime-Induced Production	$ (millions)
Drug Trafficking	160,584
Police Protection	47,129
Corrections	35,879
Prenatal Exposure to Cocaine and Heroin	28,156
Federal Agencies	23,381
Judicial and Legal Services—State & Local	18,901
Guards	17,917
Drug Control	10,951
DUI Costs to Driver	10,302
Medical Care for Victims	8,990
Computer Viruses and Security	8,000
Alarm Systems	6,478
Passes for Business Access	4,659
Locks, Safes, and Vaults	4,359
Vandalism (except Arson)	2,317
Small Arms and Small Arms Ammunition	2,252
Replacements due to Arson	1,902
Surveillance Cameras	1,471
Safety Lighting	1,466
Protective Fences and Gates	1,159
Airport Security	448
Nonlethal weaponry, e.g., Mace	324
Elec. Retail Article Surveillance	149
Theft Insurance (less indemnity)	96
Guard Dogs	49
Mothers Against Drunk Driving	49
Library Theft Detection	28
Total	397,395

Table 3

The Value of Risks to Life and Health	$ (millions)
Value of Lost Life	439,880
Value of Injuries	134,515
Total	574,395

and lost earnings (within modest bounds, victims or their spouses typically receive about two thirds of lost earnings for life or the duration of the injury). The values do capture perceived risks of pain, suffering, and mental distress associated with the health losses. If the risk of involvement in violent crime evokes more mental distress than the risk of occupational injuries and fatalities, the labor market values represent conservative estimates of the corresponding costs of crime. Similar estimates have been used in previous studies of crime costs. . . .

The average of 27 previous estimates of the implicit value of human life as reported by W. Kip Viscusi is 7.1 million. Removing two outlying estimates of just under $20 million about which the authors express reservation, the average of the remaining studies is $6.1 million. Viscusi points out that the majority of the estimates fall between $3.7 and $8.6 million ($3 and $7 million in 1990 dollars), the average of which is again $6.1 million. The $6.1 million figure was multiplied by the 72,111 crime-related deaths to obtain the $440 billion estimate of the value of lives lost to crime. Similarly, the average of 15 studies of the implicit value of non-fatal injuries, $52,637, was multiplied by the 2,555,520 reported injuries resulting from drunk driving and boating, arson, rape, robbery, and assaults to find the $135 billion estimate for the implicit cost of crime-related injuries.

Transfers

More than $603 billion worth of transfers result from crime. After the $204 billion lost to occupational fraud and the $123 billion in unpaid taxes, the $109 billion lost to health insurance fraud represents the greatest transfer by more than a factor of two, and the associated costs amount to almost ten percent of the nations' health care expenditures. Robberies, perhaps the classic crime, ironically generate a smaller volume of transfers ($775 million) than any other category of crime. The transfers of goods and money resulting from fraud and theft do not necessarily impose a net burden on society, and may in fact increase social welfare to the extent that those on the receiving end value the goods more than those losing them. Nonetheless, as Table 4 illustrates, those on the losing side bear a $603 billion annual burden. . . .

There are additional cost categories that are not included here, largely because measures that are included absorb much of their impact. Nonetheless, several are worth noting. Thaler, Hellman and Naroff, and Rizzo estimate the erosion of property values per crime. An average of their figures, $2,024, can be multiplied by the total number of crimes reported in 1994, 13,992, to estimate an aggregate housing devaluation of $28 billion. Although this figure should reflect the inability to behave as desired in the presence of crime, it also includes psychic and monetary costs imposed by criminal behavior that are already included in this [article].

It is likely that in the absence of crime including drug use, some criminals who are not presently employed in the legal workforce would be willing and able to find gainful employment. This assumption is supported by the fact that many criminals are, in a way, motivated entrepreneurs whose energy has taken an unfortunate focus. In the absence of more enticing underground activities, some of the same individuals could apply these skills successfully in the legal sector.

The Value of Risks to Life and Health

Table 3 presents estimates of the implicit costs of violent crime. The value of life and injury estimates used here reflect the amounts individuals are willing to accept to enter a work environment in which their health state might change. The labor market estimates do not include losses covered by workers' compensation, namely health care costs (usually provided without dollar or time limits)

Table 4

Transfers	$ (millions)
Occupational Fraud	203,952
Unpaid Taxes	123,108
Health Insurance Fraud	108,610
Financial Institution Fraud	52,901
Mail Fraud	35,986
Property/Casualty Insurance Fraud	20,527
Telemarketing Fraud	16,609
Business Burglary	13,229
Motor Vehicle Theft	8,913
Shoplifting	7,185
Household Burglary	4,527
Personal Theft	3,909
Household Larceny	1,996
Coupon Fraud	912
Robbery	775
Total	603,140

Table 5

The Aggregate Burden of Crime	$ (billions)
Crime-Induced Production	397
Opportunity Costs	130
Risks to Life and Health	574
Transfers	603
Gross Burden	**$1,705**
Net of Transfers	**$1,102**
Per Capita (in dollars)	**$4,118**

repercussions, the cost of crime is now seen to be more than twice as large as previously recognized.

Conclusion

Previous studies of the burden of crime have counted crimes or concentrated on direct crime costs. This paper calculates the aggregate burden of crime rather than absolute numbers, includes indirect costs, and recognizes that transfers resulting from theft should not be included in the net burden of crime to society. The accuracy of society's perspective on crime costs will improve with the understanding that these costs extend beyond victims' losses and the cost of law enforcement to include the opportunity costs of criminals' and prisoners' time, our inability to behave as desired, and the private costs of crime deterrence.

As criminals acquire an estimated $603 billion dollars worth of assets from their victims, they generate an additional $1,102 billion worth of lost productivity, crime-related expenses, and diminished quality of life. The net losses represent an annual per capita burden of $4,118. Including transfers, the aggregate burden of crime is $1,705 billion. In the United States, this is of the same order of magnitude as life insurance purchases ($1,680 billion), the outstanding mortgage debt to commercial banks and savings institutions ($1,853 billion), and annual expenditures on health ($1,038 billion).

As the enormity of this negative-sum game comes to light, so, too, will the need for countervailing efforts to redefine legal policy and forge new ethical standards. Periodic estimates of the full cost of crime could speak to the success of national strategies to encourage decorum, including increased expenditures on law enforcement, new community strategic approaches, technological innovations, legal reform, education, and the development of ethics curricula. Economic theory dictates that resources should be devoted to moral enhancement until the benefits from marginal efforts are surpassed by their costs. Programs that decrease the burden of crime by more than the cost of implementation should be continued, while those associated with negligible or positive net increments in the cost of crime should be altered to better serve societal goals.

Julie Berry Cullen and Stephen D. Levitt discuss urban flight resulting from crime. They report a nearly one-to-one relationship between serious crimes and individuals parting from major cities. The cost component of this is difficult to assess because higher commuting costs must be measured against lower property costs in rural areas, and the conveniences of city living must be compared with the amenities of suburbia. Several other categories of crime costs receive incomplete representation due to insufficient data, and therefore make the estimates here conservative. These include the costs of unreported crimes (although the National Crime Victimization Survey provides information beyond that reported to the police), lost taxes due to the underground economy, and restrictions of behavior due to crime.

When criminals' costs are estimated implicitly as the value of the assets they receive through crime, the gross cost of crime (including transfers) is estimated to exceed $2,269 billion each year, and the net cost is an estimated $1,666 billion. When criminals' costs are assumed to equal the value of time spent planning and committing crimes and in prison, the estimated annual gross and net costs of crime are $1,705 and $1,102 billion respectively. Table 5 presents the aggregate costs of crime based on the more conservative, time-based estimation method. The disaggregation of this and the previous tables facilitates the creation of customized estimates based on the reader's preferred assumptions. Each of the general studies summarized in Table 1 included transfers, so the appropriate comparison is to the gross cost estimate in the current study. As the result of a more comprehensive treatment of

UNIT 3

Groups and Roles in Transition

Unit Selections

Key Points to Consider

- Is the family in America in crisis? What indicators of family health have worsened, and what indicators have improved?

- What factors are influencing women's roles today? How are they changing women's lives?

- What do you think are the keys to successful marriages?

- Do you think that gay marriages should be legally treated as equal to heterosexual marriages?

- What factors create community? How can they be brought into being under today's conditions? What are the impediments to community? What are the consequences of weak communities? Does the Internet strengthen community?

Student Web Site

www.mhcls.com/online

Internet References

Further information regarding these Web sites may be found in this book's preface or online.

The Gallup Organization
http://www.gallup.com
Marriage and Family Therapy
http://www.aamft.org/index_nm.asp
The North-South Institute
http://www.nsi-ins.ca/english/default.asp
PsychNet/American Psychological Association
http://www.apa.org/topics/homepage.html
SocioSite: Feminism and Woman Issues
http://www.pscw.uva.nl/sociosite/TOPICS/Women.html

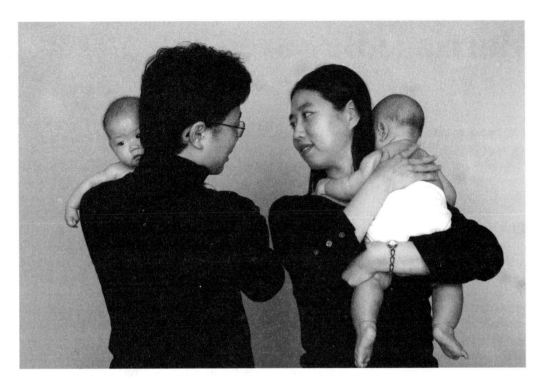

Primary groups are small, intimate, spontaneous, and personal. In contrast, secondary groups are large, formal, and impersonal. Primary groups include the family, couples, gangs, cliques, teams, and small tribes or rural villages. Primary groups are the main sources that the individual draws upon in developing values and an identity. Secondary groups include most of the organizations and bureaucracies in a modern society, and carry out most of its instrumental functions. Often primary groups are formed within secondary groups, such as a factory, school, or business.

Urbanization, geographic mobility, centralization, bureaucratization, and other aspects of modernization have had an impact on the nature of groups, the quality of the relationships between people, and individual's feelings of belonging. The family, in particular, has undergone radical transformation. The greatly increased participation of women in the paid-labor force and their increased careerism has led to severe conflicts for women between their work and family roles.

The first subsection of this unit deals with marriage and family in the context of dramatic changes in the culture and the economy. Everyone seems to agree that the family is in trouble, but Frank Furstenberg challenges this viewpoint. He recognizes that there are many marriage and family issues to be concerned about, but the modern American family is not on the rocks. It simply differs from the patterns of the 1960s, which were unusual when compared to patterns before World War II and compared to other countries. There is no universal normative family arrangement, and seldom do different classes in the same society have the same normative pattern. His major concern is the welfare of children where resources are few.

The next two articles look at current marriage issues. First, Janet Gornick reports on the time pressures on parents that are adversely affecting families. This is where government policies would be a big help, but the U.S. lags way behind other developed countries on such policies. The second article by Pepper Schwartz claims that peer marriages have become quite common in just one generation. Old patriarchal norms have been challenged and no longer provide a sure normative guide to marriage patterns because they are out of step with modern culture, society, and economic conditions. "Peer marriage offers a new formula for family and marital stability that may be . . . better adapted to the demands of contemporary culture."

The next subsection focuses on changes in gender roles. Michele Orecklin reports that more and more fathers are taking on childrearing responsibilities, and thus are struggling to balance work and family. This helps mothers but also creates new problems. In the second piece Julian Sanchez writes about how gay couples can provide a loving and supportive family to children, especially compared to the average foster home. Many states do not permit gay couples to adopt, which is unfortunate for many children.

The last subsection looks at cities and communities. The first article analyzes whether cities or country-sides are the answer to environmental problems. Cities as currently constructed are ecological disasters, but if redesigned to minimize their negative impact, they benefit the environment by concentrating population and thus reducing the extent of land conversion. In the final article Philip Langdon investigates the key urban issue of how to create cities and neighborhoods that also create communities. Many nineteenth-century cities seemed to have the answer. Houses close together and close to the street help neighbors to get to know and help each other, and more freely use public spaces.

Can Marriage Be Saved?

FRANK FURSTENBERG

A growing number of social scientists fear that marriage may be on the rocks and few doubt that matrimony, as we have known it, has undergone a wrenching period of change in the past several decades. Andrew Cherlin, a leading sociologist of the family, speaks of "the de-institutionalization of marriage," conceding a point to conservative commentators who have argued that marriage and the family have been in a state of free-fall since the 1960s.

Western Europe has experienced many of the same trends—declining rates of marriage, widespread cohabitation, and rising levels of nonmarital childbearing—but has largely shrugged them off. By contrast, concern about the state of marriage in the United States has touched a raw, political nerve. What ails marriage and what, if anything, can be done to restore this time-honored social arrangement to its former status as a cultural invention for assigning the rights and responsibilities of reproduction, including sponsorship and inheritance?

On the left side of the political spectrum, observers believe that the institutional breakdown of marriage has its roots in economic and social changes brought about by shifts in home-based production, structural changes in the economy, and the breakdown of the gender-based division of labor—trends unlikely to be reversed. The other position, championed by most conservatives, is that people have lost faith in marriage because of changes in cultural values that could be reversed or restored through shifts in the law, changes in administrative policies and practices, and public rhetoric to alter beliefs and expectations.

The Bush administration is trying to put into place a set of policies aimed at reversing the symptoms of retreat from marriage: high rates of premarital sex, nonmarital childbearing, cohabitation, and divorce. Do their policies make sense and do they have a reasonable prospect of success? To answer this question, I want to begin with the trends that Americans, including many social scientists, have found so alarming and then turn to the question of how much public policy and what kinds of policies could help to strengthen marriage.

Demographic Changes and Political Interpretations

When compared to the 1950s, the institution of marriage seems to be profoundly changed, but is the middle of the twentieth century an appropriate point of comparison? It has been widely known since the baby boom era that the period after the Second

World War was unusual demographically: the very early onset of adult transitions; unprecedented rates of marriage; high fertility; an economy that permitted a single wage earner to support a family reasonably well; and the flow of federal funding for education, housing, and jobs distinguished the 1950s and early 1960s as a particular historical moment different from any previous period and certainly different from the decades after the Vietnam War era. For a brief time, the nuclear family in the United States and throughout much of Europe reigned supreme.

If we use the middle of the twentieth century as a comparison point, it might appear that we have been witnessing a deconstruction of the two-parent biological family en masse. But such a view is historically shortsighted and simplistic. The nuclear family, though long the bourgeois ideal, had never been universally practiced, at least as it was in the middle of the last century. Only in the 1950s—and then for a very brief time—did it become the gold standard for what constitutes a healthy family. Indeed, sociologists at that time fiercely debated whether this family model represented a decline from the "traditional" extended family. Even those who argued against this proposition could not agree whether this family form was desirable ("functional" in the language of the day) or contained fatal flaws that would be its undoing.

During the 1960s and 1970s, anthropological evidence indicated that family diversity is universal, and findings from the new field of historical demography revealed that families in both the East and the West had always been changing in response to economic, political, demographic, and social conditions. In short, the nuclear family was cross-culturally and historically not "the natural unit," that many wrongly presume today.

Although it was widely known that the family had undergone considerable changes from ancient times and during the industrial revolution, that family systems varied across culture, and that social-class differences created varied forms of the family within the same society, it was not until the 1960s, when historians began to use computers to analyze census data, that the extent of this variation came into clearer focus. For the first time, family scholars from several disciplines could see the broad outlines of a new picture of how family forms and functions are intimately related to the social, cultural, and perhaps especially the economic contexts in which household and kinship systems are embedded.

From this evidence, students of the family can assert three points. First, no universal form of the family constitutes the appropriate or normative arrangement for reproduction, nurturance, socialization, and economic support. Both across and within societies, family forms, patterns, and practices vary enormously. Second, change is endemic to all family systems, and at least in the West, where we have the best evidence to date, family systems have always been in flux. Typically, these changes create tensions and often ignite public concern. Since colonial times, the family has been changing and provoking public reaction from moralists, scientists, and, of course, public authorities. Finally, family systems do not evolve in a linear fashion but become more or less complex and more elemental in different eras or among different strata of society depending on the economic and social conditions to which families must adapt.

Does this mean that we are seeing a continuation of what has always been or something different than has ever occurred in human history—the withering of kinship as an organizing feature of human society? The decline of marriage suggests to some that this round of change is unique in human history or that its consequences for children will be uniquely unsettling to society.

Many scholars weighed in on these questions. It is fair to say that there are two main camps: (1) those who have decided that the family is imperiled as a result of changes in the marriage system, a position held by such respectable social scientists as Linda Waite, Norvel Glenn, and Judith Wallerstein; and (2) those who remain skeptical and critical of those sounding the alarm, a position held by the majority of social scientists. Many in this second camp take seriously the concerns of the "alarmists" that children's welfare may be at risk if the current family regime continues. Still, they doubt that the family can be coaxed back into its 1950s form and favor adaptations in government policy to assist new forms of the family—an approach followed by most European nations.

Some portion of those skeptics are not so alarmed by changes in the family, believing that children's circumstances have not been seriously compromised by family change. They contend that children's well-being has less to do with the family form in which they reside than the resources possessed to form viable family arrangements. Lacking these resources (material and cultural), it matters little whether the children are born into a marriage, cohabitation, or a single-parent household, because they are likely not to fare as well as those whose parents possess the capacity to realize their goals.

I place myself in this latter group. Of course, children will fare better when they have two well-functioning, collaborative parents than one on average, but one well-functioning parent with resources is better than two married parents who lack the resources or skills to manage parenthood. Moreover, parents with limited cultural and material resources are unlikely to remain together in a stable marriage. Because the possession of such psychological, human, and material capital is highly related to marital stability, it is easy to confuse the effects of stable marriage with the effects of competent parenting. Finally, I believe that the best way to foster marriage stability is to support children with an array of services

that assist parents and children, regardless of the family form in which they reside.

Marriage and Good Outcomes for Children

A huge number of studies have shown that children fare better in two-biological-parent families than they do in single-biological-parent families, leading most family researchers to conclude that the nuclear family is a more effective unit for reproduction and socialization. Yet this literature reveals some troubling features that have not been adequately examined by social scientists. The most obvious of these is that such findings rule out social selection.

If parents with limited resources and low skills are less likely to enter marriage with a biological parent and remain wed when they do (which we know to be true), then it follows that children will do worse in such single-parent households than in stable marriages. We have known about this problem for decades, but researchers have not been equipped adequately to rule out selection. The standard method for doing so is by statistically controlling for prior differences, but this method is inadequate for ruling out differences because it leaves so many sources of selection unmeasured, such as sexual compatibility, substance abuse, and so on. Newer statistical methods have been employed to correct for unmeasured differences, but strong evidence exists that none of these techniques is up to the challenge. Nevertheless, it is *theoretically* possible to examine social experiments such as those being mounted in the marriage-promotion campaign and assess their long-term effects on children.

Another useful approach is to examine macro-level differences at the state or national level that would be less correlated with social selection and hence more revealing of the impact of marriage arrangements on children's well-being. To date, there is little evidence supporting a correlation between family form and children's welfare at the national level. Consider first the historical data showing that children who grew up in the 1950s (baby boomers) were not notably free of problem behavior. After all, they were the cohort who raised such hell in the 1960s and 1970s. From 1955 to 1975, indicators of social problems among children (test scores, suicide, homicide, controlled-substance use, crime) that can be tracked by vital statistics all rose. These indicators accompanied, and in some cases preceded rather than followed, change in the rates of divorce, the decline of marriage, and the rise of nonmarital childbearing during this period. Conversely, there is no evidence that the cohort of children who came of age in the 1990s and early part of this century is doing worse than previous cohorts because these children are more likely to have grown up in single-parent families. Of course, compensatory public policies or other demographic changes such as small family size, higher parental education, or lower rates of poverty may have offset the deleterious effects of family form, but such an explanation concedes that family form is not as potent a source of children's well-being as many observers seem to believe.

We might also gain some purchase on this issue by comparing the success of children under different family regimes. Do the countries with high rates of cohabitation, low marriage, high divorce, and high nonmarital fertility have the worst outcomes for children? We don't know the answer to this question, but we do know that various indicators of child well-being—health, mental health, educational attainment—do show higher scores in Northern than in Southern Europe. They appear to be linked to the level of investment in children, not the family form (which is certainly more intact in Southern Europe). Still, this question deserves more attention than it has received.

Significantly, many of the countries that continue to adhere to the nuclear model have some of the world's lowest rates of fertility—a problem that seems worse in countries with very low rates of nonmarital childbearing. I am not claiming that nonmarital childbearing is necessarily desirable as a social arrangement for propping up fertility, but it is a plausible hypothesis that nonmarital childbearing helps to keep the birth rate up in countries that would otherwise be experiencing a dangerously low level of reproduction.

Finally, it is important to recognize that family change in the United States (and in most Western countries, it appears) has not occurred evenly among all educational groups. In this country, marriage, divorce, and nonmarital childbearing have jumped since the 1960s among the bottom two-thirds of the educational distribution but have not changed much at all among the top third, consisting, today, of college graduates and postgraduates. Though marriage comes later to this group, they are barely more likely to have children out of wedlock, have high levels of marriage, and, if anything, lower levels of divorce than were experienced several decades ago. In other words, almost all the change has occurred among the segment of the population that has either not gained economically or has lost ground over the past several decades. Among the most socially disadvantaged and most marginalized segments of American society, marriage has become imperiled and family conditions have generally deteriorated, resulting in extremely high rates of union instability. The growing inequality in the United States may provide some clues for why the family, and marriage in particular, is not faring well and what to do about it.

Marriage and Public Policy

The logic of the Bush administration's approach to welfare is that by promoting and strengthening marriage, children's well-being, particularly in lower-income families will be enhanced. At first blush, this approach seems to make good sense. Economies of scale are produced when two adults live together. Two parents create healthy redundancies and perhaps help build social capital both within the household and by creating more connections to the community. The prevalence of marriage and marital stability is substantially higher among well-educated and more stably employed individuals than among those with less than a college education and lower incomes. Wouldn't it be reasonable to help the less educated enjoy the benefits of the nuclear family?

There are several reasons to be skeptical of this policy direction. First, we have the experience of the 1950s, when marriages did occur in abundance among low-income families. Divorce rates were extremely high during this era, and many of these families dissolved their unions when they had an opportunity to divorce because of chronic problems of conflict, disenchantment, and scarcity. In my own study of marriages of teen parents in the 1960s, I discovered that four out of every five women who married the father of their children got divorced before the child reached age eighteen; the rate of marital instability among those who married a stepfather was even higher. Certainly, encouraging marriage among young couples facing a choice of nonmarital childbearing or wedlock is not an easy choice when we know the outcome of the union is so precarious. If divorce is a likely outcome, it is not clear whether children are better off if their parents marry and divorce than remain unmarried, knowing as we do that family conflict and flux have adverse effects on children's welfare.

What about offering help to such couples before or after they enter marriage? This is a good idea, but don't expect any miracles from the current policies. Strong opposition exists to funding sustained and intensive premarital and postmarital counseling among many proponents of marriage-promotion programs. Conservative constituencies largely believe that education, especially under the aegis of religious or quasi-religious sponsorship is the best prescription for shoring up marriage. Yet, the evidence overwhelmingly shows that short-term programs that are largely didactic will not be effective in preserving marriages. Instead, many couples need repeated bouts of help both before and during marriage when they run into difficult straits. Most of these couples have little or no access to professional counseling.

The federal government has funded several large-scale experiments combining into a single program marital education or counseling *and* social services including job training or placement. These experiments, being conducted by the Manpower Research Demonstration Corporation, will use random assignment and have the best hope of producing some demonstrable outcomes. Yet, it is not clear at this point that even comprehensive programs with sustained services will be effective in increasing partner collaboration and reducing union instability.

There is another approach that I believe has a better prospect of improving both children's chances and probably at least an equal chance of increasing the viability of marriages or marriage-like arrangements. By directing more resources to low-income children regardless of the family form they live in, through such mechanisms as access to quality child care, health care, schooling, and income in the form of tax credits, it may be possible to increase the level of human, social, and psychological capital that children receive. And, by increasing services, work support, and especially tuition aid for adolescents and young adults to attend higher education, Americans may be able to protect children from the limitations imposed by low parental resources. Lending this type of assistance means that young adults are more likely to move into higher paying jobs and acquire through education the kinds of communication and problem-solving skills that are so useful to making marriage-like relationships last.

When we invest in children, we are not only likely to reap the direct benefits of increasing human capital but also the indirect benefits that will help preserve union stability in the next generation. This approach is more likely to increase the odds of success for children when they grow up. If I am correct, it probably follows that direct investment in children and youth has a better prospect of strengthening marriage and marriage-like relationships in the next generation by improving the skills and providing the resources to make parental relationships more rewarding and enduring.

So it comes down to a choice in strategy: invest in strengthening marriage and hope that children will benefit or invest in children and hope that marriages will benefit. I place my bet on the second approach.

FRANK FURSTENBERG, Zellerbach Family Professor of Sociology at the University of Pennsylvania, has written extensively on children, families, and public policy. His most recent book is *On the Frontier of Adulthood* (co-edited with Rick Settersten and Ruban Rumbaut), University of Chicago Press, 2005.

Overworked, Time Poor, and Abandoned by Uncle Sam

Why Don't American Parents Protest?

JANET C. GORNICK

The story of the overworked American parent is by now well-known. Every day, millions of American parents—single and partnered, low-income and affluent—scramble to coordinate the demands of employment with their children's need for care and supervision. In the majority of families in the United States, all the adults are in the workforce, more often than not working full time. It is not surprising that the stressed-out working parent is now a staple in multiple venues, from social science research to newspaper opinion columns to TV-land.

As Kathleen Gerson pointed out in these pages last year ("The Morality of Time: Women and the Expanding Work Week," Fall 2004), the common wisdom in the United States generally lays the responsibility for the work-family time bind on individuals and lets American institutional realities off the hook. Conservatives typically focus on mothers, protesting that many (middle-class and well-off) women are choosing paid work over family, indulging themselves while leaving their children and husbands unattended. (Poor single mothers, of course, have long been exempted from this criticism, as they are expected to work for pay.) And many progressives, Gerson argues, have not helped matters, too often attributing Americans' notoriously long work hours to their ever-expanding desire for consumption or their preference for the effects-oriented workplace over the strains and uncertainties of life at home.

But, in fact, the American institutional landscape deserves much of the blame. Many workplaces are still designed for workers who have no competing responsibilities, and the paucity of public policies that support working families can hardly be overstated. As Marcia Meyers and I argue in our book—*Families That Work*—the American state provides much less to working parents than do many other countries, especially the high-income countries of northern and western Europe.

For starters, parents in several European countries have access to multiple forms of paid family leave and to high-quality affordable child care. In addition, working-time regulations limit the imposition of excessively long weekly work hours and effectively cap the number of days worked each year. Furthermore, public measures in all European Union member countries require pay and benefit parity for part-time workers—making shorter-hour work a more feasible option. And a growing number of countries grant full-time workers the right to temporarily downsize to part-time work and/or to alter the scheduling of their assigned hours. These so-called work-family reconciliation measures are, of course, embedded in larger social protection systems that provide universal health insurance, among other crucial components. All told, these comprehensive policy packages allow parents ample latitude in deciding how to allocate their time between paid work and care. Public supports also indemnify families against substantial fluctuations in disposable income when parents temporarily diminish their time in paid work, or take a break altogether, to concentrate on caregiving.

In contrast, American public policy leaves the vast majority of working parents high and dry. The meager Family and Medical Leave Act of 1993 provides some parents limited rights to periods of unpaid leave to take care of infants and other family members. (Workers in small enterprises and without substantial work experience in the prior year are not eligible.) As for paid leave, only five states offer mothers any wage replacement following childbirth or adoption (through public temporary disability insurance laws) and only one (California) offers benefits for fathers. The standard work week remains set at forty hours, a level established more than six decades ago, and American working-time law is silent on equal treatment for part-time workers, on rights to part-time or flexible scheduling, and on the right to a minimum number of paid days off per year. The public child care system in the United States is among the least developed in the industrialized world.

In the absence of public supports, Americans are left with the market. With the exception of the poorest workers, parents turn to consumer markets to purchase child care—or they manage with informal arrangements. Workers who get family-friendly leave and working-time options generally get them in the labor market, sometimes as part of a standard employee benefit package, sometimes via individualized negotiation. While many workers—especially more highly educated, higher-earning workers—secure workplace benefits, many others do not. The weakness of unions in the United States, due in part to public policy, means that when American parents turn to their employers for work-family benefits, they commonly have a weak collective voice and little bargaining power.

The Problem of Private Solutions

What do American parents do in the absence of public supports? How do they manage the work-family crunch? As we argue in *Families That Work,* U.S. parents craft a range of private solutions to reconcile high rates of parental employment with their children's need for care. In many families, parents reduce the labor market attachment of one parent—in practice, overwhelmingly, the mother. Women with children often choose various forms of underemployment, opting for jobs that demand less of them than their skills would otherwise warrant; others are employed part time and/or intermittently. (The paucity of high-quality, remunerative work in the thirty-five- to thirty-nine-hour range leads many couples to end up with one long-hour worker and one part-time worker.) Other families choose a different route, opting for what Harriet Presser has dubbed "split-shift parenting." Split-shift parents—or any pair of caregivers, more generally—arrange employment schedules so that they work opposite hours; one leaves for the workplace as the other comes home. Yet another group of families makes extensive use of non-parental care, with many placing their children in child care starting in early infancy.

These private solutions are adaptive and work well for many individual families. But they also exacerbate long-standing problems of gender inequality and create new social and economic problems. The "one-parent-chooses-partial-employment" option cements gender divisions of labor, because it is mothers, and rarely fathers, who cut back on paid work to care for children. While split-shift parenting works well for some families, and may strengthen fathers' ties to their children, other social consequences are problematic—including disproportionately high rates of marital dissolution and negative effects on children's well-being. Likewise, intensive use of non-parental child care, even from early infancy, also works well for many families. But, for others, the out-of-pocket costs deplete family disposable income, and too many children end up in care of worrisome quality. And leaving child care to the market, especially with limited regulation, also means that many child care workers are very poorly paid, which places them and their own families at risk.

Finally, leaving work-family benefits to labor and consumer markets deepens inequalities. As Jody Heymann's work has demonstrated, market-based work-family benefits are not only limited in the United States, their distribution is extremely regressive. Although many highly educated, high-earning workers have ample workplace benefits—and excellent child care options—their less privileged counterparts typically have access to far less for themselves and their children. As Jason DeParle relates in heartbreaking detail in his book *American Dream,* many low-wage workers—especially those who are also solo parents—hold jobs with little in the way of workplace benefits, and high quality child care, especially for infants, remains largely out of reach.

How U.S. Parents and Children Fare

A mountain of research reveals that American working parents have a tougher job than their counterparts in other high-income countries. Among two-parent families, with two earners, U.S. couples spend just over eighty hours a week (jointly) working for pay. In a number of other rich countries—including France, Germany, and the United Kingdom—dual-earner couples with children average between seventy-three and seventy-eight hours a week, whereas Dutch and Swedish dual-earners average between sixty-five and sixty-eight hours a week, or the equivalent of nearly two fewer days per week, relative to U.S. couples. Even more remarkable, nearly two-thirds of U.S. couples work *more* than eighty hours each week jointly—a distribution that no European country even approaches.

How about gender equality in the labor market? With all that hard work, surely the United States must be the world's leader in women's engagement in paid labor. In fact, gender equality in the U.S. labor market is only fair-to-middling, relative to more than half of ten European comparison countries and Canada. Among parents with partners, U.S. mothers take home about 28 percent of total parental earnings—substantially less than the share commanded by mothers in Denmark, Sweden, Finland, Norway, France, and Belgium. And equality at home? Gender disparities in the American labor market spill over into the home: American working fathers spend forty-four minutes doing unpaid work at home for every hundred minutes invested by their working wives, a ratio that lags behind that reported in a handful of European countries.

Not surprisingly, more Americans than Europeans report dissatisfaction with their ability to balance work and family life. According to a recent national survey conducted by the Families and Work Institute, over half of American workers report that they experience conflict "in balancing work, personal life, and family life." In a recent survey, when EU parents were asked, "In general, do your working hours fit in with your family or social commitments outside work very well, fairly well, not very well or not at all well?," a remarkable 80 percent of parents responded that their work hours and private commitments fit "very well" or "fairly well."

Clearly many U.S. parents feel unbalanced, but how about our children? Does our hard work at least benefit America's children? Sadly, there is little evidence that it does—children in the United States are not doing especially well either. That is most evident at the bottom of the income distribution. Relative to many other rich countries, American children are much more likely to be poor—no matter what their family's structure and their parents' employment status. But average outcomes are none too great either. American children, on average, are also more likely to die in infancy or in young childhood, to perform poorly on international math and science tests during their adolescent years, and to conceive or bear children as teenagers. (American children also watch inordinate amounts of television, possibly because it serves as low-cost child care.) Although much research establishes that public policies have a powerful direct effect on parents' working hours, and even on gendered labor market outcomes, it is much harder to establish that the U.S. work-family policy configuration is the *cause* of our relatively poor child outcomes. Nevertheless, what we do know is that the "American model" for balancing work and family—essentially, leaving it to individuals and markets—is not associated with impressive outcomes for our children.

There Is Some Good News—Sort of

Is there some good news? Yes, to some extent. While Americans' long work hours may produce deleterious results for many parents and children, we do earn a lot. The United States ranks first among the thirty OECD (Organization for Economic Cooperation and Development) member countries in per capita income, using purchasing-power-adjusted exchange rates. That means that, on average, Americans enjoy a relatively high standard of living—when standard of living is captured by this common measure—compared to our neighbors in other rich countries. Many argue that this result closes the case: despite some distributional concerns, it is argued, the American model, overall, remains the most economically advantageous. European workers may feel good about their generous benefit packages but, in the end, so goes the argument, they and their families pay a considerable price.

That's a powerful claim, but, at the same time, average per capita income needs a second look. First of all, it doesn't account for many forms of non-market income, such as education, health care, child care, and the like—forms of income that we know lag (and are regressively distributed) in the United States. Second, some scholars argue that it is misleading to measure "standard of living" solely in monetary terms, without taking into account time investments. As Lars Osberg, a Canadian economist has argued: "'Quality of life' or 'economic well-being' may be hard to define precisely, but most would agree that they depend on both an individual's income level and the discretionary time they have in which to enjoy it."

So, American workers—on average—do take home a sizable chunk of income compared to average workers elsewhere, but for many American workers and their families, that economic payoff is compromised by the family time-poverty that enables it. It's also the case that Americans may work so hard that we are on the diminishing-returns portion of the productivity curve. While the United States leads the world in gross domestic product per worker, we are ranked eighth among the OECD countries in GDP per worker-hour. It is possible that, as

a society, we could shift some hours from work to family *and* see a rise in our hourly output. What is clear is that the current work-family arrangement—with its weak protections and limited benefits for working parents—is problematic on many fronts, and that large numbers of American parents and their children are poorly served.

Why Don't U.S. Parents Protest?

Why do American working parents accept the paltry public supports? Why don't they object to the absence of paid family leave, the weak working-time protections, and the near total absence of public investment in child care? Even more starkly, where is the public outcry as the Bush administration chips away at the Family and Medical Leave Act and weakens the Fair Labor Standards Act? Why do large numbers of Americans tell pollsters that they *want* more help from government, specifically for working parents, and then fail to form an effective social movement calling for that help? Why was work-family policy nearly invisible in the last election cycle? Why did so many who claim to want help for American working families pull the other lever?

There are no easy answers. Although there is much to argue with in *What's the Matter With Kansas?*, Thomas Frank has surely awakened us to the larger possibility that a peculiar form of cultural alienation has pushed many Americans to vote against their own material interests. Speaking more broadly, Jeff Madrick tells us that, in contemporary America, supporting government—even with a policy agenda that promises economic growth—is simply against our "national character." "The American national character," Madrick writes in *Why Economies Grow,* "has prevented the nation from adopting a new social contract to lead it forward. We do not even speak in terms of the social contract anymore because, implicitly, we do not give government sufficient status to enter into a contract with the people. These days, as large as government is, in the public mind it is an appendage and a burden, not a partner."

In addition to these dispiriting—and largely persuasive—analyses I would point to two more barriers to work-family policy development that may ultimately be more malleable. First of all, many Americans envision well-being so narrowly as to be counter-productive. As an example, in a recent *New York Times* column (January 4, 2005) David Brooks laid out the same cross-national portrait of working hours that I present to illustrate the work-family time bind in the United States. Brooks, however, told the mirror tale. He praised the fact that Americans work "50 percent more than Germans, French, and Italians." Because of our industriousness, he argued, "American GDP per capita is about 30 percent higher than Europe's and the gap, if anything, is getting wider." (Several of my progressive colleagues sent me that column, adding "Unfortunately, he's right, isn't he?") Long work hours may indeed produce a lot of output—and, of course, for many families, much-needed income—but they are also associated with an array of negative social consequences that aren't talked about enough, even on the left.

Second, Americans remain remarkably unaware that generous work-family reconciliation policies operate successfully—and with widespread political support—in many other rich countries. Unfortunately, it is not just conservatives, but often progressives as well, who have absorbed damaging misperceptions—in particular, that the European countries have cut work-family programs in recent years (not true), after concluding that these programs, along with the social safety net more generally, have negative macroeconomic consequences (also not true). In fact, a mounting body of research challenges the claim that social spending is harmful to economic growth. Peter Lindert's comprehensive new study on the impact of social spending, *Growing Public: Social Spending and Economic Growth Since the Eighteenth Century,* concludes, "Contrary to the intuition of many economists and the ideology of many politicians, social spending has contributed to, rather than inhibited, economic growth." (On top of that, Lindert argues, public investments in women's employment constitute a crucial pro-growth strategy.) Lawrence Mishel, Jared Bernstein, and Sylvia Allegretto concur that public social protections often bring macroeconomic benefits. Their own empirical results—presented in *The State of Working America 2004–2005*—lead them to conclude that "although the U.S. economy saw increased productivity in the last few years, it under-performed relative to other OECD economies for most of the past 20 years. . . . This suggests that those formulating policy may benefit from looking beyond the U.S. model."

Building a social consensus in the United States for more government support for working families will not be easy, but a few things are clear. If we want to spur change, we need a dramatically altered discourse about the role of government in the lives of American families. We need a new lexicon concerning "family values," one that includes the damaging consequences of time poverty, as well as income poverty, for American workers and their families. We need to recognize that we, as a nation, must invest in our children's care and education during the first five years of their lives—rather than waiting until they are old enough for kindergarten. We need to alert many more Americans to the extreme exceptionalism of U.S. family policy offerings relative to the other rich countries of the world—and, increasingly, from a global perspective as well. (The United States is one of five countries in the entire world without a national policy of paid maternity leave.) And, finally, we need to persuade Americans, on both the left and right, that a comprehensive package of work-family policies would be consistent with a more equitable distributional result—for women, for men, and for children—and with healthy macroeconomic outcomes as well.

Janet C. Gornick is, with Marcia K. Meyers, coauthor of *Families That Work: Policies for Reconciling Parenthood and Employment*, published by the Russell Sage Foundation in 2003 and released in paperback in April 2005.

Originally published in *Dissent Magazine,* Summer 2005, pp. 65–69. Copyright © 2005 by Foundation for Study of Independent Ideas, Inc. Reprinted by permission. www.dissentmagazine.org

Peer Marriage

PEPPER SCHWARTZ

Our generation has been the first to witness the emergence of "partnership" or "peer" marriages on a large social scale. Such marriages differ from their traditional counterparts in at least four key respects: men and women in these relationships regard each other as full social equals; both pursue careers; partners share equal authority for financial and other decision making; and, not least important, husbands typically assume far greater responsibility for child-rearing than in the past. Many of us—including much of the feminist movement, of which I have been a part—tend to regard these marriages as a major social breakthrough, the culmination of an arduous, generation-long effort to redefine women's roles and to secure for women the same freedom and dignity that society has traditionally accorded to men.

Yet in recent years conservatives, particularly the adherents of the "pro-family" or "family values" movement, have increasingly called for a rejection of the peer marriage ideal and a return by society as a whole to the traditional role-differentiated model. Bolstering their case is a significant body of traditional social theory arguing for the superior stability of the role-differentiated marriage, in which the husband serves as sole provider and main figure of authority, and the wife bears the lion's share of responsibilities for child rearing and day-to-day household maintenance.

Contemporary concerns with marital and family stability are certainly warranted. In a society with a 50 percent divorce rate—in which a host of social pathologies can be traced directly to havoc in fatherless or broken homes—policymakers and theorists are right to place a high priority on measures aimed at keeping families intact. Yet it is far from self-evident that the road to greater marital stability lies in a return to tradition. Over the past generation, I would argue, broad changes in society—and in the expectations that men and women bring to the marital relationship—have undermined much of the original basis of the traditional model of marriage. In reality, as I will try to show here, peer marriage offers a new formula for family and marital stability that may be both more durable and better adapted to the demands of contemporary culture than the older form. New data from studies that I and others have conducted support the notion that peer marriages are at least as stable as traditional unions and may in the long run prove more resilient vis-à-vis the special social pressures that marriages confront today.

Marital Stability and Marital Satisfaction

There is a close connection between marital stability and happiness or satisfaction in marriage—in both practice and theory. Even the most hard-headed theorists of the traditional model—such as sociologist Talcott Parsons or economist Gary Becker—have invariably sought to reconcile their advocacy of gender-based role differentiation with the possibility of marital satisfaction. To justify the traditional division of labor in marriage purely on the basis of men's and women's different biological aptitudes, historical experience, or cultural training is, after all, not a difficult theoretical task. But to posit happiness and mutual satisfaction as the outcome of such a union is another matter.

This is not to say that happiness was or is impossible to achieve under the traditional marital regime. Many people, especially when the larger culture supports it, find happiness in holding up their part of the marital bargain: women who like to be in charge of the kitchen, and men who want to bring home the bacon but do not want to cook it. In the past, and even today, this contract has worked for many people. Increasingly, however, it does not work as well as it used to. It did not work for me as well as it worked for my mother, and it didn't work for her all the time, either. The gender-based division of labor, so automatic for so much of history, increasingly fails to bring the promised emotional fulfillment that was supposed to be a major part of its contribution to family satisfaction and stability—emotional fulfillment which is increasingly vital to marital stability today.

We may contrast the experience of my mother's generation with that of my own. Like so many women of her era, my mother traded *service* for *support,* a transaction with which she usually seemed content. She bore almost complete responsibility for raising her children and at the same time had full charge of household upkeep: cooking, cleaning, keeping my father's closets and drawers impeccably neat, and so forth. My father, not atypical of his generation, was a man who never packed his own suitcase for a trip. In return, he provided handsomely—beyond my mother's wildest dreams, since she had grown up in poverty and was forced to drop out of high school to support her ailing mother and her youngest sisters. Having met my father as a secretary in his fledgling law office, my mother was very grateful to have been pulled from destitution into a different social class. Later she could afford to finish high school and college, raise three children, and become a docent in an art museum. Her lifestyle with my father was something secure and in a sense wonderful, exceeding all her childhood expectations.

The arrangement worked well for my father also. He was not born to privilege. The eldest of five growing up on a farm in Indiana, he put himself through law school, transferring from the University of Chicago to night school at Loyola when times got rough. He scrambled to better himself and his family. He and his wife had the same goal: to achieve the means for the good life. They entertained clients and traveled.

But my father also expected my mother to do everything he told her to do. After all, his own father had been dictatorial; it was something a woman owed a man—even though, in my grandfather's case, his wife had purchased the farm for the family. No matter. Leadership at home was owed a man as part of his birthright. When my mother—an intense, intelligent woman—would occasionally resist an order or talk back, my father's response to her was scathing and uninhibited.

What was the bargain my mother willingly made? She had a husband who loved her, who created an increasingly luxurious environment, and who ordered her around and reminded her—almost incessantly—about how lucky she was to have him. Love and what my generation of women would call patriarchal control went hand in hand. On my mother's side, gratitude, deep resentment, and anger all came in a neat package. The marriage lasted 55 years, until my mother's death. Children were launched. The marriage could be declared a success. Nevertheless, under today's circumstances, I would expect such a marriage to survive ten years at best.

Today my mother would have had a chance at her own career, at which she had the talent to excel. She would have had a new identity as a human being with core rights and her own sense of entitlement. (Surely, she promoted mine.) She would have had a different standard of equality and different ideas about equity. She would probably not have thought it enough to have been rescued from poverty. She would have felt entitled to a different style of family decision making, and she would have had the options—and the cultural support—to demand more. But if my father had remained the same man he was when I was growing up, he would not have acquiesced. Under contemporary circumstances, the marriage most probably would have broken up—much to my own, my siblings', and probably my parents' disadvantage.

And that is one reason why I believe peer marriage—a marriage founded on the principle of equality and supported by shared roles and a greater chance of shared sensibilities—is an adaptation in the direction of greater family stability rather than instability. Indeed, in contemporary culture, a peer or partner relationship between spouses has become increasingly vital to keeping families intact. It also offers new advantages to children, to which I will return in a moment.

We must be clear, however, that the mere existence of separate careers does not guarantee a peer marriage. Such a marriage also requires a comprehensive reconceptualization of the partners' roles. Dual incomes alone are insufficient to guarantee stability.

Money and Work

Indeed, much empirical research, some of it my own, indicates that labor force participation and achievement of high income by women destabilizes marriage. A number of studies, including the well-known Income Maintenance Study done out of the University of Michigan, found that when one raised the income of low-income women—hoping to stabilize families by reducing poverty—divorce increased substantially. Theorists have deduced that, under such circumstances, growth in income simply opens a new option for women to leave the relationship, an option that many of them exercise. Moreover, many studies show high-earning women with higher breakup rates. It is unclear whether high earnings make women less willing to tolerate unwanted behaviors or other disappointments on the part of their spouses, or whether men find women who are ambitious or aggressive (or who possess other traits consonant with career success) unsatisfying to be with in the long run. At any rate, the correlation is real enough.

Nor do couples necessarily adapt smoothly to equalization of income and status between partners. In *American Couples,* a study of 6,000 married, cohabiting, and lesbian and gay couples, Phil Blumstein and I found that a partner's power rose in relation to his or her relative income as compared with that of the spouse or live-in lover, but not necessarily in the ways we would have predicted. Women's power rose and became equal to their partners' when they had equal income—but only if they had a supportive ideology that allowed them to claim equal power. And power did not necessarily increase proportionally to the income differential. For example, more power did not release women from as much housework as one might expect. Higher-income career women did less, but not equivalently less, and their partners did not do proportionately more. (Male partners of high-earning women *did* feel their partners were entitled to do less housework, but did not feel required to do more themselves!) Feminists may be inclined to despair: Are men so resistant to participation in household labor that nothing will induce them to pitch in appropriately?

Yet—and this is the key point—it remains to be seen whether the tensions we found are the permanent consequence of change or merely transitional pains that arise as couples, and society as a whole, grope for a new definition of the marital relationship. Many men are clearly uncomfortable with the weakening of the traditional male role as sole provider. And, notably, there has been little effort—outside a small and probably unrepresentative "men's movement"—to reconceptualize the husband's role under these new economic circumstances. However, several changes are conspiring to move society as a whole beyond this sometimes painful transitional phase: transformations in the economy, in the attitudes of younger men, and in the cultural definition of marriage itself.

In the first place, in the contemporary economy female income has become an important ingredient of family prosperity (even, in many cases, a necessity). Economists have long recognized that household income has maintained stability in the United States over the past decades only through large-scale entry of women into the work force. The two-income household, once an exception, is now increasingly the norm.

Furthermore, corporate restructuring and downsizing have tended to intensify the trend. Women's labor force participation has become increasingly vital to family stability in a society where job security is, for all but a few, a thing of the past. Men are now beginning to realize that their hold on continuous employment after age 40 is, to say the least, shaky. By age 55, less than half of all men are still fully employed. Women, having many of the skills necessary for a service-oriented society, stay employable longer and more steadily. Indeed, in our society, the nonworking wife is increasingly becoming a symbol of exceptional wealth or conspicuous consumption—or of a major

ideological commitment either to the patriarchal family or to a vision of the female as the primary parent.

There are signs that these new economic realities are beginning to affect attitudes among men in their 20s. Young boys today are increasingly growing up in two-parent families where females are either the chief provider or an essential contributor to family income. Moreover, they understand their own economic futures as providers to be far from secure. Partly as a result, more and more young men are seeking in marriage someone to be part of an economic team rather than an exclusive parenting specialist. Just as women have in the past sought "a good provider," so, I predict, men will increasingly want to marry (and stay married to) a woman who can provide her share of economic stability.

But possibly the most important change has come in the subtle cultural redefinition of the marital relationship itself. In a society in which divorce is prevalent and the economic independence of both spouses is the rule, marital stability depends increasingly on factors of personal satisfaction and emotional fulfillment. The glue holding marriages together today is neither economic necessity nor cultural sanction, but emotion. Marital stability in contemporary society increasingly depends on sustaining the emotional satisfaction of *both* partners. It is here that peer marriage shows its special advantages.

Under these new economic and cultural circumstances, the ability of men and women to participate in each other's lives—to build companion status—becomes essential to marital survival. Equality is a crucial ingredient of this form of intimacy. When women have validation in the outside world through career, and when couples can operate as a team on both economic and home issues, partners become more similar to each other and achieve greater emotional compatibility—or so I would hypothesize on the basis of my research with peer couples. With more outside experiences to bring to the marital community, the woman becomes a more interesting companion for the long run. Moreover, whatever competition or tensions may result from this new arrangement, women today probably need some of these career-related personality traits simply to stay competitive with the women men increasingly meet in the workplace. This was less important in a society where home and family were sacrosanct and a mother and wife—no matter how far she was from being a "soul mate"—was automatically protected from outside contenders for her spouse. However, that is not the society we live in any more, nor is it likely to return. And even though income creates independence and therefore opportunities for separation, the recognition that spouses would lose their mutually constructed lifestyle if the marriage ended has its own stabilizing effect, as I have found in my interviews with dozens of peer couples.

Love Versus Money

Of course, even today, if one were to analyze marriage in purely economic terms, the traditional model can seem to offer certain advantages over the peer arrangement. Becker and others have contended that, at least during child-raising years, couples with the woman in a full-time mothering role tend to gain more income. And a few studies have shown that men with working wives have lower incomes than men with nonworking wives. Economically ambitious couples probably calculate correctly that one parent, usually the male, should be released from most parental duties to earn as much as he can; the payoff here will lie in enhanced family income and social status, in which both partners presumably will share.

But this approach fails to address the real problem at the base of today's shaky marital system—maintaining a high standard of emotional fulfillment. "Efficient" role allocation frequently leaves partners leading parallel and largely separate lives. Mom and Dad did that—each an expert in their separate spheres. It worked when there was less expectation that marriage should produce a soul mate, and when Mom's tolerance levels were higher for the habitual carping at dinner. While this system did and does work for some, it tends to diminish emotional partnership. People in such "parallel marriages," financially secure, look at each other ten years later and say, "Why you?"—and they divorce, often with children in primary grades.

Secrets of Peer Success

One key to the success of peer unions lies in *joint child rearing*—the creation of a male parenting niche in day-to-day family life. Indeed, I would go so far as to say that joint child rearing constitutes the secret of successful peer unions and a new pathway to marital and family stability in contemporary life. Joint child-rearing cements a new intimacy between husband and wife and, research shows, builds a critical and difficult-to-sever tie between the two parents and the children.

Some theorists in the past have actually argued *against* a model of significant daily paternal participation in parenting, on the grounds that male involvement will erode the natural dependence of men on women and that men, resenting the extra burden, will ultimately leave. Of course, a lot of men are leaving in any case. And certainly some studies, particularly among working-class men, show child care and household labor participation to

be associated with lower marital satisfaction. Still, other researchers have found large numbers of men whose perception of shared participation correlates with greater marital satisfaction.

On the woman's side, moreover, the picture is not at all ambiguous. Shared labor has a *major* impact on women's satisfaction in marriage—and since more women than men leave relationships, this is a significant finding. A 1996 study by Nancy K. Grote and others showed that the more traditional the division of labor, the lower marital satisfaction was for women (though *not* for men). However, *both* men and women reported higher erotic satisfaction and friendship with one another when household labor, including parenting, was shared more equitably.

My studies and others show several other important benefits to joint child rearing: First, the more men participate, the more attached they are to their children. Second, the more they parent, the more grateful wives are. Third, under joint parenting, it becomes harder for either the husband or the wife to consider leaving. And finally, unless the men are manifestly awful parents, children benefit from their father's attention, skills, and additional perspective. This extra parenting and contact with the father can represent a real boon for children.

While my study draws from interviews with only about one hundred couples, some research based on large data sets reinforces my findings. In *Bitter Choices: Blue Collar Women In and Out of Work,* E. I. Rosin showed that a substantial number of working-class women interpreted the husband's help with children and housework as an expression of love and caring. A very interesting study by Diane Lye at the University of Washington found, among other things, that men who had the lowest divorce rates had the highest interaction with their sons around traditionally male games—football, baseball, etc. Interestingly, the same was true of men who participated in similar activities with their daughters. Other studies have found a lower divorce rate among men who attended prenatal classes.

Still, one may argue that we are talking here about atypical men. Only a certain kind of fellow will participate in a prenatal class: peer men are born, not made. Yet that is not what I found in my own research. Most men I interviewed in egalitarian marriages did not come to them by way of ideological motivation, nor were they married to women who described themselves as feminists. The usual road to peer marriage was happenstance. The four most common routes: (1) A serious desire on the part of the husband to father more, and more effectively, than he himself had been fathered (men in these situations were frequently wrestling with significant pain left over from paternal abuse, neglect, or abandonment). (2) A job that *required* shift work or role sharing and which, over time, greatly attached the father to the parenting role. (3) A strong-willed working partner who presumed egalitarian marriage; men in these cases were mostly prepared to structure the marriage any way their wives (often not declared feminists) preferred to have it. (4) The experience of an unsatisfactory, highly traditional first marriage in which the wife was perceived as too emotionally dependent during the marriage and too economically helpless after it was over; men in these cases consciously selected a different kind of spouse and marital bargain in the second marriage.

Were they happy with their new bargain? Most of these men expressed pride in themselves, their wives, and their home life. Were these typical egalitarian marriages? it is impossible to say. But these marriages, while not invulnerable, looked more stable for their integration—in much the way traditional marriages often appear: integrated, independent, and satisfied.

"Near Peers"

Some of the most troubled contemporary marriages, I have found, are those, in essence, caught between the old and the new paradigm—marriages that are neither fully traditional nor fully peer. I called such couples "near peers," since they professed belief in equal participation but failed to achieve it in practice. I believe the experience of such "near peers" may lie behind some of the frustrations that lead conservatives and others today to declare, in effect, that "We have tried equality and it has failed." In reality, what many couples have tried is inequality under the label of equality—an experience which has given equality, in some quarters, a bad name.

In "near peer" marriages, the wife typically devoted vastly more energy to the children while holding down a job. Although the husband made certain contributions to child rearing and household upkeep, and professed an eagerness to do more, actual male performance fell short of the intended ideal, stirring the wife's resentment. In most cases, "near peer" men still controlled the finances and exercised veto power over the wife. The wife, performing a full-time job outside the home with little or not relief inside of it, was typically caught in a "slow burn" of inward anger. Paradoxically, such women did not long for more equality, since they assumed it would bring more of the same—increased responsibilities with no substantial male contribution. These women felt trapped and overwhelmed and many of them, I found, would have been happy to leave the work force if it were financially possible. Furthermore, all their power—and much of their pleasure—continued to reside in the mothering role. They loved their children, felt compromised at the inadequacy of parenting time, and, perhaps surprisingly, rarely considered that one answer might be greater paternal participation. In truth, many such women were unwilling to surrender hegemony at home.

In such marriages, each spouse typically clings to his or her traditional powers while simultaneously craving a more partnership-oriented relationship. The result is emotional disappointment and conflict. Women in such relationships tend to view egalitarian gender roles as oppressive—seeing more respect, security, and satisfaction in the role of full-time mother. Yet they simultaneously resent the husband's low participation and quasi-autocratic behavior, since they feel they have earned equality and crave it on an emotional level.

Roadblocks and Suggested Policy Reforms

While I have found that there are many different routes to a stable peer marriage, achievement of such a relationship is not automatic, as the experiences of the "near peers" attest. Several barriers stand in the way.

In the first place, it is often hard to avoid role differentiation, especially when partners have been strongly socialized to one or the other role. For example, it is simply not in the couple's best interests for the "bad cook" to prepare dinner while the good one does dishes. Even though cooking can be learned—quite easily, in fact—the startup costs (bad meals for a while) stop most couples in their tracks. The better the homemaker-parent and the more outstanding the provider, the less likely there is to be taste for change.

Other inhibitors to peer marriages include the gender-based organization of jobs in the outside world (which affect evaluations of each partner's career prospects), and the overall pull of the status quo. Yet in a sense, the biggest roadblock we face is our sense of the possible. Many women and men simply do not believe an egalitarian marriage is feasible—unless they happen to be in one. Even many who desire the peer model do not believe it can be achieved within ordinary working schedules. And most women expect significant male resistance and see a risk in asserting themselves, fearing that conflict with their husbands will lead to defeat and deeper resentment on their own part, or even divorce.

These are all reasonable cautions. The pleasure of sharing the day-to-day administration of home and family is not apparent to many men, especially those socialized to the older model. Nonetheless, today we find an increasing number of young men and remarried men actually yearning to be an involved parent. This represents a shift in ideology, a new view of "what is important in life."

However, women, too, need to change. Many women are used to being taken care of and are trained for submissive interaction with men. In effect, they set up during courtship many of the inequities they will complain about in marriage—and ultimately flee from. They want intimacy, yet they often establish conditions—such as maximization of male income—that subvert family time and marital closeness.

In addition, there are several public policy reforms that might assist in the formation of peer marriages and thereby help anchor families of the future. Such reforms might include classes on marriage and the family in high school, where young men and women can learn a model of partnership, equity, and friendship; more pressure on employers to offer flextime and on-site child care, so that individuals are not penalized for their parenting choices; and after-school care in the public schools (until 6 P.M.).

There also needs to be more cultural support from the larger society. Most parents do not want to see their sons in the role of primary parent, do not want their sons' careers compromised, and still view a woman's work—including care for children—as unmanly. Moreover, most women are not encouraged to think of themselves as potential providers; only recently have they come to imagine themselves as fully committed to careers. I know there is a great split of opinion over whether young mothers should work at all, much less be encouraged to be responsible for their own economic welfare. But I would suggest that too much specialization in parenting and insufficient equality of experience may be more injurious in the long run than the difficulties involved when both partners juggle work and home.

Conclusions

We must recognize that there is no one form of marital organization appropriate for all couples. But I believe the "pro-family" or "family values" movement has been needlessly antagonistic to feminist models of marriage. After all, the two sides in this dialogue share some important goals: we do not want marriages to break up unless they absolutely have to; we want children to be loved and cherished and brought to adulthood in an intact family if there is any way it can be accomplished without punishment to either the children or the parents; we want people to want to form lasting bonds that strengthen the extended family.

The big question is how best to accomplish this. I suggest that shared parenting and increased spousal satisfaction are the most effective routes to family stability. I think that newfound feelings about equity and emotional closeness are essential to modern marital durability. Peer relationships will be good for women, children, and families—and a great benefit for men as well. Peer marriage is not a feminist or elitist vision. It is a practical plan to lower the divorce rate. But in order to see how well it works, society needs to offer the cultural and structural support to permit both men and women to parent, to participate in each other's lives, and to have the time together that a strong relationship requires. Whether peer marriage will actually work better than traditional marriage is, at this point, a matter of conjecture. We do know, however, that traditional roles have failed to ensure stability. The new model is an experiment we can ill afford to ignore.

From *The Communitarian Reader: Beyond the Essentials,* by Amitai Etzioni, Andrew Volmert, and Elanit Rothschild, Eds, Rowan & Littlefield, 2004, pp. 149–160. Copyright © by Rowman & Littlefield. Reprinted by permission.

Stress and the Superdad

Like the supermoms before them, today's fathers are struggling to balance work and home

MICHELE ORECKLIN

The past 30 years have seen the emergence of the working mom, the single mom, the supermom, the soccer mom and—because full-time motherhood is often considered a choice rather than a given—the stay-at-home mom. Yet aside from the recent categorization of NASCAR dads (which more pointedly concerns the significance of NASCAR than parenting), the title of dad has rarely been linked to a modifier. It would be wrong, however, to conclude that the role of fathers has remained unaltered; the majority of men today are vastly more involved in the rearing of their children and maintenance of their households than their fathers ever were. That no phrases have been coined to describe such behavior can probably be attributed to the fact that unlike women, men have not particularly organized, united or even been pro-active to effect these reforms but, in essence, adapted to the changes the women in their lives demanded for themselves.

That is not to say men resent the transformation. Data from focus groups, conversations with men around the country and a poll conducted by the men's cable network Spike TV and shared exclusively with TIME suggest that men, most interestingly those in their early 20s through early 40s—the first generation to come of age in the postfeminist era—are adjusting to their evolving roles, and they seem to be doing so across racial and class lines. But in straining to manage their responsibilities at work and home, many men say they don't feel an adequate sense of control in either realm. "There's a push-pull," says Kevin Lee, 40, a photographer in Salt Lake City, Utah, with two small children and a wife who works part time. "I feel like when I'm with the kids, it's great, and I enjoy that time. But in the back of my mind, I'm always thinking that I've got all these other things to do, like work around the house or job-related work."

As pioneer superdads, these men have few role models. Not terribly long ago, a man went out into the world and worked alongside other men, and when he came home, the rest of the family busied itself with making him comfortable. Now, as with women of a generation ago, men are experiencing the notion of a second shift, and they are doing so at a time when downsizing, outsourcing and other vagaries of the economy have made that first shift feel disquietingly unstable. Says Dr. Scott Haltzman, 44, a psychiatrist in Barrington, R.I., with many male clients under 45: "Historically, men felt that if they applied themselves and worked hard, they would continue to rise within an organization." Now they must contend with a shaky economy, buyouts, layoffs and mergers, not to mention rapidly evolving technological advances. Of the 1,302 men polled, 75% said they were concerned about keeping up with changing job skills, and even among those 25 to 34, a presumably more tech-savvy cohort, 79% admitted to such concerns.

There are things men do that women don't see as contributing

There is also uncertainty in men's roles at home. Says Bob Silverstein, an employment consultant and personal life coach in New York City: "Home has become one more place where men feel they cannot succeed." For as much as women desire and demand their husbands' assistance in floor waxing and infant swaddling, many men complain that their wives refuse to surrender control of the domestic domain and are all too adept at critiquing the way their husbands choose to help out. Haltzman, who gathers research on husbands through his SecretsOfMarriedMen.com website, points out that "there are a lot of things men do that women don't define as contributing to the household. If a man is in the yard and notices that the basketball is flat and he pumps it up, he gets no credit because it's not something that needed to get done in the wife's eyes. But from the man's perspective, it's just as important as picking up an article of clothing or doing the wash."

But even while men chafe at not being appreciated around the house, few of them express a desire to return to the roles defined by previous generations. "I would love a reprieve from all the domestic chores," says Steve McElroy, 35, of Barrington, R.I., a father of two whose wife is a full-time professor. "But I wouldn't want it at the expense of my family and what I have with them." Asked by Spike TV to choose how they measure success, only 3% of men said through their work, while 31% said they did so through their faith in God, 26% through being the best person possible, 22% through their network of family and friends, and 17% through maintaining a balance between home and work.

In calibrating an acceptable balance between the two, men came down decisively on the side of family life, with 72%—including those who are single—saying they would sacrifice advancements at work to spend more time at home and 66% saying they would risk being perceived poorly by a superior to ask for a month's paternity leave. In 2002, Mark Carlton, 33, left his job in mechanical design and moved with his wife and two children from Evansville, Ind., to Minneapolis, Minn., when his wife got a better-paying position. While interviewing for a new job, Carlton told potential employers that he expected a "give and take. I give it my all at work, and in return if I have a family issue, I should be able to have the time."

Despite their best intentions, however, men are not necessarily curtailing their work hours. Nearly 68% of men work more than 40 hours a week, and 62% are working on weekends. And men with children are putting in more hours than those without: 60% of them work 41 to 59 hours a week, whereas only 49% of men without kids rack up that many hours.

Even though men say they spend too much time on the job, they don't seem to care about the gender or race of those they work alongside or below. This would appear to be progress over 10 years ago, when many downsized men channeled their frustration toward minorities and women whom they perceived as threats to their professional advancement. Today, the Spike poll shows that 55% of men profess to have no preference for a male or female boss, while 9% actually prefer a woman. Proof that men may now recognize the advantages of having women in the workplace is evident in another poll number: 55% say they have no problem dating someone who earns significantly more than they do. **—With reporting by Sonja Steptoe/Los Angeles and Sarah Sturmon Dale/Minneapolis**

All Happy Families

The looming battle over gay parenting

JULIAN SANCHEZ

Wayne LaRue Smith had never been so happy to be called *bitch*.

About two months earlier, Smith and his partner, Dan Skahen, had taken in a 3-year-old foster child we'll call Charlie. The boy had emerged from the caseworker's car redolent of stale cigarette smoke, hair matted and tangled, barely able to walk, and, except for the occasional raspy cry, stone silent. "We think," whispered the caseworker, leaning in, "he's retarded."

Week after week, Smith recalls, Charlie refused to say anything. Then one day, as Smith was trying to prevent the boy from climbing around on the furniture, Charlie uttered the first word Smith had heard escape his lips: "Bitch!" Nonplussed at the vocabulary ("He didn't learn that language from us!" Smith says), Smith was nevertheless delighted that the child had said *something*. His silence broken, Charlie pressed his tiny fists to his hips and added "Asshole!" before scampering away. Within weeks he was speaking in complete—and more polite—sentences.

Charlie wasn't retarded. He had simply withdrawn from a world that until then hadn't given him much reason to be engaged with it. That sort of history, sadly, is shared by many of the children who find their way into the nation's foster care systems, which included half a million kids when the Department of Health and Human Services last counted, with some 126,000 available for adoption. At the end of fiscal year 2003, 30,000 of those children were in Florida, more than in any other state except New York and California, with more than 5,000 available for adoption.

Charlie lucked out with Skahen and Smith. As of last April, Florida could not even account for the whereabouts of more than 500 children nominally in its custody. Every few years, the state's papers dutifully report an especially tragic case of a child rescued from a bad home only to be deposited by the state into some fresh hell. One such child is Yusimil Herrera, who after being moved dozens of times from one foster home to another, homes in which she was beaten and sexually abused, won a famous lawsuit against the state in 1999. (The verdict was later overturned, and Herrera settled her claim.) She now stands accused of murdering her own young daughter.

Charlie was one of 23 foster children Skahen and Smith have taken in since 1999. The two boys they're now looking after have been with them for years, and Smith and Skahen would like to adopt them, to spare them the prospect of who-knows-how-many desultory transitions from foster family to foster family.

But in Florida, thanks to orange juice pitchwoman Anita Bryant's 1977 "Save the Children" campaign, the Department of Children and Families' adoption forms carry a pair of "yes" and "no" check boxes—page 5, part II, section G—below the statements "I am a homosexual" and "I am a bisexual." Check "yes" to either and you're ineligible to adopt. The law, as its sponsor explained shortly after it passed, was meant to alert gays that "we wish you'd go back into the closet."

> **Dan Skahen and Wayne Smith can log on to the Department of Children and Families' Web site and find a photograph and description of their older boy, an offer to any nice heterosexual couple who'd like to take him away from his family.**

Thanks to this law, Skahen and Smith can log on to the Department of Children and Families' Web site and find a photograph and description of their older boy, on offer to any nice heterosexual couple who'd like to take him away from his family.

Right now only Florida explicitly prohibits any gay person from adopting, but just six states and the District of Columbia explicitly *allow* adoptions by homosexuals. In most cases there's no formal policy, and several states either are known for family judges disinclined to grant homosexuals custody or have indirect statutory barriers to gay parenting. Nebraska banned gay foster parenting in 1995. Mississippi and Utah allow only married couples to adopt, a restriction geared in both cases to exclude gay couples. Just under half of U.S. states permit "second-parent adoption," which grants parental rights to both members of an unmarried couple, in at least some jurisdictions. And more restrictions may be on the way.

From a civil libertarian perspective, it's clear enough why the unequal treatment of gay parents is objectionable: The human desire for family isn't exclusive to heterosexuals, and attempts to prevent gays from raising families both stigmatize them and threaten to deprive them of an important component of a full life. But these barriers to adoption should also offend anyone concerned about family values—about ensuring that all children, especially those who have suffered in the past, find loving homes, and that enrolling those kids in school or getting them medical care is a simple, routine procedure, not a legalistic obstacle course. Yet "family values" remains the call to arms of many who support restricted parenting.

Better an Orphanage?

In 2004 the U.S. Supreme Court refused to hear an appeal of a lower court decision upholding Florida's ban on gay adoption. The challenge was brought by the American Civil Liberties Union on behalf of Smith, Skahen, and other gay parents. Among the plaintiffs were Steve Lofton and Roger Croteau, who care for five children born with HIV. Three of the kids have been with the couple since infancy.

"Good," reacted *World* Editor Marvin Olasky on the Christian news magazine's weblog. "Maybe more states will now pass legislation protecting kids from gay adoption." Mathew D. Staver, head of Liberty Counsel, which filed an amicus brief supporting Florida's policy, agreed. "Children in Florida will be benefited," he opined to the Christian news service AgapePress, "but not only that—I think other states will follow Florida's lead to enact similar laws."

Some lawmakers and judges in other states do indeed share a horror of gay parenthood. In 2003, as he introduced a bill to ban gay foster parenting, Texas legislator Robert Talton (R-Pasadena) told the state's House of Representatives: "If it was me I would rather [leave] kids in orphanages as such—this is where they are now if they're not fostered out. At least they have a chance of learning the proper values." (Texas doesn't actually have orphanages, but you get the point.) Talton pushed a similar bill through his state's House in April, though Talton's language was later stripped from the Senate version of the law. Former Alabama Supreme Court Judge Roy Moore used uncommonly vehement language, but perhaps not uncommon logic, when he wrote in 2000 that a lesbian mother should be denied custody of her three children because homosexuality was "an evil disfavored under the law," and that the state should "use its power to prevent the subversion of children toward this lifestyle, to not encourage a criminal lifestyle."

State legislatures are now pushing to erect a variety of legal barriers to gay couples seeking to raise kids. Carrie Evans, state legislative lawyer for the Human Rights Campaign, a gay advocacy group, has tracked state legislation on gay parenting since 2000. "This year has been the worst," says Evans. "Usually we have a few, but I've never seen this many in one year." Just four months into 2005, lawmakers in seven states—Alabama, Arkansas, Indiana, Oregon, Tennessee, Texas, and Virginia—had introduced bills that would restrict the parenting rights of gay couples and individuals. This new assault seems to be the result of several complementary factors:

- **The Gay Baby Boom:** Extrapolating from 2000 census data, Urban Institute demographer Gary Gates conservatively estimates there are at least a quarter million children living in households headed by same-sex couples; 4.2 percent are either adopted or foster children, almost double the figure for heterosexual couples. (Single gay parents, of course, are not captured by those numbers.) While the increase in gay parenting can't be precisely measured, Gates estimates that one in 20 male same-sex couples and one in five female couples were raising children in 1990. By 2000 those figures had risen to one in five for male couples and one in three for female couples. A 2003 survey by the Evan B. Donaldson Adoption Institute found that 60 percent of adoption agencies place children in gay households, and a 2001 Kaiser Family Foundation survey found that, while about 8 percent of gay respondents were currently parents or guardians of children under 18, almost half of those who weren't hoped to one day adopt children of their own. As the ranks of gay parents swell, they become more visible—and more visible targets.

- **The Tipping Point:** A 2004 Harris poll found that a plurality of Americans still disapproves of adoption by same-sex couples—43 percent and 45 percent for female and male couples, respectively. But that represents a dramatic decrease in opposition since 1996, when majorities of more than 60 percent disapproved in both cases. Conservatives may worry, with good reason, that if laws restricting gay parenting aren't locked in now, perhaps drawing strength from the momentum behind anti-gay marriage legislation, their time will soon have passed.

- **The Marriage Factor:** "Among both the youngest and oldest cohorts," a 2003 study by the Pew Forum on Religion and Public Life found, "those who know someone who is gay are about twice as likely to favor gay marriage as those who do not." The expansion of gay parenting means people who might not otherwise encounter gay couples will be more likely to see them at PTA meetings and Little League games. And the Harris poll found an overwhelming majority agrees that children being raised by gay couples should "have the same rights as all other children." For practical purposes, that means ensuring that their parents have rights too. If, other things being equal, it's better for children to be raised by married couples, then as the number of kids raised by gays increases, the conservative case for expanding marriage rights becomes more potent. All of which means that as more same-sex couples raise children, opposition to gay marriage is likely to erode—a matter of concern to the social conservatives on whom Republican politicians increasingly rely for support.

- **The *Lawrence* Effect:** Until recently, sodomy laws in 13 states confirmed Judge Moore's assessment of homosexuality as "an evil disfavored under the law." But in the 2003 case *Lawrence v. Texas,* the Supreme Court held that sodomy laws were unconstitutional, yielding, in the words of the Human Rights Campaign's Evans, "rapid changes in custody and visitation case law." The *Lawrence* decision, she explains, "really helped us because for a long time, especially in adoption cases, judges restricted gay parents' rights on the grounds that sodomy was a felony." But now the baton has been passed to lawmakers, who know that courts are more deferential to legislators on questions of family policy than on issues of sexual privacy.

- **"Kids Need a Mom and Dad":** Even Americans otherwise favorably disposed to gay rights may have concerns about how growing up in a gay household affects children. Traditionalists have done their best to heighten those concerns, arguing that discriminatory laws serve the best interests of kids.

The Phantom Menace

The mantra that "children need a mother and a father" has acquired a patina of conventional wisdom through frequent repetition. Yet there is little evidence that children raised by gay couples fare worse than other children.

Gay rights opponents such as Family Research Institute chief Paul Cameron and the Family Research Council's Timothy Dailey are fond of arguing that gay men are disproportionately likely to molest children—a potent charge rejected by the serious social scientists who have directly investigated it. Large-scale studies of molestation victims have repeatedly found that abusers overwhelmingly were either heterosexual in adult relationships or lacked any sexual response to adults.

Noting that about a third of molestation cases involve male adults targeting male children, Dailey and Cameron insist those adults must, by definition, be homosexual. Since homosexual men make up a far smaller proportion of the general population, Dailey reasons, gay men must be disproportionately likely to abuse children.

The problem with this view is that psychologists generally regard pedophilia an orientation of its own. Men who molest boys are not necessarily—indeed, are almost never—"gay" in the colloquial sense. Even if one accepts a definition that calls such men "homosexual," the fact remains that there is little overlap between that group and men who pursue romantic relationships with other adult men, the relevant comparison group for gay adoption.

Most child welfare professionals don't see things Dailey and Cameron's way. After reviewing the available data in 2002, the American Academy of Pediatrics endorsed second-parent adoption rights for gay couples. A resolution passed by the American Psychological Association in 2004 declared that there was "no scientific evidence that parenting effectiveness is related to parental sexual orientation: lesbian and gay parents are as likely as heterosexual parents to provide supportive and healthy environments for their children." It also noted that "the children of lesbian and gay parents are as likely as those of heterosexual parents to flourish."

The Child Welfare League of America, an organization founded in 1920 that now comprises more than 1,100 public and private agencies providing child services, filed an amicus brief in 2004 supporting the ACLU's challenge to Florida's adoption ban, noting the consensus that "children are not adversely affected by their parents' lesbian or gay orientation" and that "all of the mainstream professional organizations in the fields of child health and welfare agree that there is no basis to exclude gay men and lesbians from adopting children." That same year, an Arkansas circuit court overturned a state Child Welfare Agency Review Board regulation prohibiting gay foster parenting after extensive fact finding, including testimony from a variety of psychologists, social workers, and sociologists, concluding that the ban contradicted the agency's mandate to serve the best interests of children.

The statistical evidence meshes with the experience of Adam Pertman, executive director of the Donaldson Institute, an adoption policy-research organization, and author of *Adoption Nation.* "The evidence on the ground, based on the markers that we have, is that these are good families," he says. "The social workers I talk to are asking how they can recruit more [gay parents], because they're working. That's the best validation I can think of, unless you think all these child welfare professionals are out to harm kids."

Opponents of gay parenting, for the most part, have been forced to fall back on the assertion that the jury's still out. Noting—correctly—that none of the research on children of gay couples made use of the large random samples that generate the most robust results, they claim studies to date provide no basis for supposing that gay parents won't be inferior. But as New York University sociologist Judith Stacey argues, "they have to stretch pretty far to find that. The studies have been very consistent and very positive." Stacey concedes that most of them are "small scale" but adds that "there are some 50 studies now, and we don't see them going the other way. I have yet to see one legitimate refereed publication or scholar come out with a generally negative finding."

As in so many other disputes, child welfare may be serving as a proxy for a values debate. Marjorie Heins, director of the Free Expression Policy Project at the National Coalition Against Censorship and author of *Not in Front of the Children: "Indecency," Censorship, and the Innocence of Youth,* puts it this way: "If you're convinced that certain attitudes and values are wrong, then you consider exposing a child to those values a harm *in itself."*

The Second-Parent Trap

Even on the assumption that heterosexual households are somehow better for children, some restrictions on gay parenting are hard to fathom. For children in Florida's foster care system, the alternative to gay parents may be no parents at all. And many policies don't *prevent* gay couples from raising children; they just make life *more difficult* for gay parents and their children.

Barriers to second-parent adoption in some states create a variety of difficulties for gay couples raising children, often allowing only one to be recognized as a legal parent. Allison Bauer is an attorney who sits on the board of the Family Pride Coalition, an advocacy group for gay families. She lived in Virginia before moving to Massachusetts, where she could adopt her partner Marie Longo's biological children, twin girls. During the pregnancy, says Bauer, "we told our friends that if Marie went into labor, they should drive her into D.C. and *then* call an ambulance—we knew D.C. would issue an amended birth certificate with both our names later, and Virginia wouldn't." Until they moved, she adds, "I spent 14 months holding my breath. One night when the kids were six months old, Rebecca woke up with a terrible barking cough. We knew it was croup, and I had to wake Marie up because I was afraid the hospital would question my authority to authorize care, even though I had a document that gave me power of attorney."

Such fears are why Anne Magro is fighting to overturn an Oklahoma law stipulating that "this state, any of its agencies, or any court of this state shall not recognize an adoption by more than one individual of the same sex from any other state or foreign jurisdiction." Magro, an accounting professor at the University of Oklahoma, had moved from New Jersey, where the state had granted her partner of 13 years, Heather Finstuen, second-parent rights over Magro's biological daughters.

The child welfare argument against gay parenting may be a proxy for a values debate. "If you're convinced that certain attitudes and values are wrong," says Marjorie Heins, "then you consider exposing a child to those values a harm in itself."

Oklahoma state Rep. Thad Balkman (R-Norman), who supported the adoption law, defends it as a "reflection of our public policy that we support one-man-one-woman adoptions. To grant privileges like birth certificates to people who aren't in that relationship is doublespeak; we have to be consistent." Yet Balkman also claims that all the rights "so-called parents" have when their adoptions are recognized can be obtained through other means, such as by obtaining durable power of attorney for the second parent.

Brian Chase, an attorney with the gay rights litigation firm Lambda Legal who is representing Magro and Finstuen, disagrees. "A final adoption decree entitles a child to Social Security benefits and medical benefits that can't be conferred by a power of attorney," he says. "Furthermore, the most important right guaranteed by a final adoption is the right to continue to care for a child if something were to happen to the other parent. No power of attorney or will confers the degree of security

that accompanies an adoption." And such workarounds, Magro adds, are often complex, time-consuming, and expensive.

New York University law professor Linda J. Silberman, an expert in interjurisdictional legal conflicts, believes policies like Oklahoma's may violate the Constitution's Full Faith and Credit Clause, which says "Full Faith and Credit shall be given in each State to the public Acts, Records, and judicial Proceedings of every other State." "If you're talking about one state applying another state's *law*," Silberman explains, "there's a public policy exception. If you have a court judgment from another state, though, you can't just say 'oh, we have a different public policy' and ignore it on that basis."

But the 1996 Defense of Marriage Act stipulates that "the United States Constitution shall not be construed to require any state or territory to give effect to any public act, record, or judicial proceeding respecting a relationship between persons of the same sex that is treated as a marriage under the laws of another state or territory." That attempt to reach judicial proceedings, normally not subject to "public policy exceptions," adds a new wrinkle, says Silberman. A state hostile to gay rights might, for instance, refuse to recognize a custody ruling from another state that allowed civil unions.

That scenario isn't just a hypothetical: It has already happened. In 2003 Lisa and Janet Miller-Jenkins, a lesbian couple who had been together since 1998 and were joined in a Vermont civil union in 2000, split up. Lisa moved to Virginia with her biological daughter and filed for dissolution of the union—and child support—in a Vermont court. Vermont awarded Janet visitation rights, as it might for a divorcing married couple. But when Virginia passed its Marriage Affirmation Act, which declared same-sex "civil unions . . . and any rights created thereby. . .void and unenforceable," Lisa appealed to Virginia to, in effect, declare that Janet was just a nice lady who once lived with Mommy. Frederick County Circuit Court Judge John Prosser did just that, and the case is now in the hands of the Virginia Court of Appeals.

Family Values

On a drizzly weekend at the end of April, some 250 gay parents, prospective parents, and their kids gathered at Sligo Middle School in Silver Spring, Maryland, for a day-long Family Pride Coalition conference on gay parenting. Standing under a scrolling rainbow LED marquee announcing "Congratulations, Honor Roll Students," Cayo Gamber, a writing professor at George Washington University, surveyed the day's dense program and quipped: "It would be wonderful if straight people came to parenting with this kind of scrutiny. . . . For us it's a choice, not an accident or a destiny."

At a breakout workshop on adoption, a few dozen participants studied the details of that choice. Panelists related their experiences adopting through private agencies, through foster care, and from the shrinking number of foreign countries open to gay parents. They recounted spending tens of thousands of dollars, waiting anxious months, sitting through lengthy and intrusive interviews and "home studies," and filling out mountains of paperwork in a process one likened to "buying a house and applying to grad school simultaneously."

Conservatives should ask a child in foster care which makes him feel more threatened: the thought of being raised by homosexuals, or the prospect of an indefinite number of years spent passing through an indefinite number of homes.

The hearts of conservatives would, one might think, be warmed by such a group. They feel the universal human need for family as deeply and acutely as anyone and are unusually determined to make committed parenting a central part of their lives.

Those behind the burgeoning assault on gay parenting would have us believe these people are a menace to the children they would take in. And had any of them visited Sligo Middle School that afternoon, they surely would have heard their share of complaints from the children and teenagers in attendance: complaints about homophobic teachers, about classmates whose peers and parents have taught them to use *gay* as an epithet. Concerned conservatives might ask those kids: Are those complaints a sign there's something wrong with your gay families, or with the broader culture?

Better still, they could visit Florida and ask a child in foster care which makes him feel more threatened: the thought of being raised by homosexuals, or the prospect of an indefinite number of years spent passing through an indefinite number of homes. They could ask whether "family values" are best served by attempting to marginalize gay couples who raise families, by "protecting" abused or sick children from people who want to give them a home, by forcing parents to worry whether they'll have the legal authority to bring their kids to the hospital in an emergency. They could ask Charlie.

Julian Sanchez (jsanchez@reason.com) is an assistant editor of *reason*.

Ecopolis Now

Forget the rural idyll. Urban living may be the best way to save the planet, says Fred Pearce

FRED PEARCE

A hundred years ago, the largest city in the world was London, with a population of 6.5 million. Today it is dwarfed by Tokyo. With barely a quarter the population of London a century ago, Japan's capital city has since mushroomed to 34 million, propelling it to pole position in the global city league table.

Tokyo's phenomenal growth is largely down to a single factor: migration from the countryside to the city. It is just one of many to have overtaken London, which with a population of 7.5 million today doesn't even make the top 20.

This rural to urban migration can now be seen in scores of cities across the globe. And it has brought us to a pivotal moment in human history. In 1900, most people lived in the countryside, with a little over 10 per cent of the world's population living in cities. From next year, the UN Population Division predicts that for the first time in history, more people will live in cities than in the country, and the biggest growth will be in "megacities," with populations over 10 million.

The meteoric growth of megacities—there are now 20 in total—has brought with it huge environmental and social problems. Cities occupy just 2 per cent of the land surface of the Earth but consume three-quarters of the resources that are used up each year, expelling the half-digested remains in clouds of greenhouse gases, billions of tonnes of solid waste and rivers of toxic effluent. Their inhabitants are making ruinous demands on soils and water supplies for food, and on forests for timber and paper. For example, London needs 125 times its own area to provide the resources it consumes, and if the new megacities in the developing world are allowed to grow in the same way that cities did in the west, their environmental impact will be catastrophic.

Scientists calculate that a sustainable ecological footprint that shares all the world's resources equally among its inhabitants would be 1.8 hectares per person. Today, the average in rural China is 1.6, in Shanghai it is already 7, and the eco-footprint of a typical American is 9.7.

"Cities have become the largest, most complex, man-made structures ever created"

Returning the world's population to the countryside isn't an option. Modern living standards mean there is little difference between the eco-footprints of rural and urban dwellers. And dividing up the planet into plots of land on which we could all live self-sufficiently would create its own natural disasters, not to mention being highly unlikely to ever happen.

If we are to protect what is left of nature, and meet the demand to improve the quality of living for the world's developing nations, a new form of city living is the only option. The size of a city creates economies of scale for things such as energy generation, recycling and public transport. It should even be possible for cities to partly feed themselves. Far from being parasites on the world, cities could hold the key to sustainable living for the world's booming population—if they are built right.

Fortunately, governments, planners, architects and engineers are beginning to wake up to this idea, and are dreaming up new ways to green the megacities. Their approaches rest on two main principles: recycle whatever possible, and cut car use to a minimum. So as well as developing energy-efficient buildings, emphasis is being placed on increasing the use of public transport and redesigning how cities are organised to integrate work and living areas into a single neighbourhood, rather than separating cities into residential, commercial and industrial zones.

The big ideas are still on the drawing board, but many cities already have showcase eco-projects. For example, at the new A\$50 million (\$40 million) home of Melbourne city council in Australia, hanging gardens and water fountains cool the air, wind turbines and solar cells generate up to 85 per cent of the electricity used in the building, and rooftop rainwater collectors supply 70 per cent of its water needs. In Berlin, Germany's new Reichstag parliament building cut its carbon dioxide emissions by 94 per cent by burning carbon-neutral vegetable oil. In San Diego, California, refuse trucks run on methane extracted from the landfills they deliver to. In Austria, 1500 free bicycles have been distributed across Vienna. Reykjavik in Iceland is among the pioneers of hydrogen-powered public transport, and Shanghai is subsidising the installation of 100,000 rooftop solar panels. The Chinese city is also about to put many of these ideas to the test by creating the first purpose-built eco-city from scratch.

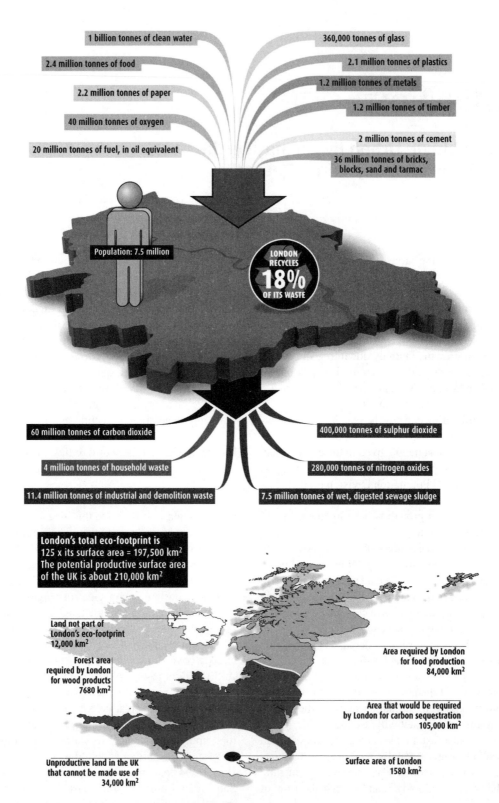

Figure 1 London's Annual Metabolism.

Source: Herbert Giradet

Unfortunately, for the past century most cities have been moving in the wrong direction. Planners have designed cities as if resources such as land, fuel and concrete were unlimited, and waste has been something to dump as cheaply and as distantly as possible. Worse, they designed cities around cars rather than people. Heading the field in this respect has been the US, where the architect Frank Lloyd Wright provided a blueprint for modern America in his "Broadacre City," a suburban idyll of homesteads connected by an endless lattice of highways. The model became a global template, stretching from Milton Keynes in the UK to Brasilia, the modernist new capital that Brazil built in the middle of its central savannah in the late 1950s.

This generation of city builders "worshipped at the altar of the automotive god, and idealised mobility and freedom," says Peter Hall, professor of planning and regeneration at University College London. They thought that community living was over and that in the future people would have no desire for local neighbourhood. This idea was embraced in the 1960s by one of the most influential figures in urban planning, Christopher Alexander, professor of architecture at the University of California, Berkeley, who said that when your friends don't live next door, neighbourhoods became not just irrelevant but stifling "military encampments designed to create discipline and rigidity."

The problem with this kind of thinking is that the resulting cities lack the flexibility that would allow them to respond to the wishes of their inhabitants. They just don't work.

As a result, Alexander's philosophy has turned many cities, especially in the US, into social and ecological disaster areas, teeming with socially deprived neighbourhoods whose inhabitants are forced to rely on the polluting, petrol-guzzling car to maintain the illusion of freedom. Cities have never grown in the way that urban planners imagined, says Michael Batty of University College London, which is why the grand plans

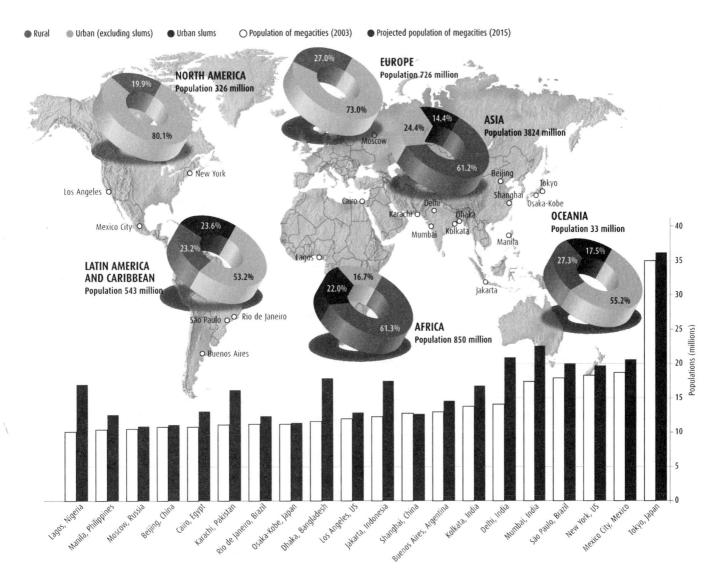

Figure 2   Where the World Lives.   Cities around the globe are growing fast; 20 now have population of over 10 million.

Source: UN Population Division

are rarely successful. The best that planners can hope for is to intervene at decisive points and let human nature and market forces do the rest.

Planners and architects now agree that to improve the social and environmental condition of cities the top priority is to cut car use. They say zero-emission cars running on electricity or burning hydrogen are not enough. "Automobiles still require massive networks of streets, freeways and parking structures to serve congested cities and far-flung suburbs," says Richard Register, founder of the non-profit campaigning organisation EcoCity Builders in Oakland, California.

What is needed is a wholesale rethink of how new cities are laid out—and how existing ones expand—to minimise the need for cars in the first place. One way of achieving this is to build cities with multiple centres where people live close to their work in high-rise blocks that are also near public transport hubs. In parts of the world this is already taking shape. That won't wash with some planners, for whom living in high-rise blocks is at odds with their vision of living in harmony with nature. People need day-to-day access to green spaces and nature to be happy and healthy, they argue. So is there an inevitable conflict between eco-efficiency and pleasant living?

"Planners now agree that to make cities eco-friendly the top priority is to cut car use."

A study by Peter Newman and Jeff Kenworthy suggests not. They found a strong inverse relationship between urban density and the amount of energy used by cars driving within the city limits . However, they also showed that super-dense is not a good thing either. Energy use in transport is far higher in a sprawling city such as Houston than in more compact, low-rise cities such as London or Copenhagen, but up the density any more and you run into another problem. Dense cities heat the air around them. Stone, concrete and asphalt absorb more solar energy, and reflect less, than natural surfaces such as grass, water and trees, so they pump up the temperature at night. Vehicles, air conditioning and electrical appliances also give off heat, while tall buildings cut down winds that can disperse the heat. So cities are usually about 1°C warmer than the surrounding countryside during the day, and can be up to 6°C warmer at night.

The denser the city, the worse the effect. In hot climates, where many of the world's super-dense megacities are found, air conditioning is used to keep the indoor temperature bearable. On a hot day in many of these cities, air conditioning can consume more energy than any other single activity.

To cut this huge use of energy, many cities are taking steps to counter the heat-island effect by redesigning buildings to reduce direct sunlight through windows, increase ventilation, cool the air with water fountains and cut energy absorption by painting external walls white. Planting trees along the streets can help reduce the air temperature too. Up to 400 litres of water can evaporate from a single tree every day, cooling the surrounding air. In Miami, researchers found that summer electricity bills were around 10 per cent lower in neighbourhoods with more than 20 per cent tree cover than in neighbourhoods with none.

While planners look at how to cut back the energy consumption of big cities, at the other end of the scale are shanty towns—organically evolved and self-built by millions of people in the developing world without a planner in sight. These shanties meet many of the ideals of eco-city designers. They are high-density but low-rise; their lanes and alleys are largely pedestrianised; and many of their inhabitants recycle waste materials from the wider city.

From a purely ecological perspective, shanties and their inhabitants are a good example of the new, green urban metabolism. Despite their sanitary and security failings, they often have a social vibrancy and ecological systems that get lost in most planned urban environments.

So perhaps something can be taken from the chaos and decentralised spontaneity embodied in shanties, and combined with the planned infrastructure of a designed eco-city. Cities built without extensive high-rise can still be dense enough to make life without a car profitable, and they can retain the economies of scale needed for the new metabolism built around efficient recycling of everything from sewage to sandwich wrappers. At the same time, they need to remain flexible enough for people to adapt them to the way they want to live. The key is to put people and ecology joint first.

Can Design Make Community?

PHILIP LANGDON

Today's leading source of ideas on how to design American communities is not a high-tech urban laboratory or a latter-day Buckminster Fuller but something much less exotic: the places Americans built in the nineteenth century and the early decades of the twentieth. Why should these older communities exert such power over designers' and planners' imaginations? Because these old places tended to be—and in many cases still are—more complete and more well-rounded than the single-purpose subdivisions of the last 40 years.

In the test of time, communities built in the early 1900s have turned out to be much more soul-satisfying than the developments churned out since World War II. Communities in the early twentieth century and before frequently had an intimacy that supplied a joyful depth (and a dollop of gossip) to everyday life: Adults knew most of their neighbors, their character, and their idiosyncrasies. Children walked to school, church, and ball fields on a grid of well-watched sidewalks. The essentials of daily life were close by—in corner stores, neighborhood bakeries and taverns, and other locally rooted enterprises. In their heyday, eloquently recounted in Alan Ehrenhalt's *The Lost City,* neighborhoods like St. Nick's parish in Chicago's "bungalow belt," or Bronzeville, in that city's not yet devastated black ghetto, possessed a combination of customs, institutions, and authority figures that helped to discourage bad behavior and encourage responsibility.

Though by no means problem-free, the neighborhoods built three or more generations ago had resources for overcoming setbacks, and offered plentiful satisfactions for people of every income level. For that reason, traditional neighborhood and town designs are increasingly being deployed against contemporary American ills: isolation, diminished community life, and inadequate guidance for the young.

The Physical Elements of Community

Those who are reapplying the principles of older communities generally choose one of three names for their work: "Traditional Neighborhood Development," "Neotraditional Development," or "New Urbanism." The first two are fairly easy to understand. Murkier is the term "New Urbanism," which was coined in an attempt to provide a common umbrella for those who want buildings and towns to look like places from the past and those who, on the other hand, believe in historically effective community layouts but prefer their buildings distinctly modern. In any case, the style of the architecture turns out to be of secondary importance. It is the community *layout,* culled from American and, in some cases, European experience, that is critical to the aims of this movement.

What are the key precepts of the New Urbanist community? Above all, a belief in the importance of the public realm—streets, sidewalks, parks, and gathering places. In a well-conceived New Urbanist community, the individual buildings work together to form coherent public spaces, where people will see and talk with one another. A New Urbanist residential area is almost always a walking neighborhood; houses are close enough together and close enough to the street that neighbors cease to be strangers. The architects who have done the most to push this movement into public consciousness, Andres Duany and Elizabeth Plater-Zyberk of Miami (allied with others such as Berkeley architect Peter Calthorpe), lay out neighborhoods on the basis of a "five-minute walk." Within a quarter-mile a resident should reach a neighborhood park, services such as a dry cleaner and a convenience store, and a spot where buses, trains, or shuttles can stop. In prominent locations within the community are schools, churches, and civic buildings—testaments to the New Urbanists' insistence on using the power of architecture to affirm civilization's highest strivings.

New Urbanist developments tend to have narrow streets (to slow the traffic), on-street parking (to shield pedestrians from the passing vehicles), front porches (preferably at least eight feet deep, to encourage people to use them), and public ways with pleasant, well-defined edges—picket fences, hedges, rows of trees. Garages are dethroned from their place of honor in the modern subdivision. No 18-foot blankness of garage door dominates the street—New Urbanists relegate the garage to the back of the lot (where it stood inconspicuously in the 1920s and 1930s), or they recess it behind the house's facade or put it on an alley, making the house once again an attractive, expressive part of the public scene.

According to the newsletter *New Urban News,* over 100 such developments are currently in planning or under construction, most of them in a broad territory from Pennsylvania and Maryland through Virginia, the Carolinas, Florida, Alabama, and Tennessee, plus Colorado and the Far West. The most ambitious development to break ground is Celebration, a town for up to 20,000 inhabitants that the Walt Disney Company began building two years ago on the outskirts of Orlando. Two notable developments closer to completion are Duany/Plater-Zyberk's Kentlands, a 356-acre undertaking begun in 1989 in Gaithersburg, Maryland, within commuting distance of Washington, D.C., and Harbor Town, a 130-acre project planned by RTKL Associates of Baltimore and begun in 1989 on Mud Island in the Mississippi River, a bridge trip away from downtown Memphis.

The Web of Community

New Urbanists seek more than pleasant aesthetic effects—they aim to create a different, more neighborly social life within their communities. The crucial question therefore is: Do their grids and buildings and design principles actually achieve this? Do these places turn out to be the cohesive neighborhoods that their developers promise? To answer this, I interviewed people living in Kentlands, Harbor Town, and older towns built along the lines the New Urbanists are trying to revive. I discovered that on the whole these communities deliver what the New Urbanists say they will. With shallow front yards and smaller house lots than in most conventional developments, residents say there is a noticeable increase in neighborliness. "If you're out doing yard work, everybody stops and chats," says Steve Christian, a Kentlands homeowner. "After a big snowfall, we helped each other shoveling the driveways and all had chili afterward. There's more of a sense of a community than anywhere else we've lived."

Steve's wife, Sandra, a stay-at-home mom, told me she had felt "terribly isolated" in the townhouse development where they lived before moving to Kentlands. "It cleared out at 9 a.m.," she recalled. By contrast, at Kentlands, where she takes care of their young son except when volunteering at the white-columned Rachel Carson Elementary School, there are a number of parents around during the day, and they are easy to meet, since the houses are close together and people frequently go out walking—to the swim club, to a nearby shopping center, to the lake, or to nowhere in particular.

Harbor Town resident Jim Howell says that in the conventional development where he previously lived, on the east side of Memphis, he and his wife "might have known two to three neighbors on each side of us. Here at Harbor Town, we know 50 neighbors. You live closer together, the streets are narrower, and you know so many more people because you're out walking and things are going on. People in the afternoon are out in the yard or on their porches. They bring grills out to the garages. There's a cocktail party in somebody's house." After Jim's wife, Amy, gave birth last summer, six- and seven-year-olds would come to the door and ask, "Is it convenient for me to come and see the baby now?" Jim observes, "It's a more protective environment."

This setting benefits children as much as adults. Youngsters in a traditional neighborhood obtain a healthy degree of autonomy—difficult to get in a cul-de-sac subdivision. More is within easy reach because of the compactness, and there are numerous routes everywhere over an extensively connected street network. Faith Kusterer, a Kentlands mother, notes that her daughter Elena *walked* to the piano lessons she took for two years in the home of her instructor, a woman they knew within the development. "She could go to the store alone on her bike to get anything from candy to school supplies," Mrs. Kusterer added. "It's afforded her some opportunities to be out in the community and to be independent."

James Krohe Jr., a writer who lived and worked for six years in Oak Park, Illinois—a grid planned Chicago suburb founded in the nineteenth century, now containing 53,000 people in its 4.5 square miles—says that in many old communities the availability of public transportation helps youngsters to explore their world and to mature. "It was not unusual for Oak Park kids 13 or 14 years old to have a relationship with the larger city—to take classes or go to private schools in the city," says Krohe. "Compared to the suburbs immediately to the northwest that were not served by Els [Chicago's elevated public transit lines] and that were less served by commuter rail, kids in Oak Park were much more comfortable moving about in the larger metropolis."

What the vast majority of developers seem to have forgotten, then, in creating the automobile-dependent suburbs of the past half-century, is that youngsters need a modulated introduction to the world beyond their block, so that they can cope with, and learn to thrive in, a country that has never been, and never will be, entirely safe or homogeneous. The typical suburban subdivision of the last few decades tries in the main to *withdraw* its children from society's difficulties, inadvertently leaving them without the skills and judgment to manage unfamiliar situations. "There's a fearfulness I find in kids in the newer suburbs," Krohe says. "They can't mix. They can't go anywhere without private transportation. The most horrific examples of violence I recall in the Chicago area were kids from the suburbs who got lost in the city and were raped or robbed because they weren't prepared and didn't know what to expect." Youngsters from Oak Park, by contrast, learn to size up situations "so they won't be bullied so easily when they are exposed to danger," Krohe observes. "It makes them competent and confident members of a larger society."

It Takes a Village

Of course, minor troubles occur everywhere. In compact traditional communities they are likely to be noticed and to stir a response. In Shorewood, Wisconsin, an early-twentieth-century Milwaukee suburb, Philip Nero tells of the time his son fell from his bike, and a man who saw the mishap comforted the boy and walked him the rest of the way to school. Would this happen in a conventional subdivision? Sometimes. But the closeness and visibility characteristic of a traditional community makes it easier for such acts of neighborly assistance to take place.

By the same token, misbehavior, when it occurs, is also likely to be noticed. "When kids do something they shouldn't, they are often caught doing it," says Barney Gorin, a Kentlands homeowner. "They're often yelled at by somebody other than their own parent. For example, one neighborhood kid set off a smoke bomb in someone's house. After that, he was in deep trouble with a big chunk of the neighborhood." For some time, his movements were closely monitored by adults leery of what would happen next. "Since then," Gorin relates happily, "his behavior has come around to where it should be."

Many New Urbanist communities feature a range of housing, not separated into rigidly exclusive tracts. Kentlands contains apartments, row houses of varying sizes, and detached houses. Above the garages of some of the detached houses are small units that can be rented out or used as home offices. Mostly these are rented to singles. The result is neighborhoods with some diversity of ages and incomes—from young renters on tight budgets to middle-aged and older people with comfortable incomes. (Duany initially argued that auxiliary apartments would enable grandmothers to live next to their children and grandchildren; so far, extended families do not appear to be in a rush to reassemble in this fashion.)

Residents of New Urbanist neighborhoods generally prefer a degree of diversity, believing it helps ward off the insularity exhibited by subdivisions containing only a thin slice of society. "I've always thought it's very important for our children to know lots of adults other than us—to have other role models, models of decent human beings—and that certainly has happened here [in Kentlands]," says Mrs. Kusterer. Family breakups do occur—whether at the same rate as elsewhere is not known. Sociologist Ray Oldenburg, in his 1989 book *The Great Good Place,* argues that an absorbing community life relieves some of the pressures on a marriage and consequently promotes family stability.

In any event, the mix of age groups, when combined with a traditional community's close-knit social structure, offers what is probably a stabilizing influence for the children of divorce. In Mariemont, Ohio, a leafy one-square-mile suburb of Cincinnati laid out in the 1920s and interwoven with apartments, row houses, duplexes, and detached dwellings, there are many older people, and a number of them volunteer for an after-school program for children, many from single-parent families. Former mayor Richard Adams says quite a few single-parent households have moved to row houses in Mariemont from other municipalities, in part because children in the village of 3,100 receive a traditional community's tremendous social asset—a balance of supervision and community-monitored freedom of movement that is hard to achieve in a conventional subdivision.

In a vigorous traditional community, institutions spring into being as conditions call for them. Fifteen years ago, for instance, Mariemont generated an organization of residents 55 and older, the MariElders, which reaches out to elderly people who have begun slipping into isolation. Supported by village taxes, the MariElders involve people in tours, lectures, card games, and other activities. The organization has been invaluable, Adams says, because "there were an awful lot of people who were eating alone all the time." Kentlands, too, is giving birth to an energetic institutional life. The three-year-old Kentlands Community Foundation promotes educational programs, as well as charitable and philanthropic work in the Gaithersburg area, including concerts, town lectures and debates, and food and clothing drives. Every time a house is sold, four months of

homeowners association dues are allocated to the all-volunteer foundation. The homeowners association so far has given the foundation more than $117,000. Traditional communities foster in their citizenry the ability to use local government to positive effect. In a place like Oak Park, Krohe says, "government is big enough to do you some good, but small enough that you feel you could have some impact on it. There is a sense of interdependence, unlike the sense in the outer suburbs that government is just a nuisance that takes your taxes."

Hopeless Nostalgia?

New Urbanists are sometimes criticized for promoting a nostalgic vision that does not square with how Americans actually live at the end of the 20th century. Many of the criticisms, however, are half-truths.

Consider the charge of "classism." Some assert that New Urbanism is an upper-middle-class phenomenon ill-suited to the majority of Americans. It is true that much of the New Urbanist housing in the suburbs is beyond the financial reach of poor families. But this is a function more of suburban real estate economics and exclusionary zoning than of some inherent flaw in New Urbanist concepts. There are New Urbanist developments that do in fact house people of modest income. In Starkville, Mississippi, for more than 20 years, Dan Camp has been building the Cotton District, a compact, pedestrianscale precinct with a charm redolent of Charleston, South Carolina—and he has been doing it with inexpensive houses and small apartments whose monthly rents range mainly between $250 to $550, with no government subsidy of any kind. A former shop teacher with a love of architecture and urban design, Camp has mastered the art of constructing dignified, well-crafted dwellings on cheap land.

If New Urbanism were just for the affluent, there would be no Cotton District. Nor would there be a renovated public housing project like Diggs Town in Norfolk, Virginia—a formerly crime-ridden slum that has been made livable through New Urbanist techniques. Pittsburgh-based UDA Architects, a practiced exponent of New Urbanism, cut new streets and sidewalks through Diggs Town's anonymous no-man's-lands and added sociable porches to the fronts of apartment buildings. Occupants were given individual front and back yards, sometimes bounded by picket fences to create the careful gradations of public and private space that fostered order and control in neighborhoods years ago. Those alterations, carried out with the intention of nurturing neighborliness and safety, have cut lawlessness substantially and generated a sense of community. Diggs Town is far from unique. Henry Cisneros, in his last year as Secretary of Housing and Urban Development, declared that New Urbanism would be a central element in the federal agency's efforts to salvage housing for the poor in cities around the country. New Urbanism is not a toy of the affluent.

A second line of criticism focuses on modern mobility: People's employment, shopping, and leisure activities are now scattered across sprawling metropolitan areas, so it is futile to try to inculcate a sense of geographic community. True, few of the people who live in Kentlands or Harbor Town also work there and form all their meaningful social connections within its boundaries. What is especially troubling is the difficulty New Urbanists have run into in their attempts to build up a cadre of local merchants and other businesspeople, who in the past were indispensable elements in a town's or neighborhood's identity. One remedy for this may be public policies that encourage developers to include employment and retailing in their plans. Developers may have to make special efforts to attract owner-operated retailers—perhaps by granting them financial concessions. Duany has argued that developers should regard local stores as an amenity, just like a park or a recreation complex, and subsidize it, at least in the beginning. He also argues that the number of stores in these developments will grow over time, since retailing follows, rather than leads, population growth.

The idea that people are destined to have ever weaker neighborhood ties seems questionable in light of the increasing number of people working at home either part- or full-time. With the growth of computers, faxes, modems, and other modern communication devices, it may be that *more* people, rather than fewer, will be both living and working in the same place. As that happens, it will be important for these home-based workers to have services and gathering places, such as cafes, close by. Neighborhood gathering places could offset the isolation of working alone and help generate a never-obsolete quality: geographic community. To accomplish that, New Urbanist instruments of physical design will be invaluable.

Of course, with a whole generation of Americans having grown up in isolated outer suburbs, such neighborly interdependence may, unfortunately, not be what most people immediately look for when they shop for a home. In the *Washington Post,* reporter Steve Twomey told of Lori and Bob Scarbrough, who had lived in Herndon, Virginia, a suburb where they and other residents would pull their car into the garage, enter the house by an interior door, and rarely have contact with the neighbors. When they first looked at Belmont Forest, a New Urbanist town that Duany/Plater-Zyberk designed in northern Virginia, the Scarbroughs, now in their early fifties, were concerned that the houses were built too close together. But they moved in, and now love the coziness and neighborly camaraderie. Libby and Walter Cable, who arrived in Belmont Forest from a similarly isolating suburb in Annandale, Virginia, were likewise concerned at first that they would lack privacy. But now, as they share the close-knit community with their two daughters and grandchildren and swap front-porch talk and visits with neighbors, they think of their new surroundings as a supportive and comforting re-creation of the small-town life of their upbringing.

Allison Bradfield, who lives with her husband and two small children in Belmont Forest, finds that the sidewalk activity, the front porch life, and the sheer proximity of dwellings in the neighborhood counteract the anonymity of the usual suburban development. She knows every one of the 12 families on her street, she reports, and "what all of them do, where they're from, and what they want of life." She acknowledges that "if you didn't want to know your neighbors, you wouldn't want to live here."

That is perhaps the biggest issue of all facing proponents of New Urbanism: Just how many Americans are there who actually want to live in a community where they will know their neighbors, and be known by them? Are walkable neighborhoods just a small market niche, or something that millions of American families would find to their liking?

Probably the strongest indication that the New Urbanist town is more than a hobbyhorse for nostalgic visionaries is the Walt Disney Company's decision to build an entire New Urbanist community near Orlando, complete with schools, parks, lakes, an old-fashioned walkable downtown, a health campus, up to one million square feet of office space, and neighborhoods full of houses in historical styles. Celebration started construction in the spring of 1995 after nine years of painstaking preparation, involving the prominent New York urban design firm Cooper, Robertson & Partners in cooperation with Robert A.M. Stern Architects. This is no minuscule niche project—its 4,900-acre tract, buffered by a 4,700-acre greenbelt, is to be developed with up to 8,000 houses and apartments. It has been estimated that by the time Celebration is completed in eight to ten years, some $2.5 billion will have been invested. Celebration elevates New Urbanism from the province of mostly small, local, and often contrarian developers to the realm of amply financed corporations. As America's leading caterer to the middle-class imagination, Disney, in its new community-building role, has already stirred great interest among architects, builders, and developers, not to mention the general public. With the level of talent that Disney is able to call on, Celebration will likely be good enough, big enough, and conspicuous enough to affect the direction of American building.

Obstacles in the Road

New Urbanist communities, then, tend to uphold central principles of good citizenship: vigorous involvement in a geographic community; interchange with people of different stations in life; a healthy combination of guidance and independence for youngsters; responsive local government; and local support of culture, charity, and philanthropy. All of this amounts to a kind of communal bulwark against the impersonality and materialism of today's mass culture. If the true test of New Urbanist design is how the people within its boundaries conduct themselves, particularly their public lives, then by that standard New Urbanism seems to be a success.

It is indisputable that for every Kentlands that is under construction, there are still a hundred newly built Isolation Estates, where the family of a physician never crosses paths with the family of a mail clerk, and where there is little incentive to stroll down the block, because it is a dead end. And even in traditional communities, whether new or old, it is a formidable task to attract and keep assortments of small, locally owned stores—in times past, the very embodiment of a neighborhood's personality and convenience. The vastly enlarged consumer marketsheds created by the automobile have caused a large decline in mom-and-pop establishments, a loss that traditionalists, despite their ambitions, are hard pressed to combat.

Nonetheless, the New Urbanist movement is the brightest hope to arise in community design in a long while. The next step is to break down the barriers that prevent developments like Kentlands and Harbor Town from being built in much of America. The inflexible hand of zoning should be loosened so that mixtures of housing—gradations of different kinds, sizes, and prices—can be included in a community, and so that small stores, cafes, and other hallmarks of a sociable neighborhood can legally be built within walking (or biking) distance of people's homes. Transportation departments must change their standards—which favor wide roads and maximum vehicular use—and start injecting pedestrian comfort into their calculations, for walking is a prime source of community consciousness.

If we are serious about building cohesive communities, we would demand that governmental and educational institutions reconsider their policies on what to build and where to build it. Branch post offices would not be oriented mainly to the convenience of 18-wheelers, but would be designed to enhance community gathering places; few services generate as much local interchange as a well-placed post office. Boards of education would integrate their schools into neighborhoods rather than granting educators their selfish wish for dozens of acres of parking, lawns, and athletic fields—a wish that consigns high schools to edge-of-town sites and prevents students from circulating through the community and its business section, the way students did in an era when town centers contained the communities' major functions.

If we take the well-being of communities seriously, we would do all these things and more. The past half-century has been spent creating a smooth, well-advertised world of shopping malls, megastores, profusely equipped houses, and the ultimate in private motorized transportation—a consumer paradise, in the view of its proponents, but in reality a centerless zone where what is on TV seems more compelling than the public life outside the door. We can do better. If we turn our energy to it, the lives of individuals, families, and communities will reverberate with the improvement.

UNIT 4

Stratification and Social Inequalities

Unit Selections

Key Points to Consider

• What inequalities do you find unacceptable and what inequalities do you find acceptable?

• Is the current level of income inequality unjust? If so, why? What negative effects does it have on society?

• Why is stratification such an important theme in sociology?

• Which social groups are likely to rise in the stratification system in the next decade? Which groups will fall? Why?

• How does stratification along income lines differ from stratification along racial or gender lines?

• Do you think women and blacks are treated fairly in America? Are changes needed in the policies that deal with discrimination? Why or why not?

• Is affirmative action no longer needed? Is it unjust or just?

Student Web Site

www.mhcls.com/online

Internet References

Further information regarding these Web sites may be found in this book's preface or online.

Americans With Disabilities Act Document Center
http://www.jan.wvu.edu/links/adalinks.htm

American Scientist
http://www.amsci.org/amsci/amsci.html

Give Five
http://www.independentsector.org/give5/givefive.html

Joint Center for Poverty Research
http://www.jcpr.org

NAACP Online: National Association for the Advancement of Colored People
http://www.naacp.org

People are ranked in many different ways—by physical strength, education, wealth, or other characteristics. Those who are rated highly often have power over others, special status, and prestige. The differences among people constitute their life chances—the probability that an individual or group will be able to obtain the valued and desired goods in a society. These differences are referred to as stratification, the system of structured inequalities in social relationships.

In most industrialized societies, income is one of the most important divisions among people. Karl Marx described stratification in terms of class rather than income. For him, social class referred mainly to two distinct groups: those who control the means of production and those who do not. This difference results in great differences in income, wealth, power, status, privileges, and opportunities. This section examines the life chances of the rich and the poor and of various other disadvantaged groups in the United States.

The first subsection of this unit deals with income inequality and the hardship of the poor. In his article, "The Rich and the Rest," Sam Pizzigati describes the great increase in the inequality of income in the past half century, and some of the adverse consequences of these inequalities. If present trends continue, the negative consequences could be so great that radical pro-egalitarian policies would begin to make sense.

Jeffrey D. Sachs maintains that extreme poverty can be eliminated throughout the world at the modest price of $160 billion a year for a couple of decades. This is a paltry sum (.5% of their GNP) for the rich countries of the world. To be successful, the money would have to be invested carefully in ways that he describes. The three articles in the next subsection explore, in interesting ways, some critical inter-group conflict issues and the cultural and attitudinal foundations of problems of racial and ethnic relations. The most poignant inequality in America is the gap between blacks and whites. Recently there has been considerable good news that the gap has been closing, and many indicators show that on average quality of life has improved for blacks. This progress, however, is limited to the black middle and upper classes while the lower class blacks are still locked into poverty and are not helped by current black politics. In the subsequent article, the authors demonstrate the prevalence of prejudice in America and show how quickly hatred toward a group can evolve. Since September 11, 2001, hatred toward Muslims has erupted despite calls for tolerance from President George W. Bush and other public leaders. One explanation of hatred and prejudice against entire groups is social identity theory. People have a powerful drive to divide people into groups, identify with one group, and develop negative views of some of the out groups. Fortunately, "people who are concerned about their prejudices have the power to correct them." The following article discusses the problem of integrating different groups in the context of massive immigration into the United States. Can so many newcomers be assimilated into American culture? According to author Anne Wortham, the United States has been quite successful in assimilating immigrants, most of whom want what America stands for when they come. They support democracy and other American institutions, and are willing to work hard to get ahead. Relatively high and rising intermarriage rates demonstrate increasing assimilation, but continuing housing segregation is one indicator of impediments to assimilation.

The last subsection of Unit 4 deals with sex inequalities. The first article of this subsection examines the persistence of the "glass ceiling." Women have the degrees, the talent, and the ambition to reach the highest levels of the corporate world, but 95% of senior managers in 1995 were men, and 92% in 2005. Several factors contribute to this imbalance. Next, Phyllis Rosser rejects the recent call for affirmative action for boys, because girls are doing so much better through college. Women are disadvantaged relative to men in so many ways that affirmative action should be in their favor. Furthermore, the disadvantage for boys in education is almost entirely a lower class phenomena and should be addressed in a different way. Alice Leuchtag describes one of the great evils that is haunting the world today—sex slavery. The sex trade system grows out of poverty and profits. Extreme poverty forces parents to sell their girls into servitude, often not knowing that they will become sex slaves. Considerable profits drive the system. The exploitation involved is horrendous, making this a worldwide human rights issue. In the final article, *The Economist* presents a special report on Arab women today. They have fewer rights than women in comparative societies, but their situation is slowly improving by many measures.

The Rich and the Rest

The Growing Concentration of Wealth

SAM PIZZIGATI

A century ago, battles against what angry Americans called plutocracy—rule by the rich—raged all across the United States. Those battles would eventually leave the world's first mass middle class by the 1950s. Today, that plutocracy is back and that middle class is hurting. What about tomorrow? In the twenty-first century, will Americans continue to tolerate enormous disparities in the property people own and the wealth individuals have accumulated?

In the United States currently, the most-affluent 1% of the population holds more wealth than the entire bottom 90% combined, according to U.S. Federal Reserve research. The most-honored captains of industry—Fortune 500 CEOs—routinely make more in a morning than their average employees earn in a year. Will our grandchildren live amid similar disparities? That future, most contemporary analysts would agree, seems likely.

Indeed, Americans have yet to begin the debate regarding just how concentrated wealth has become. In the 2004 U.S. presidential election campaign, President George W. Bush made no apologies for his tax cuts that, in 2004 alone, meant an extra $170,000 for average taxpayers in the nation's most-affluent 1%. His challenger, John Kerry, did call for a roll-back on tax cuts benefiting this top 1%, but he declined to challenge the existing distribution of income and wealth, a distribution more unequal than any seen in the United States since before the Great Depression. Kerry's stance raised no eyebrows, perhaps because no politician today considers grand accumulations of private wealth as any sort of pressing problem.

"I think it's less productive to worry about how much rich people have than to worry about how much middle-class and working people have," Howard Dean said during his 2004 presidential bid. "The thing to do is concentrate on the 90% of people who don't have what they need and make sure they have it, and not worry about the people who make $500,000 a year. Of course, it's obscene, but so what?"

Fighting Economic "Obscenity"

A century ago, most U.S. citizens who considered that they had a social conscience saw their advocacy for a better society as essentially a two-front struggle. A good and honorable republic would only emerge, they believed, if more wealth accumulated at the bottom of the social order, less at the top. Wise nations, James Madison had argued years earlier, seek to "reduce extreme wealth towards a state of mediocrity, and raise extreme indigence towards a state of comfort." Advocates for social justice a hundred years ago shared Madison's perspective. Their task appeared straightforward. They needed to "level up" the lowly and "level down" the high and mighty. They preached this egalitarian imperative at every opportunity—and found massive audiences for their message.

Just how massive can be illustrated by examining public response to Edward Bellamy's best-selling 1888 novel, *Looking Backward,* which tells the tale of an affluent Bostonian who falls asleep in 1887 and awakes in 2000 to a United States without a wealthy elite. In the new nation Bellamy describes, all working people earn the same income but work varying numbers of hours. Workers bid for jobs, and the market sets the hours of work for each job category. If no one bids for a particularly unappealing job, the hours required for that job are reduced until the job becomes appealing enough to attract bidders. In Bellamy's utopia, workers with the least-appealing jobs only have to labor a few hours a week.

In the 1890s, clubs soon sprang up around the nation to popularize the *Looking Backward* credo. The book's readers, dirt-poor populist farmers and middle-class reformers alike, thrilled to Bellamy's vision for an egalitarian future.

Those readers all lived in a profoundly unequal society. In 1861, only a handful of millionaire fortunes dotted the American landscape. By 1900, more than 4,000 fortunes had reached seven figures. Never before in U.S. history had so few become so rich so fast. One leading magnate spent $5 million erecting a mansion on Manhattan's Fifth Avenue, then found he hadn't left enough space for flower beds. He promptly had the brownstone next door demolished and replaced with a $400,000 garden. Meanwhile, elsewhere in Manhattan, half the city's people lived in tenement neighborhoods that averaged close to a thousand people per acre.

Men and women inspired by visionaries like Bellamy would not accept this gross inequality. They battled to slice the wealthy down to democratic size through checks on trusts—the grand accumulations of companies that created even grander accumulations of personal wealth—and taxes on the incomes and the estates of the wealthy.

These men and women were more right than they knew. The research of a veritable brigade of present-day analysts—economists, environmentalists, and epidemiologists—predicts a dark future indeed if policy makers in the United States continue to ignore the steadily growing gap between the wealthiest citizens and everyone else. Over recent decades, these analysts have generated an often brilliant body of work that explores just what happens when modern societies let themselves grow substantially more unequal.

Economists have put to test the most cherished chestnut of apologists for concentrated wealth, the claim that complex, modern market societies have no choice but to accept inequality. Any steps taken to reduce inequality, this claim holds, will inevitably reduce market efficiency—and leave societies less able to create new wealth for everyone. In reality, recent researchers have documented that societies tolerating inequality do not grow faster economically than more-equal societies. Princeton economist Roland Benabou counted more than a dozen "cross-country empirical analyses" that demonstrated a "negative effect of inequality on growth." Clearly, noted another analysis prepared for the Federal Reserve, "the older view, that greater inequality is associated with faster growth, is not supported by the data."

Environmental researchers, meanwhile, have been documenting how growing inequality is speeding the exhaustion of the earth's natural resources and the ability to absorb the wastes of the increasingly wasteful consumer culture. On a grotesquely unequal globe, these environmentalists point out, the desperation of those without wealth and power—and the greed of those with it—is despoiling the natural world.

We see this desperation—and despoliation—wherever wealth concentrates. In Guatemala and El Salvador, the wealthiest 2% of the population owns more than 60% of available arable land, notes environmental analyst Tom Athanasiou. Should we be surprised, he asks, when landless peasants in outrageously unequal nations like these "migrate into rain forests or onto fragile uplands" to find land to farm?

But the greatest strains on the earth's carrying capacity come not from developing nations, but from the already developed. Those living in the richest 20% of the world's nations use 17 times more energy than the bottom 20%, UN researchers report. The United States alone produces nearly a quarter of the world's greenhouse gases.

These contrasts shock, but they do not tell the whole story. Indeed, the gaps between nations may not be the biggest obstacle to environmental security. That biggest obstacle may well be the gaps *within* nations, between the rich and everyone else. These gaps—wider today in the United States than in any other developed nation—accelerate consumption and waste, as growing fortunes ratchet up the level of acquisitions that define the good life. The wider these gaps, the deeper we stamp footprints into the earth.

Epidemiologists—scientists who study the health of populations—have an even more alarming story to tell: The more unequal a country is, the less healthy its people are. People with modest incomes in relatively equal societies can actually look forward to longer, healthier lives than people with higher incomes who live in more unequal societies.

The nation with the developed world's lowest level of income inequality, Japan, currently boasts the world's highest life expectancy—and this despite atrociously high levels of cigarette smoking among Japanese men. The much more unequal United States, despite spending as much on health care as the rest of the world combined, sits twenty-seventh in current world life-span rankings. "In the developed world, it is not the richest countries which have the best health, but the most egalitarian," says British epidemiologist Richard Wilkinson.

This epidemiological research on inequality has had no impact on mainstream political discourse in the United States yet. Nor have any of the findings of equality-minded economists and environmentalists. And the political debates that figure to roil the United States during the next few years—debates over Social Security and the federal tax system—aren't likely to move the nation in a more equal direction either. In both the Social Security and tax debates, the choice before the American people is between the current top-heavy status quo and a proposal for change that would, if adopted, leave the nation's wealth more unequally distributed, not less.

Should There Be a Maximum Wage?

Fortunately, all these current political realities don't necessarily doom us to continued inequality. If we look beyond today's political mainstream into the political margins, we can see a debate beginning to take shape over how much inequality a sane society should tolerate. This debate seems to be revolving around what has become the nation's most visible manifestation of concentrated wealth and income: the explosive growth of corporate executive compensation.

Top business executives a generation ago could not possibly have imagined how fortunate their successors would turn out to be. In 1975, Reginald Jones, then CEO of General Electric and widely regarded as the nation's most talented executive, took home $500,000, a sum that equaled 36 times the income of that year's typical U.S. family. A quarter century later, in 2000, General Electric CEO Jack Welsh took home $144.5 million, a sum equal to 3,500 times the typical family income for that year. In 2004, Yahoo CEO Terry Semel cleared $231 million in the year's first 10 months alone.

Windfalls like these are prompting calls for radical action from *within* the business community, most notably from Richard C. Breeden, the former chairman of the U.S. Securities and Exchange Commission, the agency that regulates Wall Street. In 2002, a federal judge appointed Breeden to come up with a fix-it plan for WorldCom, the scandal-ridden, bankrupt telecom giant. Breeden's plan, subsequently adopted, totally dismantled WorldCom's lavish structure of executive pay incentives—a structure, Breeden charged, that had encouraged a reckless pursuit of wealth. Breeden's solution was to put a lid on total compensation from all sources for the top executive at MCI, the company that emerged out of WorldCom's ashes. Breeden fixed this maximum dollar amount at not more than $15 million a year, though the MCI board, he added quickly, would be free to set a lower number. Breeden had established, in effect, the first "maximum wage" in U.S. corporate history.

Breeden's maximum didn't win many headlines. But his advocacy for an explicit limit on executive pay did remind some observers that the United States once abounded with distinguished national leaders ready and willing to seriously discuss and debate proposals that would cap the incomes of its very richest citizens.

In 1942, a call for what amounted to a maximum wage actually came from U.S. President Franklin D. Roosevelt, who asked Congress to impose a 100% tax on all individual income above $25,000—the equivalent of about $300,000 today after adjusting for inflation. Roosevelt didn't get his 100% top tax rate, but he did get Congress to pass a 94% top tax rate on all income more than $200,000. The top tax rate on high incomes would hover around 90% for the next two decades, when the incomes of the average U.S. family would double—and when the share of the nation's income going to the richest 1% would drop by more than half.

Those high tax rates on high incomes that Roosevelt inspired have long since disappeared. In 1943, America's very richest, according to U.S. Internal Revenue Service statistics, paid 78% of their total incomes in federal income tax. In 2003, by contrast, they paid a mere 17.5% of their total incomes in federal tax.

And Roosevelt's notion of a maximum wage has largely disappeared, too. Today, no advocates for a more-equal United States see a maximum wage as a realistic possibility anytime soon. But some advocates do see a potential for more modest proposals that would shove the United States in a maximum-wage direction.

Minnesota Congressman Martin Sabo, for instance, has introduced legislation in Congress that, if enacted, would prohibit corporations from deducting from their tax bills any executive compensation that totals more than 25 times the pay of their lowest-paid workers. A similar proposal surfaced a few years ago in Connecticut. That initiative would have denied state government contracts to any corporations that pay executives more than 25 times what their workers receive.

Elsewhere in the developed world, where rising levels of executive pay have generated considerably more public outrage than they have in the United States, proposals for outright income caps have started to gain some political traction. For example, the former leader of Germany's largest political party is now suggesting that compensation at Germany's CEO summits be limited to 20 or 30 times the pay that average workers receive.

Ideas along this line might, of course, never catch on in the United States. We might continue down the road to greater inequality in the decades ahead. And if so, what would life be like in a still more-unequal United States? We need only look to Brazil to find the answer. Brazil currently boasts the overall greatest gaps in wealth and income in the world. In Brazil, the richest 10% make nearly 50 times what the poorest 10%

make—more than twice the gap between top and bottom tenths that currently exists in the United States.

Amid this stark inequality, Brazilians are spending $2 billion a year on private security. In São Paulo, a third of local residents employ private guards. People in São Paulo have good reason to be nervous. According to news reports, kidnappings have become so common that some plastic surgeons now "specialize in treating wealthy victims who return from their ordeals with sliced ears, severed fingers, and other missing body parts that were sent to family members as threats for ransom payment."

Meanwhile, in Brazil's second-largest city, Rio de Janeiro, carjackings were taking place so often in the late 1990s that police officials assured affluent drivers that they could run red lights on dark streets without facing any fines. Thousands of those drivers took no chances. They armored their cars, typically at $35,000 per automobile. "Soon the haves will circulate throughout the city in personal tanks," São Paulo novelist Ignácio de Loyola Brandão predicted right before the century turned.

That prediction would turn out to be somewhat off base. Brazil's wealthy took to the air, not tanks. São Paulo now sports 24 times more helipads than New York City, and São Paulo businessmen routinely ride helicopters to work, commuting, the *Washington Post* reports, "from their fortified offices to their fortified homes."

Could this be America's future? Could the growing numbers of gated communities in the United States morph into Latin American–style fortresses? Perhaps. But another future is possible—a more equal, stable, healthy future.

Maximum of 10 Times Minimum?

Back in the 1940s, Roosevelt found himself unable to assemble a winning coalition behind his proposal to levy a 100% tax on annual incomes greater than what today would be $300,000. His allies likely saw this as a politically impractical declaration of war against the rich. But suppose Roosevelt had asked Congress to set a cap—a maximum allowable income—not as a fixed amount, but as a fixed multiple of the nation's minimum wage, with any income above that multiple subject to a 100% tax. If this approach—an income ceiling tied to an income floor—had been proposed and adopted, the wealthy would have been able to increase their incomes even with a maximum wage in place. To realize this increase, the wealthy would have needed only to convince Congress to raise the minimum wage, because the higher the minimum, the higher the maximum. By advocating for the nation's poorest workers, the wealthy would have advocated for themselves.

Any move we might make today to link an income maximum to an income minimum would, of course, immediately raise a series of difficult questions. How wide a gap between top and bottom, maximum and minimum, makes sense? How much income is enough? How much is too much?

Philosophers over the millennia have pondered the question of how much is enough. In ancient Greece, Plato pronounced the ideal ratio between the wealth of the richest and the wealth of the poorest to be four to one. Aristotle deemed the ideal ratio five to one. Modern analysts have found that, within every developed country, about 97% of all income earners fall within a 10-to-1 income ratio of each other.

Let us assume for the moment that this 10-to-1 ratio makes sense as a set-point for an income limit. The maximum wage would then become 10 times the minimum wage. Any income more than 10 times the minimum wage would be taxed at a 100% rate.

What would this mean in actual dollars and cents? The U.S. federal minimum wage currently stands at $5.15 an hour, or $10,712 over the course of a year. A couple, with each spouse earning the minimum wage, earns twice that, or $21,424. If a "Ten Times Rule" were in effect, the maximum wage would be 10 times this annual minimum—$107,120 for single filers or $214,240 for couples filing jointly.

For people with incomes below the maximum but above the minimum, the Ten Times Rule would key income-tax rates to the minimum wage, not just the tax rate applied to the wealthiest incomes. A maximum tied to a minimum, as noted, would give rich people a vested personal interest in raising the minimum wage and improving the well-being of the poorest people. Linking all tax rates to the minimum wage would give everyone else in society that same vested interest.

In such a Ten-Times-Rule nation, taxpayers earning 10 times the minimum wage would pay 10% of their income in taxes. Taxpayers earning five times the minimum would pay a 5% tax. And if they made exactly the minimum wage, they would pay 1% of their income in taxes.

How significant a fiscal impact would Ten Times tax rates make? In 2003, the incomes of the richest 1% of U.S. citizens averaged $1.082 million for the year. If the Ten Times Rule had been in effect in 2003, these households would have paid a 10% tax on their first $214,240 and a 100% tax on all income above that. The total tax due would be $889,184, an amount that would have equaled 82% of the average top 1% income, a rate only slightly higher than the actual 78% tax America's wealthiest paid on their total incomes back in 1943.

The next richest 4% of households averaged $217,000 in 2003, just a hair more than the $214,240 that would have been the 2003 maximum. In a Ten-Times-Rule nation, the average household in this tax bracket would have paid $24,184 in federal income tax, or 11% of their total incomes.

In 2003, the middle 20% of income earners averaged $36,600 per household, less than twice the income for a minimum-wage couple. Under the Ten Times Rule, middle-bracket taxpayers would have paid federal income taxes at just a 1% rate.

If the Ten Times Rule had been in effect in 2003, all U.S. households would have paid fewer dollars in federal taxes than they actually did—all except the richest 1%. In fact, average families would have seen their taxes cut by almost three-fourths, and families making around $200,000 would have seen their taxes cut by more than a third. Furthermore, despite these cuts, the Internal Revenue Service would still have collected more total income-tax revenue, because the increase in tax collections from the nation's richest 1% would offset the decrease in revenues from the bottom 99% by about $450 billion.

The IRS, of course, would have only been able to collect those extra billions if the rich continued earning income above the Ten Times maximum after the Ten Times Rule went into effect. But why would anyone wealthy continue working to earn income that would be completely taxed away? No rational person is going to *labor* for dollars that go only to a tax collector. But the highest incomes don't come from labor. The highest incomes come overwhelmingly from the ownership of property. The wealthiest individuals owe the bulk of their incomes to their fortunes. In 2000, for instance, people who made $1 million or more averaged only 33% of their incomes from wages and salaries. Most of their incomes came from other sources, everything from interest and dividends to capital gains.

Income from labor can be turned off, like water out of a spigot, but income from wealth never stops flowing. In a Ten-Times-Rule nation, wealthy people angry about paying taxes at a 100% rate could certainly choose to stop working. But they could not stop their wealth from working. That wealth would continue to generate income. And that income, above the Ten Times maximum, would be taxed at a 100% rate.

Could any of this Ten-Times-Rule scenario ever materialize? That may hardly seem likely in the current political environment. But environments change, and U.S. society could, too, as more Americans begin to understand how outrageously high levels of inequality hurt all people—rich, poor, and everyone in between.

SAM PIZZIGATI is a Maryland-based labor journalist. He currently edits *Too Much* (www.toomuchonline.org), a weekly online journal on excessive income and wealth. His latest book is *Greed and Good: Understanding and Overcoming the Inequality That Limits Our Lives* (Apex Press, 2004). E-mail editor@toomuchonline.org.

Originally published in the July/August 2005 issue of *The Futurist*, pp. 38–43. Copyright © 2005 by World Future Society, 7910 Woodmont Avenue, Suite 450, Bethesda, MD 20814. Telephone: 301/656-8274; Fax: 301/951-0394; http://www.wfs.org. Used with permission from the World Future Society.

Can Extreme Poverty Be Eliminated?

Market economics and globalization are lifting the bulk of humanity out of extreme poverty, but special meaures are needed to help the poorest of the poor

Jeffrey D. Sachs

Almost everyone who ever lived was wretchedly poor. Famine, death from childbirth, infectious disease and countless other hazards were the norm for most of history. Humanity's sad plight started to change with the Industrial Revolution, beginning around 1750. New scientific insights and technological innovations enabled a growing proportion of the global population to break free of extreme poverty.

Two and a half centuries later more than five billion of the world's 6.5 billion people can reliably meet their basic living needs and thus can be said to have escaped from the precarious conditions that once governed everyday life. One out of six inhabitants of this planet, however, still struggles daily to meet some or all of such critical requirements as adequate nutrition, uncontaminated drinking water, safe shelter and sanitation as well as access to basic health care. These people get by on $1 a day or less and are overlooked by public services for health, education and infrastructure. Every day more than 20,000 die of dire poverty, for want of food, safe drinking water, medicine or other essential needs.

For the first time in history, global economic prosperity, brought on by continuing scientific and technological progress and the self-reinforcing accumulation of wealth, has placed the world within reach of eliminating extreme poverty altogether. This prospect will seem fanciful to some, but the dramatic economic progress made by China, India and other low-income parts of Asia over the past 25 years demonstrates that it is realistic. Moreover, the predicted stabilization of the world's population toward the middle of this century will help by easing pressures on Earth's climate, ecosystems and natural resources—pressures that might otherwise undo economic gains.

Although economic growth has shown a remarkable capacity to lift vast numbers of people out of extreme poverty, progress is neither automatic nor inevitable. Market forces and free trade are not enough. Many of the poorest regions are ensnared in a poverty trap: they lack the financial means to make the necessary investments in infrastructure, education, health care systems and other vital needs. Yet the end of such poverty is feasible if a concerted global effort is undertaken, as the nations of the world promised when they adopted the Millennium Development Goals at the United Nations Millennium Summit in 2000. A dedicated cadre of development agencies, international financial institutions, nongovernmental organizations and communities throughout the developing world already constitute a global network of expertise and goodwill to help achieve this objective.

Extreme poverty could become a thing of the past in a few decades if the affluent countries of the world pony up a small percentage of their wealth to help the planet's 1.1 billion indigent populations out of conditions of dire poverty.

This past January my colleagues and I on the U.N. Millennium Project published a plan to halve the rate of extreme poverty by 2015 (compared with 1990) and to achieve other quantitative targets for reducing hunger, disease and environmental degradation. In my recent book, *The End of Poverty,* I argue that a large-scale and targeted public investment effort could in fact eliminate this problem by 2025, much as smallpox was eradicated globally. This hypothesis is controversial, so I am pleased to have the opportunity to clarify its main arguments and to respond to various concerns that have been raised about it.

Beyond Business as Usual

Economists have learned a great deal during the past few years about how countries develop and what roadblocks can stand in their way. A new kind of development economics needs to emerge, one that is better grounded in science—a "clinical economics" akin to modern medicine. Today's medical professionals understand that disease results from a vast array of

Crossroads for Poverty

The Problem:

- Much of humankind has succeeded in dragging itself out of severe poverty since the onset of the Industrial Revolution in the mid-18th century, but about 1.1 billion out of today's 6.5 billion global inhabitants are utterly destitute in a world of plenty.
- These unfortunates, who get by on less than $1 a day, have little access to adequate nutrition, safe drinking water and shelter, as well as basic sanitation and health care services. What can the developed world do to lift this huge segment of the human population out of extreme poverty?

The Plan:

- Doubling affluent nations' international poverty assistance to about $160 billion a year would go a long way toward ameliorating the terrible predicament faced by one in six humans. This figure would constitute about 0.5 percent of the gross national product (GNP) of the planet's rich countries. Because these investments do not include other categories of aid, such as spending on major infrastructure projects, climate change mitigation or post conflict reconstruction, donors should commit to reaching the long stand target of 0.7 percent of GNP by 2015.
- These donations, often provided to local groups, would need to be closely monitored and audited to ensure that they are correctly targeted toward those truly in need.

interacting factors and conditions: pathogens, nutrition, environment, aging, individual and population genetics, lifestyle. They also know that one key to proper treatment is the ability to make an individualized diagnosis of the source of illness. Likewise, development economists need better diagnostic skills to recognize that economic pathologies have a wide variety of causes, including many outside the traditional ken of economic practice.

Public opinion in affluent countries often attributes extreme poverty to faults with the poor themselves—or at least with their governments. Race was once thought the deciding factor. Then it was culture: religious divisions and taboos, caste systems, a lack of entrepreneurship, gender inequities. Such theories have waned as societies of an ever widening range of religions and cultures have achieved relative prosperity. Moreover, certain supposedly immutable aspects of culture (such as fertility choices and gender and caste roles) in fact change, often dramatically, as societies become urban and develop economically.

Most recently, commentators have zeroed in on "poor governance," often code words for corruption. They argue that extreme poverty persists because governments fail to open up their markets, provide public services and clamp down on bribe

taking. It is said that if these regimes cleaned up their acts, they, too, would flourish. Development assistance efforts have become largely a series of good governance lectures.

The availability of cross-country and time-series data now allows experts to make much more systematic analyses. Although debate continues, the weight of the evidence indicates that governance makes a difference but is not the sole determinant of economic growth. According to surveys conducted by Transparency International, business leaders actually perceive many fast-growing Asian countries to be more corrupt than some slow-growing African ones.

Geography—including natural resources, climate, topography, and proximity to trade routes and major markets—is at least as important as good governance. As early as 1776, Adam Smith argued that high transport costs inhibited development in the inland areas of Africa and Asia. Other geographic features, such as the heavy disease burden of the tropics, also interfere. One recent study by my Columbia University colleague Xavier Sala-i-Martin demonstrated once again that tropical countries saddled with malaria have experienced slower growth than those free from the disease. The good news is that geographic factors shape, but do not decide, a country's economic fate. Technology can offset them: drought can be fought with irrigation systems, isolation with roads and mobile telephones, diseases with preventive and therapeutic measures.

The other major insight is that although the most powerful mechanism for reducing extreme poverty is to encourage overall economic growth, a rising tide does not necessarily lift all boats. Average income can rise, but if the income is distributed unevenly the poor may benefit little, and pockets of extreme poverty may persist (especially in geographically disadvantaged regions). Moreover, growth is not simply a free-market phenomenon. It requires basic government services: infrastructure, health, education, and scientific and technological innovation. Thus, many of the recommendations of the past two decades emanating from Washington—that governments in low-income countries should cut back on their spending to make room for the private sector—miss the point. Government spending, directed at investment in critical areas, is itself a vital spur to growth, especially if its effects are to reach the poorest of the poor.

The Poverty Trap

So what do these insights tell us about the region most afflicted by poverty today, Africa? Fifty years ago tropical Africa was roughly as rich as subtropical and tropical Asia. As Asia boomed, Africa stagnated. Special geographic factors have played a crucial role.

Foremost among these is the existence of the Himalaya Mountains, which produce southern Asia's monsoon climate and vast river systems. Well-watered farmlands served as the starting points for Asia's rapid escape from extreme poverty during the past five decades. The Green Revolution of the 1960s and 1970s introduced high-yield grains, irrigation and fertilizers, which ended the cycle of famine, disease and despair.

Globalization, Poverty and Foreign Aid

Average citizens in affluent nations often have many questions about the effects of economic globalization on rich and poor nations and about how developing countries spend the aid they receive. Here are a few brief answers:

Is Globalization Making the Rich Richer and the Poor Poorer?

Generally, the answer is no. Economic globalization is supporting very rapid advances of many impoverished economies, notably in Asia. International trade and foreign investment inflows have been major factors in China's remarkable economic growth during the past quarter century and in India's fast economic growth since the early 1990s. The poorest of the poor, notably in sub-Saharan Africa, are not held back by globalization; they are largely bypassed by it.

Is Poverty the Result of Exploitation of the Poor by the Rich?

Affluent nations have repeatedly plundered and exploited poor countries through slavery, colonial rule and unfair trade practices. Yet it is perhaps more accurate to say that exploitation is the result of poverty (which leaves impoverished countries vulnerable to abuse) rather than the cause of it. Poverty is generally the result of low productivity per worker, which reflects poor health, lack of job-market skills, patchiness of infrastructure (roads, power plants, utility lines, shipping ports), chronic malnutrition and the like. Exploitation has played a role in producing some of these conditions, but deeper factors [geographic isolation, endemic disease, ecological destruction, challenging conditions for food production] have tended to be more important and difficult to overcome without external help.

Will Higher Incomes in Poor Countries Mean Lower Incomes in Rich Countries?

By and large, economic development is a positive-sum process, meaning that all can partake in it without causing some to suffer. In the past 200 years, the world as a whole has achieved a massive increase in economic output rather than a shift in economic output to one region at the expense of another. To be sure, global environmental constraints are already starting to impose themselves. As today's poor countries develop, the climate, fisheries and forests are coming under increased strain. Overall global economic growth is compatible with sustainable management of the ecosystems or which all humans depend—indeed, wealth can be good for the environment—but only if public policy and technologies encourage sound practices and the necessary investments are made in environmental sustainability.

Do U.S. Private Contributions Make Up for the Low Levels of U.S. Official Aid?

Some have claimed that while the U.S. government budget provides relatively little assistance to the poorest countries, the private sector makes up the gap. In fact, the Organization for Economic Cooperation and Development has estimated that private foundations and nongovernmental organizations give roughly $6 billion a year in international assistance, or 0.05 percent of U.S. gross national product (GNP). In that case, total U.S. international aid is around 0.21 percent of GNP—still among the lowest ratios of all donor nations.

—J.D.S.

It also freed a significant proportion of the labor force to seek manufacturing jobs in the cities. Urbanization, in turn, spurred growth, not only by providing a home for industry and innovation but also by prompting greater investment in a healthy and skilled labor force. Urban residents cut their fertility rates and thus were able to spend more for the health, nutrition and education of each child. City kids went to school at a higher rate than their rural cousins. And with the emergence of urban infrastructure and public health systems, city populations became less disease-prone than their counterparts in the countryside, where people typically lack safe drinking water, modern sanitation, professional health care and protection from vector-borne ailments such as malaria.

Africa did not experience a green revolution. Tropical Africa lacks the massive floodplains that facilitate the large-scale and low-cost irrigation found in Asia. Also, its rainfall is highly variable, and impoverished farmers have been unable to purchase fertilizer. The initial Green Revolution research featured crops, especially paddy rice and wheat, not widely grown in Africa (high-yield varieties suitable for it have been developed in recent years, but they have not yet been disseminated sufficiently). The continent's food production per person has actually been falling, and Africans' caloric intake is the lowest in the world; food insecurity is rampant. Its labor force has remained tethered to subsistence agriculture.

Compounding its agricultural woes, Africa bears an overwhelming burden of tropical diseases. Because of climate and the endemic mosquito species, malaria is more intensively transmitted in Africa than anywhere else. And high transport costs isolate Africa economically. In East Africa, for example, the rainfall is greatest in the interior of the continent, so most people live there, far from ports and international trade routes.

Much the same situation applies to other impoverished parts of the world, notably the Andean and Central American highlands and the landlocked countries of Central Asia. Being economically isolated, they are unable to attract much foreign

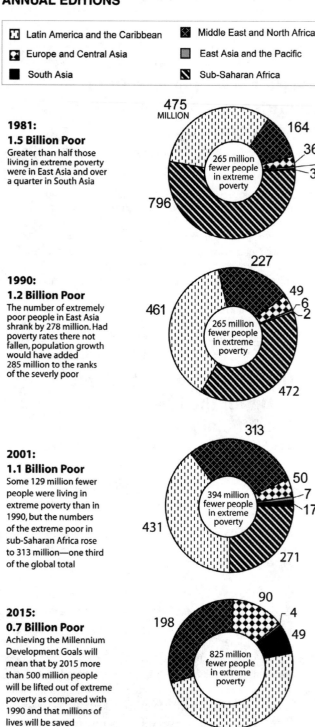

Legend:
- Latin America and the Caribbean
- Europe and Central Asia
- South Asia
- Middle East and North Africa
- East Asia and the Pacific
- Sub-Saharan Africa

1981:
1.5 Billion Poor
Greater than half those living in extreme poverty were in East Asia and over a quarter in South Asia

265 million fewer people in extreme poverty
475 MILLION · 164 · 36 · 9 · 3 · 796

1990:
1.2 Billion Poor
The number of extremely poor people in East Asia shrank by 278 million. Had poverty rates there not fallen, population growth would have added 285 million to the ranks of the severly poor

265 million fewer people in extreme poverty
227 · 49 · 6 · 2 · 472 · 461

2001:
1.1 Billion Poor
Some 129 million fewer people were living in extreme poverty than in 1990, but the numbers of the extreme poor in sub-Saharan Africa rose to 313 million—one third of the global total

394 million fewer people in extreme poverty
313 · 50 · 7 · 17 · 271 · 431

2015:
0.7 Billion Poor
Achieving the Millennium Development Goals will mean that by 2015 more than 500 million people will be lifted out of extreme poverty as compared with 1990 and that millions of lives will be saved

825 million fewer people in extreme poverty
90 · 4 · 49 · 317 · 198

Figure 1   Extreme Poverty: Where We Stand.   The number of people mired in the lowest depths of poverty has shrunk since the early 1980s, as the global economy has grown stronger. But these gains were concentrated in East Asia, leaving behind more than a billion unfortunates in sub-Saharan Africa, Central Asia and the mountainous parts of Central America and the Andean region. A determined push to help those lagging populations during the coming decade could cut the ranks of poor in half. The numbers below indicate millions of people.

investment (other than for the extraction of oil, gas and precious minerals). Investors tend to be dissuaded by the high transport costs associated with the interior regions. Rural areas therefore

remain stuck in a vicious cycle of poverty, hunger, illness and illiteracy. Impoverished areas lack adequate internal savings to make the needed investments because most households live hand to mouth. The few high-income families, who do accumulate savings, park them overseas rather than at home. This capital flight includes not only financial capital but also the human variety, in the form of skilled workers—doctors, nurses, scientists and engineers, who frequently leave in search of improved economic opportunities abroad. The poorest countries are often, perversely, net exporters of capital.

Put Money Where Mouths Are

The Technology to overcome these handicaps and jump-start economic development exists. Malaria can be controlled using bed nets, indoor pesticide spraying and improved medicines. Drought-prone countries in Africa with nutrient depleted soils can benefit enormously from drip irrigation and greater use of fertilizers. Landlocked countries can be connected by paved highway networks, airports and fiber-optic cables. All these projects cost money, of course.

Many larger countries, such as China, have prosperous regions that can help support their own lagging areas. Coastal eastern China, for instance, is now financing massive public investments in western China. Most of today's successfully developing countries, especially smaller ones, received at least some backing from external donors at crucial times. The critical scientific innovations that formed the underpinnings of the Green Revolution were bankrolled by the Rockefeller Foundation, and the spread of these technologies in India and elsewhere in Asia was funded by the U.S. and other donor governments and international development institutions.

We in the U.N. Millennium Project have listed the investments required to help today's impoverished regions cover basic needs in health, education, water, sanitation, food production, roads and other key areas. We have put an approximate price tag on that assistance and estimated how much could be financed by poor households themselves and by domestic institutions. The remaining cost is the "financing gap" that international donors need to make up.

For tropical Africa, the total investment comes to $110 per person a year. To place this into context, the average income in this part of the world is $350 per annum, most or all of which is required just to stay alive. The full cost of the total investment is clearly beyond the funding reach of these countries. Of the $110, perhaps $40 could be financed domestically, so that $70 per capita would be required in the form of international aid.

Adding it all up, the total requirement for assistance across the globe is around $160 billion a year, double the current rich-country aid budget of $80 billion. This figure amounts to approximately 0.5 percent of the combined gross national product (GNP) of the affluent donor nations. It does not include other humanitarian projects such as postwar Iraqi reconstruction or Indian Ocean tsunami relief. To meet these needs as well, a reasonable figure would be 0.7 percent of GNP, which is what all donor countries have long promised but few have fulfilled.

Other organizations, including the International Monetary Fund, the World Bank and the British government, have reached much the same conclusion.

We believe these investments would enable the poorest countries to cut poverty by half by 2015 and, if continued, to eliminate it altogether by 2025. They would not be "welfare payments" from rich to poor but instead something far more important and durable. People living above mere subsistence levels would be able to save for their futures; they could join the virtuous cycle of rising incomes, savings and technological inflows. We would be giving a billion people a hand up instead of a handout.

GOAL 1 ERADICATE EXTREME POVERTY AND HUNGER

Target: Halve the proportion of people living on less than $1 a day and the proportion of those who suffer chronic hunger.
Status: Between 1990 and 2001, the fraction of the populations in sub-Saharan Africa, Latin America and the Caribbean living in extreme poverty remained stagnant and, ominously, increased in Central Asia. Food intake is rising, but hunger is still widespread in several regions.

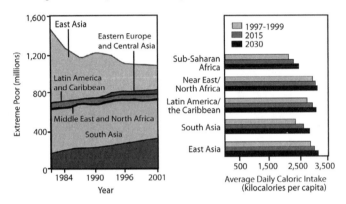

GOAL 2 ACHIEVE UNIVERSAL PRIMARY EDUCATION

Target: Ensure that by 2015 all children complete a full course of primary education.

GOAL 3 PROMOTE GENDER EQUALITY AND EMPOWER WOMEN

Target: Eliminate gender disparity in primary, secondary and tertiary education by 2015.
Status: Education is probably the best way to promote gender equality. The greatest challenges are in sub-Saharan Africa, where overall school completion rates have hovered around 50 percent. Women and girls fare even worse, as shown below by the ration of literate females to males on the African continent.

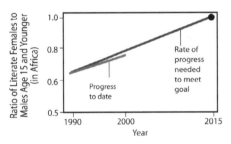

GOAL 4 REDUCE CHILD MORTALITY

Target: Reduce by two thirds the mortality rate of children younger than five years
Status: Child mortality rates fell in every region except the former Soviet republics in the Commonwealth of independent States (CIS), but rates remain high in sub-Saharan Africa and in South Asia. For comparison, the child mortality rate in high-income countries in 2000 was about six per 1,000 births.

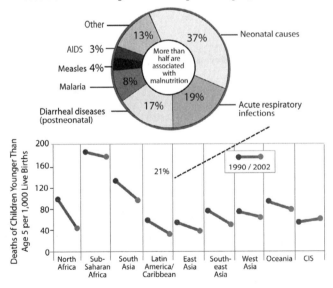

GOAL 5 IMPROVE MATERNAL HEALTH

Target: Reduce by 75 percent the maternal mortality rate by 2015.
Status: Maternal mortality rates remain shockingly high in every developing region of the world. Increasing the proportion of deliveries attended by skilled health workers will be critical to lowering maternal mortality.

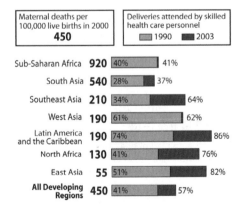

Figure 2 The Millennium Development Goals: How Are We Doing? At the United Nations Millennium Summit in 2000, the nations of the world promised to make the investments necessary to help today's impoverished regions improve their residents' welfare in key areas, including health, education, water, sanitation and food production. The U.N. specified eight broad Millennium Development Goals (MDG) to reduce extreme poverty substantially across the globe by 2015. The data on these two pages illustrate the challenges of meeting those goals. Measurement of progress is based on statistical levels that existed in 1990.

SARA BEARDSLEY (data compilation); SOURCES: GOAL 1: WWW.WORLDBANK.ORG/DATA/W012005/WDITEXT/SECTION1_1_1.HTM (graph): WWW.FAD. ORG/00CREP/007/Y5650E/Y5650ED4.HTM (bar chart); GOALS 2 AND 3: ACHIEVING THE MILLENNIUM DEVELOPMENT GOALS IN AFRICA, JUNE 2002 (graph); GOAL 4: THE MDG REPORT 2005 [pie chart] HTTP://UNSTATS.UN.ORG/UNS0/MI/MI_COVERFINAL.HTM (line graph); GOAL 5: THE MDG REPORT 2005 (bar chart)

GOAL 6 COMBAT HIV/AIDS, MALARIA AND OTHER DISEASES

Targets: Halt and begin to reverse the spread of HIV/AIDS. Slow the spread of malaria and other diseases.
Status: HIV, now affecting about 40 million people, is widespread in parts of sub-Saharan Africa and poses a serious threat to other developing regions. Meanwhile malaria kills around three million people a year, mostly in Africa, the vast majority of them children. In recent years, the distribution of mosquito nets has expanded, but hundreds of millions in malarious regions still need nets.

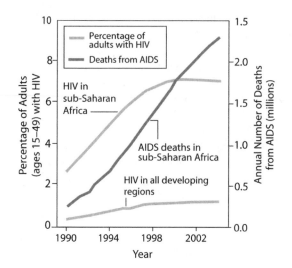

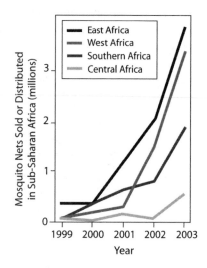

GOAL 7 ENSURE ENVIRONMENTAL SUSTAINABILITY

Target: Halve by 2015 the proportion of people without sustainable access to safe drinking water and basic sanitation.
Status: With the exception of sub-Saharan Africa, access to drinking water in urban areas is generally relatively high, although rural access remains limited. Low availability of sanitation services in sub-Saharan African and South Asia contributes to widespread diarrheal disease.

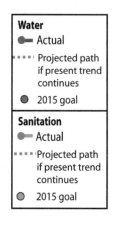

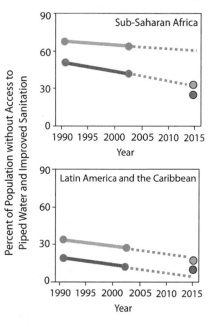

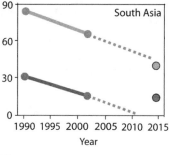

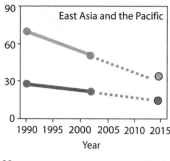

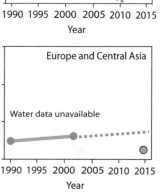

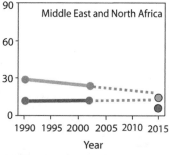

GOAL 8 DEVELOP A GLOBAL PARTNERSHIP FOR DEVELOPMENT

Targets: Address the special needs of the least developed countries (including more generous development assistnace).
Status: Rich countries have repeatedly pledged to give 0.7 percent of their national income as foreign aid, yet 17 of 22 donors have failed to reach that target. Some progress has occurred, however; European Union countries recently committed to attaining the 0.7 percent mark by 2015. Meanwhile other donors claim that poor countries are too corrupt to achieve economic growth. The table at the right helps to dispel that myth; in fact, many fast-growing Asian economies have higher levels of perceived corruption than some slow-growing African ones.

CORRUPTION AND ECONOMIC GROWTH		Rank of perceived corruption levels (lower means less corrupt)	Average yearly percent growth in GDP per capita, 1980–2000
Sub-Saharan Africa	Ghana	70	0.3
	Senegal	76	0.5
	Mali	78	−0.5
	Malawi	83	0.2
East Asia	India	83	3.5
	Pakistan	92	2.4
	Indonesia	122	3.5
	Bangladesh	133	2.0

GOAL 6: *THE MDG REPORT 2005 (graphs)*; GOAL 7: *GLOBAL MONITORING REPORT 2005: MDG: FROM CONSENSUS TO MOMENTUM (data)*; GOAL 8: *GLOBAL CORRUPTION REPORT*, BY TRANSPARENCY INTERNATIONAL, 2004 (table)

Figure 2 *continued*

Table 1   Foreign Aid: How Should the Money Be Spent?

Here is a breakdown of the needed investment for three typical low-income African countries to help them achieve the Millennium Development Goals. For all nations given aid, the average total annual assistance per person would come to around $110 a year. These investments would be financed by both foreign aid and the countries themselves.

Investment Area	Average per Year between 2005–2015 ($ per capita)		
	Ghana	Tanzania	Uganda
Hunger	7	8	6
Education	19	14	5
Gender equality	3	3	3
Health	25	35	34
Water supply and sanitation	8	7	5
Improving slum conditions	2	3	2
Energy	15	16	12
Roads	10	22	20
Other	10	10	10
Total	**100**	**117**	**106**

Calculated from data from *Investing in Development* [U.N. Millennium Project, Earthscan Publications, 2005]. Numbers do not sum to totals because of rounding.

If rich nations fail to make these investments, they will be called on to provide emergency assistance more or less indefinitely. They will face famine, epidemics, regional conflicts and the spread of terrorist havens. And they will condemn not only the impoverished countries but themselves as well to chronic political instability, humanitarian emergencies and security risks.

When polled, Americans greatly overestimate how much foreign aid the U.S. gives—by as much as 30 times.

The debate is now shifting from the basic diagnosis of extreme poverty and the calculations of financing needs to the practical matter of how assistance can best be delivered. Many people believe that aid efforts failed in the past and that care is needed to avoid the repetition of failure. Some of these concerns are well grounded, but others are fueled by misunderstandings.

When pollsters ask Americans how much foreign aid they think the U.S. gives, they greatly overestimate the amount by as much as 30 times. Believing that so much money has been donated and so little has been done with it, the public concludes that these programs have "failed." The reality is rather different. U.S. official assistance to sub-Saharan Africa has been running at $2 billion to $4 billion a year, or roughly $3 to $6 for every African. Most of this aid has come in the form of "technical cooperation" (which goes into the pockets of consultants), food contributions for famine victims and the cancellation of unpaid debts. Little of this support has come in a form that can be invested in systems that improve health, nutrition, food production and transport. We should give foreign aid a fair chance before deciding whether it works or not.

A second common misunderstanding concerns the extent to which corruption is likely to eat up the donated money. Some foreign aid in the past has indeed ended up in the equivalent of Swiss bank accounts. That happened when the funds were provided for geopolitical reasons rather than development; a good example was U.S. support for the corrupt regime of Mobutu Sese Seko of Zaire (now the Democratic Republic of the Congo) during part of the cold war. When assistance has been targeted at development rather than political goals, the outcomes have been favorable, ranging from the Green Revolution to the eradication of smallpox and the recent near-eradication of polio.

The aid package we advocate would be directed toward those countries with a reasonable degree of good governance and operational transparency. In Africa, these countries include Ethiopia, Ghana, Mali, Mozambique, Senegal and Tanzania. The money would not be merely thrown at them. It would be provided according to a detailed and monitored plan, and new rounds of financing would be delivered only as the work actually got done. Much of the funds would be given directly to villages and towns to minimize the chances of their getting diverted by central governments. All these programs should be closely audited.

Western society tends to think of foreign aid as money lost. But if supplied properly, it is an investment that will one day yield huge returns, much as U.S. assistance to western Europe and East Asia after World War II did. By prospering, today's impoverished countries will wean themselves from endless charity. They will contribute to the international advance of science, technology and trade. They will escape political instability, which leaves many of them vulnerable to violence, narcotics trafficking, civil war and even terrorist takeover. Our own security will be bolstered as well. As U.N. Secretary-General Kofi Annan wrote earlier this year: "There will be no development without security, and no security without development."

The author, **Jeffrey D. Sachs,** directs the Earth Institute at Columbia University and the United Nations Millennium Project. An economist, Sachs is well known for advising governments in Latin America, eastern Europe, the former Soviet Union, Asia and Africa on economic reforms and for his work with international agencies to promote poverty reduction, disease control and debt reduction in poor countries. A native of Detroit, he received his B.A., M.A. and Ph.D. degrees from Harvard University.

Welfare Redux

Back in 1996, we were pessimistic about reform. We were wrong. But new rules pushed through this year may confirm our worst fears.

CHRISTOPHER JENCKS, JOE SWINGLE, AND SCOTT WINSHIP

When welfare reform passed in 1996, critics (including all of us) feared a substantial increase in material hardship among single mothers and their children. We were wrong. Six years ago, after reviewing dozens of government surveys, two of us wrote in these pages that the record was neither as grim as critics had feared nor as encouraging as advocates had promised. [See Christopher Jencks and Joe Swingle, "Without a Net," *TAP*, January 2000.] The welfare rolls had been cut by almost half, material hardship had declined, and the rise in out-of-wedlock childbearing seemed to have slowed.

At that time, however, the economy was still booming and the most stringent requirements of the 1996 legislation had not yet been implemented. Skeptics therefore continued to fear that once the next recession arrived and the new law's requirements were fully implemented a lot more single mothers would start turning up in homeless shelters or would have to send their children to live with grandma.

Now the economy has been through a fairly long (though rather shallow) recession, and the requirements of the 1996 legislation are all in effect. Reviewing the evidence collected since 2000, we have found that single mothers were indeed worse off when unemployment peaked in 2003 than they had been in 2000. (Could it have been otherwise?) But single mothers were no worse off in 2003 than they had been in 1996, before welfare reform.

About 4.5 million families were getting welfare in 1996. Today, as chart 1 shows, that figure has fallen by two-thirds. Because the welfare rolls have dropped so dramatically, welfare is no longer a major political issue. As far as the public is concerned, the problem has gone away. Nonetheless, when the 1996 legislation had to be renewed in 2002, Congress was so polarized that it could not agree

on what to do. With Republicans in control of Congress and the White House, the obvious solution might have been to declare welfare reform a success and leave the law unchanged. Had the three of us been in charge, the obvious solution would have been to make work-supports more generous. But conservative Republicans wanted to make it even harder for single mothers to get welfare, and most Democrats objected.

This impasse was finally broken last fall when the Republicans incorporated their welfare proposals into the budget reconciliation agreement for 2006. This maneuver prevented a Democratic filibuster in the Senate, and the changes passed in February. The biggest change is a requirement that the number of people receiving Temporary Assistance to Needy Families (TANF) without engaging in "work-related activities" should be no more than half a state's 2005 caseload. States can meet this requirement either by putting recipients to work or pushing them off the rolls entirely. Since today's TANF recipients are mostly hard to employ, putting them to work will be difficult and expensive. Pushing them off the rolls will be cheaper and easier.

State officials' temptation to choose the cheap alternative will be exacerbated if Congress adopts the administration's recent budget proposals for the next five years. After adjusting for inflation, these proposals would reduce federal grants to the states by 8 to 13 percent over the next five years. If the economy continues to grow—a big "if"—state revenues should grow enough to cover the reductions in federal funding. But given all the competing claims on states' resources, the new federal work requirements for single mothers may well bring about the hardships that liberals have been predicting since 1996. Before turning to that possibility, however, we need to say a little more about what has happened over the past decade.

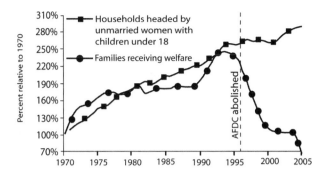

Chart 1: The Number of Households Receiving Welfare. At a 35-year low.

Sources: U.S. Department of Health and Human Services and Current Population Reports

Declining Poverty

Until 1996, most cash assistance for single mothers came from Aid to Families with Dependent Children (AFDC). In 1996 Congress replaced AFDC with a new program called Temporary Assistance to Needy Families. TANF established federal time limits and work requirements, and it allowed states to set requirements even more stringent than the federal ones. Several million single mothers left the welfare rolls between 1996 and 2000, and many other women who had recently become single mothers or lost their job decided not to apply for benefits or applied but were "diverted" into a job-search program. (Unlike AFDC, TANF does not give indigent mothers a "right" to welfare.)

Chart 2 shows our estimates of how the poverty rate changed for single mothers. Unlike the official poverty count, our estimates subtract taxes from income and add the Earned Income Tax Credit (EITC), food stamps, and

the estimated value of school lunches and housing subsidies. Our estimates are also based on household income rather than family income, so they include the income of live-in boyfriends. Finally, our estimates adjust the poverty thresholds for inflation using a slightly better price index than the one used to make the official estimates.

The square line in chart 2 shows that our measure of poverty among single mothers fell from 21 percent in 1996 to 15 percent in 2000. The rate rose again during the recession, but it was still only 17 percent when unemployment peaked in 2003. The Census Bureau has not yet released the data we need to calculate our poverty rate for 2004 but the official rate for single mothers rose slightly between 2003 and 2004, and we predict ours will do the same thing. No poverty data for 2005 will be available until next fall.

The circle line in chart 2 tells a different story. It shows the percentage of single mothers with incomes less than 70 percent of the poverty line, a condition we call "severe" poverty. Instead of falling between 1996 and 2003, severe poverty rose slightly. This apparent contradiction reflects a crucial fact about the past decade. While most single mothers have more money today than their counterparts had in 1996, the poorest mothers do not. Tighter work requirements will make this problem even worse if states meet the new federal requirements by pushing families off the welfare rolls entirely.

Chart 3 helps explain why these changes occurred. The square line shows a dramatic increase in the fraction of single mothers who reported that they had worked during the previous year and that no one in their household had received money from public assistance. The poverty rate for such mothers was 7.6 percent in 1996 and 7.4 percent in 2003, so as more single mothers moved into this category the poverty rate for all single mothers fell. (Readers should bear in mind that our poverty counts include live-in boyfriends' earnings. The poverty rate for single mothers who had to rely entirely on their own earnings would be more than 7 percent.)

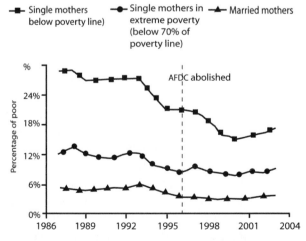

Chart 2: Poverty Among Single Mothers. Risen slightly since 2000 but still much lower than 1996; extreme poverty slightly higher than 1996.

Source: Annual March Current Population Surveys

Chart 3: Employment Among Single Mothers. Down since 2000, but much higher than in 1996.

Sources: Annual March Current Population Surveys and authors' tabulations

The circle line in chart 3 shows the fraction of single mothers who reported no income during the previous year from *either* work *or* welfare. This group also grew. Fortunately, most of these mothers lived with someone else who helped pay their bills, so "only" 44 percent of them had household incomes below the poverty line. But some of these mothers were very poor indeed. In the years between 1996 and 2003, roughly one in 10 reported that her total household income was less than $2,500. The growth of this group helps explain the rise in severe poverty.

Of course, $2,500 worth of goods and services is not enough to keep a mother and child alive for a year, so we cannot take these reports literally. Some of these mothers had other income that they did not report, either because it was illegal, because they worked off the books, because they had a boyfriend whose presence they did not mention, because they got money from a parent about whom the Census Bureau does not ask, or because the household's principal breadwinner had recently moved out. (The Census does not ask about the income of people who lived in the household last year but no longer live there at the time of its March survey.) That said, we still need to know far more than we now do about who these mothers are, why they are not getting TANF benefits, how they survive, and how their children are faring.

Not Moving in Tandem

Although chart 2 suggests that most single mothers had slightly more resources in 2003 than in 1996, those who went to work also had more expenses. Working mothers usually have to pay for transportation from home to work, and most of them also have to spend more on clothing. Furthermore, while child care subsidies rose between 1995 and 2003, subsidized child care is not always available at the time and place where a working mother needs it, so out-of-pocket spending on child care often rose. If single mothers' work-related expenses rose as much as their incomes, they would not have had any more money left for food, housing, or children's sneakers than they did before. Indeed, some of them may have ended up with less discretionary income than before.

Health-insurance coverage is another important determinant of a mother's expenses. If going to work meant that fewer single mothers were covered, as it did right after welfare reform, medical bills could have eaten up working mothers' extra income. Indeed, some mothers might have gone without the medical care they previously would have received. We measure trends in health-insurance coverage by calculating the proportion of the people with insurance in each single mother's household. This proportion hardly changed: It averaged 79.7 percent in 1996, 80.2 percent

Major Conditions Attached to TANF Block Grants

Work Requirements: States must have a plan to make recipients engage in "work-related activities" once they have received TANF for 24 months. States also had to ensure that the number of recipients engaged in such activities was equal to a specified share of their 1995 caseload, which reached 50 percent in 2002. Reductions in the caseload since 1995 could, however, also be counted toward this goal. Under the legislation adopted in February 2006, states must ensure that the number of recipients engaged in work-related activities is half their 2005 caseload rather than their 1995 caseload, and they can only count caseload reductions since 2005 toward this goal.

Lifetime Limits: Families may receive federally funded benefits for a maximum of five years. TANF allows states to set shorter lifetime limits. It also allows states to exempt up to 20 percent of their caseload from the five-year limit.

Eligibility: Legal immigrants with less than five years of residence, unmarried teenage mothers not living with a parent or guardian, and unmarried teenage mothers who have dropped out of high school cannot receive *federal* benefits, although states can (and often do) provide recent immigrants with benefits from state funds.

in 2000, and 80 percent in 2004. The proportion of single mothers with Medicaid coverage fell from 1996 to 2000, but by 2004 it had climbed back to its 1996 level. These statistics do not suggest that welfare reform cut single mothers' insurance coverage. But insurance does not cover everything. Because the cost of medical care rose faster than most other prices during these years, single mothers' out-of-pocket costs probably rose too.

One way to see if single mothers *felt* richer in 2004 than in 1996 is to see whether more of them thought they could afford a place of their own. This is not a measure of material well-being. A single mother who lives in someone else's home often has more creature comforts than a mother who has a place of her own. Single mothers want their own place because they want control. If a mother has a place of her own with her name on the lease, she can evict a boyfriend who misbehaves or stops helping pay the rent. If his name is on the lease, her material standard of living may be higher, but he has the whip hand in domestic negotiations. The same logic applies when a single mother lives with her mother. If a single mother lives in her mother's home, her mother is in charge and she may often be treated as if she were still a child. If she has her own place and lets her mother live with her, she feels like a grown-up.

The proportion of single mothers who headed their own households showed no clear trend between 1995 and 2005. About a sixth of all single mothers lived with relatives (usually one or both parents). Another 4 or 5 percent lived in a non-relative's household. The rest headed their own household. The fact that declining poverty was not accompanied by an increase in the fraction of mothers with their own household suggests that discretionary income did not rise much in the bottom part of the distribution.

Getting Enough to Eat

The U.S. Department of Agriculture (USDA) has paid the Census Bureau to conduct a "food security" survey every year since 1995. The survey asks more than 40 questions about whether households had trouble getting enough to eat during the previous 12 months. The April 1997 survey covers the period just before and after August 1996, when Congress replaced AFDC with TANF.

The problem that single mothers reported most frequently was running short of money and having to "stretch" food. Except for an upward blip in the December 2001 survey, this problem declined steadily, affecting only 44 percent of single mothers in 2003 compared to 57 percent in 1995. In 1995 even households near the middle of the income distribution for single mothers often reported this problem. Since these mothers' real income rose 15 percent between 1995 and 2003, the fact that they were less likely to report such problems in 2003 is no surprise.

Other problems the USDA asks about range from worrying that food will run out before the end of the month to reporting that a child went hungry for an entire day. Almost all these problems declined between April 1995 and April 2001. Almost all of them also rose during the recession. They were about as common in December 2003 as they had been in April 1997, but less common than they had been in April 1995. In 1997, for example, 26.9 percent of single mothers said they had worried that they would run out of food before the end of the month. In 2003 the figure was 27.6 percent—a tiny increase. At the other end of the severity scale, 2.4 percent of mothers said in April 1997 that a child in their household had gone hungry for an entire day during the past 12 months. In December 2003 the figure was 2 percent—a tiny decrease. The stability of these numbers is consistent with what we saw when we looked at health insurance and at having a place of one's own in which to live. Taken together, these facts suggest that living standards did not change much between 1996 and 2003 for single mothers in the bottom part of the income distribution.

If living standards have not changed for low-income single mothers, the apparent fall in the poverty rate shown in chart 2 is obviously misleading. The same must be true of the Census Bureau's poverty estimates for single mothers, which declined even more than ours and have been widely cited by defenders of welfare reform. The most obvious way of reconciling a declining poverty rate with stable levels of material hardship is to recognize that work-related expenses, which the Census Bureau does not measure, rose after 1996.

But work-related expenses may not be the only reason why our measures of living conditions failed to improve. Because of the EITC, most single mothers with jobs get a substantial check soon after they file their tax return. (Recipients are allowed to take the credit monthly rather than annually, but few do.) Recipients often use their EITC check to make a down payment on a car they can use to get to a better job, on a new living room set, or on other "big-ticket" items. As a result, the monthly income they use for food and rent may then be no higher than it was when they were on welfare.

One final caveat. Our findings do not show that welfare reform per se lowered poverty or left living conditions largely unchanged. Welfare reform was not a laboratory experiment in which everything else remained constant. It was accompanied by a lot of other legislation aimed at helping low-wage workers and their children. Congress had raised the Earned Income Tax Credit in 1993, and single mothers got more EITC money as more of them went to work. Medicaid coverage of low-income children expanded steadily because of changes enacted before 1996. Congress also raised the minimum wage within days of passing welfare reform. Low-wage workers' access to Medicaid also improved after 1996. Without all these changes, welfare reform might well have lowered living standards, just as liberals feared.

Defending the Two-Parent Family

For many conservatives the primary goal of welfare reform was not to improve single mothers' standard of living but to make them work for what they already got. This idea had overwhelming public support, and the United States has clearly moved in that direction since 1996. The late 1990s were the first economic boom in decades when employment increased faster among single mothers than married mothers. After the boom ended, some single mothers lost their jobs and had a hard time finding new ones. But work remains more common than it has ever been before.

But some conservatives also hoped that forcing single mothers to work would discourage out-of-wedlock childbearing and encourage marriage. For these traditionalists, welfare-reform legislation that raised single mothers' material standard of living would have seemed counterproductive, because it would have made single motherhood even more economically attractive than AFDC had.

According to the National Center for Health Statistics, the birth rate among unmarried women of childbearing age rose almost continuously from 1940 until 1994. It declined briefly between 1994 and 1996, *before* TANF replaced AFDC, and was basically flat from 1996 to 2002. It jumped in both 2003 and 2004, however, and was higher in 2004 than in 1992. The timing of these changes has no obvious relationship to the timing of welfare reform, but that may be because lots of other things also changed during these years.

If we compare blacks to non-Hispanic whites, we see a more striking pattern. In 1994, unmarried black mothers were considerably more likely than unmarried white mothers to receive AFDC. Thus if welfare reform made single motherhood less attractive, blacks should have been more affected than whites. And that may be what we see. The birth rate among unmarried white women was flat between 1994 and 2003. The birth rate among unmarried black women declined 18 percent. As a result, nonmarital births have accounted for a declining fraction of all black births since 1994. These racial differences suggest that welfare reform may have had an impact on nonmarital childbearing after all—a small impact among whites that is offset by other factors, but a larger impact among blacks that is not fully offset by those factors. Still, the evidence is hardly conclusive.

What Next?

Welfare reform may not have had a big impact on single mothers' typical living conditions, but it transformed the political landscape. For the past 10 years the political action has almost all been in state capitals, not Washington, D.C. Once TANF gave states more control over welfare, most governors concluded that the best way to look good to the electorate was to cut the welfare rolls as rapidly as possible, and that was what they did. Unlike AFDC, which gave a state more federal money when it spent more of its own money, TANF gave states a fixed amount of federal money based on what they had received in the last years of AFDC. Under TANF, therefore, cutting the welfare rolls left states with more federal money for child care, job training, and other programs that help single mothers hold jobs.

In theory, TANF block grants were always contingent on a state's meeting federal work requirements and enforcing federal time limits. Since 2002 states have had to ensure that the number of families getting TANF and not participating in "work-related activities" was less than

half the number getting AFDC in 1995. Now they will have to ensure that the number of people getting TANF and not participating in work-related activities is less than half the number getting TANF in 2005. The Congressional Research Service estimates that the new rules will raise the number of families facing work requirements by 70 percent. Because today's TANF recipients tend to have more problems than the typical AFDC recipient had in 1995, moving today's recipients into the labor force will be harder. It is unclear how many states will resist the temptation to just push these families off the rolls entirely.

> **Welfare is no longer the poverty trap that it was, but it is less of a safety net. As other federal funds are cut, the safety net will become more threadbare.**

For welfare reform's critics, time limits have traditionally been an even bigger worry than work requirements. States can exempt 20 percent of their caseload from the five-year lifetime limit on TANF benefits. But the 20 percent figure was not based on much evidence about how many recipients could really be expected to work. Nobody knew. Critics of welfare reform therefore worried about what would happen to mothers who reached their lifetime limit but were caring for a sick child or a frail parent; were sick themselves; or were too disturbed, too addicted to alcohol or drugs, or too slow-witted to hold a job.

Mothers began hitting the TANF time limit in 2001. Thus far, states appear to have managed this problem pretty successfully, using a combination of the 20 percent exemption, transfers to disability programs, and transfers to state-funded programs for the hard-to-employ. Recent reports by the Department of Health and Human Services indicate that very few TANF cases have been closed due to time limits, and some of those cases were transferred to state-funded programs.

The main reason welfare reform has hurt so few families is that the combination of rising wages and work supports like the EITC and child-care subsidies made work an economically viable option for single mothers who could hold a job. But the damage was also limited by the fact that states had enough flexibility to shelter mothers they judged incapable of working. That flexibility is now being reduced dramatically. The economic fate of single mothers is now tied to the business cycle in the same way as that of other working-age parents. Welfare is no longer the poverty trap that it was, but it is also less of a safety net. As other federal funds aimed at the poor are cut, the safety net will become even more threadbare.

By the time Congress abolished AFDC in 1996, everyone hated it. Liberals hated it for being too stingy. Conservatives hated it for supporting the undeserving. The public hated it for promoting idleness instead of work. Recipients hated it for forcing them to cheat in order to survive and then treating them like dirt because it suspected them of cheating. Nobody wept when it died.

But TANF was also a compromise that pleased neither liberals nor conservatives. Liberals thought that its time limits and work requirements would, as Senator Daniel Patrick Moynihan famously said, leave "tens on tens of thousands" of children sleeping on grates. Gingrich Republicans thought it was nowhere near tough enough.

President Bill Clinton, who vetoed the Republicans' initial proposals, eventually signed the bill even though he thought it was a bad piece of legislation—because he thought it was still better than AFDC. For the past decade that has probably been true. Whether it will remain true is an open question.

CHRISTOPHER JENCKS teaches social policy at Harvard University's Kennedy School of Government. He is working on a book about the social consequences of economic inequality. JOSEPH SWINGLE is Visiting Assistant Professor of Sociology at Wellesley College. SCOTT WINSHIP is a doctoral candidate in social policy at Harvard's Kennedy School, and a co-founder of New Vision, a new student-led think tank on social policy (see www.newvisioninstitute.org).

Virtual Equality, Virtual Segregation

NORMAN KELLEY

If one reads Charles Johnson's essay regarding the black American condition, one can see the critical fault lines. Despite a number of blacks doing well or okay (just a pay check or two from disaster), roughly 25 to 33 percent of African Americans are still stuck in poverty and social dysfunction. Bill Cosby's comments regarding the black poor merely underscored the subterranean class conflict in black America. Sociologist E. Essien-Udom, however, aptly outlined this situation in *Black Nationalism: A Search for Identity* (1962). Essien-Udom saw how lower-class blacks were defining themselves differently from the ideals and mores of middle-class blacks (and this may well be the roots of hip-hop culture):

> . . . [L]ower class Negroes are beginning to define themselves in relationship to the Negro "image" portrayed by the middle-class and are attracted to it[;] they are also repelled by it because their actual conditions do not permit identification with the middle-class Negroes. As it is in their relations with the white society, lower-class Negroes tend to withdraw and disassociate themselves from the middle and upper class Negroes. This estrangement suggests the beginning of class conflict among the Negro masses, directed not against white, but against the Negro middle and upper classes. This development aggravates tensions in the Negro community and produces distrust of the middle-class leadership among lower class Negroes. . . . These Negroes feel powerless not only in relation to the white power complex but also to what appears to them as the monopoly of power by middle-class Negro leadership.

The condition of black America is mixed: success and failure. While Mr. Johnson spends a great deal of time looking at what some people call the lack of "personal responsibility" in the black community, both African American politics and civil society—the bonds of solidarity in chains—have collapsed, and blacks refuse to deal openly with their class chasm. African Americans are in deep denial or ignorance as to what has and hasn't been accomplished in the last 40 years. Embarrassingly

for today's black middle class, hip-hop music and culture has been the most dynamic but problematic creation that blacks have produced while effective black politics and leadership itself has come to a dead end.

A greater failure, however, is black leadership's inability and unwillingness to confront this as a problem and devise something new; this situation underscores how utterly bankrupt black leadership is. Perhaps that should not be too surprising. As Robert C. Smith wrote in *We Have No Leaders,* "Black leaders are integrated but their core community is segregated, impoverished and increasingly in the post-civil rights era marginalized, denigrated and criminalized."

This became abundantly clear when thousands of mostly black New Orleanians were left stranded during Hurricane Katrina; those who survived were treated as mere afterthoughts as it took four or five days to provide them with emergency provisions and evacuation. That President Bush could even joke about his partying days in Houston at a press briefing on the tarmac of New Orleans' airport, at a time of tragedy, underscores his callous disregard for a group of people who neither look like him nor share his class position, neither his Christian piety nor "compassionate conservatism" with much standing.

That swatches of American society are locked into Third World-like poverty conditions became evident in the aftermath of Hurricane Katrina. Those who had cars could easily leave the city, but those without immediate transportation, mostly blacks, had to ride out the storm and suffer the consequences of incompetent disaster planning and coordination. While it may be understandable that some blacks looted stores to get necessary provisions, it didn't help that some were running riot on other blacks, impeding rescue operations.

As reported by the *New York Times:* "Little attention was paid to moving out New Orleans's 'low-mobility' population—the elderly, the infirm and the poor without cars or other means of fleeing the city, about 100,000 people. At disaster planning meetings, said [a consultant to the state's evacuation plan], 'the answer was often silence.'" Yet the fact that that city's black leaders—elected officials and those of civil society (churches, social organizations, businesses)—never sought to improvise an evacuation plan within that 'low mobility' population may well underscore how black leadership and mobilization have atrophied.

New York *Daily News* columnist Errol Louis said in regard to "The ugly truth":

> In far too many cities, including New Orleans, the marching orders on the front lines of American race relations are to control and contain the very poor in ghettos as cheaply as possible; ignore them completely if possible; and call in the troops if the brutes get out of line.

Put another way, the "core community" of black leaders exists in *virtual segregation* while the black middle class enjoys *virtual equality,* and the black elite, which includes most black leaders, are truly integrated. The core community, however, is in the throes of "asset accumulation deficiency." In addition to addressing this issue, black leadership, local and national, elected and non-elected leaders, will also have to address the problem of lawlessness in some impoverished black communities. While noting that the affects of racism are legitimate, African-American leadership has long neglected or shunned any effort or debate regarding internal redevelopment of impoverished black communities.

At this point in time and history, African Americans have no viable political and economic program or platform to withstand the resurgent phenomenon of white nationalism, an aspect of the conservative movement that has been developing in the country in plain sight for the last four decades. As Carol Swain noted in *The New White Nationalism in America:*

> Republicans have repeatedly demonstrated the party's ability to attract a significant majority of white votes whenever it champions racially tinged issues such as welfare and immigration reform, affirmative action, and crime reduction. Many of these Republican supporters have been attracted to the party's racially conservative policies out of a concern and belief that the interests of white people are being trampled on by an insensitive government, a theme common among white nationalists.

And one can be sure that among such people, especially bloggers, the criminal-minded activities of some blacks in New Orleans were highlighted more so than the general plight of those who were left stranded.

Since the 1960s black America has banked its well-being and advancement in alliance with what Bayard Rustin called the coalition that staged the "March on Washington." In a 1965 *Commentary* article, "From Protest to Politics," Rustin wrote: "We need allies. The future of the Negro struggle depends on whether the contradictions of this society can be resolved by a coalition of progressive forces which becomes the effective political majority in the United States. I speak of the same coalition which staged the March on Washington, passed the Civil Rights Act, and laid the basis for the Johnson landslide—Negroes, trade unionists, liberals and religious groups." That alliance has netted very little in the last 25 years since the rise of the New Right to power and influence.

Coalitions and Allies

Except for *Brown v. the Board of Education* (1954) and the two landmark pieces of civil rights legislation of 1964 and 1965, nearly everything that had been legislated to ameliorate the situation of blacks and others has been chipped away, undermined, or de-legitimized. Effective black politics has come to a dead end, which was, sotto voce, an objective of the conservative movement.

The 2004 election consolidated the conservatives' grip on the White House, the two chambers of Congress, the judiciary, the governorships, and state legislatures. The recent election was the triumph of conservative politics, which had crashed and burned during the 1964 election of Barry Goldwater. But it steadily marched onward to the election of Ronald Reagan as the first leader of post-civil rights "redeemer" government; Bush is merely the second, but with a more profound agenda, which seems to have imploded.

With the Clinton years as an interregnum, the Republicans have held power during most of the last 25 years, and have consistently organized at the top—think tanks and media infrastructure—and have developed "boots on the ground": evangelical Christian social conservatives. Their achievement has been spectacular. After World War II, conservatism was routinely disregarded by pundits and by the liberal consensus as the disposition of cranks that once dominated American political discourse from the Civil War until the Depression.

But as former Democratic party national chairman Donald L. Fowler admitted, in light of the 2004 election: "I think we have come to an ending point in the long transition that began in 1968. During that time, the old Roosevelt Democratic majority has creaked and cracked away under various kinds of racial, religious, social and international forces, and this election was the end point in that transition. I think we live in a country that is majority Republican now."

The country has entered into a postmodern version of the Jim Crow era. Blacks now have an edgy virtual equality with whites in a country that purports to be about "color-blindness" equal opportunity. In reality, however, it practices white nationalism, which uses unofficial power and official power of the state to maintain white privilege.

Race was less of a wedge in the 2004 election because "racial issues"—affirmative action, crime, and welfare (codes for blacks)—had been neutralized, no longer seen as an albatross around the necks of Democrats, courtesy of Bill Clinton and the Democratic Leadership Council. Instead, the new "black issue" or major wedge issue was gay marriage. This election was also a black-and-white replay of 1960s white backlash politics in response to the Civil Rights movement. However, this time the beast that stirred the ire of good, decent, Christian (read mostly white) folk was not the threat of miscegenation but of same-sex. The boogeyman of social conservatives, the "homosexual agenda," had materialized in a Massachusetts court that sanctioned equality for homosexuals in regard to marriage, which became the red meat drawing the faithful to the polls.

That racial issues were de-politicized did not mean that blacks and whites had achieved comity. In reality, it meant that blacks and black aspirations were no longer an issue that had to be contended with or addressed. Blacks had already been neutralized during the Clinton years, and the voting interests of blacks were not vigorously protected by the Democrats during the 2000 election. John Kerry even threw in the towel when there were still outstanding votes to be counted in the 2004 election.

As black nationalism came to an impasse in the mid-1970s, suppressed by the state and also due to its own ideological incoherence, a more resurgent nationalism has made itself known, and it has had a profound effect on American society, and on African Americans in particular. The rise of conservatism in the last 40 years is predicated on the reemergence of white nationalism, rooted in the backlash politics of the civil rights era.

Ronald Walters, a political scientist at the University of Maryland (College Park), has outlined this phenomenon in *White Nationalism, Black Interests* (Wayne State University Press, 2003). Walters defines white nationalism as a "radical aspect of the Conservatism movement to use both unofficial power and the official power of the state to maintain White Supremacy by subordinating Blacks and other non-whites."

Walters argues that the reemergence of white nationalism came about due to the rising status of African Americans, and the use of the federal government to assist blacks. In the world of zero sum politics, a positive change in the status of blacks meant a loss for whites either psychologically or in redistributive policies. And one can see the outlines of such in the claims of "reverse racism," the use of the Confederate flag, and Christianity, as a rallying banner in the "cultural wars" against the homosexual and multicultural agenda. One should also note the use of Christianity in the ideological meandering of some on the

extreme right who consider whites the real chosen people and blacks and others as "mud people."

Almost every policy—affirmative action, welfare, minority set-asides, etc.—that has come into existence via the federal government to assist blacks has been attacked, chipped away, de-legitimized by the conservative movement, some using coded racial references ("welfare," "underclass," "crime," "quota queen," Willie Horton).

This resurgence has its roots in white southerners decamping the Democratic party and becoming Republicans, and Republicans using a "southern strategy" to attract them. Ronald Reagan began his 1980 presidential campaign in the same county in Mississippi where three civil rights workers had been slain by the Klan. Reagan even talked about states rights, often used by white southerners to keep blacks in a subordinate position without the benefit of federal intervention.

The Reagan-Bush years are often viewed as the first triumph of the New Right, the obtainment of state power, which led to the diminution of federal power and programs to help blacks. The recent reelection of George W. Bush is the consolidation of that power, assisted by his base of mostly white Christian evangelicals (who mostly attend all white churches). While some cited gay rights and abortion as evidence of lack of morality in America, a fair amount of them began voting GOP when the Democrats assisted blacks in obtaining their right to vote and become full citizens during the 1960s.

Historian Dan Carter outlined such in *From George Wallace to Newt Gingrich: Race in the Counter-Revolution, 1963–1993*. Carter noted how the GOP, especially the Darth Vader of American politics, Richard Nixon, understood the impact that Alabama democrat Governor George Wallace's volatile mixture of race, populism, and anti-intellectualism was having on American politics, and how it attracted whites outside of the South. Since then, Republicans have engaged in what Carter terms the "soft porn of racism," the coded use of race for political purpose, a legacy bequeathed to them by Wallace and the political culture of the South.

Tucked away, hidden in the psycho and political dynamics of race, is the phenomenon of metaracism, coined by Joel Kovel (*White Racism*, 1984). American society has progressed to the point where dominative racism, direct oppression, has mostly ceased. Instead, today, metaracism is the mode of action, and this mode of action accommodates indirect racial oppression or exclusion through economic and technocratic means. Lopping off millions from the welfare rolls, the high rate of black incarceration, or the bogus disenfranchisement of blacks are coldly performed by public policies, law, technocrats, or by the structure of the economy. Little does it matter whether the intent is to cause harm to blacks as long as the outcome is such. Race was not sublimated in this election; it just no longer mattered. Rather, the black political agenda, predicated on what Rustin saw as needing allies, has gone down to a resounding defeat.

Roots of Virtual Segregation

No one can deny that some racial reforms have been made, but when American public schools are as segregated as they were fifty years ago, the touting of progress rings hollow. And it is no small wonder that the greatest unrecognized achievement of the Civil Rights movement is the unintended consequences of convincing white Americans that racism is no longer a serious social and structural problem in the United States.

Racism has always been defined and viewed, at least by whites, as personal prejudice expressed by one individual against another, not as a concept that benefits the vast number of whites at the expense of blacks.

The ambiguity of contemporary racial practices can be described as "now you see it, now you don't." The most egregious forms of white racism have been eradicated (but reinforced through the economy and public policy). Most white Americans, convinced that they themselves have lived up to Martin Luther King's soaring rhetoric more so than blacks, particularly in regard to judging people "by the contents of their character," see no need to deal with the problem of racism. To many of them, racism has meant a white individual doing something bad against a black individual, and blacks have become a class of chronic complainers.

Yet structural inequality (a.k.a. white privilege) remains and it is that which has been the hardest to confront because it tends to be invisible, and whites have a vested interest in keeping it invisible. It provides whites with the privilege of being white, or, more exactly, not being black. One aspect of a "Plausible Deniability" program, as Debra Dickerson explained in *The End of Blackness,* is to see racism solely as an intentional individual phenomenon, but not as "a sense of group position" or the "organized accumulation of racial advantage." And it is "a system," argues Michael Brown and others in *Whitewashing Race: The Myth of a Colorblind Society,* "best understood by observing actual behavior."

Written by a team of seven scholars with expertise in sociology, economics, law, education, and political science, *Whitewashing* challenges the conventional wisdom that has been propagated by those whom the authors call "racial realists": Jim Sleeper, Tamar Jacoby, Dinesh D'Souza, Shelby Steele and, most importantly, Abigail and Stephen Thernstrom. The conventional wisdom of this group is argued under the rubric of individual black failure or "personal responsibility."

Whitewashing builds its case on the related concepts of "accumulation" and "disaccumulation." Ever since the founding of the republic, whites, then white males, have been invested in, given preferential treatment merely by being considered citizens under the U.S. Constitution, which did not apply to blacks, free or enslaved, as argued by the infamous 1857 Dred Scott case. In labor markets and in other realms, whites engage in "opportunity hoarding" which allows a group to "acquire and monopolize access to valuable resources and privileges." People understand that access to jobs and important information are also predicated on personal, familial, and network associations that tend to keep others outside those informal relationships.

By a process of inversion, blacks, collectively and as individuals, have been disinvested. This has been going on for three centuries prior to the civil rights era. Now, in the last 30 years or so, years of disaccumulation are discounted as malingering. Considered less than whites, denied opportunities in or access to education, work, housing, healthcare, political representation, disinvestment has accumulated over the years for blacks, even for those who are considered to have made it.

Blacks are still discriminated against in housing, and housing segregation, despite whites rhetoric to the contrary, still confirms that most whites do not care to be neighbors of even the most successful blacks, the very people who supposedly epitomize personal responsibility. This situation has had a cumulative effect on education since most taxes for education are derived from local property taxes, which means that blacks, especially those segregated in inner cities, are given an inferior education. As Brown noted: "White Americans may support the principle of fair housing, but less than half say they are willing to act on this principle. In fact, when actual patterns of racial isolations are examined, it is clear that very few whites prefer integrated to segregated neighborhoods."

Examining crime and justice, employment, education, housing, poverty, political representation and their intersection with race, the scholars of *Whitewashing* peel away the cloak of invisibility and show empirically, by way of facts and figures, that present-day racial inequalities have little to do with individual black failure. They are rooted in the sociological reality that whites, as a group, have advantages for themselves and "because these benefits seem so natural that they are taken for granted, experienced as wholly legitimate."

Whites simultaneously see and refuse to acknowledge "how race permeates America's institutions—the very rules of the game—and its distribution of opportunities and wealth." Blacks, however, are noticed as the "other," as a race, but whiteness is invisible. It has only become noticed recently, however, because the historic investment in "whiteness," challenged by policies like affirmative action or greater political representation, threatens previously uncontested racial monopolization in regard to work, income, education and cultural capital. And it is white nationalism, a radical aspect of conservatism, which seeks to maintain its supremacy.

Virtual Equality

With the 13th, 14th and 15th Amendments that were added to the Constitution, along with Reconstruction era civil rights laws, the *Brown* decision, and the 1964 and 1965 Civil Rights Acts, blacks now have achieved virtual equality with their white counterparts. This form of equality comes with an emphasis on *virtual,* defined as being such in force or effect, though not actually or expressly such.

What does this mean exactly? It means that most blacks, while not living in an overt climate of racial exclusion, may have their abilities to maneuver only somewhat constricted by conservative politics, which preaches "colorblindness" but often uses official and unofficial power to hamper and constrict black aspirations via white nationalism or metaracism.

If one wants a general idea as to how this may come about, take, for example, the nearly 1,000 conservative lawyers that gathered at an annual convention of the Federalist Society in the aftermath of the GOP's victory. They celebrated Bush's reelection and the opportunities a second term would bring. Their views, as reported by the *New York Times,* "generally include opposition to affirmative action and abortion, support of stronger rights for property owners who complain that they are besieged by federal regulations, and insistence on greater respect for state powers relative to those of the federal government."

These 1,000 conservative lawyers are the foot soldiers that may well become jurists and officials at the Justice Department, people not too predisposed to the black political agenda as they have defined it. African Americans will not be discriminated against as a class, but as discrete individuals who will suffer the slings and arrows of policies that just happen to affect them more so than any set of individuals of a particular persuasion.

Except for a few friends, blacks are now alone, existing in a world somewhat analogous to the post-Reconstruction era, a situation that could have been predicted if people were willing to pay attention to the laws of African-American history: Any period of progress or racial reform will be followed by an era of reaction, as indicated by the last four decades of conservative politics.

The last four decades of American politics have seen the rise of conservative politics and the decline of the alliance that staged the March on Washington. Even more troubling, however, has been the decline of effective black politics in which the likes of Al Sharpton have risen to the position of the latest "Head Negro in Charge" (HNIC) of symbolic black politics.

White Shadows, Black Substance

Banking on black progress being in coalition with the usual suspects of American liberalism, African-American leadership never had to consider the necessity of internal redevelopment, of wrestling with the twin problems of social disorganization of the poor, and lack of black economic development. Welfare payments were supposed to attend to those on the bottom of the social well; affirmative action and minority set-asides would do the rest for the black middle class.

African-America leadership, ignoring the possibility of a return to a post-civil rights era of hostility to black advancement, never sat down and tried to strategize ideas and policies that would deal with the poor and economics. Today, a swath of the black population is still enmeshed in a web of social dysfunction, which DuBois outlined over a hundred years ago:

The great deficiency of the Negro, however, is his small knowledge of the art of social life—that last expression of human culture. His development in group life was abruptly broken off by the slave ship, directed into abnormal channels and dwarfed by the Black Codes, and suddenly wrenched anew by the Emancipation Proclamation. He finds himself, therefore, peculiarly weak in that nice adaptation of individual life to the life of the group which is the essence of civilization. This is shown in the grosser forms of sexual immorality, disease and crime, and also in the difficulty of race organization for common ends economic or in intellectual lines.

The numbers have gone down since the civil rights era, but as Bill Cosby put it: "The lower economic people are not holding up their end in this deal." Neither is the leadership class "holding up its end in this deal," Mr. Cosby. Today it has failed, and no better example of such a failure is the rise of Al Sharpton as a spokesman for blacks and/or the Democratic party, despite his years of corruption and cronyism, as well as dalliances with the Republican party. Despite the *Village Voice* and the *New York Times* reporting that Sharpton was playing footsie with the GOP, the black political elite said nothing. Despite his meager showing, lack of ideas and vote-getting in the primaries, he was rewarded by the party for one reason and one reason only at the Democratic National Convention: being entertaining.

Effective black politics came to an end when the Reagan administration assumed the reigns of power and blacks did not sufficiently mobilize the black community or rethink the paradigm of civil rights politics. What Sharpton represents is merely the rot and hollowness of black politics in full view, aided and abetted by whites (and market intellectuals like Cornel West) who know but refuse to say anything lest they be called racist. Here is liberal racism in full force.

African Americans are going to have to create a new vision for themselves beyond HNIC politics. In this vision, whites are going to have to be reduced to being white shadows; they are there but blacks are too busy focusing on black substance to care. A major problem is the lack of economic development, of which blacks are going to have to use their vaunted improvisational skills in music and sports to fashion a new economic arrangement or one conducive to their needs in a market society.

At this point and time in history, it is well understood that 25 percent to 33 percent of black Americans are still mired in poverty, yet roughly 60 percent are middle class (with 10 percent in the elite). It is questionable, however, whether the black middle class, which historically has been the leadership class, can socially and economically reproduce itself without programs such as affirmative action and minority set-asides, which have previously aided them.

Melvin Oliver and Thomas Shapiro have pointed out in *Black Wealth/White Wealth* that while middle-class blacks now enjoy higher incomes, they "earn seventy cents for every dollar earned by middle-class whites but they possess only fifteen cents for every dollar of wealth held by middle-class whites."

Despite a growing black middle class over the last forty years, African Americans tend to lag in business development, a major source of wealth opposed to mere income. According to a 2000 Milken Institute minority business report (prepared for the U.S. Commerce Dept.), blacks, while comprising 12.5 percent of the U.S. population, accounted for only 3.6 percent of businesses (according to recent Census data black business is 5 percent of all U.S. business). Hispanics (who have become the largest minority since 2000) were 11.0, but accounted for 4.5 percent of businesses. Asian Americans, 4.0 percent of the U.S. population, a third of the black population figure, held 3.5 percent of businesses in the United States. Also, according to the report, there were 1.4 million Latino-owned business, 1.1 million Asian and Native American businesses, but only 880,000 black-owned enterprises.

While highlighting that immigrant and minority firms were making inroads into "breakthrough industries,"

African Americans were noticeably absent in the report: "Someone of Indian or Chinese origin starts one in four of every new business endeavors." In other words, blacks are behind in the moneymaking technologies that have fueled economic activities in the last decade. Or put another way: black America needs to produce generations of nerds who'll invent products and applications more so than future generations of bling-blinging hip-hop artists and brawling athletes.

Most Africans Americans have achieved virtual equality, meaning they are no longer by dint of law or custom held in a permanent caste position and subjected to rank discrimination. Conversely, the black poor are virtually segregated not by law or custom but by circumstances (a combination of personal habits and structural inequities).

Perhaps Booker T. Washington's observation that "No race that has anything to offer to the markets of the world is long in any degree ostracized" ought to be reexamined. The Washington-DuBois debate was essentially over what sort of social/public policies or avenue of engagement would best benefit blacks. Washington advocated an industrial one, eschewing "social equality" as an "extreme folly." Once Washington passed from the scene, DuBois and the NAACP's (National Association for the Advancement of Colored People) agitation for integration became the dominant mode of social interaction—at the expense of establishing a set of ideas or policies regarding economic self-sufficiency.

DuBois, however, began to rethink his position on economics and segregation in light of the Great Depression. He began to advocate segregation as a means to defend black dignity and to argue for an economic agenda ("Cooperative Commonwealth"). However, the dominant mode of political mobilization was based on integration but there was no significant discussion regarding black economic development save for that coming under the rubric of "economic justice."

Economic justice is a naïve concept in an aggressive capitalist society like America. As Harold Cruse once pointed out, "Negro intellectuals produce . . . no original economic theorists who can cope realistically with either capitalism or socialism from a Negro point of view." No better example of this is the lack of promotion of "esusu" (or rotating credit association) as a way to help individuals accumulate capital when denied by lending institutions. Interestingly, this form of primitive accumulation is used by West Africans and West Indians. Yet despite years of Kwanzaa and Afrocentric thinking, most African Americans know nothing of this, and black leadership and intellectuals do not promote this as a form of collective financial mobilization. Even more astounding is that so-called hip-hop intellectuals—Cornel West, Michael Eric

Dyson, Mark Anthony Neal, and others—have never used their "critical" intellect to develop public policy proposals that could possibly have linked hip-hop entrepreneurship to empowerment/enterprise zones in the blighted areas of urban Bantustans.

The past presidential election underscores that the black political agenda of the last forty years, trying to use politics to influence the machinery of the federal government, has failed. This failure, however, does not mean that blacks ought totally to abandon politics; politics and economics in American society go hand in hand. Instead, blacks should also focus on developing ideas, policies, programs, and business models that will help themselves engage in an internal process of economic development (a.k.a. wealth creation), and deal with the social dysfunction of urban black communities.

However, this would entail an incredible level of introspection on behalf of black America, which has often oriented itself towards dealing with race and racism, but not with internal matters of self-criticism, reevaluation, and introspection. The lack of these critical abilities has been aided and abetted, despite increasing black consumer power, by a dearth of critical information/media infrastructure. Blacks have no real critical popular journals or websites of thought, politics, and economics compared to the cross-section of the mainstream: the *Nation, New Republic, Weekly Standard, Atlantic Monthly.*

For every *Negro Digest, Freedom Ways* or *Emerge* that has come and gone, more and more hair care, hiphop or fashion magazines have taken their place. African Americans, despite having so-called public intellectuals who have established no significant independent think tanks or critical research institutes, have invested a great deal and time and money in a critical mass of stupidity that has left them ill-prepared for the challenges of the twenty-first century.

One would be hard pressed to single out any book from black America expounding a new public or political philosophy that tries to deal with the issues that confront African Americans in the post-civil rights era. For every book such as Debra Dickerson's *The End of Blackness* there are inconsequential works like Dyson's *Is Bill Cosby Right?,* Neal's *New Black Man* or Kitwana's *Why White Kids Love Hip-Hop,* or West's *Democracy Matters.*

Ironically, though, this school of cultural criticism, which also cites structural iniquities that underscore black lower-class behavior, may even be prompting a *kulturkampf* of its own. Columnist Errol Lewis has argued for a black "culture war" against an "ancient enemy: a bold, seductive street culture that exalts lawlessness, addiction and anti-family behavior, sexual promiscuity, ignorance and personal selfishness." In a word: hip-hop.

Increasingly, African Americans prefer to discuss issues of class, poverty, and political direction in the guise of "cultural criticism," which means they prefer to have debates about pop culture, ebonics, hip-hop, or dead-end discussions about identity or blackness, or how the media portrays blacks. Yet the social condition of black poor, like those in New Orleans, elicits no call for a rethinking or political mobilization. Has serious thought about African Americans disappeared from the black public sphere despite more so-called black public intellectuals?

Black America has no future-oriented vision of itself within the context of American reality. Forty years ago, blacks talked about power. As of late it is reparations, which means a significant portion of black America is still locked in the past. Both the AFL-CIO and the gay rights movement have been rethinking and arguing over their strategies in the wake of the 2004 elections. Outside of the United States, Muslims are debating the interpretation of the Koran and how extremists have hijacked it. Even in the pro-choice movement some have begun reassessing their approach to abortion advocacy. Black political leadership? Where is the open debate and discussion in black America about, as Marvin Gaye once said, "What's going on?" Has anyone noticed that the Congressional Black Caucus is MIA?

Black politics of the last forty years has come to a halt and the leaders of those years have offered nothing of programmatic substance—and nothing but symbolic posturing in the last twenty years. If the rank and file wants solutions to problems and a reasonable level of economic well-being they are going to have to cast down their own buckets in the clear waters of organizational efficiency, political accountability and self-generated economic mobilization. At this time and point in history, there doesn't seem to be any other way.

NORMAN KELLEY is author of *The Head Negro in Charge Syndrome: The Dead End of Black Politics* (Nation Books, 2004). His most recent book is the paperback edition of *Rhythm and Business: The Political Economy of Black Music* (Akashic Books, 2005).

Why We Hate

We may not admit it, but we are plagued with xenophobic tendencies. Our hidden prejudices run so deep, we are quick to judge, fear and even hate the unknown.

Margo Monteith, Ph.D. and Jeffrey Winters

Balbir Singh Sodhi was shot to death on September 15 in Mesa, Arizona. His killer claimed to be exacting revenge for the terrorist attacks of September 11. Upon his arrest, the murderer shouted, "I stand for America all the way." Though Sodhi wore a turban and could trace his ancestry to South Asia, he shared neither ethnicity nor religion with the suicide hijackers. Sodhi—who was killed at the gas station where he worked—died just for being different in a nation gripped with fear.

For Arab and Muslim Americans, the months after the terrorist attacks have been trying. They have been harassed at work and their property has been vandalized. An Arab San Francisco shop owner recalled with anger that his five-year-old daughter was taunted by name-callers. Classmates would yell "terrorist" as she walked by.

Public leaders from President George W. Bush on down have called for tolerance. But the Center for American-Islamic Relations in Washington, D.C., has tallied some 1,700 incidents of abuse against Muslims in the five months following September 11. Despite our better nature, it seems, fear of foreigners or other strange-seeming people comes out when we are under stress. That fear, known as xenophobia, seems almost hardwired into the human psyche.

Researchers are discovering the extent to which xenophobia can be easily—even arbitrarily—turned on. In just hours, we can be conditioned to fear or discriminate against those who differ from ourselves by characteristics as superficial as eye color. Even ideas we believe are just common sense can have deep xenophobic underpinnings. Research conducted this winter at Harvard reveals that even among people who claim to have no bias, the more strongly one supports the ethnic profiling of Arabs at airport-security checkpoints, the more hidden prejudice one has against Muslims.

But other research shows that when it comes to whom we fear and how we react, we do have a choice. We can, it seems, choose not to give in to our xenophobic tendencies.

The Melting Pot

America prides itself on being a melting pot of cultures, but how we react to newcomers is often at odds with that self-image. A few years ago, psychologist Markus Kemmelmeier, Ph.D., now at the University of Nevada at Reno, stuck stamped letters under the windshield wipers of parked cars in a suburb of Detroit. Half were addressed to a fictitious Christian organization, half to a made-up Muslim group. Of all the letters, half had little stickers of the American flag.

Would the addresses and stickers affect the rate at which the letters would be mailed? Kemmelmeier wondered. Without the flag stickers, both sets of letters were mailed at the same rate, about 75 percent of the time. With the stickers, however, the rates changed: Almost all the Christian letters were forwarded, but only half of the Muslim letters were mailed. "The flag is seen as a sacred object," Kemmelmeier says. "And it made people think about what it means to be a good American."

In short, the Muslims didn't make the cut.

Not mailing a letter seems like a small slight. Yet in the last century, there have been shocking examples of xenophobia in our own back yard. Perhaps the most famous in American history was the fear of the Japanese during World War II. This particular wave of hysteria lead to the rise of slurs and bigoted depictions in the media, and more alarmingly, the mass internment of 120,000 people of Japanese ancestry beginning in 1942. The internments have become a national embarrassment: Most of the Japanese held were American citizens, and there is little evidence that the imprisonments had any real strategic impact.

Today the targets of xenophobia—derived from the Greek word for *stranger*—aren't the Japanese. Instead, they are Muslim immigrants. Or Mexicans. Or Chinese. Or whichever group we have come to fear.

Just how arbitrary are these xenophobic feelings? Two famous public-school experiments show how easy it is to turn one "group" against another. In the late 1960s, California high school history teacher Ron Jones recruited students to participate in an exclusive new cultural program called "the Wave." Within weeks, these students were separating themselves from others and aggressively intimidating critics. Eventually, Jones confronted the students with the reality that they were unwitting participants in an experiment demonstrating the power of nationalist movements.

Sonam Wangmo:
"Am I fearful of Arab men in turbans? No, I am not. I was born and raised in India, and I am familiar with other races. I have learned to be attuned to different cultures. I find that there are always new, positive things to be learned from other people; it brings out the best in us."

A few years later, a teacher in Iowa discovered how quickly group distinctions are made. The teacher, Jane Elliott, divided her class into two groups—those with blue eyes and those with brown or green eyes. The brown-eyed group received privileges and treats, while the blue-eyed students were denied rewards and told they were inferior. Within hours, the once-harmonious classroom became two camps, full of mutual fear and resentment. Yet, what is especially shocking is that the students were only in the third grade.

Social Identity

The drive to completely and quickly divide the world into "us" and "them" is so powerful that it must surely come from some deep-seated need. The exact identity of that need, however, has been subject to debate. In the 1970s, the late Henri Tajfel, Ph.D., of the University of Bristol in England, and John Turner, Ph.D., now of the Australian National University, devised a theory to explain the psychology behind a range of prejudices and biases, not just xenophobia. Their theory was based, in part, on the desire to think highly of oneself. One way to lift your self-esteem is to be part of a distinctive group, like a winning team; another is to play up the qualities of your own group and denigrate the attributes of others so that you feel your group is better.

Terry Kalish:
"I am planning a trip to Florida, and I'm nervous about flying with my kids; I'm scared. If an Arab man sat next to me, I would feel nervous. I would wonder, 'Does he have explosives?' But then I feel ashamed to think this way. These poor people must get so scrutinized. It's wrong."

Tajfel and Turner called their insight "social identity theory," which has proved valuable for understanding how prejudices develop. Given even the slenderest of criteria, we naturally split people into two groups—an "in-group" and an "out-group." The categories can be of geopolitical importance—nationality, religion, race, language—or they can be as seemingly inconsequential as handedness, hair color or even height.

Once the division is made, the inferences and projections begin to occur. For one, we tend to think more highly of people in the in-group than those in the out-group, a belief based only on group identity. Also, a person tends to feel that others in the in-group are similar to one's self in ways that—although stereotypical—may have little to do with the original criteria used to split the groups. Someone with glasses may believe that other people who wear glasses are more voracious readers—even more intelligent—than those who don't, in spite of the fact that all he really knows is that they don't see very well. On the other hand, people in the out-group are believed to be less distinct and less complex than are cohorts in the in-group.

Although Tajfel and Turner found that identity and categorization were the root cause of social bias, other researchers have tried to find evolutionary explanations for discrimination. After all, in the distant past, people who shared cultural similarities were found to be more genetically related than those who did not. Therefore, favoring the in-group was a way of helping perpetuate one's genes. Evolutionary explanations seem appealing, since they rely on the simplest biological urges to drive complicated behavior. But this fact also makes them hard

to prove. Ironically, there is ample evidence backing up the "softer" science behind social identity theory.

Hidden Bias

Not many of us will admit to having strong racist or xenophobic biases. Even in cases where bias becomes public debate—such as the profiling of Arab Muslims at airport-security screenings—proponents of prejudice claim that they are merely promoting common sense. That reluctance to admit to bias makes the issue tricky to study.

To get around this problem, psychologists Anthony Greenwald, Ph.D., of the University of Washington in Seattle, and Mahzarin Banaji, Ph.D., of Harvard, developed the Implicit Association Test. The IAT is a simple test that measures reaction time: The subject sees various words or images projected on a screen, then classifies the images into one of two groups by pressing buttons. The words and images need not be racial or ethnic in nature—one group of researchers tested attitudes toward presidential candidates. The string of images is interspersed with words having either pleasant or unpleasant connotations, then the participant must group the words and images in various ways—Democrats are placed with unpleasant words, for instance.

Rangr:
"For the months following 9/11, I had to endure my daily walk to work along New York City's Sixth Avenue. It seemed that half the people stared at me with accusation. It became unbearable. Yet others showed tremendous empathy. Friends, co-workers and neighbors, even people I had never met, stopped to say, 'I hope your turban has not caused you any trouble.' At heart, this is a great country."

The differences in reaction time are small but telling. Again and again, researchers found that subjects readily tie in-group images with pleasant words and out-group images with unpleasant words. One study compares such groups as whites and blacks, Jews and Christians, and young people and old people. And researchers found that if you identify yourself in one group, it's easier to pair images of that group with pleasant words—and easier to pair the opposite group with unpleasant imagery. This reveals the underlying biases and enables us to study how quickly they can form.

Really though, we need to know very little about a person to discriminate against him. One of the authors of this story, psychologist Margo Monteith, Ph.D., performed an IAT experiment comparing attitudes toward two sets of made-up names; one set was supposedly "American," the other from the fictitious country of Marisat. Even though the subjects knew nothing about Marisat, they showed a consistent bias against it.

While this type of research may seem out in left field, other work may have more "real-world" applications. The Southern Poverty Law Center runs a Web version of the IAT that measures biases based on race, age and gender. Its survey has, for instance, found that respondents are far more likely to associate European faces, rather than Asian faces, with so-called American images. The implication being that Asians are seen as less "American" than Caucasians.

Similarly, Harvard's Banaji has studied the attitudes of people who favor the racial profiling of Arab Muslims to deter terrorism, and her results run contrary to the belief that such profiling is not driven by xenophobic fears. "We show that those who endorse racial profiling also score high on both explicit and implicit measures of prejudice toward Arab Muslims," Banaji says. "Endorsement of profiling is an indicator of level of prejudice."

Beyond Xenophobia

If categorization and bias come so easily, are people doomed to xenophobia and racism? It's pretty clear that we are susceptible to prejudice and that there is an unconscious desire to divide the world into "us" and "them." Fortunately, however, new research also shows that prejudices are fluid and that when we become conscious of our biases we can take active—and successful—steps to combat them.

Researchers have long known that when observing racially mixed groups, people are more likely to confuse the identity of two black individuals or two white ones, rather than a white with a black. But Leda Cosmides, Ph.D., and John Tooby, Ph.D., of the Center for Evolutionary Psychology at the University of California at Santa Barbara, and anthropologist Robert Kurzban, Ph.D., of the University of California at Los Angeles, wanted to test whether this was innate or whether it was just an artifact of how society groups individuals by race.

To do this, Cosmides and her colleagues made a video of two racially integrated basketball teams locked in conversation, then they showed it to study participants. As reported in the *Proceedings of the National Academy of Sciences,* the researchers discovered that subjects were more likely to confuse two players on the same team, regardless of race, rather than two players of the same race on opposite teams.

Cosmides says that this points to one way of attacking racism and xenophobia: changing the way society imposes group labels. American society divides people by race and by ethnicity; that's how lines of prejudice form. But simple steps, such as integrating the basketball teams, can reset mental divisions, rendering race and ethnicity less important.

This finding supports earlier research by psychologists Samuel Gaertner, Ph.D., of the University of Delaware in Newark, and John Dovidio, Ph.D., of Colgate University in Hamilton, New York. Gaertner and Dovidio have studied how bias changes when members of racially mixed groups must cooperate to accomplish shared goals. In situations where team members had to work together, bias could be reduced by significant amounts.

Monteith has also found that people who are concerned about their prejudices have the power to correct them. In experiments, she told subjects that they had performed poorly on tests that measured belief in stereotypes. She discovered that the worse a subject felt about her performance, the better she scored on subsequent tests. The guilt behind learning about their own prejudices made the subjects try harder not to be biased.

This suggests that the guilt of mistaking individuals for their group stereotype—such as falsely believing an Arab is a terrorist—can lead to the breakdown of the belief in that stereotype. Unfortunately, such stereotypes are reinforced so often that they can become ingrained. It is difficult to escape conventional wisdom and treat all people as individuals, rather than members of a group. But that seems to be the best way to avoid the trap of dividing the world in two—and discriminating against one part of humanity.

Read More About It:

Nobody Left to Hate: Teaching Compassion After Columbine, Elliot Aronson (W.H. Freeman and Company, 2000)

The Racist Mind: Portraits of American Neo-Nazis and Klansmen, Madonna Kolbenschlag (Penguin Books, 1996)

MARGO MONTEITH, PH.D., is an associate professor of psychology at the University of Kentucky. **JEFFREY WINTERS** is a New York-based science writer.

The Melting Pot

Part I: Are We There Yet?

ANNE WORTHAM

In the years following the American Revolution the expectation developed that over time the best traditions of Europe would be blended or amalgamated into a dynamic unity; that Englishmen, Germans, Italians, Irishmen, and Russians[1] would all become Americans, a new group that would be different from any of the original groups but also a combination of them all.[2] This was the vision of a young French nobleman, Michel Guillaume Jean de Crèvecoeur (1735–1813), who immigrated to the United States in 1759 and in 1782 published a book on life in America entitled *Letters From an American Farmer.* "What, then, is the American, this new man?" asked Crèvecoeur. "He is neither an European nor the descendant of an European; hence that strange mixture of blood which you will find in no other country. . . . Here individuals of all nations are melted into a new race of men whose labor and posterity will one day cause great changes in the world."[3]

> "What, then, is the American, this new man?" asked Crèvecoeur. "He is neither an European nor the descendant of an European; hence that strange mixture of blood which you will find in no other country. . . . Here individuals of all nations are melted into a new race of men whose labor and posterity will one day cause great changes in the world."

Crèvecoeur's image of the United States as a melting pot had little basis in fact. For one thing, by restricting his application of the melting pot to whites, he omitted American Indians and Negroes, who made up about 20 percent of the total colonial population. Extensive cultural diversity had been characteristic of the aboriginal North American peoples long before European colonialization.[4] Crèvecoeur's model also ignored the cultural and regional differences among the diverse Europeans who immigrated to the New World in the seventeenth century:

they were no more homogeneous than the indigenous people of many cultures who already populated the land.

In contrast to Crèvecoeur's vision, which reflected his romanticized perception of his times, Ralph Waldo Emerson (1803–1882) saw the melting pot as a promise to be fulfilled in the future. Unlike Crèvecoeur, he included Negroes in the mix. For Emerson the United States was the "asylum of all nations," and he predicted that "the energy of Irish, Swedes, Poles, and Cossacks, and all the European tribes—of the Africans, and of the Polynesians, will construct a new race, a new religion, a new state, a new literature, which will be as vigorous as the new Europe which came out of the smelting-pot of the Dark Ages, or that which earlier emerged from Pelasgic and Etruscan barbarism."[5]

More Melting Pot Visions

Yet another melting-pot vision was promoted by the influential historian Frederick Jackson Turner (1861–1932). In 1893, Turner argued that American identity was not Anglo-Saxon in origin and was forged in the Middle West, which he saw as "a newer and richer civilization" from which "a new product, which held the promise of world brotherhood" had emerged. The frontier had been the catalyst that had already fused the immigrants into a composite new national stock, argued Turner.[6] But his model was an inaccurate depiction of frontier reality. As Vincent Parrillo points out, "The pioneers did adapt to their new environment but the culture remained Anglo-American in form and content. Furthermore, in many areas of the Middle West Turner speaks about, culturally homogeneous settlements of Germans or Scandinavians often maintained distinct subcultures for generations."[7]

Perhaps the most quoted melting-pot idealist is Israel Zangwill (1864–1926), a British-born Jew, whose 1908 play *The Melting Pot* portrayed America as "God's crucible, the great melting pot where all the races of Europe are melting and re-forming!" To the immigrants entering Ellis Island, Zangwill's protagonist exhorted: "A fig for your feuds and vendettas! German and Frenchman, Irishman and Englishman, Jews, Russians—into the crucible with you all! God is making the American . . . He will be the fusion of all the races, the coming superman."[8] The politician William Jennings Bryan (1860–1925) echoed Zangwill's sentiments: "Great has been the Greek, the Latin, the Slav, the Celt, the Teuton, and the Saxon; but greater than any of these is the American, who combines the virtues of them all."[9]

Reflecting on the plausibility of the melting-pot ideal, Milton Gordon notes that, given a population drawn from many nations, "was it not possible then, to think of the evolving American society not simply as a slightly modified England but rather as a totally new blend, culturally and biologically, in which the stocks and folkways of Europe were, figuratively speaking, indiscriminately mixed in the political pot of the emerging nation and melted together by the fires of American influence and interaction into a distinctly new type?"[10]

It became apparent during the decades before World War I that immigrants were not giving up the ways of their origins as the price of assimilation and were not mixing together in the great crucible to form the new American.

This frame of mind was certainly plausible, but the vision itself could not be realized. When it became apparent during the decades before World War I that immigrants were not giving up the ways of their origins as the price of assimilation and were not mixing together in the great crucible to form the new American, the melting-pot idea as a natural laissez-faire process was abandoned. At the turn of the twentieth century, the policy of coerced assimilation, known as "Americanization," was inaugurated. Public schools, patriotic societies, chambers of commerce, women's clubs, public libraries, social settlements, and even industrial plants were enlisted to divest the immigrant of his foreign heritage, suppress his native language, teach him English, make him a naturalized citizen, and inject into him a loyalty to American institutions.[11]

The Americanization movement was coercive, condescending, and suppressive; it implied that American culture was a finished product, in an Anglo-Saxon pattern, that it was superior to all others, and that immigrants should adapt to Anglo-American culture as fast as possible. Immigrants were under no illusion; they knew that Americanization was the precondition for access to better jobs, higher education, political participation, and other opportunities. Nevertheless, the policy fell into disrepute. The most celebrated opponent of the melting pot and Americanization was the philosopher Horace Kallen, who developed the theory of cultural pluralism. The real meaning of American history, argued Kallen, was cultural pluralism, freedom, and unity through group diversity.[12]

Since the appearance of Kallen's theory, most of the major studies of American minority groups have been alternately guided by the theories of assimilation and cultural pluralism. Yet the failure of the melting-pot thesis to become policy has not prevented it from being of great ideological influence, becoming the utopian lens through which Americans view their society.

Melting-Pot Theory

Theoretically, the melting-pot model is one of several answers to the question: What is the best way of integrating disparate peoples into a single nation? The form of this question is as old as questions posed by the founders of Western philosophy; but in modern thought it dates back to Thomas Hobbes' question: How and why is society possible? The issue, known as the Hobbesian "problem of order," was central in the thought of eighteenth- and nineteenth-century social philosophers and sociologists. It was no less the preoccupation of the framers of the American nation, whose particular concern was the creation of one nation out of thirteen colonies: Would the United States be politically one nation, or would it not? Their answer is represented in the motto on the face of the Great Seal of the United States: *E pluribus unum* (out of many, one).[13] Although *E pluribus unum* shares with the melting-pot metaphor the same species (the problem of social organization), they are of different genera. The former expresses the political ideal of fashioning one nation out of many states, and is more appropriate to today's federal system; the latter refers to the biological and cultural amalgamation of groups into a new group.

In the extreme form of cultural assimilation, the previously distinct cultural groups would lose all their distinguishable behavior and values.

Although technically the concept of the melting pot refers to the amalgamation of groups, it is also used variously to refer to two different patterns of assimilation: (1) unidimensional, one-way assimilation, or Anglo-conformity, by which immigrants relinquish their own culture in favor of the dominant culture and are remade according to the idealized Anglo-Saxon mold;[14] and (2) reciprocal assimilation or acculturation, which may involve either direct social interaction or exposure to other cultures by means of mass media. As the outcome of such contact, the dominant group adopts some traits of minorities while the cultural patterns of the dominant group are taken over by minority groups. An example of Anglo-conformity is learning the English language; acculturation can be seen in the Americanization of foreign cuisine.

Suppose the plausibility of the melting-pot model. Given a structural environment of democratic political institutions, voluntary association, and a relatively free and open economic system, exactly what attitudes and behavior would be necessary to realize the blending, melting, and fusing processes portrayed by melting-pot visionaries? Gordon has identified subprocesses of assimilation that, when linked together, could theoretically produce a culturally and biologically amalgamated people. Foremost among these processes would be "the complete mixture of the various stocks through intermarriage—in other words, *marital* assimilation, or amalgamation."[15] *Cultural* assimilation or acculturation would involve the intermixing of cultural traits (language, values, religion, everyday norms, dress, diet) of various groups to "form a blend somewhat different from the cultures of any one of the groups separately." This is the process by which Italians become Italian Americans, Poles become Polish Americans, and Haitians become Haitian Americans. In the extreme form of cultural assimilation, the previously distinct cultural groups would lose all their distinguishable behavior and values.

Large-scale intermarriage presupposes *structural* assimilation of immigrants; that they have "entered into cliques, clubs, and other primary groups, and institutions of the host society and, in addition, placed their own impress upon these social structures to some extent." Melting would most certainly require *identificational* assimilation "in the form of all groups merging their previous sense of peoplehood into a new and larger ethnic identity which, in some fashion, honors its multiple origins at the same time that it constitutes an entity distinct from them all." Individuals would no longer see themselves as distinctive and would stake their personal identities to participation and success in the mainstream institutions of the society; they may maintain what Herbert Gans calls "symbolic ethnicity," which can be taken on or off without any real social cost to the individual, but they would think of themselves as Americans.[16]

> ## When the melting-pot vision is measured against these combined processes that are the necessary conditions of its creation, it has no basis in reality.

Since, as a consequence of amalgamation, there would not be any identifiably separate groups to be a target, attitude-receptional assimilation would be evident in the absence of prejudicial attitudes and stereotyping on the part of both dominant and minority ethnic groups. Behavioral-receptional assimilation would be apparent in the absence of intentional discrimination against groups. Finally, civic assimilation would have taken place, "since disparate cultural values are assumed to have merged and power conflict between groups would be neither necessary nor possible."

An example of assimilation using these dimensions is as follows. An immigrant arrives in the United States, takes on American customs, and learns to speak flawless English (cultural assimilation). She encounters no prejudice from neighbors or employers (*attitude-receptional* assimilation), and is able to live and work where she pleases (behavioral-receptional assimilation). She observes that no political or social issues separate her group from the host society (civic assimilation). Increasingly she no longer thinks of herself as an immigrant, or as having ties to "the old country," but sees herself as an American (identificational assimilation). She marries a member of the dominant group (marital assimilation) and joins bridge clubs, professional societies, and sororities that are composed entirely of core society members (structural assimilation).[17]

Such a detailed account of the subprocesses of assimilation indicates just how difficult assimilation is for an individual, let

Black slaves on the deck of the bark *Wildfire*. Its arrival into Key West, Florida, on April 30, 1860, violated the 1809 law prohibiting the importation of slaves.
Library of Congress/Harper's Weekly, June 2, 1860

alone an entire ethnic group, particularly racially visible groups such as Negroes, Indians, and Asians. When the melting-pot vision is measured against these combined processes that are the necessary conditions of its creation, it has no basis in reality. If all the assimilation processes that the melting pot entails were completed, says Martin Marger, the result would be a homogeneous society

> in which ethnicity plays no role in the distribution of wealth, power, and prestige. This does not mean, of course, that other forms of social differentiation and stratification such as age, sex, and class would not exist; it means only that the ethnic forms would no longer be operative. In essence, a society in which all groups have perfectly assimilated is no longer a multiethnic society. However, this complete form of assimilation is rarely achieved, either for the society as a whole or for specific groups and individuals. Instead, assimilation takes different forms and is evident in different degrees.[18]

Sociologist Seymour Martin Lipset believes that the melting pot is validated by intermarriage statistics, which, as he surmises, "indicate that majorities of Catholics, Jews, Italians, Irish, and Japanese Americans marry out of their ancestral groups."[19] Indeed, demographic data also show greater tolerance for black-white intermarriages, although they are the least common form of racial intermarriage for whites.[20] However, while some degree of amalgamation occurs between groups in a pluralistic society, it is not often a total societal process in the sense meant by the melting-pot theory. As for the emergence of a distinct new national culture evolving from elements of all other cultures, Marger notes: "Ideologically, societies may advocate some kind of ethnic melting pot wherein all groups contribute in proportionate amounts to form a new social system, but such a cultural and, particularly, structural fusion is a chimera."[21]

Assimilation Impediments

An example of the demographic and socioeconomic variability with which groups assimilate is Frances Fitzgerald's description of the impact of the movement of ethnic groups to the suburbs. When members of European ethnic communities left the cities in the wake of the flight of manufacturing, they did not "melt" into the white middle class; rather, instead of a melting pot, what they experienced was "a centrifuge that spun them around and distributed them out again across the landscape according to new principles: families with incomes of, say, thirty to sixty thousand dollars a year went to one suburb; families with incomes of, say, sixty to a hundred thousand dollars went to another; and young, single people were flung, en masse, into the recently vacated downtown neighborhoods." Ethnicity, class, and lifestyle were no longer correlated. Many of the young people came from blue-collar backgrounds but were college educated and did not think of themselves as hyphenated Americans. "By the mid-sixties the whole deck of white middle-class society had been reshuffled, and the old cards of identity—Italian-American, WASP, Russian Jewish-American—had lost much of their meaning."[22]

The situation for lower-class minorities in the central cities—where ethnicity, class, and lifestyle remain highly correlated—has been just the opposite of the suburbanization experience of the white ethnics Fitzgerald describes. Data from a study of seventy-four of the country's largest cities and metropolitan areas from 1970 to 1990 show that despite an increase in employment opportunities and a decline in formal discrimination in the wake of civil rights legislation, low wages and lack of access and opportunity continue to plague minorities concentrated in central cities. The housing patterns of minorities, particularly blacks, have not kept pace with the movement of employment to the suburbs. The percent of employment in the suburbs has been rising faster than the percent of population moving to the suburbs.[23] William Julius Wilson refers to this trend in which minorities live where the jobs aren't as "spatial mismatch."[24] The situation is exacerbated by the lack of rail and bus lines that accommodate commuting from the city to the suburbs.

Housing segregation such as this means that minorities lack the social networks and resources that are conducive to fostering entry into the mainstream. It illustrates the difficulty of achieving structural assimilation, particularly to the degree that is necessary for the realization of the other processes of assimilation. Yet, despite the assimilation problems of inner-city minorities, demographic data show modest declines in racial residential segregation in most metropolitan areas, and the growing suburbanization of blacks, Hispanics, and Asians matches the broad shift in attitudes on residential integration and openness to racial mixing in neighborhoods.

> **In the 1970s scholars found that although there had been considerable "melting" of ideas and cultural attributes, the ethnics themselves had proved "unmeltable" in any ultimate sense.**

In the 1970s scholars found that although there had been considerable "melting" of ideas and cultural attributes, the ethnics themselves had proved "unmeltable" in any ultimate sense. Not only had ethnic belonging survived, but so had the subjective evaluations of ethnic categories in the community. A decade later, as noted above, Fitzgerald observed that for later-generation white ethnics, ethnicity was not something that influenced their lives unless they wanted it to. Mary Waters, who has studied patterns of "optional ethnicity," writes that "for an increasing number of European-origin individuals whose parents and grandparents have intermarried, the ethnicity they claim is largely a matter of personal choice as they sort through all of the possible combinations of groups in their genealogies."[25]

But the situation is quite different for visible minorities. Waters writes that the freedom to include or exclude ancestries in one's identification is not the same for those defined racially in American society. Racially defined minorities "are constrained to identify with the part of their ancestry that has been socially defined as the 'essential' part. African Americans, for example, have been highly socially constrained to identify as blacks, without other options available to them, even when they know that their forebears included many people of American Indian or European background."[26]

Being a white ethnic is not entirely unproblematic. That researchers do not include them among "racially-defined groups" does not mean that they are not racially defined by others and that there are no negative consequences for being so defined. While the ethnic components of white identity are receding with each generation's increased distance from its immigrant ancestors, the racial component of their identity is a handicap for many. As Michael Omni and Howard Winant point out, whites have been racialized in the post-civil rights movement era, and "now, the very meaning of 'white' has become a matter of anxiety and concern."[27]

In a study of racial diversity at the University of California at Berkeley, students expressed several themes and dilemmas of contemporary white identity. Lacking a sense of ethnic identity, one student said, "I think that I may be missing something that other people have, that I am not experiencing." Another identified the disadvantages of being white with respect to the distribution of resources: "Being white means that you're less likely to get financial aid. . . . It means that there are all sorts of tutoring groups and special programs that you can't get into, because you're not a minority." Said another: "If you want to go with stereotypes, Asians are the smart people, the blacks are great athletes, what is white? We're just here. We're the oppressors of the nation."[28]

> **Caribbean-American immigrants even push their children to adopt strategies, such as invoking their accents or other references to French or British colonial culture, to differentiate themselves from U.S.-born blacks and avoid the stigma of "blackness."**

As the authors point out, although white Americans have not been immune to the process of racialization, unlike "people of color," they are prohibited from asserting their racial identity in political life.[29] In the aftermath of the civil rights movement, a double standard developed by which the reification of racial identity was deemed appropriate for everyone but whites. Blacks, Hispanics, and American Indians are expected to assert racial and ethnic pride, and whites are expected to concede their collective culpability for the plight of minorities, accept their stigma without protest, and to applaud minorities for resisting their stigma.

The stereotyping of *white* to mean "oppressor" and "racist" causes identity problems for colored minorities as well—ironically, because "white" is also associated with rationality, the work ethic, and intellectual achievement. Min Zhou describes how it plays out in the generational conflict between immigrant parents and their U.S.-born children in the Asian-American and Caribbean-American communities. "Ironically, the parent generation consciously struggles to push children to become 'white' by moving their families to white neighborhoods, sending their children to white schools, and discouraging their children from playing basketball and mimicking hip-hop culture. But becoming 'white' is politically incorrect, and thus unacceptable for the U.S.-born generation."[30]

Caribbean-American immigrants even push their children to adopt strategies, such as invoking their accents or other references to French or British colonial culture, to differentiate themselves from U.S.-born blacks and avoid the stigma of "blackness."[31] A common concern among Haitians in south Florida is that their children will adopt the attitudes of the inner city's underclass. Vietnamese parents in New Orleans often try to keep their children immersed in their ethnic enclave, discouraging them from assimilating too fast.[32]

The absurdity of this kind of stereotyping extends to high-achieving native black children, especially college students, who feel they must camouflage their strivings and achievements to avoid the stigma of "whiteness."

The definition of *American* to mean "white," which can be traced to the writings of melting-pot visionaries like Crèvecoeur, also has a negative impact on the identificational assimilation of "people of color." In a study of children of Haitians, Cubans,

West Indians, Mexicans, and Vietnamese in south Florida and Southern California, the researchers asked repondents how they identified themselves. Most chose categories of hyphenated Americans, few chose "American" as their identity. Asked if they believed the United States was the best country in the world, most of them answered no.[33]

On the other hand, as Min Zhou points out, U.S.-born children and grandchildren of Asian and Hispanic ancestry find that although they are already assimilated and think of themselves as American, their American identity is often questioned because they look like the contemporary influx of "colored" immigrants. "Suddenly they are confronted with the renewed image of themselves as 'foreigners'," notes Zhou. "Harassment of a Mexican American accused of being an undocumented immigrant, or comments about a third-generation Japanese American's 'good English' are frequently reported."[34]

The Pluralist Reality

As the sources of tension and conflict in intergroup relations indicate, assimilation is not an inevitable outcome of immigration. Most groups in America are incompletely assimilated. Although there has been widespread cultural assimilation in American society—due, in part, to mass communications, mass transportation, and education—structural assimilation has not yet occurred on a grand scale. Gordon stresses that structural assimilation is more difficult to achieve than cultural assimilation because it involves penetration into the close interactions and associations of dominant ethnic groups. Even when members of ethnic groups penetrate secondary and formal organizational structures—schools, workplaces, and political arenas—they may still lack more primary and personal ties with members of dominant ethnic groups.

Nathan Glazer and Daniel Moynihan were among the first to emphasize that even as many of their customs are replaced with those of the dominant American society, white ethnic groups continue to reveal residential, behavioral, organizational, and cultural patterns that mark their distinctive ethnic identity, one that subtly separates them from the middle-class, American Protestant core.[35] They think of themselves as Americans sharing one national culture and as members of distinct groups with distinctive ways of life.

America has always been a pluralistic society. In its rejection of ethnic exclusivity and denial of the political recognition or formal status of ethnic groups, the American political system has made ethnic-group formation and maintenance a voluntary matter. Despite many policies of exclusivism, the history of American society has been such that the structural basis for ethnic preservation has been progressively undermined by a system of justice based on individual rights and the demands of a market economy. However, while ethnicity (as a sense of peoplehood) has been undermined by the forces of modernization and transformed by acculturation, and while social mobility has taken members of ethnic groups across boundaries of the ethnic structural network, ethnic belonging has persisted and considerable structural pluralism exists along racial and religious lines.

> **This reality of regional differentiation as well as national origin has been totally ignored by the U.S. Census Bureau's lumping together persons from Central America, Mexico, Puerto Rico, and Cuba into a superethnic group called "Hispanics."**

Gordon attempted to capture the complexity of simultaneous assimilation and pluralism by focusing on ethnic group subcultures that are to some extent organized within subsocieties. While assimilation takes place within economic, political, and educational institutions, ethnic subsocieties are maintained in the institutional areas of religion, family, and recreation. It is in this sense that Gordon sees both assimilation and cultural pluralism occurring. Moreover, while race, religion, and nationality are important determinants of these subsocieties, these three variables are intersected by three others: social class, urban-rural residence, and regional residence. The various combinations of these dimensions of differentiation create what Gordon calls "ethclasses." Examples of such ethclasses include southern, lower-class, Protestant, rural blacks; northern, upper-class, white, urban Jews; northern, lower-class, white, urban, Catholics; and western, middle-class, suburban, third-generation Japanese.[36]

Viewing the assimilation process from the vantage point of the ethclass reveals that immigrants do not assimilate American culture in general; rather, they tend to adopt the folkways of the regions in which they settle. So it is, for instance, that there are Yankee Jews, Philadelphia Jews, southern Jews, and back-slapping Texas Jews in cowboy boots and ten-gallon hats. Such cases of regional assimilation illustrate the fact that assimilation is itself pluralistic. This reality of regional differentiation as well as national origin has been totally ignored by the U.S. Census Bureau's lumping together persons from Central America, Mexico, Puerto Rico, and Cuba into a superethnic group called "Hispanics." The ethclass also casts light on the multidimensional nature of intergroup relations in America. For instance, the factors of social class, urban-rural residence, and regional residence enable us to understand that groups that are the object of prejudice and discrimination vary according to those differences. The experiences of blacks in the South vary from those of blacks and Puerto Ricans in the North, and their experiences differ from those of Mexican Americans in the Southwest or Vietnamese in the West.

Because of the prevalence of incomplete assimilation—of the simultaneous integration into the societal mainstream and retention of ethnic group identification—it is more accurate to apply the model of pluralism in understanding American intergroup relations. The general meaning of pluralism is the coexistence and mutual toleration of groups that retain their separate identities. There are three dimensions of the generic pluralist model of intergroup relations: cultural, structural, and political. At the cultural level, each group is free to maintain and develop its own culture, not totally separated but voluntarily segregated to a considerable degree. At the structural level, groups participate in different institutions and informal arrangements rather than in the same ones. Political pluralism is the distribution of political power among various interest groups and organizations, not equally, but with equal rights to organize or join coalitions to influence political decisions that have bearing on their perceived interests.[37]

America's Pluralist Paradox

In these definitions, the concept of pluralism has a sociological connotation. Pluralism also refers to an ideological position that takes the view that the cultures and identities of different groups ought to be preserved.

In his monumental study of American race relations, Gunnar Myrdal concluded that a key characteristic of American life was the contradiction between the political ideals of the American creed, which call for just treatment of all people, regardless of race, creed, or color, and the practices of prejudice and differential treatment of people on the basis of race.[38] In the six and one-half decades since Myrdal's report, the United States has clearly moved a considerable distance toward implementing the implications of the American creed for race relations. However, in the aftermath of the civil rights and immigration legislation of the mid-1960s, America has been facing what Gordon calls a new dilemma that "is oriented toward a choice of the kinds of group pluralism which American governmental action and the attitudes of the American people will foster and encourage."[39]

The question for Gordon is "which type of pluralist society is most appropriate and most beneficial for a nation composed of many ethnic groups." America has always been a pluralistic society. What causes the current dilemma of choice, says Gordon, is "the role of government in racial and ethnic relations, together with ethical and philosophical issues revolving around just rewards and whether to treat persons as individuals or as members of a categorically defined group." Nathan Glazer characterizes the situation as follows:

> We have a complex of education, culture, law, administration, and political institutions which has deflected us onto a course in which we publicly establish ethnic and racial categories for differential treatment, and believe that by so doing we are establishing a just and good society. . . . But this has meant that we abandon the first principle of a liberal society, that the individual's interests and good and welfare are the test of a good society, for we now attach benefits and penalities to individuals simply on the basis of their race, color, and national origin. The implications of the new course are an increasing consciousness of the significance of group membership, increasing divisiveness on the basis of race,

color, and national origin, and a spreading resentment against the favored groups.[40]

Liberal pluralism seeks equality between individuals, inequality of result, and unity out of group diversity by means of individual rights.

It is these issues that point to the competing frameworks of pluralism that he distinguishes as *liberal* pluralism and *corporate* pluralism. Liberal pluralism seeks equality between individuals, inequality of result, and unity out of group diversity by means of individual rights. Corporate pluralism seeks equality between groups, equality of result, and unity out of group diversity by means of group rights. The conflict between liberal and corporate pluralism arises in part out of what Peter Berger calls "the concurrence of modernizing and demodernizing impulses in the contemporary situation." The modernizing impulse entails an aspiration for liberation from restrictive solidarities of collective life and ideologies. The demodernizing impulse, whether it looks backward into the past or forward into the future, seeks a reversal of the modern trends that its adherents believe have alienated the individual. Their aim is to liberate the individual from what they believe are the dehumanizing excesses of individualism, capitalism, and democracy.[41]

Where Are We?

Gordon ended his essay on the conflicting models of pluralism with the prediction that "what the American people decide about this patterned complex of issues in the last twenty years of the twentieth century will have much to do with determining the nature, shape, and destiny of racial and ethnic relations in America in the twenty-first century." Lipset thinks of the future of American ethnicity in terms of an ongoing conflict between two different perspectives of equality expressed in the mass behavior of average Americans on the one hand, and in the discussions and proposals of intellectuals and the ideological Left on the other.

Lipset insists that for the masses, the melting-pot image "remains as appropriate as ever."[42] By melting pot, Lipset means American universalism, the desire to incorporate groups into one culturally unified whole, [which] is inherent in the founding ideology—the American Creed."[43] Although melting pot is not technically the term that describes what Lipset means, it is clearly a vision that is consistent with the option of liberal pluralism that Gordon identifies. (My qualification of Lipset rests on the understanding of melting pot to mean a biologically and/or culturally amalgamated whole, whereas Lipset's usage refers to a culturally unified whole, which he understands to be a democratic pluralistic society.)

The liberal pluralistic society that Gordon proposes (and that Lipset calls universalistic pluralism) is characterized by David Sears as

a "cosmopolitan liberal" society in which diverse groups comfortably coexist, tolerating each other's modest differences but sharing a strong bond of loyalty to the superordinate nation. This universalist traditional ideal of American integration is perhaps most often captured in the idea of the 'melting pot.' To its adherents, the melting pot means the intermingling of varied cultural streams in the crucible of American life. Immigrants enrich popular culture without threatening the distinctive core of national identity, a Lockean commitment to individual rights shared by all citizens. In principle, though less fully in practice, this conception of American identity is ethnically inclusive, its adherents believing that American society could assimilate all newcomers.[44]

The second option of corporate pluralism, which Lipset asserts is promoted by intellectuals and the ideological Left, is "particularism, the preservation of subnational group loyalties," which entails the right of ethnic groups to cultural survival.[45] "The emphasis on univeralism has declined in political discourse, while particularism—described by some as multiculturalism—has become more important," says Lipset. In the vision of multiculturalism, writes David Sears, "the differences between groups are not appreciated but institutionalized, in formal power-sharing coalitions." The term *multiculturalism* was first advanced in Canada. Its guiding political principles "are the recognition of and respect for individuals' cultural identity, the primacy of ethnic identity in defining political interests, the idea of communal representation, and the importance of public policies that respond to the claims of subordinate cultural groups. In that sense, multiculturalism is a redistributive ideology that justifies the claims of subordinate groups to a greater share of society's goods. It does so by invoking the notion of group rather than individual rights."

Indeed, what might be called "identity politics" goes beyond ethnicity to include such groups as women, gays, and the disabled.

Multiculturalism, which Sears calls the "'hard' particularistic version" of pluralism, "asserts the viability and merit of multiple cultures within a society and advocates government action to maintain these equally worthy cultures. As an ideal image of society, multiculturalism rejects the assimilationist ethos of the melting pot in favor of the mosaic, which typically consists of differently colored tiles isolated from each other by impenetrable grout. It construes racial or ethnic identity as the preferred choice of self-definition." Although its roots are in the black civil rights movement, Sears notes that "multiculturalism extends the model of blacks' struggle for equality in two senses. First, it regards all the distinct cultures within the country as morally and intellectually equal, most notably including the new immigrants from Latin America and Asia. Indeed, what might be called 'identity politics' goes beyond ethnicity to include such groups as women, gays, and the disabled. Second, it advocates official action to achieve equality for all groups."[46]

> **Clearly, it is toward mutuality and respect for differences that we should be headed, not toward melting or politicized "diversity."**

The success of the multiculturalists in promoting their vision is indicated by Aguirre and Turner's observation that "it is now politically incorrect to question pluralism or, worse, to extol the virtues of integration of ethnics into an Anglo-Saxon cultural core—at least within academia. But if there is no cultural core to which each wave of immigrants adjusts, or if ethnic populations of any size refuse or cannot adjust, then societal integration will be tenuous."[47] This is not a rejection of the reality of ethnic pluralism but recognition of the requirement of a democratic republic (and capitalism) that ethnic pluralism revolve around weak ethnic identification.

Public opinion research indicates that the vast majority of Americans believe that this is still the land of opportunity, where meritorious achievement is possible. Their opposition to government-enforced pluralism should be seen as a reflection of loyalty to an idealized and seemingly threatened civic culture in which individual equality was enshrined as a core democratic principle. Omni and Winant believe that culture, which was espoused across the political and cultural spectrum as a central ideal, seems to many Americans to be a receding ideal. Yet, they argue, "Avoiding racial polarization in our society may well depend on resuscitating and rearticulating that very vision so as to go beyond race-specific demands to a society of greater social justice for all."[48] There is some hope in the paradoxical reality, as Marger points out, that "while groups extoll the need to retain an ethnic culture and encounter declining resistance to its retention from the dominant group, societal trends continue to erode those cultural differences," compressing cultural singularities into common forms.[49] We may also hope that the erosion of cultural differences will reveal the unique "Americanness" that is a key component of our cultural core. It has the capacity to facilitate the universalism of the American creed.

Denying the existence of the melting pot leaves much to be explained. No denial has been made here of the existence of a metaphorical "pot," only that the processes occurring within amount to a universal "melting." Australian author and art critic Robert Hughes correctly argues that it is too simplistic to say that America is, or ever was, a melting pot. "But it is also too simple to say none of its contents actually melted," writes Hughes. "No single metaphor can do justice to the complexity of cultural crossing and perfusion in America."[50] To be sure, there is some melting (marital and cultural assimilation); however, as pointed out, there is also unevenly spread structural, identificational, attitude-receptional, behavior-receptional, and civic assimilation.

For utopians who dream of a unified, monoethnic, homogenous society, the lack of universal melting is a pathological situation that must be overcome. For realists, to say universal melting is not occurring is not to claim an unnecessary failure but to assert that the facts of human nature, history, and voluntary human association preclude universal melting. However, this is not to deny the possibility of cohesion and unity. Peace, harmony, prosperity, and unity do not require homogeneity, but they do require cohesion. What many Americans experience, and some resist, is not melting but mutuality—a mutuality that, as Hughes points out, "has no choice but to live in recognition of difference."[51] Whether differences persist as distinctions, or are intermingled or merged into something unlike the original form, is no threat to social order so long as mutuality is maintained and distinctions are not used as political clubs of tribal warfare. If mutuality is destroyed, however, differences become the "cultural ramparts" of the current cultural wars. Clearly, it is toward mutuality and respect for differences that we should be headed, not toward melting or politicized "diversity."

Notes

1. Actually numerous waves of immigrants came from many nations to America, including but not confined to these.

2. William Newman, American Pluralism: *A Study of Minority Groups and Social Theory* (New York: Harper & Row, 1973), 63.

3. J. Hector St. John (Michel-Guillaume-Jean de Crèvecoeur), *Letters From an American Farmer* (New York: Fox, Duffield & Co., 1904), 54–55.

4. Vincent Parrillo, *Diversity in America* (Thousand Oaks, California: Pine Forge Press, 1996), 18.

5. *The Journals and Miscellaneous Notebooks of Ralph Waldo Emerson,* ed. Ralph Orth and Alfred Ferguson (Cambridge: Belknap, 1971), 9; 299–300.

6. Frederick Jackson Turner, *The Frontier in American History* (New York: Henry Holt, 1920), 3–4.

7. Vincent Parrillo, *Strangers to These Shores,* 5th ed. (Boston: Allyn and Bacon, 1997), 11.

8. Israel Zangwill, *The Melting Pot* (New York: Macmillan, 1909).

9. As quoted in Peter Rose, *They and We: Racial and Ethnic Relations in the United States,* 3rd ed. (New York: Random House, 1981), 64.

10. Milton Gordon, *Assimilation in American Life* (New York: Oxford University Press, 1964), 115.

11. Brewton Berry, *Race and Ethnic Relations,* 3rd ed. (Boston: Houghton Mifflin, 1965), 212–13.

12. Horace Kallen, "Democracy Versus the Melting Pot," *The Nation,* 25 Feb., 1915, 220.

13. The phrase, which can be traced back to Horace's *Epistles,* was suggested by the designer of the Great Seal, Philadelphia artist and painter Pierre Eugene Du Simitiere, who became a naturalized citizen in 1769. Du Simitiere was consultant to Benjamin Franklin, John Adams, and Thomas Jefferson, members of the first committee for the selection of the seal. The official motto of the United States is "In God We Trust," adopted on July 30, 1956.

14. The term "Anglo-conformity" was introduced by Stewart G. Cole and Mildred Wise Cole, *Minorities and the American Promise* (New York: Harper & Row, 1937).

15. This quotation and those that follow in this paragraph are from Gordon, *Assimilation in American Life,* 124–26.

16. Herbert Gans, "Symbolic Ethnicity: The Future of Ethnic Groups and Cultures in America," *Ethnic and Racial Studies* 2 (January 1979): 1–20.

17. From Richard Schaefer, *Racial and Ethnic Groups* (Boston: Little, Brown, 1979), 40–41.

18. Martin Marger, *Race and Ethnic Relations: American and Global Perspectives,* (Belmont, California: Wadsworth Publishing, 1985), 71.

19. Seymour Martin Lipset, *American Exceptionalism: A Double-Edged Sword* (New York: W.W. Norton, 1996), 249. See also Seymour Martin Lipset and Earl Raab, *Jews and the New American Scene* (Cambridge: Harvard University Press, 1995); Stanley Lieberson and Mary Waters, *From Many Strands: Ethnic and Racial Groups in Contemporary America* (New York: Russell Sage Foundation, 1989); and Mary Waters, *Ethnic Options: Choosing Identities in America* (Berkeley: University of California Press, 1990).

20. Lawrence Bobo, "Racial Attitudes and Relations," in *America Becoming: Racial Trends and Their Consequences,* vol. I, ed. Neil Smelser, William Wilson, and Faith Mitchell (Washington, D.C.: National Academy Press, 2001), 295.

21. Marger, *Race and Ethnic Relations,* 78.

22. Frances Fitzgerald, Cities on a Hill: *A Journey Through Contemporary American Cultures* (New York: Simon & Schuster, 1981), 16–17, 387.

23. Manuel Pastor Jr., "Geography and Opportunity," in *America Becoming,* 435–67. See also Douglas Massey, "Residential Segregation and Neighborhood Conditions in U.S. Metropolitan Areas," in *America Becoming,* 391–434.

24. William Julius Wilson, *The Truly Disadvantaged: The Inner City, the Underclass, and Public Policy* (Chicago: University of Chicago Press, 1987).

25. Mary Waters, "Optional Ethnicities: For Whites Only?" in *Origins and Destinies: Immigration, Race and Ethnicity in America,* ed. Silvia Pedraza and Ruben G. Rumbaut (Belmont, California: Wadsworth, 1996), 447.

26. Waters, "Optional Ethnicities."

27. Michael Omni and Howard Winant, "Contesting the Meanings of Race in the Post-Civil Rights Movement Era," in *Origins and Destinies.*

28. Omni and Winant, "Contesting the Meaning of Race."

29. Omni and Winant, "Contesting the Meaning of Race."

30. Min Zhou, "Immigration and the Dynamics of Race and Ethnicity," *America Becoming,* 222–23.

31. Alejandro Portes and A. Stepick, *City on the Edge: The Transformation of Miami* (Berkeley: University of California Press, 1993).

32. William Booth, "The Myth of the Melting Pot, Part 1: One Nation, Indivisible: Is It History?" *Washington Post,* February 22, 1998.

33. Alejandro Portes and Rubin Rumbaut, *Immigrant America: A Portrait,* 2nd ed. (Berkeley: University of California Press, 1996).

34. Zhou, "Immigration and the Dynamics of Race and Ethnicity."

35. Nathan Glazer and Daniel Moynihan, *Beyond the Melting Pot,* 2nd ed. (Cambridge: MIT Press, 1970).

36. Gordon, *Assimilation in American Life,* 18–54.

37. F. James Davis, *Minority-Dominant Relations: A Sociological Analysis* (Arlington Heights, Illinois: AHM Publishing, 1979), 152–54.

38. Gunnar Myrdal, *An American Dilemma* (New York: Harper and Brothers, 1944).

39. Milton Gordon, "Models of Pluralism: The New American Dilemma," *Annals of the American Academy of Political and Social Science,* March 1981.

40. Nathan Glazer, *Affirmative Discrimination: Ethnic Inequality and Public Policy* (New York: Basic Books, 1976), 220.

41. Peter Berger, Brigitte Berger, and Hansfried Kellner, *The Homeless Mind* (New York: Vintage, 1974), 196.

42. Lipset, *American Exceptionalism,* 249–50.

43. Seymour Martin Lipset, "Historical Traditions and National Characteristics: A Comparative Analysis of Canada and the United States," in *Patterns of Modernity, Volume I: The West,* ed. S.N. Eisenstadt, (New York: New York University Press, 1987), 77–78.

44. David Sears, Jack Citrin, Sharmaaine Cheleden, and Colette van Laar, "Cultural Diversity and Multicultural Politics: Is Ethnic Balkanization Psychologically Inevitable?" in *Cultural Divides: Understanding and Overcoming Group Conflict,* ed. Deborah Prentice and Dale Miller, (New York: Russell Sage Foundation, 1999), 35–79.

45. Lipset, "Historical Traditions and National Characteristics."

46. Sears et al., "Cultural Diversity and Multicultural Politics."

47. Adalberto Aguirre Jr. and Jonathan Turner, *American Ethnicity: The Dynamics and Consequences of Discrimination,* 2nd ed. (Boston: McGraw-Hill, 1998), 247.

48. Omni and Winant, "Contesting the Meaning of Race," 476.

49. Marger, *Race and Ethnic Relations,* 290–91.

50. Robert Hughes, *Culture of Complaint: The Fraying of America* (New York: Oxford University Press, 1993), 12–13.

51. Hughes, *Culture of Complaint,* 12–13.

ANNE WORTHAM is associate professor of sociology at Illinois State University.

* Part II of this article [was] published in a subsequent issue.

The Conundrum of the Glass Ceiling

Why are women so persistently absent from top corporate jobs?

The Economist

It is 20 years since the term "glass ceiling" was coined by the Wall Street Journal to describe the apparent barriers that prevent women from reaching the top of the corporate hierarchy; and it is ten years since the American government's specially appointed Glass Ceiling Commission published its recommendations. In 1995 the commission said that the barrier was continuing "to deny untold numbers of qualified people the opportunity to compete for and hold executive level positions in the private sector." It found that women had 45.7% of America's jobs and more than half of master's degrees being awarded. Yet 95% of senior managers were men, and female managers' earnings were on average a mere 68% of their male counterparts'.

Ten years on, women account for 46.5% of America's workforce and for less than 8% of its top managers, although at big *Fortune* 500 companies the figure is a bit higher. Female managers' earnings now average 72% of their male colleagues'. Booz Allen Hamilton, a consulting firm that monitors departing chief executives in America, found that 0.7% of them were women in 1998, and 0.7% of them were women in 2004. In between, the figure fluctuated. But the firm says that one thing is clear: the number is "very low and not getting higher."

In other countries the picture is similar. Not a single woman featured in Fortune magazine's list this June of the 25 highest-paid CEOs in Europe. Although Laurence Parisot, the chief executive of Ifop, an opinion pollster, was chosen recently to head Medef, the French employers' association, she is a rare exception. Corinne Maier, an economist with EDF, a French energy group, gave a scathing description of French corporate life in last year's bestseller, "Bonjour Paresse." "Among the well-heeled battalions of executives," she wrote, "only 5% are women." Equality in the French workplace, claimed Ms Maier, "is a far-off dream."

It is even farther off in Japan where, until 20–30 years ago, it was generally unacceptable for women to stay in the office after 5pm. One ambitious employee of a foreign multinational dared to hide in the ladies room until the men had left before returning to her desk to finish her work. There has been some progress since. This year two women have been appointed to head big Japanese companies. Fumiko Hayashi is now chairman and CEO of Daiei, a troubled supermarket chain; and Tomoyo Nonaka, a former newscaster, has been appointed boss of Sanyo Electric. Nissan has a general manager for "diversity development" who, when asked recently what has changed least in Japanese business in the past 20 years, replied: "The mindset of Japanese gentlemen."

In Britain, the number of female executive directors of FTSE100 companies rose from 11 in 2000 to 17 in 2004, according to Cranfield, a business school—17 women as against almost 400 men. A larger sample of British quoted companies found that 65% had no women on their board at all in 2003. No British woman has yet headed a big British company, although 44% of the workforce is female. Marjorie Scardino, CEO of Pearson, owner of the *Financial Times* which owns 50% of *The Economist,* is American, as is Laura Tyson, who heads the London Business School. Clara Furse, boss of London's stock exchange, was born in Canada.

It is progress of a sort—but of a glacially slow sort. The glass-ceiling phenomenon is proving peculiarly persistent. The top of the corporate ladder remains stubbornly male, and the few women who reach it are paid significantly less than the men that they join there.

This is despite the fact that companies are trying harder than ever to help women to climb higher. So-called "diversity programmes" (which are aimed at promoting minorities as well as women) are as common as diversity on the board is rare, and not just among service industries such as finance and retailing. No-nonsense formerly male clubs such as IBM (where two decades ago blue-suited identikit white men drove the company close to bankruptcy), GE (where the culture was not exactly female-friendly during the long rule of its legendary leader Jack Welch) and BP (where long hours at sea on windy oil rigs were a career booster), have appointed senior executives to be in charge of diversity. The three firms were the unlikely joint sponsors of a recent conference on "Women in Leadership."

Diversity Pays

Such companies no longer see the promotion of women solely as a moral issue of equal opportunity and equal pay. They have been persuaded of the business case for diversity. It has long been known that mixed groups are better at problem solving than like-minded ones. But the benefits of diversity are greater than this. Research by Catalyst, an American organisation that aims to expand "opportunities for women and business," found a strong correlation between the number of women in top executive positions and financial performance among *Fortune* 500 companies between 1996 and 2000.

For some companies the push towards greater diversity has come from their customers. Lou Gerstner, the man who turned around IBM partly by promoting diversity within the company, has said "we made diversity a market-based issue . . . it's about understanding our markets, which are diverse and multicultural." Lisa Bondesio, head of diversity in Britain for Deloitte, a big firm of accountants, says that diversity is "about how we differentiate ourselves in the marketplace."

Other companies surprisingly fail to reflect the diversity of their customers. Procter & Gamble (P&G), for example, the manufacturer of Pampers nappies, Max Factor and Tampax, boasts in its 2004 annual report that it was ranked "among the top companies for executive women" by the National Association for Female Executives. Yet it has only two women on its 16-person board, both of them non-executives, and out of the 45 people it lists as its top "corporate officers" only three are women—ie, 93% of them are men. P&G is an enormously successful company and its management programmes are widely admired. Its shareholders may wonder if it would do even better if the gender ratios at the top were less skewed.

Many companies have been motivated by a desire to broaden the pool of "talent" that their human-resources departments can fish in. They worry in general about the ageing populations of the developed world. But particular industries have other reasons for broadening their recruitment trawl. The big accounting firms, for example, had their reputations seriously dented by the demise of Enron and its auditor Arthur Andersen just before they had an unprecedented increase in business as a consequence of the extra duties imposed by the Sarbanes-Oxley act. They became the "employer of choice" for far fewer graduates at a time when they needed to attract far more. A consequence is that they have had to extend their recruitment and promotion efforts to more women.

The management-consulting business, where firms tend to follow the career strategy of "up or out," would like to hold on to many more of its women. But up or out can scarcely accommodate maternity leave, so it is no surprise that the industry loses twice as many women as men from the middle rungs of its career ladder.

Booz Allen Hamilton, a leading consulting firm, regularly wonders how to alter the fact that only 1–2% of its partners are women. Orit Gadiesh, the chairman of Bain, a rival, is a notable exception to the general exclusion of women from the top ranks. However, an earlier career in the Israeli army may have provided essential skills for her to reach the top.

Some firms' diversity programmes are working. At IBM, there are now seven women among its 40 top executives. GE says that 14% of its "senior executives" are now women, although none of them featured in the chief executive's recent reshuffle at the very top. The firm's six new business divisions are all headed by men.

By contrast, Alcan, a Canadian multinational metal manufacturer, has made extraordinary progress. Three out of its four main businesses are now headed by women (including the bauxite and alumina business). Steven Price, the company's HR director, says "it's been a long journey" to reach this point. Crucial has been "the tone at the top" and a determination to break down the perception that working long hours and wearing air miles like a "battle medal" are ways to get ahead in the company.

Why is it proving so difficult for women to reach the top of corporations? Are they simply less ambitious, less excited by the idea of limitless (albeit first-class) travel, late nights and the onerous responsibilities imposed by mounting regulation? A 2002 survey of top executives in American multinationals around the world did find them to be less ambitious, at least for the very top job: 19% of the men interviewed aspired to be CEO, whereas only 9% of the women did. At a slightly lower level there was less difference: 43% of women hoped to join a senior management committee, compared with 54% of the men. Catalyst, on the other hand, says that its research shows that women and men have equal desires to have the CEO job. "Ambition knows no gender," says Ilene Lang, the president of Catalyst and once a senior executive in Silicon Valley.

Who's in the Club?

Top businesswomen in America give three main explanations for why so few of them reach "C-level"—that group of executives who preface their titles with the word "chief." First comes the exclusion from informal networks. In many firms jock-talk and late-night boozing still oil the wheels of progress. In America and elsewhere it has become almost traditional for sales teams to take potential clients to strip clubs and the like. These activities specifically exclude most women.

Yasmin Jetha, a Muslim of Asian origin who made it to the board of Abbey, a British bank and a FTSE100 company until it was taken over last year by Spain's Banco Santander, says that although she neither drinks alcohol nor supports a rugby team, she made a point in her career of participating in industry-wide events where the opportunities for exclusion are less. More and more women in business are forming their own networks, which also help to counter male clubbishness.

The second hurdle is what Ms Lang calls "pervasive stereotyping of women's capacity for leadership". Everyone is unconsciously biased and there is strong evidence that men are biased against promoting women inside companies. This was a central point in the landmark 1989 case in America of *Price Waterhouse v Hopkins*, where Ann Hopkins sued her employer when she was not given a partnership. She eventually won her case in the Supreme Court. Since then some companies have begun to take special steps to guard against bias. Deloitte, for example, carefully scrutinises its pay and promotion decisions for bias, especially its list of new partners announced annually in June.

The third hurdle is the lack of role models. There are too few women in top jobs to show how it is done. Helen Alexander, the chief executive of The Economist Group and one of very few female CEOs to have succeeded a female CEO (Ms Scardino) says, however, that the role models that matter come earlier in life—at school or in the family. In addition, it seems to be important for many successful businesswomen to have had a supportive father.

Chris Bones, a senior human-resources executive with Cadbury Schweppes before he took over as head of Henley Management College at the beginning of this year, suggests another reason. The flattening of organisations in recent years, as layers of management have been stripped out, has meant that promotions now are far steeper steps than they used to be. This leaves fewer opportunities for people to re-enter the workforce at higher levels. And many women inevitably need to take time off during their careers. In America, there is evidence to suggest that more women with children under the age of one are taking time off work than was the case some years ago.

More and more too are withdrawing to care for elderly parents at a time when they are on the cusp of the higher echelons. Ben Rosen, a professor at the Kenan-Flagler Business School in North Carolina who has done research on the topic, says that many women bail out of corporate life to become self-employed consultants and entrepreneurs, roles where they can have greater freedom and autonomy to manage the rest of their lives. This may be reinforcing companies' long-held belief that they should invest less in women's careers because they are unlikely to stay the course.

Ms Maier's Gallic analysis of the issue is that French men spend more time at work than women, which "can be explained by their insatiable predatory instincts as well as by their casual approach to banal household chores." This leaves women with so much to do at home that they are more than twice as likely as men to work part-time, "which makes it all the more impossible to break the glass ceiling." In America a survey by the Centre for Work-Life Policy found that 40% of highly qualified women with spouses felt that their husbands did less work around the home than they created.

Another finding of the study was that qualified women leave work for a mixture of reasons—some pull them away (home and family life), and some push them away (the type of work, the people they are working with). In business, the push factors were found to be particularly powerful, "unlike, say, in medicine or teaching." The vast majority of women (93%) said they wanted to return to work, but found the options available to them "few and far between, and extremely costly." Across sectors, women lost 37% of their earning power when they spent three or more years out of the workforce.

Very few (5%) wanted to return to the companies they had left, claiming the work they had been doing there was not particularly satisfying. In Britain, women are increasingly dissatisfied with work. A recent study by the University of Bath of female workers between 1992 and 2003 showed an overall decline in their stated levels of job satisfaction. For full-time female managers the decline was an above-average 6%. For men, job satisfaction over the same period went up.

The only category of female workers with a significant rise in satisfaction (of 19%) was that of part-time craft workers. It has become a lot more rewarding to blow glass or design gardens than to strive forever in a vain bid to reach the boardroom.

Change Needed

Will time alone erode the gap between men and women? The steep decline among women in the popularity of MBA degrees, the *sine qua non* (at least in America) of a fast-track corporate career, suggests not. What is more, women with MBAs are fast dropping out of the workforce. One study in America found that one out of every three such qualified women is not working full-time. For men, the comparable figure is one in 20.

What can be done to improve the gender balance at the top? In Norway, legislation has been passed decreeing that by the end of 2006 all companies must have at least two women on their boards. Norway already leads the world in the number of women on its company boards.

In Britain a group of businesswomen has set up an organisation called WDOB, or Women Directors on Boards, whose aim is "to change the face of UK plc." Jacey Graham, its director, hopes to see the almost static percentage of female executive directors in Britain more than double (to 10%) by 2010.

Ms Graham says that such change "won't just happen". It needs specific intervention within companies—intervention that is led from the top. Opportunities for flexible working are particularly helpful in keeping women in the workforce. KPMG, one of the Big Four accounting firms, is aiming to double the percentage of its partners who are women (currently 13%). It says flexible working is a key measure to help it achieve this goal. Three-quarters of all requests for flexible working over the past 12 months have been from women.

Mentoring is also helpful. The WDOB has initiated a programme in which the chairmen and CEOs of 25 FTSE100 companies have agreed to mentor women who have been identified from other companies among the group as having boardroom potential. "The sad thing," says Ms Graham, "is that some companies could not find a woman to put forward for mentoring." Women are enthusiastic mentors of each other. Colleen Arnold, the general manager of IBM Europe, Middle East and Africa, mentors 27 people formally and more than 100 informally. "Mentoring," she says, "is penalty-free."

Chief executives are appointed by sub-committees of companies' boards, often advised by headhunters. More of them will be women when more members of the sub-committees are women and when fewer headhunters are old white men. As Catalyst's Ms Lang puts it: "There are so many women qualified to be on boards who are out there, under the radar screen." Heidrick & Struggles, a firm of headhunters, says that boards may need to look beyond the top-management structures from which non-executive directors are usually drawn if they are "to increase markedly the ratio of female to male directors."

Some think the task is particularly urgent. Chris Clarke, the America-based CEO of Boyden, a firm of headhunters, and a visiting professor at Henley Management College in England, argues that women are superior to men at multi-tasking, team-building and communicating, which have become the essential skills for running a 21st-century corporation. Maria Wisniewska, who headed a Polish bank, Bank Pekao, and is an international adviser to the Conference Board, says: "The links between the rational and emotional parts of the brain are greater in women than in men. If so, and if leadership is about making links between emotion and intelligence, then maybe women are better at it than men."

Too Many Women in College?

Suddenly, the media—and Laura Bush—are concerned about an education gender gap. Funny, no one was scared when men were on top.

PHYLLIS ROSSER

Although American women still struggle for parity in many arenas, we have outpaced men in at least one: undergraduate college education. Currently, 57.4 percent of bachelor's degrees in the United States are earned by women, 42.6 percent by men. This is an almost exact reversal from 1970, when 56.9 percent of college graduates were males and 43.1 percent females.

We should be celebrated for this landmark achievement, but instead it has engendered fear. Read the headlines: "Falling Male College Matriculation an Alarming Trend," or "Admissions Officers Weigh a Heretical Idea: Affirmative Action for Men." Notice, too, that a major focus of first lady Laura Bush's new anti-gang task force is education for boys. As she's been quoted, "The statistics are pretty alarming. Girls are going to college much more than boys."

Few worried when college students were two-thirds men. But as early as February 1999, *U.S. News & World Report* predicted that the rising tide of women college grads could close the salary gap and move women into positions of power as heads of corporations, presidents of universities and political leaders. At the other extreme, the article suggested, college education might become devalued—considered "a foolhardy economic decision"—as has happened in other fields after women begin to predominate.

Still Rare at the Top

What *U.S. News* failed to mention was that women are still a rare presence at the top ranks of the corporate and professional world despite earning more college degrees than men for 23 years. Women undertake stronger academic programs than men in high school, and receive higher average grades than men in both high school and college, but haven't been able to translate that success into equitable money and power. Consider these disparities as well:

- Women currently earn nearly 59 percent of master's degrees, but men outstrip women in advanced degrees for business, engineering and computer-science degrees—fields which lead to much higher-paying jobs than education, health and psychology, the areas where women predominate.
- Despite women's larger numbers as undergrads and in master's programs, men outnumber women in earning doctorates (54 percent) and professional degrees (53 percent).
- This year, the number of women applying to medical school outpaced men for the second time, but they are only predicted to be 33 percent of doctors by 2010.
- Women comprise nearly half of the students entering law schools, but they're miles from parity as law partners, professors and judges.

Tests Don't Tell the Whole Tale

Women may lose a step on the career ladder even before they enter college. That's because, despite their greater number of bachelor's and master's degrees, women remain at a disadvantage in college admissions testing—which affects their acceptance at elite schools. The main purpose of the SAT—on which women averaged 44 points lower than men last year—is to predict first-year grades. However, it consistently underpredicts the college performance of women, who earn higher college grades than men.

Women's lower scores on the SAT have been shown to arise from several factors biased toward male performance, including the fact that it's a timed test and rewards guessing—and men tend to be more confident and risk-taking than women in such test situations. Also, the SAT puts many of the questions in a male context (such as sports), which can further lower female confidence about knowing the material.

In an attempt to even the gender playing field, a writing section that includes language questions and an essay was added to the SAT this year, after the University of California insisted that the test be more attuned to the skills necessary for college success. This may raise women's SAT scores somewhat, since writing tests are an area in which they have traditionally out performed males.

Lower SAT scores keep qualified women from both attending the most competitive schools and from receiving National Merit Scholarships and other awards based on PSAT and SAT scores. The test biases against women then continue in graduate education, with such instruments as the Graduate Record Exam (GRE), Graduate Management Admissions Test (GMAT) and Law School Admissions Test (LSAT).

Thus, women have yet to predominate at the most prestigious colleges and universities, where graduates are tracked toward top leadership positions in society. With enormous numbers of both sexes applying to these schools, the admissions offices can choose their gender ratio. In 2005, men outnumbered women at all the Ivy League schools except Brown and Columbia. Women are also significantly outnumbered at universities specializing in engineering and physical science, such as Massachusetts Institute of Technology in Cambridge and California Institute of Technology in Pasadena.

Affirmative Action—for Men?

The greater percentage of women earning bachelor's degrees has given rise to some reactionary theories explaining why. Conservative analyst Christina Hoff Sommers insists the gap takes root in the more "girl-friendly" elementary school environment where boys are turned off to learning. In *The War Against Boys: How Misguided Feminism Is Harming Our Young Men* (Simon & Schuster, 2000), Hoff Sommers claims that schoolboys are "routinely regarded as protosexists, potential harassers and perpetuators of gender inequity" who "live under a cloud of censure."

Even higher-education policy analyst Tom Mortensen, who has a special concern with underrepresented populations in higher education, also sees the college gender gap as part of a larger societal problem for men and boys. Mortensen says K–12 teachers, 75 percent of whom are women, are not providing the role models and learning styles boys need. Of course, this was never an issue during the decades when college graduates were mainly men, and hasn't drawn much notice since the end of the Civil War—the time when women began their continuing predominance as elementary school teachers.

If these theories seem to spring from a blame-the-women viewpoint, there is a legitimate concern about the decline in male graduates at private colleges, where the gap has been greatest (although public universities have also been affected). Admissions officers worry that their colleges' value will be lowered by an imbalance of female students: The larger the female majority, some say, the less likely either males or females will want to apply.

Speaking at a College Board conference several years ago, admissions officers agreed that a 60-40 female-to-male gender ratio was their upper limit. After that, said former Macalester College president Michael McPherson, "students will take notice." Small private colleges are now using what can only be called "male affirmative action" to increase male enrollment: actively recruiting men by emphasizing their science, math and engineering courses, adding sports programs (in violation of Title IX), sending extra mailings designed to attract men and even calling men to remind them of the admissions deadline.

"Probably no one will admit it, but I know lots of places try to get some gender balance by having easier admissions standards for boys than for girls," said Columbia University Teachers College president Arthur Levine to *The New York Times* national correspondent Tamar Lewin. Robert Massa, vice president of Dickinson College in Carlisle, Penn., has said that the school now evaluates prospective male students less on grades and more on measures where they typically do better, such as SAT scores. Adds Goucher College admissions vice president Barbara Fritze, "Men are being admitted to schools they never got into before, and offered financial aid they hadn't gotten before."

Massa reported that the number of first-year males at Dickinson rose from 36 percent to 43 percent in 2001 after they took affirmative action toward men, who were admitted with lower grades but comparable SAT scores. Women, meanwhile, had to be much better than men to make the cut: Nearly 62 percent of the women accepted to the school ranked in the top 10 percent of their high school class, compared to 42 percent of the men.

This new form of affirmative action, even if begun with all good intentions, could lead to bad college-admissions policy. What if a university decides it doesn't just want more men in attendance, but more white men? The whole notion of affirmative action as a way to help disadvantaged populations succeed could be turned on its head.

The Income Gap

The real reason behind the undergrad gender gap may have much less to do with one's sex and more to do with income, race and class.

Jacqueline King, director of the Center for Policy Analysis at the American Council on Education in Washington, D.C., decided that media stories about the decline of white male enrollment didn't intuitively jibe with what she saw happening, so she took a closer look at college student data, analyzing it by sex, age, race/ethnicity and socioeconomic status. She found the gender gap in college enrollment for students 18 to 24 years of age in 1995–96 occurred among low-income students of all racial/ethnic groups except Asian Americans.

There has been no *decline* in bachelor's degrees awarded to men, the numbers awarded to women have simply increased.

In fact, since 1995, many more women than men from households making less than $30,000 attend college. The latest available data, from 2003–04, shows there is an even smaller percentage of low-income males attending college than there were in 1995, and they are from every racial/ethnic group.

African American and Native American students have the largest gender gaps—males comprise just 37 percent of all low-income African American students and 36 percent of low-income Native Americans. Low-income Hispanic men reach a slightly higher 39 percent, and low-income white males 41 percent (a drop from 46 percent in 1995). Asian Americans have the smallest gender gap, with 47 percent of that group's low-income college students being male.

Middle-income ($30,000–$70,000) male students maintained gender parity with females 10 years ago, but since then the numbers have dropped somewhat. This may mean that fewer men from the lower end of this income bracket are attending college, says Eugene Anderson, senior research associate at the American Council on Education. At the highest income level ($70,000 or more), though, men and women in all ethnic groups attend college in nearly equal numbers.

No studies have been done to determine why more low-income women than men attend college, but there are theories. Economist Lester Thurow suggests that low-income men have been lured to the comfortable salaries of mechanical maintenance jobs. Low-income women, on the other hand, don't have such opportunities, and without a college degree, see themselves getting trapped in low-pay sales or service jobs, says King. Also, more men than women work in computer support or high-tech factories—jobs that don't require bachelor's degrees.

Overall, an increasing number of poor and working-class people are dropping out of college because of such reasons as escalating tuition and the attraction of high-paying factory work, according to a May piece in *The New York Times* ("The College Dropout Boom: Diploma's Absence Strands Many in the Working Class"). Harvard president Lawrence H. Summers goes so far as to call this widening of the education gap between rich and poor our "most serious domestic problem"—and recent changes in federal grant formulas may exacerbate it even further.

Uprising: Minorities and Older Women

On the bright side, ethnic minorities have made impressive gains as college students since 1976, increasing their percentage in the total student body from 10 percent to 23 percent. Minority men's share of all bachelor's degrees has gone from 5 percent to 9 percent. But, again, minority women have outstripped them, more than doubling their share of bachelor's degrees, from 5 percent to 14 percent of the total degrees awarded.

Not only is that statistic a contributing factor to the overall gender gap, but another contributing factor is that women are the majority of older (25+) students—and that demographic has been returning to college in record numbers. The "oldsters" now make up 27 percent of the undergraduate student body, and 61 percent of older students are women. King found that many of these students were African American or Latina, attending community colleges to improve future earnings in health-related fields.

"This story is not one of male failure, or even lack of opportunity," says King, "but rather one of increased academic opportunity and success among females and minorities." Indeed, there has been no decline in bachelor's degrees awarded to men; the numbers awarded to women have simply increased.

Feminists should continue to be concerned about encouraging low-income and minority students to attend college, using the current momentum to give these problems the attention they deserve. But in the meantime, we must remain vigilant about attempts to roll back our educational gains. The fact is, we're a long way from threatening corporate America, so don't put the onus on women. Maybe it's just time to let men try to catch up to us, for a change.

Human Rights, Sex Trafficking, and Prostitution

ALICE LEUCHTAG

Despite laws against slavery in practically every country, an estimated twenty-seven million people live as slaves. Kevin Bales, in his book *Disposable People: New Slavery in the Global Economy* (University of California Press, Berkeley, 1999), describes those who endure modern forms of slavery. These include indentured servants, persons held in hereditary bondage, child slaves who pick plantation crops, child soldiers, and adults and children trafficked and sold into sex slavery.

A Life Narrative

Of all forms of slavery, sex slavery is one of the most exploitative and lucrative with some 200,000 sex slaves worldwide bringing their slaveholders an annual profit of $10.5 billion. Although the great preponderance of sex slaves are women and girls, a smaller but significant number of males—both adult and children—are enslaved for homosexual prostitution.

The life narrative of a Thai girl named Siri, as told to Bales, illustrates how sex slavery happens to vulnerable girls and women. Siri is born in northeastern Thailand to a poor family that farms a small plot of land, barely eking out a living. Economic policies of structural adjustment pursued by the Thai government under the aegis of the World Bank and the International Monetary Fund have taken former government subsidies away from rice farmers, leaving them to compete against imported, subsidized rice that keeps the market price artificially depressed.

Siri attends four years of school, then is kept at home to help care for her three younger siblings. When Siri is fourteen, a well-dressed woman visits her village. She offers to find Siri a "good job," advancing her parents $2,000 against future earnings. This represents at least a year's income for the family. In a town in another province the woman, a trafficker, "sells" Siri to a brothel for $4,000. Owned by an "investment club" whose members are business and professional men—government bureaucrats and local politicians—the brothel is extremely profitable. In a typical thirty-day period it nets its investors $88,000.

To maintain the appearance that their hands are clean, members of the club's board of directors leave the management of the brothel to a pimp and a bookkeeper. Siri is initiated into prostitution by the pimp who rapes her. After being abused by her first "customer," Siri escapes, but a policeman—who gets a percentage of the brothel profits—brings her back, whereupon the pimp beats her up. As further punishment, her "debt" is doubled from $4,000 to $8,000. She must now repay this, along with her monthly rent and food, all from her earnings of $4 per customer. She will have to have sex with three hundred men a month just to pay her rent. Realizing she will never be able to get out of debt, Siri tries to build a relationship with the pimp simply in order to survive.

The pimp uses culture and religion to reinforce his control over Siri. He tells her she must have committed terrible sins in a past life to have been born a female; she must have accumulated a karmic debt to deserve the enslavement and abuse to which she must reconcile herself. Gradually Siri begins to see herself from the point of view of the slaveholder—as someone unworthy and deserving of punishment. By age fifteen she no longer protests or runs away. Her physical enslavement has become psychological as well, a common occurrence in chronic abuse.

Siri is administered regular injections of the contraceptive drug Depo-Provera for which she is charged. As the same needle is used for all the girls, there is a high risk of HIV and other sexual diseases from the injections. Siri knows that a serious illness threatens her and she prays to Buddha at the little shrine in her room, hoping to earn merit so he will protect her from dreaded disease. Once a month she and the others, at their own expense, are tested for HIV. So far Siri's tests have been negative. When Siri tries to get the male customers to wear condoms—distributed free to brothels by the Thai Ministry of Health—some resist wearing them and she can't make them do so.

As one of an estimated 35,000 women working as brothel slaves in Thailand—a country where 500,000 to one million prostituted women and girls work in conditions of degradation and exploitation short of brothel slavery—Siri faces at least a 40 percent chance of contracting the HIV virus. If she is lucky, she can look forward to live more years before she becomes too ill to work and is pushed out into the street.

Thailand's Sex Tourism

Though the Thai government denies it, the World Health Organization finds that HIV is epidemic in Thailand, with the largest segment of new cases among wives and girlfriends of men who buy prostitute sex. Viewing its women as a cash crop to be exploited, and depending on sex tourism for foreign exchange dollars to help pay interest on the foreign debt, the Thai government can't acknowledge the epidemic without contradicting the continued promotion of sex tourism and prostitution.

By encouraging investment in the sex industry, sex tourism creates a business climate conducive to the trafficking and enslavement of vulnerable girls such as Siri. In 1996 nearly five million sex tourists from the United States, Western Europe, Australia, and Japan visited Thailand. These transactions brought in about $26.2 billion—thirteen times more than Thailand earned by building and exporting computers.

In her 1999 report *Pimps and Predators on the Internet: Globalizing the Sexual Exploitation of Women and Children,* published by the Coalition Against Trafficking in Women (CATW), Donna Hughes quotes from postings on an Internet site where sex tourists share experiences and advise one another. The following is one man's description of having sex with a fourteen-year-old prostituted girl in Bangkok:

> "Even though I've had a lot of better massages . . . after fifteen minutes, I was much more relaxed . . . Then I asked for a condom and I fucked her for another thirty minutes. Her face looked like she was feeling a lot of pain. . . . She blocked my way when I wanted to leave the room and she asked for a tip. I gave her 600 bath. Altogether, not a good experience."

Hughes says, "To the men who buy sex, a 'bad experience' evidently means not getting their money's worth, or that the prostituted woman or girl didn't keep up the act of enjoying what she had to do. . . one glimpses the humiliation and physical pain most girls and women in prostitution endure."

Nor are the men oblivious to the existence of sexual slavery. One customer states, "Girls in Bangkok virtually get sold by their families into the industry; they work against their will." His knowledge of their sexual slavery and lack of sensitivity thereof is evident in that he then names the hotels in which girls are kept and describes how much they cost!

As Hughes observes, sex tourists apparently feel they have a right to prostitute sex, perceiving prostitution only from a self-interested perspective in which they commodify and objectify women of other cultures, nationalities, and ethnic groups. Their awareness of racism, colonialism, global economic inequalities, and sexism seems limited to the way these realities benefit them as sex consumers.

Sex Traffickers Cast Their Nets

According to the *Guide to the New UN Trafficking Protocol* by Janice Raymond, published by the CATW in 2001, the United Nations estimates that sex trafficking in human beings is a $5 billion to $7 billion operation annually. Four million persons are moved illegally from one country to another and within countries each year, a large proportion of them women and girls being trafficked into prostitution. The United Nations International Children's Emergency Fund (UNICEF) estimates that some 30 percent of women being trafficked are minors, many under age thirteen. The International Organization on Migration estimates

that some 500,000 women per year are trafficked into Western Europe from poorer regions of the world. According to *Sex Trafficking of Women in the United States: International and Domestic Trends,* also published by the CATW in 2001, some 50,000 women and children are trafficked into the United States each year, mainly from Asia and Latin America.

Because prostitution as a system of organized sexual exploitation depends on a continuous supply of new "recruits," trafficking is essential to its continued existence. When the pool of available women and girls dries up, new women must be procured. Traffickers cast their nets ever wide and become ever more sophisticated. The Italian Camorra, Chinese Triads, Russian Mafia, and Japanese Yakuza are powerful criminal syndicates consisting of traffickers, pimps, brothel keepers, forced labor lords, and gangs which operate globally.

After the breakdown of the Soviet Union, an estimated five thousand criminal groups formed the Russian Mafia, which operates in thirty countries. The Russian Mafia trafficks women from African countries, the Ukraine, the Russian Federation, and Eastern Europe into Western Europe, the United States, and Israel. The Triads traffick women from China, Korea, Thailand, and other Southeast Asian countries into the United States and Europe. The Camorra trafficks women from Latin America into Europe. The Yakuza trafficks women from the Philipines, Thailand, Burma, Cambodia, Korea, Nepal, and Laos into Japan.

A Global Problem Meets a Global Response

Despite these appalling facts, until recently no generally agreed upon definition of trafficking in human beings was written into international law. In Vienna, Austria, during 1999 and 2000, 120 countries participated in debates over a definition of trafficking. A few nongovernmental organizations (NGOs) and a minority of governments—including Australia, Canada, Denmark, Germany, Ireland, Japan, the Netherlands, Spain, Switzerland, Thailand, and the United Kingdom—wanted to separate issues of trafficking from issues of prostitution. They argued that persons being trafficked should be divided into those who are forced and those who give their consent, with the burden of proof being placed on persons being trafficked. They also urged that the less explicit means of control over trafficked persons—such as abuse of a victim's vulnerability—not be included in the definition of trafficking and that the word *exploitation* not be used. Generally supporters of this position were wealthier countries where large numbers of women were being trafficked and countries in which prostitution was legalized or sex tourism encouraged.

People being trafficked shouldn't be divided into those who are forced and those who give their consent because trafficked persons are in no position to give meaningful consent.

The CATW—140 other NGOs that make up the International Human Rights Network plus many governments (including those of Algeria, Bangladesh, Belgium, China, Columbia, Cuba, Egypt, Finland, France, India, Mexico, Norway, Pakistan, the Philippines, Sweden, Syria, Venezuela, and Vietnam)—maintains that trafficking can't be separated from prostitution. Persons being trafficked shouldn't be divided into those who are forced and those who give their consent because trafficked persons are in no position to give meaningful consent. The subtler methods used by traffickers, such as abuse of a victim's vulnerability, should be included in the definition of trafficking and the word *exploitation* be an essential part of the definition. Generally supporters of this majority view were poorer countries from which large numbers of women were being trafficked or countries in which strong feminist, anti-colonialist, or socialist influences existed. The United States, though initially critical of the majority position, agreed to support a definition of trafficking that would be agreed upon by consensus.

The struggle—led by the CATW to create a definition of trafficking that would penalize traffickers while ensuring that all victims of trafficking would be protected—succeeded when a compromise proposal by Sweden was agreed to. A strongly worded and inclusive *UN Protocol to Prevent, Suppress, and Punish Trafficking in Persons*—especially women and children—was drafted by an ad hoc committee of the UN as a supplement to the Convention Against Transnational Organized Crime. The UN protocol specifically addresses the trade in human beings for purposes of prostitution and other forms of sexual exploitation, forced labor or services, slavery or practices similar to slavery, servitude, and the removal of organs. The protocol defines trafficking as:

The recruitment, transportation, transfer, harboring or receipt of persons, by means of the threat or use of force or other forms of coercion, of abduction, of fraud, of deception, of the abuse of power or of a position of vulnerability or of the giving or receiving of payments or benefits to achieve the consent of a person having control over another person, for the purpose of exploitation.

While recognizing that the largest amount of trafficking involves women and children, the wording of the UN protocol clearly is gender and age neutral, inclusive of trafficking in both males and females, adults and children.

In 2000 the UN General Assembly adopted this convention and its supplementary protocol; 121 countries signed the convention and eighty countries signed the protocol. For the convention and protocol to become international law, forty countries must ratify them.

Highlights

Some highlights of the new convention and protocol are: For the first time there is an accepted international definition of trafficking and an agreed-upon set of prosecution, protection, and prevention mechanisms on which countries can base their national legislation.

- The various criminal means by which trafficking takes place, including indirect and subtle forms of coercion, are covered.
- Trafficked persons, especially women in prostitution and child laborers, are no longer viewed as illegal migrants but as victims of a crime.

For the first time there is an accepted international definition of trafficking and an agreed-upon set of prosecution, protection, and prevention mechanisms on which countries can base their national legislation.

- The convention doesn't limit its scope to criminal syndicates but defines an organized criminal group as "any structured group of three or more persons which engages in criminal activities such as trafficking and pimping."
- All victims of trafficking in persons are protected, not just those who can prove that force was used against them.
- The consent of a victim of trafficking is meaningless and irrelevant.
- Victims of trafficking won't have to bear the burden of proof.
- Trafficking and sexual exploitation are intrinsically connected and not to be separated.
- Because women trafficked domestically into local sex industries suffer harmful effects similar to those experienced by women trafficked transnationally, these women also come under the protections of the protocol.
- The key element in trafficking is the exploitative purpose rather than the movement across a border.

The protocol is the first UN instrument to address the demand for prostitution sex, a demand that results in the human rights abuses of women and children being trafficked. The protocol recognizes an urgent need for governments to put the buyers of prostitution sex on their policy and legislative agendas, and it calls upon countries to take or strengthen legislative or other measures to discourage demand, which fosters all the forms of sexual exploitation of women and children.

As Raymond says in the *Guide to the New UN Trafficking Protocol:*

"The least discussed part of the prostitution and trafficking chain has been the men who buy women for sexual exploitation in prostitution. . . . If we are to find a permanent path to ending these human rights abuses, then we cannot just shrug our shoulders and say, "men are like this," or "boys will be boys," or "prostitution has always been around." Or tell women and girls in prostitution that they must continue to do what they do because prostitution is inevitable. Rather, our responsibility is to make men change their behavior, by all means available—educational, cultural and legal."

Two U.S. feminist, human rights organizations—Captive Daughters and Equality Now—have been working toward that goal. Surita Sandosham of Equality Now says that when her organization asked women's groups in Thailand and the Philippines how it could assist them, the answer came back, "Do something about the demand." Since then the two organizations have legally challenged sex tours originating in the United States and have succeeded in closing down at least one operation.

Refugees, Not Illegal Aliens

In October 2000 the U.S. Congress passed a bill, the Victims of Trafficking and Violence Protection Act of 2000, introduced by New Jersey republican representative Chris Smith. Under this law penalties for traffickers are raised and protections for victims increased. Reasoning that desperate women are unable to give meaningful consent to their own sexual exploitation, the law adopts a broad definition of sex trafficking so as not to exclude so-called consensual prostitution or trafficking that occurs solely within the United States. In these respects the new federal law conforms to the UN protocol.

Two features of the law are particularly noteworthy:

- In order to pressure other countries to end sex trafficking, the U.S. State Department is to make a yearly assessment of other countries' anti-trafficking efforts and to rank them according to how well they discourage trafficking. After two years of failing to meet even minimal standards, countries are subject to sanctions, although not sanctions on humanitarian aid. "Tier 3" countries—those failing to meet even minimal standards—include Greece, Indonesia, Israel, Pakistan, Russia, Saudi Arabia, South Korea, and Thailand.

- Among persons being trafficked into the United States, special T-visas will be provided to those who meet the criteria for having suffered the most serious trafficking abuses. These visas will protect them from deportation so they can testify against their traffickers. T-non immigrant status allows eligible aliens to remain in the United States temporarily and grants specific non-immigrant benefits. Those acquiring T-1 non-immigrant status will be able to remain for a period of three years and will be eligible to receive certain kinds of public assistance—to the same extent as refugees. They will also be issued employment authorization to "assist them in finding safe, legal employment while they attempt to retake control of their lives."

A Debate Rages

A worldwide debate rages about legalization of prostitution fueled by a 1998 International Labor Organization (ILO) report

entitled *The Sex Sector: The Economic and Social Bases of Prostitution in Southeast Asia.* The report follows years of lobbying by the sex industry for recognition of prostitution as "sex work." Citing the sex industry's unrecognized contribution to the gross domestic product of four countries in Southeast Asia, the ILO urges governments to officially recognize the "sex sector" and "extend taxation nets to cover many of the lucrative activities connected with it." Though the ILO report says it stops short of calling for legalization of prostitution, official recognition of the sex industry would be impossible without it.

Raymond points out that the ILO's push to redefine prostitution as sex work ignores legislation demonstrating that countries can reduce organized sexual exploitation rather than capitulate to it. For example, Sweden prohibits the purchase of sexual services with punishments of still fines or imprisonment, thus declaring that prostitution isn't a desirable economic and labor sector. The government also helps women getting out of prostitution to rebuild their lives. Venezuela's Ministry of Labor has ruled that prostitution can't be considered work because it lacks the basic elements of dignity and social justice. The Socialist Republic of Vietnam punishes pimps, traffickers, brothel owners, and buyers—sometimes publishing buyer's names in the mass media. For women in prostitution, the government finances medical, educational, and economic rehabilitation.

> **Instead of transforming the male buyer into a legitmate customer, the ILO should give thought to innovative programs that make the buyer accountable for his sexual exploitation.**

Raymond suggests that instead of transforming the male buyer into a legitimate customer, the ILO should give thought to innovative programs that make the buyer accountable for his sexual exploitation. She cites the Sage Project, Inc. (SAGE) program in San Francisco, California, which educates men arrested for soliciting women in prostitution about the risks and impacts of their behavior.

Legalization advocates argue that the violence, exploitation, and health effects suffered by women in prostitution aren't inherent to prostitution but simply result from the random behaviors of bad pimps or buyers, and that if prostitution were regulated by the state these harms would diminish. But examples show these arguments to be false.

> **Prostituted women are even more marginalized and tightly locked into the system of organized sexual exploitation while the state, now an official party to the exploitation, has become the biggest pimp of all.**

In the pamphlet entitled *Legalizing Prostitution Is Not the Answer: The Example of Victoria, Australia,* published by the CATW in 2001, Mary Sullivan and Sheila Jeffreys describe the way legalization in Australia has perpetuated and strengthened the culture of violence and exploitation inherent in prostitution. Under legalization, legal and illegal brothels have proliferated, and trafficking in women has accelerated to meet the increased demand. Pimps, having even more power, continue threatening and brutalizing the women they control. Buyers continue to abuse women, refuse to wear condoms, and spread the HIV virus—and other sexually transmitted diseases—to their wives and girlfriends. Stigmatized by identity cards and medial inspections, prostituted women are even more marginalized and tightly locked into the system of organized sexual exploitation while the state, now an official party to the exploitation, has become the biggest pimp of all.

The government of the Netherlands has legalized prostitution, doesn't enforce laws against pimping, and virtually lives off taxes from the earnings of prostituted women. In the book *Making the Harm Visible* (published by the CATW in 1999), Marie-Victoire Louis describes the effects on prostituted women of municipal regulation of brothels in Amsterdam and other Dutch cities. Her article entitled "Legalizing Pimping, Dutch Style" explains the way immigration policies in the Netherlands are shaped to fit the needs of the prostitution industry so that traffickers are seldom prosecuted and a continuous supply of women is guaranteed. In Amsterdam's 250 officially listed brothels, 80 percent of the prostitutes have been trafficked in from other countries and 70 percent possess no legal papers. Without money, papers, or contact with the outside world, these immigrant women live in terror instead of being protected by the regulations governing brothels, prostituted women are frequently beaten up and raped by pimps. These "prostitution managers" have practically been given a free hand by the state and by buyers who, as "consumers of prostitution," feel themselves entitled to abuse the women they buy. Sadly and ironically the "Amsterdam model" of legalization and regulation is touted by the Netherlands and Germany as "self-determination and empowerment for women." In reality it simply legitimizes the "right" to buy, sexually use, and profit from the sexual exploitation of someone else's body.

A Human Rights Approach

As part of a system of organized sexual exploitation, prostitution can be visualized along a continuum of abuse with brothel slavery at the furthest extreme. All along the continuum, fine lines divide the degrees of harm done to those caught up in the system. At the core lies a great social injustice no cosmetic reforms can right: the setting aside of a segment of people whose bodies can be purchased for sexual use by others. When this basic injustice is legitimized and regulated by the state and when the state profits from it, that injustice is compounded.

In her book *The Prostitution of Sexuality* (New York University Press, 1995), Kathleen Barry details a feminist human rights approach to prostitution that points the way to the future. Ethically it recognizes prostitution, sex trafficking, and the globalized industrialization of sex as massive violations of women's human rights. Sociologically it considers how and to what extent prostitution promotes sex discrimination against individual women, against different racial categories of women, and against women as a group. Politically it calls for decriminalizing prostitutes while penalizing pimps, traffickers, brothel owners, and buyers.

Understanding that human rights and restorative justice go hand in hand, the feminist human rights approach to prostitution addresses the harm and the need to repair the damage. As Barry says:

> "Legal proposals to criminalize customers, based on the recognition that prostitution violates and harms women, must . . . include social-service, health and counseling and job retraining programs. Where states would be closing down brothels if customers were criminalized, the economic resources poured into the former prostitution areas could be turned toward producing gainful employment for women."

With the help of women's projects in many countries—such as Buklod in the Philippines and the Council for Prostitution Alternatives in the United States—some women have begun to confront their condition by leaving prostitution, speaking out against it, revealing their experiences, and helping other women leave the sex industry.

Ending the sexual exploitation of trafficking and prostitution will mean the beginning of a new chapter in building, a humanist future—a more peaceful and just future in which men and women can join together in love and respect, recognizing one another's essential dignity and humanity. Humanity's sexuality then will no longer be hijacked and distorted.

Freelance writer **ALICE LEUCHTAG** has worked as a social worker, counselor, college instructor, and researcher. Active in the civil rights, peace, socialist, feminist, and humanist movements, she has helped organize women in Houston to oppose sex trafficking.

UNIT 5

Social Institutions: Issues, Crises, and Changes

Unit Selections

Key Points to Consider

- Discuss whether or not it is important to preserve some continuity in institutions.

- How can institutions outlive their usefulness? How can they be changed for the better?

- Why are institutions so difficult to change? Cite examples where changes are instituted from the top down, and others where they are instituted from the bottom up. Do you see a similar pattern of development for these types of changes?

- Is it possible to reform the political system to greatly reduce the corrupting role of money in politics? Why or why not?

- What basic changes in the economic system are evident in the things that you observe daily?

- How would you reform the educational system in America?

- How would you change the health care system?

Student Web Site

www.mhcls.com/online

Internet References

Further information regarding these Web sites may be found in this book's preface or online.

Center for the Study of Group Processes
  http://www.uiowa.edu/~grpproc
International Labour Organization (ILO)
  http://www.ilo.org
IRIS Center
  http://www.iris.umd.edu
National Center for Policy Analysis
  http://www.ncpa.org
National Institutes of Health (NIH)
  http://www.nih.gov

Social institutions are the building blocks of social structure. They accomplish the important tasks of society—for example, regulation of reproduction, socialization of children, production and distribution of economic goods, law enforcement and social control, and organization of religion and other value systems.

Social institutions are not rigid arrangements; they reflect changing social conditions. Institutions generally change slowly. At the present time, however, many of the social institutions in the United States and in many other parts of the world are in crisis and are undergoing rapid change. Eastern European countries are literally transforming their political and economic institutions. Economic institutions, such as stock markets, are becoming truly international, and when a major country experiences a recession, many other countries feel the effects. In the United States, major reform movements are active in political, economic, family, medical, and educational institutions.

The first subsection of Unit 5 examines American political institutions. Bill Moyers tells moving stories documenting the tragic inequalities in America and the institutions that generate these inequalities in society. A half-century ago institutions, culture, and policies worked to soften the inequalities; not so today. Now, the rich and powerful control the political institutions so that they generate lavish benefits for themselves while the benefits for lower classes shrink. How do the rich and powerful control the political institutions? The next article provides a major part of the answer. It examines the operation of special interests in obtaining "pork" through the legislative process, and details a shocking story because the corruption of our democracy is much worse than we realize.

The following subsection deals with major issues and problems of the economy. The first tackles the big question of how "good" the U.S. economy is. W. Michael Cox and Richard Alm provide an assessment that includes, and goes beyond, economic statistics. The authors reveal that we are the world's wealthiest nation with the highest consumption (e.g., home ownership) but also have a balanced life. This includes more leisure, more pleasant work, greater safety, more convenience, a cleaner environment, and more variety. All this supports the authors' thesis that our type of free enterprise system is one of the best in the world. The subsequent article discusses business outsourcing, which has created fear about declining jobs for the middle class. Not so, says Pete Engardio, because outsourcing greatly benefits American businesses and expands jobs. Without it, more businesses would fail and shrink the job market. The next selection focuses on consumption. It explains how consumption, and the materialistic values that under-gird it, have some seriously negative effects on us without increasing our happiness.

The social sphere is also in turmoil, as illustrated by the articles in the last subsection. A key issue for many parents and children is the quality of education, and the public's perception is rather negative. Chester E. Finn, Jr. addresses the failure of American high schools. He identifies six major problems, and offers his solutions for each. The medical sphere is also in turmoil and plagued with problems. John Carey points out that most medical decisions are based on very little, if any, evidence. He supports the crusade of Dr. David Eddy for evidence-based medicine. In the final article, the spiritual realm is addressed. Jerry Adler reports on spirituality in America in an article which covers both statistics and practices.

Who Rules America?

G. WILLIAM DOMHOFF

Power and Class in the United States

Power and *class* are terms that make Americans a little uneasy, and concepts like *power elite* and *dominant class* immediately put people on guard. The idea that a relatively fixed group of privileged people might shape the economy and government for their own benefit goes against the American grain. Nevertheless, . . . the owners and top-level managers in large income-producing properties are far and away the dominant power figures in the United States. Their corporations, banks, and agribusinesses come together as a *corporate community* that dominates the federal government in Washington. Their real estate, construction, and land development companies form *growth coalitions* that dominate most local governments. Granted, there is competition within both the corporate community and the local growth coalitions for profits and investment opportunities, and there are sometimes tensions between national corporations and local growth coalitions, but both are cohesive on policy issues affecting their general welfare, and in the face of demands by organized workers, liberals, environmentalists, and neighborhoods.

As a result of their ability to organize and defend their interests, the owners and managers of large income-producing properties have a very great share of all income and wealth in the United States, greater than in any other industrial democracy. Making up at best 1 percent of the total population, by the early 1990s they earned 15.7 percent of the nation's yearly income and owned 37.2 percent of all privately held wealth, including 49.6 percent of all corporate stocks and 62.4 percent of all bonds. Due to their wealth and the lifestyle it makes possible, these owners and managers draw closer as a common social group. They belong to the same exclusive social clubs, frequent the same summer and winter resorts, and send their children to a relative handful of private schools. Members of the corporate community thereby become a *corporate rich* who create a nationwide *social upper class* through their social interaction. . . . Members of the growth coalitions, on the other hand, are *place entrepreneurs,* people who sell locations and buildings. They come together as local upper classes in their respective cities and sometimes mingle with the corporate rich in educational or resort settings.

The corporate rich and the growth entrepreneurs supplement their small numbers by developing and directing a wide variety of nonprofit organizations, the most important of which are a set of tax-free charitable foundations, think tanks, and policy-discussion groups. These specialized nonprofit groups constitute a *policy-formation network* at the national level. Chambers of commerce and policy groups affiliated with them form similar policy-formation networks at the local level, aided by a few national-level city development organizations that are available for local consulting.

Those corporate owners who have the interest and ability to take part in general governance join with top-level executives in the corporate community and the policy-formation network to form the *power elite,* which is the leadership group for the corporate rich as a whole. The concept of a power elite makes clear that not all members of the upper class are involved in governance; some of them simply enjoy the lifestyle that their great wealth affords them. At the same time, the focus on a leadership group allows for the fact that not all those in the power elite are members of the upper class; many of them are high-level employees in profit and nonprofit organizations controlled by the corporate rich. . . .

The power elite is not united on all issues because it includes both moderate conservatives and ultraconservatives. Although both factions favor minimal reliance on government on all domestic issues, the moderate conservatives sometimes agree to legislation advocated by liberal elements of the society, especially in times of social upheaval like the Great Depression of the 1930s and the Civil Rights Movement of the early 1960s. Except on defense spending, ultraconservatives are characterized by a complete distaste for any kind of government programs under any circumstances—even to the point of opposing government support for corporations on some issues. Moderate conservatives often favor foreign aid, working through the United Nations, and making attempts to win over foreign enemies through patient diplomacy, treaties, and trade agreements. Historically, ultraconservatives have opposed most forms of foreign involvement, although they have become more tolerant of foreign trade agreements over the past thirty or forty years. At the same time, their hostility to the United Nations continues unabated.

Members of the power elite enter into the electoral arena as the leaders within a *corporate-conservative coalition,* where they are aided by a wide variety of patriotic, anti-tax, and other single-issue organizations. These conservative advocacy organizations are funded in varying degrees by the corporate rich, direct-mail appeals, and middle-class conservatives. This coalition has played a large role in both political parties at the presidential level and usually succeeds in electing a conservative majority to both houses of Congress. Historically, the conservative majority in Congress was made up of most Northern Republicans and most Southern Democrats, but that arrangement has been changing gradually since the 1960s as the conservative Democrats of the South are replaced by even more conservative Southern Republicans. The corporate-conservative coalition also has access to the federal government in Washington through lobbying and the appointment of its members to top positions in the executive branch. . . .

Despite their preponderant power within the federal government and the many useful policies it carries out for them, members of the power elite are constantly critical of government as an alleged enemy of freedom and economic growth. Although their wariness toward government is expressed in terms of a dislike for taxes and government regulations, I believe their underlying concern is that government could change the power relations in the private sphere by aiding average Americans through a number of different avenues: (1) creating government jobs for the unemployed; (2) making health, unemployment, and welfare benefits more generous; (3) helping employees gain greater workplace rights and protections; and (4) helping workers organize unions. All of these initiatives are opposed by members of the power elite because they would increase wages and taxes, but the deepest opposition is toward any government support for unions because unions are a potential organizational base for advocating the whole range of issues opposed by the corporate rich. . . .

Where Does Democracy Fit In?

. . . [T]o claim that the corporate rich have enough power to be considered a dominant class does not imply that lower social classes are totally powerless. *Domination* means the power to set the terms under which other groups and classes must operate, not total control. Highly trained professionals with an interest in environmental and consumer issues have been able to couple their technical information and their understanding of the legislative and judicial processes with well-timed publicity, lobbying, and lawsuits to win governmental restrictions on some corporate practices. Wage and salary employees, when they are organized into unions and have the right to strike, have been able to gain pay increases, shorter hours, better working conditions, and social benefits such as health insurance. Even the most powerless of people—the very poor and those discriminated against—sometimes develop the capacity to influence the power structure through sit-ins, demonstrations, social movements, and other forms of social disruption, and there is evidence that such activities do bring about some redress of grievances, at least for a short time.

More generally, the various challengers to the power elite sometimes work together on policy issues as a *liberal-labor coalition* that is based in unions, local environmental organizations, some minority group communities, university and arts communities, liberal churches, and small newspapers and magazines. Despite a decline in membership over the past twenty years, unions

are the largest and best-financed part of the coalition, and the largest organized social force in the country (aside from churches). They also cut across racial and ethnic lines more than any other institutionalized sector of American society. . . .

The policy conflicts between the corporate-conservative and liberal-labor coalitions are best described as *class conflicts* because they primarily concern the distribution of profits and wages, the rate and progressivity of taxation, the usefulness of labor unions, and the degree to which business should be regulated by government. The liberal-labor coalition wants corporations to pay higher wages to employees and higher taxes to government. It wants government to regulate a wide range of business practices, including many that are related to the environment, and help employees to organize unions. The corporate-conservative coalition resists all these policy objectives to a greater or lesser degree, claiming they endanger the freedom of individuals and the efficient workings of the economic marketplace. The conflicts these disagreements generate can manifest themselves in many different ways: workplace protests, industrywide boycotts, massive demonstrations in cities, pressure on Congress, and the outcome of elections.

Neither the corporate-conservative nor the liberal-labor coalition includes a very large percentage of the American population, although each has the regular support of about 25–30 percent of the voters. Both coalitions are made up primarily of financial donors, policy experts, political consultants, and party activists. . . .

Pluralism. The main alternative theory [I] address. . . . claims that power is more widely dispersed among groups and classes than a class-dominance theory allows. This general perspective is usually called *pluralism,* meaning there is no one dominant power group. It is the theory most favored by social scientists. In its strongest version, pluralism holds that power is held by the general public through the pressure that public opinion and voting put on elected officials. According to this version, citizens form voluntary groups and pressure groups that shape public opinion, lobby elected officials, and back sympathetic political candidates in the electoral process. . . .

The second version of pluralism sees power as rooted in a wide range of well-organized "interest groups" that are often based in economic interests (e.g., industrialists, bankers, labor unions), but also in other interests as well (e.g., environmental, consumer, and civil rights groups). These interest groups join together in different coalitions depending on the specific issues. Proponents of this version of pluralism sometimes concede that public opinion and voting have only a minimal or indirect influence, but they see business groups as too fragmented and antagonistic to form a cohesive dominant class. They also claim that some business interest groups occasionally join coalitions with liberal or labor groups on specific issues, and that business-dominated coalitions sometimes lose. Furthermore, some proponents of this version of pluralism believe that the Democratic Party is responsive to the wishes of liberal and labor interest groups.

In contrast, I argue that the business interest groups are part of a tightly knit corporate community that is able to develop classwide cohesion on the issues of greatest concern to it:

opposition to unions, high taxes, and government regulation. When a business group loses on a specific issue, it is often because other business groups have been opposed; in other words, there are arguments within the corporate community, and these arguments are usually settled within the governmental arena. I also claim that liberal and labor groups are rarely part of coalitions with business groups and that for most of its history the Democratic Party has been dominated by corporate and agribusiness interests in the Southern states, in partnership with the growth coalitions in large urban areas outside the South. Finally, I show that business interests rarely lose on labor and regulatory issues except in times of extreme social disruption like the 1930s and 1960s, when differences of opinion between Northern and Southern corporate leaders made victories for the liberal-labor coalition possible. . . .

How the Power Elite Dominates Government

This [section] shows how the power elite builds on the ideas developed in the policy-formation process and its success in the electoral arena to dominate the federal government. Lobbyists from corporations, law firms, and trade associations play a key role in shaping government on narrow issues of concern to specific corporations or business sectors, but their importance should not be overestimated because a majority of those elected to Congress are predisposed to agree with them. The corporate community and the policy-formation network supply top-level governmental appointees and new policy directions on major issues.

Once again, as seen in the battles for public opinion and electoral success, the power elite faces opposition from a minority of elected officials and their supporters in labor unions and liberal advocacy groups. These opponents are sometimes successful in blocking ultra-conservative initiatives, but most of the victories for the liberal-labor coalition are the result of support from moderate conservatives. . . .

Appointees to Government

The first way to test a class-dominance view of the federal government is to study the social and occupational backgrounds of the people who are appointed to manage the major departments of the executive branch, such as state, treasury, defense, and justice. If pluralists are correct, these appointees should come from a wide range of interest groups. If the state autonomy theorists are correct, they should be disproportionately former elected officials or longtime government employees. If the class-dominance view is correct, they should come disproportionately from the upper class, the corporate community, and the policy-formation network.

There have been numerous studies over the years of major governmental appointees under both Republican and Democratic administrations, usually focusing on the top appointees in the departments that are represented in the president's cabinet.

These studies are unanimous in their conclusion that most top appointees in both Republican and Democratic administrations are corporate executives and corporate lawyers—and hence members of the power elite. . . .

Conclusion

This [section] has demonstrated the power elite's wide-ranging access to government through the interest-group and policy-formation processes, as well as through its ability to influence appointments to major government positions. When coupled with the several different kinds of power discussed in earlier [sections] this access and involvement add up to power elite domination of the federal government.

By *domination,* as stated in the first [section], social scientists mean the ability of a class or group to set the terms under which other classes or groups within a social system must operate. By this definition, domination does not mean control on each and every issue, and it does not rest solely on involvement in government. Influence over government is only the final and most visible aspect of power elite domination, which has its roots in the class structure, the corporate control of the investment function, and the operation of the policy-formation network. If government officials did not have to wait for corporate leaders to decide where and when they will invest, and if government officials were not further limited by the general public's acceptance of policy recommendations from the policy-formation network, then power elite involvement in elections and government would count for a lot less than they do under present conditions.

Domination by the power elite does not negate the reality of continuing conflict over government policies, but few conflicts, it has been shown, involve challenges to the rules that create privileges for the upper class and domination by the power elite. Most of the numerous battles within the interest-group process, for example, are only over specific spoils and favors; they often involve disagreements among competing business interests.

Similarly, conflicts within the policy-making process of government often involve differences between the moderate conservative and ultraconservative segments of the dominant class. At other times they involve issues in which the needs of the corporate community as a whole come into conflict with the needs of specific industries, which is what happens to some extent on tariff policies and also on some environmental legislation. In neither case does the nature of the conflict call into question the domination of government by the power elite.

. . . Contrary to what pluralists claim, there is not a single case study on any issue of any significance that shows a liberal-labor victory over a united corporate-conservative coalition, which is strong evidence for a class-domination theory on the "Who wins?" power indicator. The classic case studies frequently cited by pluralists have been shown to be gravely deficient as evidence for their views. Most of these studies reveal either conflicts among rival groups within the power elite or situations in which the moderate conservatives have decided for their own reasons to side with the liberal-labor coalition. . . .

More generally, it now can be concluded that all four indicators of power introduced in [the first section] point to the corporate rich and their power elite as the dominant organizational structure in American society. First, the wealth and income distributions are skewed in their favor more than in any other industrialized democracy. They are clearly the most powerful group in American society in terms of "Who benefits?" Second, the appointees to government come overwhelmingly from the corporate community and its associated policy-formation network. Thus, the power elite is clearly the most powerful in terms of "Who sits?"

Third, the power elite wins far more often than it loses on policy issues resolved in the federal government. Thus, it is the most powerful in terms of "Who wins?" Finally, as shown in reputational studies in the 1950s and 1970s, . . . corporate leaders are the most powerful group in terms of "Who shines?" By the usual rules of evidence in a social science investigation using multiple indicators, the owners and managers of large income-producing properties are the dominant class in the United States.

Still, as noted at the end of the first [section], power structures are not immutable. Societies change and power structures evolve or crumble from time to unpredictable time, especially in the face of challenge. When it is added that the liberal-labor coalition persists in the face of its numerous defeats, and that free speech and free elections are not at risk, there remains the possibility that class domination could be replaced by a greater sharing of power in the future.

The Great American Pork Barrel

Washington Streamlines the Means of Corruption

KEN SILVERSTEIN

How the $16 billion was absconded with we will never entirely know, at least not in all the particulars. What we do know is this: At approximately 2:00 P.M. last November 17, a Wednesday, a small group of senators and representatives from the congressional appropriations committees gathered in a meeting room under the Capitol dome, where they were to finalize one of thirteen bills that fund the annual affairs of the U.S. government. According to eyewitnesses, only a few members made statements about the bill in question—the Foreign Operations bill, which pays for everything from the Peace Corps to the aerial fumigation of Colombian coca. The only notable break from protocol was made by Robert Byrd of West Virginia, who delivered an impromptu speech in praise of the women of Congress; the senator was particularly fulsome in regard to Rep. Marcy Kaptur of Ohio, of whom he remarked that he "would have fallen in love with her" had he met her earlier in life. The meeting ended less than half an hour after it began, as this very straightforward piece of legislation was approved by the conferees.

Over the next seventy-two hours, by way of meetings and measures obscured from the public, this simple bill would undergo a startling metastasis. Because Congress had failed, for the third year in a row, to pass most of the bills that keep the government running, members of the appropriations committees folded eight as yet unapproved bills—those that fund the Departments of Justice, State, Energy, Labor, Commerce, Education, Agriculture, Transportation, the Treasury, the Interior, Veterans Affairs, Health and Human Services, and Housing and Urban Development, as well as the entire legislative and judiciary branches—into the Foreign Operations bill. Even to assemble the text of the resulting piece of legislation, called an omnibus appropriations bill, was an epic task. Teams of staffers labored long into the night to edit the various bills that would be folded in, after which the mass of pages was fed through copier machines across Capitol Hill. There was no time to produce a clean copy, so the version of the omnibus bill that Congress voted on was a

fourteen-inch-thick clump of papers with corrections, deletions, and additions on virtually every page. Handwritten notes peppered the margins; typefaces varied from section to section and from paragraph to paragraph. First made available to lawmakers at around 12:15 A.M. on November 20 (and only to those who happened to be browsing the House Rules Committee website, where it was posted), the omnibus bill came to a vote before the full House some sixteen hours later, at approximately 4:00 that afternoon, and before the Senate at 8:42 that evening. For the legislators who approved it—by a margin of 344–51 in the House and 65–30 in the Senate—reading the 3,320-page bill before the vote would have been a mathematical impossibility.

Only later, after the approved bill had been shuffled off to the President for signature, could lawmakers and laymen alike peruse its contents in earnest. Scattered throughout the bill were hundreds of hastily inserted pages of "earmarks," or allocations for local projects that are tucked into federal budgets. As approved at the November 17 appropriations meeting, the Foreign Operations bill had contained a mere nine earmarks. The omnibus measure, which was completed after two feverish days of work, allocated money for 11,772 separate earmarks. There was $100,000 for goat-meat research in Texas, $549,000 for "Future Foods" development in Illinois, $569,000 for "Cool Season Legume Research" in Idaho and Washington, $63,000 for a program to combat noxious weeds in the desert Southwest, $175,000 for obesity research in Texas. In the end, the bill's earmarks were worth a combined total of nearly $16 billion—a figure almost as large as the annual budget of the Department of Agriculture and roughly twice that of the Environmental Protection Agency. It was the biggest single piece of pork-barrel legislation in American history.

Of who added these grants, no public record exists. Except in rare cases, members of Congress will refuse to discuss their involvement in establishing earmarks, and the appropriations committees have a blanket rule against commenting. Often it is difficult to discern even who is receiving the funds: earmarks are itemized in bills but generally without disclosure of the direct recipient—just a dollar amount, destination, and broad purpose. Indeed, in the matter of the $16 billion burglary, and the similar acts of mass theft plotted for this year, the only certainty seems to be this: that lawmakers and lobbyists collude to conceal, to the utmost extent possible, their actions from the American taxpayer, who serves as the ultimate benefactor to their chronic bouts of generosity.

"Pork-barreling" as a legislative epithet is a pre–Civil War coinage that referred to the custom of handing out salt pork to slaves, who would crowd around the barrels that held it; and indeed, members of Congress have raided the federal treasury for home-district boondoggles ever since the earliest days of the republic. By 1822, President James Monroe warned that financial support from Washington should henceforth be granted "to great national works only, since if it were unlimited it would be liable to abuse and might be productive of evil." The pork barrel was to become as central to our national political culture as the gerrymander or the filibuster; it has long been a foregone conclusion that whenever the federal government builds a road, or erects a dam, or constructs a power plant, members of Congress will artfully pad the bill with hometown "pork."

In the past two decades, though, the pastime has become breathtaking in its profligacy. Even as the federal deficit soars to record heights, the sums of money being diverted from the treasury have grown ever larger. Last year, 15,584 separate earmarks worth a combined $32.7 billion were attached to appropriations bills—more than twice the dollar amount in 2001, when 7,803 earmarks accounted for $15 billion; and more than three times the amount in 1998, when roughly 2,000 earmarks totaled $10.6 billion. To be sure, not every project that receives an earmark is an utter waste of money. Such appropriations can fund after-school programs, park conservation, public health. "What some people call 'pork' may be as essential as a lock on a dam that creates hydropower, or [support for] a bridge, road, or other critical infrastructure," said Zack Wamp, a Tennessee Republican on the House Appropriations Committee. "Sometimes we have to direct spending because the executive branch is not doing its job."

But the process is so willfully murky that abuse has become not the exception but the rule. Earmarks are added anonymously, frequently during last-minute, closed-door sessions of the appropriations committees. An especially attractive feature for those private interests seeking earmarks is that they are awarded on a noncompetitive basis and recipients need not meet any performance standards. In other words, applicants need not demonstrate that their project, program, or company actually delivers a useful good or service.

Although there are a number of legislative instruments that moneyed interests can use to raid the federal treasury, appropriations bills have become the vehicle of choice, both because they are regularly scheduled—they must be passed, or else the government shuts down—and because their staggering size and scope deter public scrutiny of individual line items. Unsurprisingly, seats on the appropriations committees are among the most desirable sinecures in Congress. Of the sixty-six seats on the House committee (thirty-seven Republican, twenty-nine Democrat), twenty-eight are held by members from the electoral-rich states of California, Florida, Michigan, New York, Ohio, Pennsylvania, and Texas. On the Senate committee (where Republicans hold a 15–13 advantage) sit many of the most influential members of the upper chamber: Republicans Thad Cochran of Mississippi, Ted Stevens of Alaska, and Pete Domenici of New Mexico, along with Democrats Robert Byrd of West Virginia, Minority Leader Harry Reid of Nevada, and Dianne Feinstein of California.

That appropriations bills have emerged as the premier venue for private interests also owes something to Tom DeLay, the embattled House majority leader. Traditionally, seats on the appropriations committee had been granted on the basis of seniority; but when the GOP won control of the House in 1994, DeLay (who himself served on the appropriations committee between 1987 and 2003) helped craft a new strategy under which the Republican seats were, as circumstances required, strategically assigned to "at risk" members; i.e., to those who had narrowly won office. This lent wobbly new lawmakers two vital assets: first, the ability to direct pork projects to their home districts, thereby impressing constituents with their ability to bring home federal monies; second, a fail-safe method of filling campaign war chests—namely, by tapping earmark seekers for donations.

The strategy has been eminently successful, as seen in the case of Anne Northup, a Republican from Kentucky who first won office in 1996 when she squeaked past a Democratic candidate by 1,299 votes. It was the first time in nearly three decades that a Republican had represented Kentucky's Third District, which encompasses the Democratic stronghold of Louisville. Northup was deemed to be highly vulnerable, but she was immediately assigned a slot on the appropriations committee and has held the seat ever since. In 1998, the first year she ran for reelection, Northup raised $1.9 million and won with 51.5 percent of the vote. By last November, Northup was vice-chair of one of the major pork-dispensing subcommittees—Labor, Health and Human Services, and Education—and Louisville was, not by coincidence, receiving more earmarked funds than the entire state of Delaware or Nebraska, states with no representation on the appropriations committees. Having raised $3.3 million, Northup sailed to reelection 60 percent of the vote.

As earmarking has proliferated, it has become less ad hoc and more efficient; it is now an accepted Washington industry, with its own standardized rules and procedures. Whereas in the past we had isolated thefts on behalf of constituents, what we have today is a professional crime syndicate with tentacles not only in long-established pork-barrel sectors such as public works and defense but in such relatively unspoiled fields as academic research and community programs. Those seeking government largesse no longer need to procure backroom meetings through congressional aides; most members of Congress now have simple "appropriations-request forms," which are as easy to complete as a typical job or credit-card application. The form for the office of Sen. Dianne Feinstein (which is similar to the other forms I've seen) asks earmark seekers for the name of the individual making the request, a letter from that person, a description of the project, the amount sought, a budget, and the specific appropriations bill to which the request should be attached. "Multiple requests . . . must be ranked in priority," reads the instruction sheet.

By far the most significant change of recent years has been the incursion of lobbying firms, many of which have been set up expressly for this purpose. Like attorneys at hospital bedsides, earmarking lobbyists aggressively court customers with boasts of their ability to deliver easy cash. "Shepherding appropriations requests through Congress is a priority for many clients," trumpets the website of B&D Sagamore, one such earmarking specialist. B&D's site furthermore promises to arrange "discussions between clients and members of Congress" and track legislation so that the firm can intervene "at critical points in the process."

Last year more than 3,000 private companies or institutions hired lobbying firms such as B&D to pursue earmarks. Because federal disclosure laws are minimal, to say the least, it is difficult to estimate exactly how much money in total was doled out to lobbyists. But Keith Ashdown, of Taxpayers for Common Sense, a Washington group that tracks the earmarking process, says the typical earmark seeker pays a retainer ranging from the tens of thousands up to more than $100,000 per year, with the total easily reaching tens of millions of dollars. Large though that sum may seem, as investments such retainers are undeniably savvy: the overall payout in pork is many times that, totaling into the billions.

For the aspiring pork recipient, mastering the appropriations process is hardly a difficult task. First, one needs simply to identify the correct member of Congress to approach with one's request. Almost always this will be a member whose district or state is home to the company or entity that will receive the money. Mark McIntyre, an appropriations lobbyist at the Russ Reid Company, wrote a 2003 how-to guide to appropriations for a web publication called *OnPhilanthropy,* in which he said that lining up the best congressional "champion" often means the difference between success and failure. "It is extremely helpful," McIntyre pointedly noted, "if

your U.S. Representative or one of your U.S. Senators serves on the Appropriations Committee."

Helpful indeed, as seen in the case of Ted Stevens, the senior senator from Alaska and chairman of the Senate Appropriations Committee from 1997 to 2004. Last year's vast omnibus bill contained hundreds of earmarks for Alaska, including grants for projects on seafood waste ($160,000), salmon quality standards ($167,000), and alternative salmon products ($1.1 million, of which $443,000 was specifically set aside for the "development of baby food containing salmon"). Alaska's total haul came to $2,211.07 per capita, about twenty-two times the national average.

Mississippi, home of Senator Thad Cochran, the new chairman, also happens to be a leading recipient of appropriations bounty. Grants to his state last year included $900,000 for "cattle and nutrient management in stream crossings," $248,000 for a study to prevent the spread of cogon grass, and $2.6 million for—the surest of sure bets—Mississippi State University's Thad Cochran Research, Technology and Economic Development Park. West Virginia, home of the top Democratic appropriations mastermind, Senator Byrd, always receives ample funds as well. "You may as well slap my wife as take away my transportation funding," Byrd once remarked. The senator's most memorable achievement was when he won a Coast Guard facility for his conspicuously landlocked state.

In recent years the most daring pursuer of earmarks has been former Rep. Bob Livingston of Louisiana, who headed the House Appropriations Committee in the late 1990s before resigning from Congress in 1999; his departure, which occurred just as he was helping to spearhead the call for Bill Clinton's impeachment, became necessary when Livingston was forced to acknowledge that he himself had "on occasion" committed the sin of adultery. Livingston's disgrace proved to be short-lived: he immediately turned to lobbying and signed up a drove of clients. Among the first of these was a Louisiana firm called JRL Enterprises, which since has had remarkable success winning earmarks for its "I CAN Learn" mathematics software. Last year's omnibus bill contained three separate earmarks for JRL—none named the company, only the software program—worth a combined $5.5 million.

For JRL to have hired Livingston in the first place was a natural move: the year before he resigned, Livingston had slipped JRL's original earmark into an appropriations bill, a $7.3 million grant that provided the then-floundering firm with virtually all of its income for 1998. Since becoming a lobbyist, Livingston has received nearly $1 million in fees from JRL, which, in turn, has since received $38 million in earmarks.

Yet there is very little (excluding JRL's own extravagant claims) to suggest that I CAN Learn significantly helps the learning of anyone at all. A story last fall in the *Fort Worth Star-Telegram* found that students in the local school district, which has invested heavily in I CAN Learn, weren't learning math any more successfully than students elsewhere in the state. Meanwhile, local teachers complained that the software was freezing in the middle of lessons and sometimes provided the wrong answers to test questions. Nonetheless, Congress year after year has awarded ever more money to JRL—perhaps because company executives have year after year awarded ever more money to members of the appropriations committees. Between 1999 and 2004, of JRL's $81,460 in political contributions, at least $14,500 went to appropriations members.

The link between lawmaker and earmark is virtually impossible to make definitively. A clear paper trail, however, does exist: when requesting an earmark, lawmakers must make their request in writing to the relevant appropriations committee. But because all congressional correspondence is exempt from the Freedom of Information Act, would-be watchdogs—such as Ashdown's group, Taxpayers for Common Sense (which provided much of the hard data for this story)—have no way to obtain earmark requests unless they are leaked. Ashdown, whose whole job is to monitor the appropriations process, says he has never seen more than "a handful" of the official requests himself.

Sometimes, though, circumstantial evidence will allow for the construction of a probable scenario. For example, federal lobby-disclosure records show that last year the Rajant Corporation, based in Wayne, Pennsylvania, retained three lobbying shops to seek appropriations money for a defense contract. The campaign was successful; the defense appropriations bills approved in July awarded the company $2 million for the project.

Numerous clues suggested that Rep. Curt Weldon of Pennsylvania played a role in Rajant's earmark. Consider that Weldon is vice-chairman of the House Armed Services Committee, and Rajant is based in his district. Consider also that a former Weldon staffer, John McNichol, is now a lobbyist at Greenlee Partners, and was retained by Rajant to push for the earmark. And that Blank Rome, the second lobby shop on Rajant's payroll, is a major donor to Weldon; lobbyists at the firm, including two on the Rajant account, gave Weldon $9,300 between 2000 and 2004. And that Rajant's lobbyist at the third firm, David Urban of American Continental Group, is another Weldon donor.

Russ Caso, Weldon's chief of staff, confirmed that Weldon submitted an earmark request for Rajant but said a number of other congressional offices did as well. He added that the congressman's office "accepts all [earmark] requests and we have a vetting process." Caso said that on military-related items the office checks to see whether the product is useful and "submits requests only for items that the military wants."

Securing an earmark is never a given; only about one in four requests makes the final cut, and so steps must be taken to ensure that lawmakers are sufficiently stimulated. The most effective means is, of course, direct cash disbursements. As McIntyre forthrightly states in his how-to guide, "Money has become the oxygen supply of political campaigns. For better or for worse, perhaps the best way to show your support for a Senator or Representative is to make a campaign contribution."

And yet direct contributions to lawmakers can get one only so far. Choosing the right lobbyist is as important as choosing the right lawmaker, if not more important. Because so many lobbyists have past experience on Capitol Hill, they usually have personal ties both to members of Congress and to their key staffers, who vet and prioritize the earmark requests. "You need to hire someone who understands the process and knows the pressure points," says a Beltway lobbyist who specializes in winning appropriations money. "There's a lot of horse-trading going on, so you need someone who is hounding the staffers, calling up every week or every day if necessary."

A full taxonomy of the lobbyists of Washington would necessitate a book-length field guide, but a few of the more salient species can be considered here. The most effective ally for the earmark-seeker is a lobbyist who is actually related, by blood or marriage, to a powerful member of an appropriations committee. For years many Alaskan firms, and even huge corporations such as Lockheed Martin, have retained the services of William Bittner, brother-in-law of Senator Stevens. In one case reported by the *Los Angeles Times* in 2003, Stevens inserted a single line into an appropriations bill that awarded $9.6 million to a program whose chief beneficiary was a Hyundai subsidiary represented by Bittner. The brother of Rep. John Murtha, the top Democrat on the House Appropriations Defense Subcommittee, has lobbied for at least sixteen defense manufacturers on appropriations issues. Craig Obey, the son of Rep. David Obey, the top Democrat on the House Appropriations Committee, seeks money for the National Parks & Conservation Association.

Retired members and staffers from the appropriations committees also make particularly effective lobbyists, because they enjoy guaranteed access to the friends and colleagues they left behind. Jim Dyer, who became the Republican staff director of the House Appropriations Committee in 1995, was long considered to be one of the most powerful aides on the Hill. "Jim's job was to broker deals between members," a lobbyist and friend of Dyer's told me earlier this year. "He knew where every dime was. He's been hounded for years with big money offers." In February, just weeks after we spoke, Dyer was hired by a lobby shop called Clark & Weinstock, where he joined two former appropriations committee members, Vin Weber and Vic Fazio.

Some lobbyists specialize in winning specific types of appropriations. If your seaside community wants taxpayers to pay to have its beach restored, the man to see is Howard Marlowe. He has won dozens of such earmarks, mostly for underprivileged communities like Florida's Venice and New York's Fire Island. In late October 2001, on behalf of the American Shore & Beach Preservation Association, Marlowe's firm helped prepare a letter to Congress that bemoaned the economic toll that the events of September 11 had taken on the nation. "While these financial troubles pale in comparison with the unspeakable human losses of that day, they pose a significant problem," the letter went on. Urgent action was therefore required—specifically, lavishing money on beach communities in order to lure foreign and domestic tourists to America's shorelines. "Many national leaders have stated that increased tourism is imperative to the recovery of our economic strength," the letter claimed.

Diane Blagman, a former staffer at the House Appropriations Committee, and currently of Greenberg Traurig, was the congressional liaison for the 9/11 Memorial Concert in Washington and serves on the board of the Grateful Dead's charitable foundation. She has become adept at winning money for her entertainment-industry clients, such as the $150,000 earmark she picked up last fall to fund the Santa Monica–based Grammy Foundation's "educational activities."

Van Scoyoc Associates—headed by Stu van Scoyoc, a prominent donor to politicians of both parties—specializes in winning research money for university clients. This is an especially fast-growing field: the *Chronicle of Higher Education* estimated that academic earmarks topped $2 billion in 2003, six times more than in 1996. James Savage, a professor of politics at the University of Virginia, says academic earmarks are particularly insidious. "Academic research is supposed to be peer-reviewed, with the idea being that the best science wins out. But with earmarks, quality has nothing to do with it. Schools get research funds simply because they are in a powerful member's district or have the money to hire a lobbyist." Savage has come across cases in which universities from different states team up to submit joint requests for earmarks, knowing that their chances for funding go up by bundling together the largest number of powerful lawmakers. Many universities, he says, have received earmarks for advanced research even though they don't have graduate-studies programs in the relevant fields.

Wexler and Walker Public Policy Associates has a flourishing practice in the transportation field. One of the best-connected firms in town, Public Policy Associates' name partners are Anne Wexler, a prominent Democrat who once upon a time helped organize Eugene McCarthy's 1968 antiwar presidential campaign and who now lobbies for a fair portion of the Fortune 500, and former G.O.P. congressman Robert Walker, who was one of Newt Gingrich's closest allies during the latter's reign as House speaker.

Back in 1997, Public Policy Associates put together a musical revue about lobbying that it offered clients as an educational tool, and the show gives a pretty good idea of how the firm courts Washington. One skit, performed for a group of Burger King operators called the National Franchise Association (NFA), included a song performed to the tune of "Matchmaker, Matchmaker":

> Congressman, senator we've formed a PAC
> Now we can act, no need for tact,
> Pooling resources makes very good sense
> So we formed a little PAC
> When NFA's membership starts to pitch in
> Growing the fund, access begins
> Should ever a congressman put up his guard
> The PAC is our calling card . . .
> Any lawmaker ignoring our PAC
> Risks being fried like a Big Mac
> Working together's the tried and true way to
> Deliver the facts, give pats on the back
> Favors attract, enemies sacked
> Through NFA's brand new PAC!

Public Policy Associates knows of which it sings. During the last three election cycles, the company's own PAC doled out more than $315,000 in political contributions; its employees gave an additional $255,000.

The firm's rainmaker on transportation issues is Timothy Hannegan, a former aviation expert at the General Accounting Office. Hannegan, who is described on the firm website as "a prolific Democratic fundraiser," helped secure passage of the congressional airline-aid package in the aftermath of the September 11 attacks. Another Hannegan client, the Mammoth Mountain Ski Area, in California's Sierra Nevada range, recently underwent what *Ski Magazine* termed "the biggest makeover in the history of skiing." The makeover, intended to transform the resort's image from a family-oriented ski park to a retreat for the superrich, included new lodges, luxury chalets, and high-priced condominiums. Mammoth Mountain wanted to see the local transportation network upgraded to help move in the new upscale clientele, and so last year its home town won a $1 million earmark for a bus-maintainance facility that primarily services the resort. Hannegan, who is being paid a $40,000 annual retainer by Mammoth Mountain, says that he did not lobby for that earmark but acknowledges that he is currently soliciting appropriations money for a controversial new regional airport on the resort's behalf.

The defense appropriations bill is, as one might imagine, a particularly popular target for seekers of pork. In 1980 there were just 62 earmarks in the defense appropriations bill; last year there were 2,671, worth a combined $12.2 billion. That included $3 million to develop bathrooms made entirely of stainless steel; $3.75 million for alcoholism research (at, of all places, the Ernest Gallo Clinic and Research Center, in San Francisco); and $1 million to help eradicate brown tree snakes in Guam. It also contained $13.85 million for textile companies in North Carolina that produce clothing for the Pentagon, including Odor Signature Reduction Products for Special Forces and Smart Apparel for Warriors.

That latter line of clothing, which will be subsidized with $1 million in taxpayer money, is being developed by the Sara Lee Corp., which—though better known for its frozen cheesecake, pies, and "brownie bites"—also has an apparel division based in Winston-Salem, North Carolina, that manufactures Playtex, L'eggs, and Wonderbra. I was never able to determine exactly what Smart Apparel for Warriors is, since no one at Sara Lee's headquarters in Chicago or in Winston-Salem was willing to talk about it: they claimed that the project, as a Pentagon contract, was too sensitive to discuss. But I was able to determine, through lobby-disclosure forms, that the company obtained the money with the help (for a $20,000 retainer) of The PMA Group, a lobby shop that, according to its website, is "the premier Washington consulting organization in the defense arena."

Paul Magliocchetti, a former top staffer at the appropriations committees and nine-year veteran of the defense subcommittee, is the founder and president of PMA, which is strategically located on the Metro's Blue Line, two stops from the Pentagon. The move to the private sector has paid off quite handsomely for Magliocchetti, who had been forced to eke out a living on his $65,200-a-year salary at House appropriations. Since 1998, by contrast, Magliocchetti's firm has received $21.7 million in fees from large defense companies—the most paid to any lobbying firm, according to a study by the Center for Public Integrity. PMA has thirty-two lobbyists, and all but one of them are revolving-door alumni from the Defense Department or Capitol Hill. Ten have experience on one of the two appropriations committees. PMA's website is not terribly subtle about the company's ability to rig the system. "No one understands the inner workings of our nation's capital better than The PMA Group," it says. "Many of our associates have formulated or helped to shape the policies that are in place today."

The firm's PAC is one of the defense industry's most generous, doling out more than $975,000 to 340 House and Senate lawmakers, according to the Center for Public Integrity. Of direct contributions from PMA lobbyists, the three top recipients—Reps. Pete Visclosky, John Murtha, and James Moran—are all key players on the appropriations committees. Collectively they received about $87,250 from PMA between 1998 and 2003.

No immediate suspect emerges in the question of which member of Congress inserted Sara Lee's earmark. In the case of another winner in last year's defense-earmarks sweepstakes, Night Vision Equipment Company of Allentown, Pennsylvania, there is not only a suspect but one with motive and means as well: Arlen Specter, the third-ranking Republican on the Senate Appropriations Committee.

Night Vision won a $1.25 million earmark in the defense bill, funding lobbied for by IKON Public Affairs, to which Night Vision paid $60,000. IKON deployed two lobbyists to work the Night Vision account, Peter Grollman and Craig Snyder, both of whom previously held senior posts on Specter's staff. Between 2000 and 2004, IKON donated $13,250 to Specter, with $7,250 of that coming directly from Snyder and Grollman. During that same period, Night Vision's then president, William Grube (along with his wife), kicked in $8,000 to Specter.

Just months before the defense appropriations bill passed, Snyder helped Specter fight off a fierce primary challenge from Pat Toomey. The electoral hopes of Toomey, who favors a ban on abortion, rested on his trouncing Specter in the state's conservative heartland, where the senator's pro-choice politics have made him a pariah. Shortly before the primary vote, Snyder put together a PAC called Pennsylvanians for Honest Politics, which promptly raised $17,750, with one third coming directly from Snyder and Grube. Almost all of that money was spent to produce and air a radio ad that ran in the last few days of the campaign—on just a single Christian station that airs only in conservative areas. The ad savaged Toomey for failing to call, during an interview with Chris Matthews on *Hardball,* for criminal sanctions against a woman who gets an abortion. "Somebody who claims to be on our side had the opportunity to say abortion is murder," says the ad's protagonist. "Instead of showing the nation real pro-life leadership, Toomey shrunk like a frightened turtle." Specter won by just 17,146 votes out of more than a million ballots cast and did far better in conservative counties than expected.

Less than three months later it was Specter, along with Sen. Rick Santorum, who announced that Night Vision had won the earmarks. "These projects, key to our nation's defense, will be invaluable in our continuing war against terror," he declared. So was it Specter who inserted the earmark for Night Vision? No one knows for certain, since neither the company, Specter, nor the Senate Appropriations Committee would comment.

Members of Congress are, of course, perpetually decrying the spending excesses of the body they compose; the late Illinois Senator Paul Douglas, who served between 1949 and 1967, archly likened his colleagues to "drunkards who shout for temperance in the intervals between cocktails." Just as with campaign finance, Congress in fact has little incentive to reform a system that protects incumbents, Republicans and Democrats alike. "Getting between a lawmaker and an earmark is like trying to take a ribeye away from a dog," says Keith Ashdown. "Congress sees it as one of its most fundamental rights."

Anyone who imagines that Congress could discipline itself on pork should consider the case of the $32 billion

Department of Homeland Security budget. When DHS was created in 2003, congressional leaders agreed that its appropriations bill would not be earmarked, so that pork-barreling would not muddle the priorities of the incipient War on Terror. That first year the ban held—only eighteen earmarks, worth $423 million, were attached, despite the more than seven hundred lobbyists who had registered to work on homeland-security issues. The lobbyists, however, kept their chins up. "This is a stage where people are still cultivating relationships," one hopeful told a reporter for *Congressional Quarterly* in July 2003. Said another lobbyist, a former representative named Steven Kuykendall: "It's a challenge, but that's what guys like me get paid to do."

Two years of persistence have apparently paid off. This spring, as the 2006 appropriations process got under way, Capitol Hill was awash with rumors that the informal moratorium would soon be abandoned. *Congress Daily* reported in April that the heads of the appropriations subcommittees on homeland security—Rep. Harold Rogers (R., Ky.) and Sen. Judd Gregg (R., N.H.)—were debating whether to end the ban, and thereby to allow earmarks to bloom within DHS with the same fecundity as elsewhere in the federal budget. One lobbyist opined, no doubt with great gravity of tone, that homeland-security agencies could benefit from "additional Congressional oversight."

Congress, no doubt, will soon concur; even if the moratorium survives another year or two, its days are surely numbered. Thirty-two billion dollars, when none have been siphoned off for friends, are overdue for oversight indeed.

KEN SILVERSTEIN is a reporter for the *Los Angeles Times.* His series "The Politics of Petroleum," co-written with T. Christian Miller, was the winner of a 2004 Overseas Press Club Award.

Off the Books

The benefits of free enterprise that economic statistics miss

W. Michael Cox and Richard Alm

America's consumer culture is all around us. It's along our highways, studded with shopping malls, fast food joints, and flashy neon signs. It's in our homes, filled with gadgets, furnishings, toys, and closets of clothes. It permeates the media, where ads tell us happiness and sex appeal are as close as the nearest store. It's even within us, at least to the extent that we tie status and identity to the cars we drive, the clothes we wear, and the food we eat.

That's our reputation: a consumer-driven, somewhat crass, shop-'til-you-drop society. As the world's wealthiest nation, we *should* consume a lot, but the portrait of Americans as consumption crazed misses as much as it captures. We're not working just to acquire more goods and services. Most of us strive for something broader: a balanced life.

Consumption is part of that, of course. We buy myriad things: Chevrolet cars, Sony TV sets, Levi's jeans, Nike sneakers, McDonald's hamburgers, Dell computers. But our wish list doesn't stop there. We also want leisure time, a respite to enjoy life. We want pleasant working conditions and good jobs, so earning a living isn't too arduous. We want safety and Security, so we don't live in fear. We want variety, the spice of life. We want convenience, which makes everyday life a little easier. We want a cleaner environment, which enhances health and recreation.

A full description of a balanced life would entail much more, with considerations for family and friends, perhaps even spirituality. Here we want to focus on the components of happiness that clearly depend on the market but are not reflected in the gross domestic product (GDP). Our free enterprise system provides much more than the goods and services we consume; it furnishes ingredients of a balanced life that are often overlooked in discussions of economic performance.

Capitalism creates wealth. During the last two centuries, the United States became the world's richest nation as it embraced an economic system that promotes growth, efficiency, and innovation. Real GDP per capita tripled from 1900 to 1950; then it tripled again from 1950 to 2000, reaching $35,970.

The wealth didn't benefit just a few. It spread throughout society. For many people, owning a home defines the American Dream, and 68 percent of families now do—the highest percentage on record. Three-quarters of Americans drive their own cars. The vast majority of households possess color televisions (98 percent), videocassette recorders (94 percent), microwave ovens (90 percent), frost-free refrigerators (87 percent), washing machines (83 percent), and clothes dryers (75 percent). In the past decade or so, computers and cell phones have become commonplace.

As people become wealthier, they continue to consume more, but they also look to take care of other needs and wants. They typically choose to forgo at least some additional goods and services, taking a portion of their new wealth in other forms.

Compared to previous generations, today's Americans are starting work later in life, spending less time on chores at home, and living longer after retirement. All told, 70 percent of a typical American's waking life-time hours are available for leisure, up from 55 percent in 1950.

Consider a nation that rapidly increases its productive capacity with each passing generation. Workers could toil the same number of hours, taking all of the gains as consumption. They may choose to do so for a while, but eventually they will give up some potential material gains for better working conditions or additional leisure. Hours of work shrink. Workplaces become more comfortable. In the same way, we give up consumption in favor of safety, security, variety, convenience, and a cleaner environment.

Less Work, More Play

In the early years of the Industrial Revolution, most Americans were poor, and they wanted, above all, more goods and services. These factory workers sharply improved their lives as consumers, even though for most of them it meant long hours of toil in surroundings we'd consider abominable today. As America grew richer, what workers wanted began to change, and leisure became a higher priority.

Few of us want to dedicate every waking hour to earning money. Free time allows us to relax and enjoy ourselves, spend time with family and friends. Higher pay means that each hour of work yields more consumption—in essence, the price for an hour of leisure is going up—but we're still choosing to work less than ever before. According to economists' estimates and Department of Labor figures, the average workweek shrank from 59 hours in 1890 to 40 hours in 1950. Although today we hear stories about harried, overworked Americans who never seem to have enough time, the proportion of time spent on the job has continued to fall. Average weekly hours for production workers dropped from 39 in 1960 to 34 in 2001.

Since 1950 time off for holidays has doubled, to an average of 12 days a year. We've added an average of four vacation days a year. Compared to previous generations, today's Americans are starting work later in life, spending less time on chores at home, and living longer after retirement. All told, 70 percent of a typical American's waking lifetime hours are available for leisure, up from 55 percent in 1950.

Even at work, Americans aren't always doing the boss's bidding. According to University of Michigan time diary studies, the average worker spends more than an hour a day engaged in something other than assigned work while on the job. Employees run errands, socialize with colleagues, make personal telephone calls, send e-mail, and surf the Internet. More than a third of American workers, a total of 42 million, access the Internet during working hours. The peak hours for submitting bids on eBay, the popular online auction site, come between noon and 6 p.m., when most Americans are supposedly hard at work.

With added leisure, the United States has turned arts, entertainment, and recreation into a huge industry. Since 1970, attendance per 100,000 people has risen for symphonies, operas, and theaters as well as for national parks and big-league sporting events. The annual *Communications Industry Forecast,* compiled by New York-based Veronis, Suhler & Associates, indicates that we watch an average of 58 hours of movies at home each year. Yet Americans go out to an average of 5.4 movies a year, up from 4.5 three decades ago.

Adjusted for inflation, per capita spending on recreation nearly quadrupled in the last three decades. Leisure and recreation are even important enough to have become an academic subject: 350 colleges and universities offer degree programs in it.

The number of amusement parks has increased from 362 in 1970 to 1,164 today. The number of health and fitness facilities has more than doubled, to 11,241. Adjusted for inflation, per capita spending on recreation nearly quadrupled in the last three decades. Leisure and recreation are even important enough to have become an academic subject: 350 colleges and universities offer degree programs in it.

The explosion of leisure spending and activities confirms the addition of more free time to our lives. If we hadn't reduced our hours of work, we couldn't spend as much time and money as we do on entertainment and recreation. Americans may find themselves pressed for time, but it's not because we're working harder than we used to. We're busy having fun.

Better Work Too

As the Industrial Revolution arrived in the 19th century, workers migrated from family farms to factories, from the Old World to the New World. They saw their paychecks rise but became, like Charlie Chaplin's character in *Modern Times,* mere cogs in a vast engine of mass production. Work was often brutal. Early factories were noisy, smelly, and dirty; they were cold in the winter and hot in the summer. The labor itself was repetitive, physically exhausting, and often dangerous. It was a time of mind-numbing repetition, standing on assembly lines, nose to the conveyor belt. To eke out a meager living, employees toiled an average of 10 hours a day, Monday through Friday, plus another half-day on the weekend. Breaks were few and far between. Work rules were draconian: no talking, no eating or drinking, not a minute late punching the time clock.

We've come a long way since then. For the most part, modern work takes place in a clean, well-lit, and air conditioned environment. A growing number of modern workplaces offer on-the-job amenities previous generations didn't even contemplate, such as on-site day care for children, exercise facilities, and concierge services. More and more employees are getting paternity leave, stock options, personal days off, and paid sabbaticals.

Jeans, sport shirts, and slacks are in. Ties and pantyhose are out. A July 2000 survey by the catalog retailer Land's End found that dress had become more casual in the previous five years at more than 80 percent of *Fortune* 500 firms.

More Americans than ever are free to choose the time and place for work, as long as the job gets done. In 1997, 28 percent of American workers were on flexible schedules, double the percentage in 1985. With laptop computers, cell phones, fax machines, electronic mail, and the Internet, fewer employees are tethered to the office. Telecommuting began with a handful of workers three decades ago. By 2001, 29 million Americans worked at least part of the time away from their companies' places of business.

Work isn't just more pleasant. It's also safer. Occupational injuries and illnesses, as tallied by the National Safety Council, are at an all-time low of 63 per 1,000 workers. The number of Americans killed on the job has fallen to a record low of 38 per million workers, down from 87 in 1990 and 214 in 1960.

Safer workplaces come in part from fewer accidents in such dangerous occupations as construction and manufacturing. At the same time, our economic base is shifting toward services, where jobs are less risky. The nature of the work we do is changing too. For most Americans in past generations, long days on the job involved tasks that were repetitive, physically exhausting, and often dangerous. Modern work is more likely to require analytical and interpersonal skills. Fewer employees make their livings with their backs and hands.

Jobs Rated Almanac 2001 provides a handy database of 300 occupations, ranked from best to worst. To focus on working conditions rather than pay, wages are taken out of the equation. Once that's done, it's clear our employment base is shifting in a positive direction. Since 1970 the 30 best jobs—including computer scientist, legal assistant, and engineer—have risen from 9 percent to 13 percent of total employment. At the same time, the 30 worst occupations—from logger to textile mill worker—have declined from 13 percent to 9 percent of all jobs. The trend toward better jobs is likely to continue. The Bureau of Labor Statistics estimates that the 10 best jobs will grow by 27 percent through 2008, while the 30 worst jobs will expand by just 7 percent.

Making workplaces more pleasant takes money. The added expense figures, along with wages, into the overall bill for labor. Companies pay it to attract new workers and retain those already on board. Employers shouldn't care whether the money goes for wages, time off, or working conditions. By their decisions on where to work, employees reveal their preferences.

Safer Lives

Although concerns about security have come to the fore since September 11, we shouldn't forget how far the United States has already come in making life safer. The toll of death and disease has been steadily reduced. Annual deaths per 1 million people are at an all-time low. The age-adjusted death rate has fallen by two-thirds since 1900. Fatalities from nearly all major diseases, tracked by the U.S. Centers for Disease Control and Prevention, have declined sharply from their peak rates. The rate of fatalities per 100,000 due to natural causes has fallen from 767 in 1950 to 422 in 1998, the most recent year for which data are available. The incidence of accidental deaths, both at home and on the job, is declining. So are fatalities associated with floods, tornadoes, and hurricanes.

Gains in transportation safety have been dramatic. In the five-year period ending in 2000, according to the Federal Highway Administration, annual deaths on American roads averaged 16 per billion miles driven, compared with 53 in the five years ending in 1970 and 83 for the post-World War II years. The Air Transportation Association reports that deaths per billion passenger miles flown fell from 16.7 a year in 1946–50 to 1.3 in 1966–70 to 0.14 in 1996–2000.

As a wealthy nation, we can afford to spend time and money to reduce life's risks. We can buy alarms for our homes and cars. We can buy insurance on our property and our lives. We can reduce the financial risks of illness and old age by taking part of our pay in health benefits and retirement savings.

We can also shift resources to the military to create an even more fearsome fighting force. During World War 11, defense spending per capita averaged $3,475 a year in today's dollars, or 29 percent of total output. Today, each American's share of the defense budget comes to $1,079, just 3 percent of GDP.

A Safer, Healthier Life

	1970	The Latest*
Age-adjusted death rate per 100,000 people	1,222.6	872.4
Deaths per 100,000 people from 15 leading diseases	**731.6**	**605.3**
Accidental deaths in the home per 1 million people	132.0	107.0
Work-related deaths per 1 million workers	**178.0**	**38.0**
Deaths per billion miles driven	53.3	15.9
Deaths per billion miles flown	**1.3**	**0.14**
Homicide deaths per 1 million people	79.0	57.0
Deaths per 100 tornadoes per 100,000 people	**6.8**	**1.8**
Deaths per hurricane per 100,000 people	10.1	3.3
Life expectancy at birth	**70.8**	**77.1**
Median age of the population	28.1	35.3
Injuries per 100 full-time workers in manufacturing	**15.2**	**7.8**
Incidence per 100,000 people of 14 reportable diseases	659.0	184.0

* Years range from 1999 to 2000 depending on the original source.
Source: Federal Reserve Bank of Dallas

Making America a safer place owes much to advances in engineering and technology. Divided highways, better roads, anti-lock brakes, radial tires, and air bags are reducing the highway death toll. More-sophisticated weather forecasting gear provides warnings of severe weather, so we can take refuge in time.

New medicines and treatments have reduced the incidence of fatal diseases. More are probably on the way. The stock market values the nation's 10 largest pharmaceutical companies at more than $1 trillion, an indication that we expect their sales to grow from future advances in health.

Greater safety and security didn't come about by accident. It's what we, as a people, wanted. We put a high value on our lives and physical well-being, and we're willing to pay the costs of protecting ourselves against the sometimes unpleasant facts of life.

Life is inherently risky, and protecting ourselves must be weighed against the considerations of cost and convenience. We'll never achieve a perfect safety record. In an uncertain world, we possess the wealth to afford more safety and security and the know-how to provide it, if that's what we decide we want.

Convenience and Variety

By introducing industrial efficiency to his factories, Henry Ford brought the automobile within the reach of an emerging middle class. The miracle of mass production delivered the goods but didn't adapt easily, so all Model T's looked alike. Ford's attitude can be summed up in what he reputedly said about the car's paint: "The consumer can have any color he wants, as long as it's black." Ford's company still makes black cars for drivers who want them, but it now offers a rainbow of colors: red, green, aquamarine, white, silver, purple.

The U.S. marketplace teems with variety. Just since the early 1970s, there's been an explosion of choice: The number of car models is up from 140 to 239, soft drinks from 50 to more than 450, toothpaste brands from four to 35, over-the-counter pain relievers from two to 41.

The market offers 7,563 prescription drugs, 3,000 beers, 340 kinds of breakfast cereal, 50 brands of bottled water. Plain milk sits on the supermarket shelf beside skim milk, 0.5-percent-fat milk, 1-percent-fat milk, 2-percent-fat milk, lactose-reduced milk, hormone-free milk, chocolate milk, buttermilk, and milk with a shelf life of six months. Not long ago, the typical TV viewer had access to little more than NBC, CBS, ABC, and PBS. Today, more than 400 channels target virtually every consumer interest—science, history, women's issues, Congress, travel, animals, foreign news, and more.

Like variety, convenience has emerged as a hallmark of our times. Companies compete for business by putting their products and services within easy reach of their customers.

In 1970 the nation's lone automated teller machine was at the main office of the Chemical Bank in New York. Now ATMS are ubiquitous—not just at banks but at supermarkets, service stations, workplaces, sports facilities, and airports. All told, 273,000 machines offer access to cash 24 hours a day.

Remote controls are proliferating, the newest models incorporating voice-activated technology. Computers and digital devices go with us everywhere. A cell phone is no longer a pricey luxury: The average bill fell from $150 a month in 1988 to $45 in 2001 in constant dollars. No wonder 135 million Americans now own mobile telephones. The number will continue to rise as prices continue to decline and more of us seek the peace of mind and convenience that come with communications in the pocket or purse.

Convenience stores are in nearly every neighborhood. Just one firm, industry leader 7-Eleven, has increased its locations from 3,734, in 1970 to 21,142 today. The Internet may be the ultimate convenience store, bringing shopping into the home. We're buying music, clothing, software, shoes, toys, flowers, and other products with a click of the mouse. Last year, a third of all computers and a fifth of all peripherals were sold online. Thirty-three million buyers ordered books on the Internet, accounting for $1 of every $8 spent in that category.

Convenience and variety aren't trivial extravagances. They're a wealthy, sophisticated society's way of improving consumers' lot. The more choices, the easier access to goods and services, the better. A wide selection of goods and services increases the chance that each of us will find, somewhere among all the shelves, showrooms, and Web sites, products that meet our requirements. Convenience allows us to economize on the valuable commodity of time, getting what we want more quickly and easily.

A Cleaner Environment

The environment presents a textbook case for tradeoffs between consumption and other aspects of life. Traditionally, economists teach that markets undervalue clean air, fresh water, pristine vistas, and endangered species because they aren't owned, like factories, houses, or other private property. Without clear title and market prices, there's little economic incentive to reduce pollution or husband resources. The nation's natural assets end up underpriced and overexploited.

GDP may be accurate as a tally of how much our farms, factories, and offices produce, but it's increasingly inadequate as a measure of how well the economy provides us with what we want. Our ability to choose a balanced life is one of the market's most important success stories.

Our desire for a balanced life mitigates the classic dilemma of market failure and the environment. A wealthier nation possesses the time, money, and inclination to shift the balance from exploiting the environment to preserving it. We want clean air and water for reasons of health, recreation, and aesthetics. We've developed a sense of moral obligation toward lesser species. We find unspoiled nature pleasant—although we tend to want clean linens and good food along with it.

Our desires have had a dramatic effect in recent decades. Levels of such major air pollutants as particulate matter, sulfur oxides, volatile organic compounds, carbon monoxide, and lead were at their peaks in 1970 or earlier. Levels of nitrogen oxides peaked in 1980. Water quality has improved since the 1960s, when authorities banned fishing in Lake Erie. Through government and private foundations, we're spending billions of dollars every year to preserve natural areas from development and save threatened species from extinction.

Capitalism's penchant for innovation is helping us act on our concern for the environment. We've developed less polluting gases for air conditioning systems, so we can stay cool at a lower cost to air quality. Fish farms are creating another compromise, providing salmon for our dinner tables while reducing fishing for wild species.

Taking better care of the environment is a natural extension of economic progress. At one time, the air in Pittsburgh was very dirty. It was the price we were willing to pay for all those consumer goods the industrial age offered. It wasn't that we liked pollution; it was just that the price of cleaner air was too high. Today, having grown richer, we can afford the pollution controls that have made Pittsburgh's air sweeter than an ocean breeze. Exploitation of the environment is worst in poor countries, where the economic imperative lies in producing the food, goods, and services needed for daily life. Wealthier countries possess the means and motive for a balanced life, and they do a better job of taking care of their surroundings.

Beyond Statistics

The statistics that measure our economy are reasonably good at counting the value of the cars, clothing, food, sports gear, jewelry, and other goods and services we buy. When we choose an additional hour off over additional income, though, GDP shrinks with the loss of the hour's income and output. We don't count leisure as an economic benefit because we haven't assigned a dollar value to it, even though we opt for time off because it improves our lives.

When it comes to many aspects of a balanced life, our economic barometers come up short. Safety and security are all about preventing bad things from happening. Increased spending on highway safety registers in GDP, but we don't track how much better off we are because of the accidents, injuries, and deaths we avoid. If investing in prevention works, it can actually reduce total output, at least the way we measure it, because less money is spent treating the sick and injured, repairing damage, and replacing lost property.

Variety makes products more valuable by giving us the designs, colors, and features that fit our preferences, but the statistics count everything as plain vanilla. How conveniently our wants and needs are fulfilled doesn't matter to GDP. A cleaner environment makes for a better country, but it may come at the cost of economic growth.

Inflation-adjusted GDP figures indicate economic growth at an annual average of 3 percent during the last two decades. GDP may be entirely accurate as a tally of how much our farms, factories, and offices produce, but it's increasingly inadequate as a measure of how well the economy provides us with what we want. Our ability to choose a balanced life is one of the market's most important success stories.

Some may argue that it isn't the market that makes a balanced life possible. They might concede that our economy produces abundant goods and services, but they credit government agencies, with their regulations, and unions and pressure groups, with their advocacy, for everything else. History tells us government and advocates play their roles, but they aren't the ultimate source of progress. They don't foot the bill for the choices we make to gain a balanced life. Whatever we want must be paid for, and money ultimately comes from the economy.

Companies improve working conditions because they can afford to, not simply because workers, unions, or government agencies demand it. The dismal work environments in now-defunct socialist nations—all supposedly designed to benefit the worker and eradicate the capitalist—provide a powerful testament to the fact that good intentions are hollow without the ability to pay.

The main role of collective action has been to act as a voice for what we want. Environmental groups formed as the result of our desire for cleaner air and water. When we take our preferences for leisure and better working conditions to unions or elected officials, they help create consensus among employees and lower the cost of communicating these desires to employers.

In the long run, we cannot afford any component of a balanced life—be it consumption, leisure, easier workdays, safety and security, variety and convenience, or environmental cleanup—that we don't earn by becoming more productive. When counting our blessings, we should first thank the economic system. Not federal agencies, not advocacy groups, not unions.

Our quest for a balanced life will never end. The U.S. economy, now recovering from its first recession in a decade, will make our society wealthier in the years ahead. We'll take some of our gains in goods and services, but we will also continue to satisfy our desires for the less tangible aspects of life.

W. Michael Cox (wm.cox@dal.frb.org), senior vice president and chief economist at the Federal Reserve Bank of Dallas, and **Richard Alm** (rgalm@aol.com), a business writer for *The Dallas Morning News,* are the authors of *Myths of Rich and Poor: Why We're Better Off Than We Think* (Basic Books).

The Future of Outsourcing

How it's transforming whole industries and changing the way we work

P ETE E NGARDIO

G lobalization has been brutal to midwestern manufacturers like the Paper Converting Machine Co. For decades, PCMC's Green Bay (Wis.) factory, its oiled wooden factory floors worn smooth by work boots, thrived by making ever-more-complex equipment to weave, fold, and print packaging for everything from potato chips to baby wipes.

But PCMC has fallen on hard times. First came the 2001 recession. Then, two years ago, one of the company's biggest customers told it to slash its machinery prices by 40% and urged it to move production to China. Last year, a St. Louis holding company, Barry-Wehmiller Cos., acquired the manufacturer and promptly cut workers and nonunion pay. In five years sales have plunged by 40%, to $170 million, and the workforce has shrunk from 2,000 to 1,100. Employees have been traumatized, says operations manager Craig Compton, a muscular former hockey player. "All you hear about is China and all these companies closing or taking their operations overseas."

But now, Compton says, he is "probably the most optimistic I've been in five years." Hope is coming from an unusual source. As part of its turnaround strategy, Barry-Wehmiller plans to shift some design work to its 160-engineer center in Chennai, India. By having U.S. and Indian designers collaborate 24/7, explains Vasant Bennett, president of Barry-Wehmiller's engineering services unit, PCMC hopes to slash development costs and time, win orders it often missed due to engineering constraints—and keep production in Green Bay. Barry-Wehmiller says the strategy already has boosted profits at some of the 32 other midsize U.S. machinery makers it has bought. "We can compete and create great American jobs," vows CEO Robert Chapman. "But not without offshoring."

Come again? Ever since the offshore shift of skilled work sparked widespread debate and a political firestorm three years ago, it has been portrayed as the killer of good-paying American jobs. "Benedict Arnold CEOs" hire software engineers, computer help staff, and credit-card bill collectors to exploit the low wages of poor nations. U.S. workers suddenly face a grave new threat, with even highly educated tech and service professionals having to compete against legions of hungry college grads in India, China, and the Philippines willing to work twice as hard for one-fifth the pay.

Workers' fears have some grounding in fact. The prime motive of most corporate bean counters jumping on the offshoring bandwagon has been to take advantage of such "labor arbitrage"—the huge wage gap between industrialized and developing nations. And without doubt, big layoffs often accompany big outsourcing deals.

Offshoring can free up expensive talent so they can spend more of their time innovating.

The changes can be harsh and deep. But a more enlightened, strategic view of global sourcing is starting to emerge as managers get a better fix on its potential. The new buzzword is "transformational outsourcing." Many executives are discovering offshoring is really about corporate growth, making better use of skilled U.S. staff, and even job creation in the U.S., not just cheap wages abroad. True, the labor savings from global sourcing can still be substantial. But it's peanuts compared to the enormous gains in efficiency, productivity, quality, and revenues that can be achieved by fully leveraging offshore talent.

Thus entrepreneurs such as Chapman see a chance to turn around dying businesses, speed up their pace of innovation, or fund development projects that otherwise would have been unaffordable. More aggressive outsourcers are aiming to create radical business models that can give them an edge and change the game in their industries. Old-line multinationals see offshoring as a catalyst for a broader plan to overhaul outdated office operations and prepare for new competitive battles. And while some want to downsize, others are keen to liberate expensive analysts, engineers, and salesmen from routine tasks so they can spend more time innovating and dealing with customers. "This isn't about labor cost," says Daniel Marovitz, technology managing director for Deutsche Bank's global businesses. "The issue is that if you don't do it, you won't survive."

The new attitude is emerging in corporations across the U.S. and Europe in virtually every industry. Ask executives at Penske Truck Leasing why the company outsources dozens of business processes to Mexico and India, and they cite greater efficiency and customer service. Ask managers at U.S.-Dutch professional publishing giant Wolters Kluwer why they're racing to shift software development and editorial work to India and the Philippines, and they will say it's about being able to pump out a greater variety of books, journals, and Web-based content more rapidly. Ask Wachovia Corp., the Charlotte (N.C.)-based bank, why it just inked a $1.1 billion deal with India's Genpact to outsource finance and accounting jobs and why it handed over administration of its human-resources programs to Lincolnshire (Ill.)-based Hewitt Associates. It's "what we need to do to become a great customer-relationship company," says Director of Corporate Development Peter

The Modular Corporation

Work Processes in practically every big department of a corporation can now be outsourced and managed to some degree offshore. Some of the biggest sectors in terms of global spending in 2005:

Human Resources

$13 BILLION

Includes payroll administration, benefits, and training programs.

Engineering

$27 BILLION

Testing and design of electronics, chips, machinery, car parts, etc.

Info Tech

$90 BILLION

Software development, tech support, Web site design, IT infrastructure

Analytics

$12 BILLION

Includes market research, financial analysis, and risk calculation

Customer Care

$41 BILLION

Call centers for tech support, air bookings, bill collection, etc.

Manufacturing

$170 BILLION*

Contract production of everything from electronics to medical devices

Finance & Accounting

$14 BILLION

Includes accounts payable, billing, and financial and tax statements

Logistics & Procurement

$179 BILLION

Includes just-in-time shipping, parts purchasing, and after-sales repairs

Data: IDC estimates. Analytics estimates by Evalueserve

*Manufacturing estimate only for electronics

J. Sidebottom. Wachovia aims to reinvest up to 40% of the $600 million to $1 billion it hopes to take out in costs over three years into branches, ATMs, and personnel to boost its core business.

Here's what such transformations typically entail: Genpact, Accenture, IBM Services, or another big outsourcing specialist dispatches teams to meticulously dissect the workflow of an entire human resources, finance, or info tech department. The team then helps build a new IT platform, redesigns all processes, and administers programs, acting as a virtual subsidiary. The contractor then disperses work among global networks of staff ranging from the U.S. to Asia to Eastern Europe.

In recent years, Procter & Gamble, DuPont, Cisco Systems, ABN Amro, Unilever, Rockwell Collins, and Marriott were among those that signed such megadeals, worth billions. In 2004, for example, drugmaker Wyeth Pharmaceuticals transferred its entire clinical-testing operation to Accenture Ltd. "Boards of directors of virtually every big company now are insisting on very articulated outsourcing strategies," says Peter Allen, global services managing director of TPI, a consulting firm that advised on 15 major outsourcing contracts last year worth $14 billion. "Many CEOs are saying, 'Don't tell me how much I can save. Show me how we can grow by 40% without increasing our capacity in the U.S.,'" says Atul Vashistha, CEO of outsourcing consultant neoIT and co-author of the book *The Offshore Nation*.

Some observers even believe Big Business is on the cusp of a new burst of productivity growth, ignited in part by offshore outsourcing as a catalyst. "Once this transformation is done," predicts Arthur H. Harper, former CEO of General Electric Co.'s equipment management businesses, "I think we will end up with companies that deliver products faster at lower costs, and are better able to compete against anyone in the world." As executives shed more operations, they also are spurring new debate about how the future corporation will look. Some management pundits theorize about the "totally disaggregated corporation," wherein every function not regarded as crucial is stripped away.

Processes, Now on Sale

In theory, it is becoming possible to buy, off the shelf, practically any function you need to run a company. Want to start a budget airline but don't want to invest in a huge back office? Accenture's Navitaire unit can manage reservations, plan routes, assign crew, and calculate optimal prices for each seat.

Have a cool new telecom or medical device but lack market researchers? For about $5,000, analytics outfits such as New Delhi-based Evalueserve Inc. will, within a day, assemble a team of Indian patent attorneys, engineers, and business analysts, start mining global databases, and call dozens of U.S. experts and wholesalers to provide an independent appraisal.

Want to market quickly a new mutual fund or insurance policy? IT services providers such as India's Tata Consultancy Services Ltd. are building software platforms that furnish every business process needed and secure all regulatory approvals. A sister company, Tata Technologies, boasts 2,000 Indian engineers and recently bought 700-employee Novi (Mich.) auto- and aerospace-engineering firm Incat International PLC. Tata Technologies can now handle everything from turning a conceptual design into detailed specs for interiors, chassis, and electrical systems to designing the tooling and factory-floor layout. "If you map out the entire vehicle-development process, we have the capability to supply every piece of it," says Chief Operating Officer Jeffrey D. Sage, an IBM and General Motors Corp. veteran. Tata is designing all doors for a future truck, for example, and the power train for a U.S. sedan. The company is hiring 100 experienced U.S. engineers at salaries of $100,000 and up.

Few big companies have tried all these options yet. But some, like Procter & Gamble, are showing that the ideas are not far-fetched. Over the past three years the $57 billion consumer-products company has outsourced everything from IT infrastructure and human resources to management of its offices from Cincinnati to Moscow. CEO Alan G. Lafley also has announced he wants half of all new P&G products to come from outside by 2010, vs. 20% now. In the near future, some analysts predict, Detroit and European carmakers will go the way of the PC industry, relying on outsiders to develop new models bearing their brand names. BMW has done just that with a sport-utility vehicle. And Big Pharma will bring blockbuster drugs to market at a fraction of the current $1 billion average cost by allying with partners in India, China, and Russia in molecular research and clinical testing.

Of course, corporations have been outsourcing management of IT systems to the likes of Electronic Data Systems, IBM, and Accenture for more than a decade, while Detroit has long given engineering jobs to outside design firms. Futurists have envisioned "hollow" and "virtual" corporations since the 1980s.

It hasn't happened yet. Reengineering a company may make sense on paper, but it's extremely expensive and entails big risks if executed poorly. Corporations can't simply be snapped apart and reconfigured like LEGO sets, after all. They are complex, living organisms that can be thrown into convulsions if a transplant operation is botched. Valued employees send out their résumés, customers are outraged at deteriorating service, a brand name can be damaged. In consultant surveys, what's more, many U.S. managers complain about the quality of offshored work and unexpected costs.

But as companies work out such kinks, the rise of the offshore option is dramatically changing the economics of reengineering. With millions of low-cost engineers, financial analysts, consumer marketers, and architects now readily available via the Web, CEOs can see a quicker payoff. "It used to be that companies struggled for a few years to show a 5% or 10% increase in productivity from outsourcing," says Pramod Bhasin, CEO of Genpact, the 19,000-employee back-office-processing unit spun off by GE last year. "But by offshoring work, they can see savings of 30% to 40% in the first year" in labor costs. Then the efficiency gains kick in. A $10 billion company might initially only shave a few million dollars in wages after transferring back-office procurement or bill collection overseas. But better management of these processes could free up hundreds of millions in cash flow annually.

Those savings, in turn, help underwrite far broader corporate restructuring that can be truly transformational. DuPont has long wanted to fix its unwieldy system for administering records, payroll, and benefits for its 60,000 employees in 70 nations, with data scattered among different software platforms and global business units. By awarding a long-term contract to Cincinnati-based Convergys Corp., the world's biggest call-center operator, to redesign and administer its human resources programs, it expects to cut costs 20% in the first year and 30% a year afterward. To get corporate backing for the move, "it certainly helps a lot to have savings from the outset," says DuPont Senior Human Resources Vice-President James C. Borel.

Creative new companies can exploit the possibilities of offshoring even faster than established players. Crimson Consulting Group is a good example. The Los Altos (Calif.) firm, which performs global market research on everything from routers to software for clients including Cisco, HP, and Microsoft, has only 14 full-time employees. But it farms out research to India's Evalueserve and some 5,000 other independent experts from Silicon Valley to China, the Czech Republic, and South Africa. "This allows a small firm like us to compete with

McKinsey and Bain on a very global basis with very low costs," says CEO Glenn Gow. Former GE exec Harper is on the same wavelength. Like Barry-Wehmiller, his new five-partner private-equity firm plans to buy struggling midsize manufacturers and use offshore outsourcing to help revitalize them. Harper's NexGen Capital Partners also plans to farm out most of its own office work. "The people who understand this will start from Day One and never build a back room," Harper says. "They will outsource everything they can."

Some aggressive outsourcers are using their low-cost, superefficient business models to challenge incumbents. Pasadena, (Calif.)-based IndyMac Bancorp Inc., founded in 1985, illustrates the new breed of financial services company. In three years, IndyMac has risen from 22nd-largest U.S. mortgage issuer to No. 9, while its 18% return on equity in 2004 outpaced most rivals. The thrift's initial edge was its technology to process, price, and approve loan applications in less than a minute.

But IndyMac also credits its aggressive offshore outsourcing strategy, which Consumer Banking CEO Ashwin Adarkar says has helped make it "more productive, cost-efficient, and flexible than our competitors, with better customer service." IndyMac is using 250 mostly Indian staff from New York-based Cognizant Technology Solutions Corp. to help build a next-generation software platform and applications that, it expects, will boost efficiency at least 20% by 2008. IndyMac has also begun shifting tasks, ranging from bill collection to "welcome calls" that help U.S. borrowers make their first mortgage payments on time, to India's Exlservice Holdings Inc. and its 5,000-strong staff. In all, Exlservice and other Indian providers handle 33 back-office processes offshore. Yet rather than losing any American jobs, IndyMac has doubled its U.S. workforce to nearly 6,000 in four years—and is still hiring.

Superior Service

Smart use of offshoring can juice the performance of established players, too. Five years ago, Penske Truck Leasing, a joint venture between GE and Penske Corp., paid $768 million for trucker Rollins Truck Leasing Corp.—just in time for the recession. Customer service, spread among four U.S. call centers, was inconsistent. "I realized our business needed a transformation," says CFO Frank Cocuzza. He began by shifting a few dozen data-processing jobs to GE's huge

---

A Virtual Subsidiary at Work

Some companies and global outsourcing partners work so tightly that they practically are part of the same organization. Here's a look at how Penske and India's Genpact collaborate on one process.

- When Penske buys a truck and leases it, Genpact's Indian staff remotely secures state titles, registrations, and permits electronically.
- After the truck is returned, the driver's log and taxes, fuel, and toll documents are sent to Genpact. The paperwork is forwarded to Genpact's office in Juarez, Mexico. There, the staff enters data from the drivers' logs into Penske's computer system.
- Workers in Genpact's office in Hyderabad, India, process all the data for tax filings and accounting.

Hot Players in the Offshore Outsourcing World

Consultant Gartner Inc.'s clients ask most about these companies' offshore offerings. For estimates of outsourcing revenues, areas of specialty, and location of operations, go to www.businessweek.com/go/outsourcing

Business Services

1. Hewitt Associates U.S.
2. ACS U.S.
3. Accenture U.S.
4. IBM U.S.
5. EDS U.S.
6. Hewlett-Packard U.S.
7. Wipro INDIA
8. HCL Technologies INDIA
9. Tata Consultancy Services INDIA
10. WNS Global Services INDIA

Software Development

1. Tata Consultancy Services INDIA
2. Infosys Technologies INDIA
3. Wipro INDIA
4. Accenture U.S.
5. IBM U.S.
6. Cognizant Technology Solutions U.S.
7. Satyam INDIA
8. Patni Computer Systems INDIA
9. EDS U.S.
10. CSC U.S.

Call Centers

1. Convergys U.S.
2. Wipro INDIA
3. ICICI OneSource INDIA
4. ClientLogic U.S.
5. 24/7 Customer INDIA
6. SR.Teleperformance FRANCE
7. eTelecare International U.S.
8. SITEL U.S.
9. Teletech U.S.
10. CustomerCorp. U.S.

Data: Gartner Inc. Ranking based on frequency of queries from Gartner's 10,000 global clients

Mexican and Indian call centers, now called Genpact. He then hired Genpact to help restructure most of his back office. That relationship now spans 30 processes involved in leasing 216,000 trucks and providing logistical services for customers.

Now, if a Penske truck is held up at a weigh station because it lacks a certain permit, for example, the driver calls an 800 number. Genpact staff in India obtains the document over the Web. The weigh station is notified electronically, and the truck is back on the road within 30 minutes. Before, Penske thought it did well if it accomplished that in two hours. And when a driver finishes his job, his entire log, including records of mileage, tolls, and fuel purchases, is shipped to Mexico, punched into computers, and processed in Hyderabad. In all, 60% of the 1,000 workers handling Penske back-office process are in India or Mexico, and Penske is still ramping up. Under a new program, when a manufacturer asks Penske to arrange for a delivery to a buyer, Indian staff helps with the scheduling, billing, and invoices. The $15 million in direct labor-cost savings are small compared with the gains in efficiency and customer service, Cocuzza says.

Big Pharma is pursuing huge boosts in efficiency as well. Eli Lilly & Co.'s labs are more productive than most, having released eight major drugs in the past five years. But for each new drug, Lilly estimates it invests a hefty $1.1 billion. That could reach $1.5 billion in four years. "Those kinds of costs are fundamentally unsustainable," says Steven M. Paul, Lilly's science and tech executive vice-president. Outsourcing figures heavily in Lilly's strategy to lower that cost to $800 million. The drugmaker now does 20% of its chemistry work in China for one-quarter the U.S. cost and helped fund a startup lab, Shanghai's Chem-Explorer Co., with 230 chemists. Lilly now is trying to slash the costs of clinical trials on human patients, which range from $50 million to $300 million per drug, and is expanding such efforts in Brazil, Russia, China, and India.

Other manufacturers and tech companies are learning to capitalize on global talent pools to rush products to market sooner at lower costs. OnStor Inc., a Los Gatos (Calif.) developer of storage systems, says its tie-up with Bangalore engineering-services outfit HCL Technologies Ltd. enables it to get customized products to clients twice as fast as its major rivals. "If we want to recruit a great engineer in Silicon Valley, our lead time is three months," says CEO Bob Miller. "With HCL, we can pick up the phone and get somebody in two or three days."

Such strategies offer a glimpse into the productive uses of global outsourcing. But most experts remain cautious. The McKinsey Global Institute estimates $18.4 billion in global IT work and $11.4 billion in business-process services have been shifted abroad so far—just one-tenth of the potential offshore market. One reason is that executives still have a lot to learn about using offshore talent to boost productivity. Professor Mohanbir Sawhney of Northwestern University's Kellogg School of Management, a self-proclaimed "big believer in total disaggregation," says: "One of our tasks in business schools is to train people to manage the virtual, globally distributed corporation. How do you manage employees you can't even see?"

The management challenges will grow more urgent as rising global salaries dissipate the easy cost gains from offshore outsourcing. The winning companies of the future will be those most adept at leveraging global talent to transform themselves and their industries, creating better jobs for everyone—*With Michael Arndt in Green Bay, Wis., and Dean Foust in Charlotte, N.C.*

Born to Buy

Interview with Juliet Schor

JAMES WOOLMAN

Americans love to shop. We own roughly one TV per person and acquire an average of 48 new pieces of apparel a year. We also work longer hours than people in any other industrial country, and 1.5 million U.S. households declare bankruptcy every year. Economist Juliet B. Schor has studied the work-and-spend phenomenon in her popular books *The Overworked American* and *The Overspent American*. In her new book, *Born to Buy: The Commercialized Child and the New Consumer Culture*, Schor looks at how corporations enlist schools, cultural institutions, and even other kids to transform children into consumers.   —James Woolman

DOLLARS & SENSE: In *The Overworked American* you found that Americans are working more than they used to. Could you describe what you found and what's behind those trends?

JULIET SCHOR: I began *The Overworked American* from a theoretical point of view, which was that in a capitalist economy there are structural biases in the way the labor market and the firm operate that lead to using productivity growth to produce more output rather than to give people more free time. Because with productivity growth, you always have the option of either producing the same amount with fewer hours of work or keeping work hours constant and producing more. What I found was that beginning with the 1970s, you start to see a small increase in the annual hours of work, particularly once you correct for a simultaneous growth in structural underemployment and unemployment. So you had one group of people not getting enough work, either no job at all or working part-year or part-time, and another group, the majority, working more and more hours, more than they wanted to. This trend, which is very modest in the 70s, picks up steam in the 80s and 90s, so what you have is a long-term trajectory of growing hours of work.

> **"You could be invited to a friend's slumber party and it could turn out to be a marketing opportunity. Most parents have no idea that this kind of stuff is going on."**

I came to think of those changes as very analogous to the first industrial revolution, which was a period of rapid technical change, but which also saw very big increases in hours of work. Employers want workers to work more hours, because those technical innovations, which are theoretically labor-saving innovations, represent a possibility for increased productivity, but they need to harness the labor to them. My view is that we're going through something like a second industrial revolution in terms of the demand of the market economy for more and more hours and also more people working those long hours. So the message of the first book was, why aren't we getting the benefits of increased productivity in the form of shorter hours of work, which is what everybody thought would happen.

D&S: How does this relate to your study of consumer culture in *The Overspent American?*

JS: The second book took up a question that was raised in the first one. In the first book, I developed what I called the "cycle of work and spend," which was about how workers don't have the option to reduce their hours of work. Typically they would get higher incomes, and then spend those incomes and get locked into that spending. The second book is an attempt to understand why it is that people spend rising levels of income. Of course not everyone's getting increased incomes. Particularly over the 80s and 90s you start to see that dramatic worsening of the income distribution. But with the rising work effort of women, you see family incomes growing. So *The Overspent American* is about the social pressures to spend, and the ways in which consumption is really a very social process, and Americans have basically been in a situation where the pressures to ratchet up spending have become extremely intense.

D&S: What effect has this increase in consumerism and consumption had on people's well-being?

JS: What happens is you have the majority of the population which in relative terms is doing worse because you've got this worsening income distribution. Twenty percent are doing better—they're setting the standards. Part of my argument was that the consumption patterns of the top 20% became the norm that people throughout the society are trying to emulate. For the other 80% of households who are trying to keep up, it becomes harder and harder because the norms are rising faster than their purchasing power. So they end up adding more workers to the labor force to keep up, their savings diminish, you have record levels of consumer debt, record levels of bankruptcy, high levels of stress as people feel they're running harder and harder to stay in place because there is a gap between what you need to keep up and the purchasing power that the system is delivering to you. Plus, now there is lots of research showing that materialism as a value system undermines well-being in lots of different ways. It undermines physical well-being, it undermines your emotional and social well-being. People who are more materialistic are more depressed, they're more anxious, they have less vitality, they connect less well with people, they have more stomach aches and headaches.

D&S: Why did you decide to write a book about children and marketing?

JS: Well, when I started working on *The Overspent American* in the early 90s, one of the things I started seeing was that a lot of the "action" in consumer markets was happening in youth consumer markets. Youth marketing was being transformed from a relative backwater to something where a lot of cutting-edge trends were happening. It was also the case that youth were being targeted increasingly for what had historically been adult products, so that you get the influence of youth in cars, and hotels, tourist destinations, a whole range of products that parents and adults are buying, not kids. Why are they advertising these products on Nickelodeon? The other important thing for me was that I had my first child at the time that I started working on consumer issues, so I was interested in this as a parent—my kids were being born into a childhood culture that was increasingly commercialized, and I didn't like it.

D&S: How have marketing and products directed at children changed, and what makes marketing directed at children today so different from what it used to be?

JS: Some of it is similar to what went on in the 1950s, for example, Saturday morning television: there are still sugared cereal commercials, and toy commercials for boys with lots of crashes, and toy commercials for girls that are all pink and sweet. The marketing people want to keep our attention focused on that, because that's where they can say, well, there's nothing new.

I found that the kids who are more involved in consumer culture are much worse off psychologically. They're more depressed, they're more anxious, they have less self-esteem.

What's different is, number one, the quantity of advertising. You've had very rapid increases. There's now about $15 billion a year in child-directed advertising. When I started doing this work about ten years ago, the estimates that I was seeing were more on the order of $1 to $2 billion.

There's been a big increase in the number of places where kids are advertised to. TV turns out to be just the tip of the iceberg now. Kids are advertised to almost everywhere. Schools have become a huge area of advertising. You have coercive advertising in schools, such as Channel One, which gives schools

televisions if they play their programs. If you're in a Channel One school, you have to watch a 10-minute broadcast every day, which is two minutes of advertising and eight minutes of so-called news that also has a lot of advertising in it. Channel One is in 12,000 schools, so 8 million middle and high school students are forced to watch ads for junk food, movies, even military recruiting. There is a lot of other advertising going on in schools: curriculum being written by corporations and a lot of freebie, give-away advertising, book covers and so forth.

You see advertising in cultural institutions like museums and zoos. There's a lot of what's called peer-to-peer advertising in which companies are enlisting kids to market to their friends. You could be invited to a slumber party by a friend, if you're an 11-year-old girl, and it could turn out to be a marketing opportunity. Most parents have no idea that this kind of stuff is going on.

D&S: Has the content of advertising changed?

JS: The messages that are used are different now, and there's a wider range of messages. The marketers have figured out peer dynamics. As kids move through elementary school and then especially into middle and high school, the peer dynamics are so important. And they've figured out how to insinuate themselves into that and to make products a really central part of a kid's social experiences. Kids today have access to more money, and they are much more status conscious then they used to be. Brands have become more important to kids than function. Marketers tap into this on purpose. The number one theme that's marketed to kids now is "cool," which is really about inequality, exclusion, having something others don't have or can't afford.

D&S: Why should we be concerned about the growth in marketing to children, or the trends in children's consumption?

JS: The literature on children and consumer culture has focused on two things. One is whether advertising to kids is inherently unfair, because kids can't resist advertising. We need a lot more research, but the old research at least showed that kids have a hard time resisting advertising.

The second question is the kinds of products that are being advertised to kids. A lot of them are not healthy. The number one product that is marketed to kids is junk food. And of course we've seen a huge increase in obesity and obesity-related diseases. You also have cigarette advertising, alcohol advertising, other kinds of drug advertising, advertising of violent products. So most of the products being sold by consumer culture aren't things that are good for kids.

The third aspect of it, which the study I did for my book addresses, is that advertising is getting kids more and more involved in consumer culture, in the values of consumer culture, in the practices, in the aspirations. Does that have an impact on kids' well-being? I studied a sample of mostly fifth and sixth graders and interviewed a smaller sample of their parents, and what I found was that the kids who are more involved in consumer culture, who care more about the stuff, who care more about money, and labels, and collecting, and all of those things are much worse off psychologically. They're more depressed, they're more anxious, they have less self-esteem. In some cases they had worse relations with their parents, they had worse peer self-esteem, they were more likely to have stomach aches and headaches, to feel bored. There's just a wide range of bad outcomes associated with being heavily involved in consumer culture.

D&S: What specific policies or actions can be taken to combat the child marketing industry and child consumerism?

JS: There are different types of things. Just today, I believe, Tom Harkin introduced a bill into the Senate that would restore to the FTC its ability to regulate children's advertising. That ability was stripped from the FTC in 1980, I believe, when they came close to advocating a ban on advertising sugared cereals and sugared foods. It's very early, but there is a growing coalition of activists who are trying to push for federal legislation, on a variety of things, whether it's disclosing of product placement; disclosing the authorship of ads, so that people and agencies will have to take more responsibility for their messages; getting commercial marketing out of schools. There's been a lot on the soft drinks in schools, vending machines, and other kinds of junk food within schools. A really good source, reproduced in an appendix to my book, is something called the "Parents' Bill of Rights," which is a series of proposed legislation put together by a group called Commercial Alert. They advocate things like banning advertising to kids younger than 12, keeping advertising out of schools, and requiring labeling of fast food content.

I advocate a tax on advertising to children which could be deployed to create publicly-owned, child-controlled media, where kids could write and produce their own shows. I think one of the big challenges is to change the kind of media that kids have, and to make it much more child-friendly, oriented not to making money off kids but to actually doing well by kids. We need to genuinely empower kids to gain more control over their environment, whether we're talking about the media environment or their actual spatial environment. One of the reasons that corporate-dominated childhood has come to pass is that kids have been restricted to the indoors, and electronic media has supplanted outdoor play. It is important that we give kids the ability to play outside safely with other kids, and not only in adult-supervised environments. The third key area we need to change is food, replacing the junk food culture that kids live in with really healthy food that kids are excited about and participate in growing, cooking, and eating. These are the really broad scale sort of cultural changes in childhood that I think are necessary to move away from corporate childhood.

Juliet Schor is professor of sociology at Boston College. She is the author of *The Overworked American: The Unexpected Decline of Leisure* and *The Overspent American: Why We Want What We Don't Need*. She co-edited *The Golden Age of Capitalism: Reinterpreting the Postwar Experience, The Consumer Society Reader*, and *Sustainable Planet: Solutions for the 21st Century*. Her new book, *Born to Buy: The Commercialized Child and the New Consumer Culture*, was published in September by Scribner.

James Woolman is a member of the *Dollars & Sense* collective.

From *Dollars & Sense,* September/October 2004, pp. 24–28. Reprinted by permission of Dollars & Sense, a progressive economics magazine. www.dollarsandsense.org

Can the Center Find a Solution That Will Hold?

The High School Experience: Proposals for Improvement

CHESTER E. FINN, JR.

The year 2005 began with high schools taking center stage in Washington's continuing drama concerning education reform. President George W. Bush started things off in January, when he delivered a ringing address at a suburban D.C. high school about the urgency of reforming American high schools and offered a bold $1.5 billion plan for doing so. A month after the presidential call to arms for high-school reform, 45 governors and a host of education leaders and CEOs met in a downtown Washington, D.C., hotel for a summit devoted to the subject.

In his keynote address to that gathering, Microsoft chairman Bill Gates pronounced current U.S. high schools "obsolete" and said, "Even when they are working as designed, they cannot teach all our students what they need to know today." At the same conclave, the new secretary of education, Margaret Spellings, declared that America "must make a high-school diploma a ticket to success in the 21st century." The summit concluded by adopting a five-part state "action agenda": restoring value to the diploma; redesigning the high school as an institution; strengthening the quality of high-school teachers and principals; holding high schools accountable for their results; and streamlining "education governance."

With all these powerful people talking high-school reform, it seemed that the planets had aligned to make high schools, the lost child of public education, the featured attraction on the U.S. education-policy agenda. But the universe then began to shift and the planets were knocked out of alignment. First, House Education Committee chairman John Boehner, a Republican from Ohio and longtime proponent of education reform, expressed doubts about the federal government's role in leading the high-school reform effort. "The current system," Boehner remarked at a late-May committee hearing, "isn't getting the job done.

But that doesn't necessarily mean the solution to the problem should be driven from Washington." Another senior member of that committee, former Delaware governor Michael Castle, also a Republican, was blunter. "Frankly," he said, "there's political opposition to it, and it's not just Democrats. It's within the Republican Party as well." And on the other side of the Capitol a spokesman for Senator Mike Enzi, chairman of the Senate Education Committee, noted, "Senator Enzi has made several other education issues the first priority."

As if that weren't trouble enough, the president's $1.5 billion plan entailed shifting to his high-school reform plan funds traditionally spent on vocational education, a move that riled many members of Congress since "voc ed" remains popular back home.

What happened? Has the White House initiative been stopped at the starting gate? Is high-school reform a dead issue?

The Need Is Great, the Political Will Weak

As nearly everyone in education knows, something is wrong with our high schools. And, for the most part, the Bush administration's proposal seemed built on that consensus, much the same accord that brought us No Child Left Behind and the determination that schools need a regimen of standards, testing, and accountability.

"Out of a hundred 9th graders in our public schools," said Mr. Bush in his January speech, "only 68 will complete high school on time. Now, we live in a competitive world, and a 68 percent graduation rate for 9th graders is not good enough to be able to compete in this competitive world. In math and science, the problem is especially urgent. A recent study showed that American 15-year-olds ranked 27th out of 39 countries in math literacy. I don't know about you, but I want to be ranked first in the world, not 27th."

The president proposed a series of programs to help high-school students graduate with "skills necessary to succeed." The plan included money to identify at-risk 8th graders and intervene in their academic lives "before it's too late." But the centerpiece was a call for tests in reading and math in the 9th, 10th, and 11th grades. "Testing at high-school levels will help us to become more competitive as the years go by," said Bush. "Testing in high schools will make sure that our children are employable for the jobs of the 21st century. Testing will allow teachers to improve their classes. Testing will enable schools to track. Testing will make sure that a diploma is not merely a sign of endurance, but the mark of a young person ready to succeed."

The plan seemed sensible enough. And it is possible, of course, that parts of the president's plan could reemerge when No Child Left Behind is reauthorized. At present, though, Congress seems to think it has done plenty to make over K–12 education and is loath to extend NCLB's scope at the very time that the ambitious statute is facing so many implementation challenges as well as so much opposition from states and districts. Indeed, the controversies surrounding NCLB have at least delayed, if not doomed, both the administration's version of high-school reform and any other bold federal entry into that territory.

Maximum Feasible Myopia

The real question, then, though perhaps born of necessity, is whether it's such a bad thing that responsibility for revitalizing U.S. high schools has been thrust back on states and districts, private funders, and diverse reform architects. Could the federal government's failure to mount a political consensus open the way to useful experimentation with various potential solutions?

Indeed, much experimenting is already under way across the land. And remembering the warning of the French political commentator George Bernanos may enhance the chances of finding useful solutions: "The worst, the most corrupting of lies, are problems poorly stated." In other words, if a problem is misrepresented or its definition is disputed, any given solution is unlikely to solve it to everyone's satisfaction.

A vivid American example of this policy perplexity was embodied in a famous 1969 book, *Maximum Feasible Misunderstanding,* by the late senator Daniel Patrick Moynihan. The title was a play on a key phrase in the Economic Opportunity Act of 1964 (which launched LBJ's "war on poverty") calling for the "maximum feasible participation" of residents and groups affected by the legislation's centerpiece Community Action Program. Moynihan's point was that the program's architects didn't actually agree on what the problem was, so the legislation they created fell apart when the time came for its implementation. It was, if you will, a modern public-policy rendition of the tale of the blind men and the elephant, wherein each sightless man had a different notion of the essential nature of this beast depending on which part he was touching. Moynihan contended that the Community Action Program was doomed because the rush to legislate had led people to reach superficial agreement on the definition of the policy problem.

Trying to Define the Problem

As America embarks on high-school reform, it runs a similar risk. The nation is awash in different solutions to the high-school problem. But mostly we are still grappling with trying to define the problem. Sure, from 30,000 feet we can reach broad agreement as to what's wrong. Nearly everyone shares the concern of the president and the governors that U.S. high-school students are not learning enough; that they're being surpassed by their peers in other lands; that too many are bored to death; that too many drop out; that few of those who graduate are well prepared for college and employment. And so on. From six miles up, we know we have a problem and can even reach a meeting of minds as to its most vivid manifestations.

Yes, there's a problem, several problems, in fact, and the rationale for high-school reform would seem compelling. But as we get closer to the ground, the picture loses focus. Is the problem with high school that it is not engaging students or that it is not academically challenging enough? Can we *simultaneously* reduce dropouts and beef up academic achievement? Will stiffer graduation requirements and more high-stakes testing cause even more young people to quit? Are these complementary goals, or are they trade-offs? Are these even the right questions?

One thing we do know is that if we get the answers wrong, we invite a new maximum feasible misunderstanding, and high-school reform will be declared a failure. Thus I sense that it's just as well Uncle Sam is not rushing in with a predetermined, nationwide strategy and that we're giving states, communities, and private organizations some leeway to work out different approaches. If we monitor and evaluate their efforts, we stand to learn more about what works for whom in what circumstances.

Knowing What's Wrong

How many options are there, really? Allowing for mixing and matching, I can identify at least six versions of the problem, each giving rise to different theories of action and strategies for solving it. The now-dormant White House proposals tapped into several of these, as did the summit communiqué released by the National Governors Association. At the end of the day, we will likely conclude that the high-school problem is actually a tangle of problems in need of a multipart solution. Well and good. First, though, all the blind men should come to understand the many-faceted nature of this particular beast.

Problem 1:
Achievement Is Too Low.

Solution: Extend standards-based reform to high schools by making them accountable for their students' achievement and completion rates. A number of states have begun to do this, and the Bush proposal is focused here, bringing high schools under the NCLB umbrella, primarily via testing and public accountability. This is a familiar, government-driven, top-down, standards-based, institution-centered approach, already fairly well established in the primary and middle schools.

Problem 2:
Students Aren't Working Hard Enough, Taking the Right Courses, or Learning Enough.

Solution: Since all they need do to get a diploma is go through the motions and rack up the course credits, no real reward follows from studying hard (save for the small fraction seeking entry to competitive colleges), and no unpleasantness results from taking it easy. We thus need to establish high-stakes graduation tests that students must pass to earn their diplomas. This, too, is a behaviorist, top-down, results-based, accountability-driven system, but this version bears down primarily on the kids rather than on their schools. About half the states have already put into place some form of statewide graduation test. Some also supply carrots along with the sticks via positive inducements such as college scholarships for those with B averages. The Bush administration suggested fatter Pell grants for those who complete a challenging curriculum.

Problem 3:
High School Is a Lockstep Bore, and Consequently Too Many Kids Turn Off, Tune Out, and Quit. If They Don't Stick Around (or Come Back), There's No Way They'll Learn.

Solution: Prevent dropouts and maximize completions by making the high-school experience more appealing: individualize it, let students move at their own pace.

This was the thrust of a recent task force report in Ohio titled "High-Quality High Schools"; it was the point of the president's proposed $200 million Performance Plan Fund (part of the $1.5 billion initiative); and it's the essence of any number of private-sector initiatives. With it, sometimes, comes the idea of creating new education options for out-of-school youth and dropout recovery programs for those who have fallen by the wayside. (Indeed, we could identify seven reform strategies rather than six by bisecting this one and distinguishing between prevention and retrieval schemes.) The underlying theory of action is that, if young people like school more (and, presumably, succeed at it), they'll hang in there. Well-conceived specialty schools and programs can reengage young people who have already had it with formal education.

Problem 4:
The Circa-1950s, One-Size-Fits-All, Comprehensive High School Is Itself Dysfunctional, an Inefficient, Outmoded Vehicle for Teaching Young People What They Need to Learn.

Solution: Devise new institutional forms for delivering secondary education, using technology, modern organization theory, and outsourcing. Give young people choices among the formats: early-college high schools; smaller schools; schools within schools; charter schools; KIPP schools; high-tech high schools; virtual high schools; and more. Much has been tried on this front, and the innovations take many shapes, as do the schemes whereby young people and their parents can access the version that works best for them.

Problem 5:
The Courses Are Too Easy, Pointless, and Ill Matched to the Demands of the Real World.

Solution: Beef up the curriculum. Broaden access to Advanced Placement courses and propagate the International Baccalaureate. Strengthen state standards. Revise the textbooks. Team up with colleges to create K–16 programs. Make college-prep the default curriculum. Blend higher-education's expectations with those of modern jobs, à la the American Diploma Project, and work backward through the K–12 grades.

Problem 6:
Academic Work and Intellectual Activity Are No Way to the Adolescent Heart.

Solution: Since teenagers are animated by things with tangible rewards and sleeves-rolled-up engagement, we need to get practical. Focus on tech-prep programs, ventures that join high schools to community colleges, work-study, schedules that blend school with jobs, voluntarism and community service, and kindred ways of tapping into the "affective," pecuniary, and social sides of young people.

High School Is Different

To be sure, we could slice these strategies differently and combine them in any number of packages. And yes, with a bit of effort they can be loosely grouped under the two familiar headings that we know as standards-based and choice-based reform. But that may not be the most useful way to frame them. Indeed, it may invite people to slip into familiar ideological postures rather than to think closely about high schools.

The fact is that high schools pose challenges distinct from those of K–8. Their students don't really have to be there. Even where state compulsory attendance laws extend to age 17 or 18, our sky-high dropout rate proves those statutes are unenforceable. High schools are larger than elementary schools and there are fewer of them, which makes choice-based strategies harder. For every person who believes that the high school's mission is to supply all students with a solid liberal arts education, someone else is convinced that young people's differing tastes and aspirations should preclude uniformity of academic standards and curriculum. On a major national survey conducted in April 2005, for example, 76 percent of Americans opposed making college prep the universal high-school curriculum and instead favored "career/technical education to equip students who don't go to college with real-world skills." (Hence the continuing appeal of voc ed.) By the high-school years, moreover, achievement levels range widely: some students still need basic reading and arithmetic, while others crave university-level coursework and Intel science competitions.

Adult World Problems Not Addressed

Adolescents also have much on their minds besides school: money, sports, and socializing, for starters. More than a few have tangled with such adult-world problems as drugs, crime, and pregnancy. And many have scant use for authority (or even advice) proffered by grown-ups—their parents, teachers, or anybody else.

As if that did not present a sufficiently daunting picture for would-be reformers, lots of Americans don't really see a big problem with high schools in their present form, at least not with the schools they know best. Parents typically give high marks to their own children's high schools, institutions that also anchor many communities, provide Friday-night football games, and seem to be doing an adequate job of turning out graduates who go on to college, even if some must take remedial courses when they

get there. The dropout rate means that the high schools' most acute failures largely vanish from sight. At the top, honors students fret not about boredom or weak achievement, but about the stress that attends all that cramming and homework as they compete for entry into high-status universities. And just about everyone who sticks it out can at least attend the local community college, join the military, or find an entry-level job of some sort. "What, exactly, is the problem with our high school?" ask the residents of River City, U.S.A.

Considering all the impediments to wholesale high-school reform and the absence of true consensus as to the nature and urgency of the problem, I conclude that diversity and experimentation are a reasonable way to proceed in mid-decade, rather than pressing for elusive agreement about a single national strategy. That doesn't mean I'm complacent about today's high schools. They are not, in fact, getting us where we need to go as a country. But neither are they going to be turned around from Washington, which lacks the political will to make this problem its own. Instead, let us welcome the mixing of strategies and matching of solutions, the combining of ideas and refining of programs. Let us try all six (or five or seven) of the aforementioned reform notions and any number of permutations and combinations of them and seek to determine what works best for whom in which circumstances. High-school reform may resemble welfare reform, where it was important that states had the freedom and incentive to try various approaches before the time was ripe for a national strategy.

Let us acknowledge, though, that a decentralized, piecemeal approach invites its own messy confusion, the more so if we have no common metrics by which to gauge progress, compare results, or define success from one place to another.

Multiple reform strategies cast the greatest light when they at least share measures of performance. For which purpose, let us return to 30,000 feet and suggest that the two essential sets of data for tracking America's progress or lack thereof in revitalizing the high school are objective test scores and graduation rates.

Neither, alas, is easy to come by nor itself the object of wide consensus.

Results Not Reported

Twelfth-grade scores on the National Assessment of Educational Progress (NAEP), aka the nation's report card, are not even reported by state, though 4th- and 8th-grade results are, and have long been shadowed by doubts as to their accuracy, considering that many high-school seniors don't take the exams seriously. They do not, after all, "count" for anything in the student's own life. Other national tests used for college entrance—SATs, ACTs, Advanced Placement—are taken only by a subset of juniors and seniors. And of course none is taken by the horde of young people who don't complete high school.

Though many states have instigated graduation tests, these often have low passing levels and, in any case, are not readily compared from one jurisdiction to the next.

International tests such as the Trends in International Mathematics and Science Study (TIMSS) are valuable for purposes of comparing U.S. student performance with their overseas counterparts, but these do not occur on a predictable cycle.

As for graduation and dropout rates, the National Center for Education Statistics has multiple definitions and measures; the Census Bureau counts "high-school equivalency" certificates along with actual, on-time graduates; and several independent analysts insist that the true graduation rate is far lower than federal data suggest, very different from state to state, often even different from what states think it is. (Fortunately, this may change over the next few years, as all but a handful of governors, declining to wait for Uncle Sam, announced in July 2005 that they would collaborate on a single, simplified graduation gauge.)

Thus it will be no small challenge even to monitor and evaluate U.S. high-school reform initiatives if we don't have measures that people agree on. And that's without resolving the policy paradox of whether achievement scores and graduation rates can realistically be raised at the same time, along with the level of student engagement, or whether those worthy goals tend to cancel one another.

At day's end, the multifaceted challenge of high-school reform seems to be a problem that needs to ripen before any comprehensive solution can drop from the policy tree. Americans hold disparate goals for high schools, conflicting priorities for strengthening them, and dissimilar yardsticks for tracking progress.

This is not to say the problem doesn't cry for a solution or that complacency rules the day. In a survey of high-school students released by the National Governors Association in July 2005, more than a third of respondents said their school had not done a good job of challenging them academically or preparing them for college; almost two-thirds said they would work harder if the courses were more demanding or interesting. A month earlier, the Educational Testing Service released a survey indicating that 51 percent of the general public think U.S. high schools need either "major changes" or a "complete overhaul," even if there's considerable dissonance as to what those changes should be. Furthermore, the imperative to make any changes may not extend to their own community high school.

That more and more people are discontented with today's high schools and their results is surely a good thing. This issue deserves to be on the national stage. But first it has to play in the provinces, in summer stock, and in off-off Broadway theaters, where actors, directors, investors, critics, and audiences alike can come to understand it.

CHESTER E. FINN, JR. is president of the Thomas B. Fordham Foundation, a senior fellow at the Hoover Institution, and senior editor of *Education Next*.

Medical Guesswork

From heart surgery to prostate care, the health industry knows little about which common treatments really work.

JOHN CAREY

The signs at the meeting were not propitious. Half the board members of Kaiser Permanente's Care Management Institute left before Dr. David Eddy finally got the 10 minutes he had pleaded for. But the message Eddy delivered was riveting. With a groundbreaking computer simulation, Eddy showed that the conventional approach to treating diabetes did little to prevent the heart attacks and strokes that are complications of the disease. In contrast, a simple regimen of aspirin and generic drugs to lower blood pressure and cholesterol sent the rate of such incidents plunging. The payoff: healthier lives and hundreds of millions in savings. "I told them: 'This is as good as it gets to improve care and lower costs, which doesn't happen often in medicine,'" Eddy recalls. "'If you don't implement this,' I said, 'you might as well close up shop.'"

The message got through. Three years later, Kaiser is in the midst of a major initiative to change the treatment of the diabetics in its care. "We're trying to put nearly a million people on these drugs," says Dr. Paul Wallace, senior adviser to the Care Management Institute. The early results: The strategy is indeed improving care and cutting costs, just as Eddy's model predicted.

For Eddy, this is one small step toward solving the thorniest riddle in medicine—a dark secret he has spent his career exposing. "The problem is that we don't know what we are doing," he says. Even today, with a high-tech health-care system that costs the nation $2 trillion a year, there is little or no evidence that many widely used treatments and procedures actually work better than various cheaper alternatives.

This judgment pertains to a shocking number of conditions or diseases, from cardiovascular woes to back pain to prostate cancer. During his long and controversial career proving that the practice of medicine is more guesswork than science, Eddy has repeatedly punctured cherished physician myths. He showed, for instance, that the annual chest X-ray was worthless, over the objections of doctors who made money off the regular visit. He proved that doctors had little clue about the success rate of procedures such as surgery for enlarged prostates. He traced one common practice—preventing women from giving birth vaginally if they had previously had a cesarean—to the recommendation of one lone doctor. Indeed, when he began taking on medicine's sacred cows, Eddy liked to cite a figure that only 15% of what doctors did was backed by hard evidence.

A great many doctors and health-care quality experts have come to endorse Eddy's critique. And while there has been progress in recent years, most of these physicians say the portion of medicine that has been proven effective is still outrageously low—in the range of 20% to 25%. "We don't have the evidence [that treatments work], and we are not investing very much in getting the evidence," says Dr. Stephen C. Schoenbaum, executive vice-president of the Commonwealth Fund and former president of Harvard Pilgrim Health Care Inc. "Clearly, there is a lot in medicine we don't have definitive answers to," adds Dr. I. Steven Udvarhelyi, senior vice-president and chief medical officer at Pennsylvania's Independence Blue Cross.

What's required is a revolution called "evidence-based medicine," says Eddy, a heart surgeon turned mathematician and health-care economist. Tall, lean, and fit at 64, Eddy has the athletic stride and catlike reflexes of the ace rock climber he still is. He also exhibits the competitive drive of someone who once obsessively recorded his time on every training run, and who still likes to be first on a brisk walk up a hill near his home in Aspen, Colo. In his career, he has never been afraid to take a difficult path or an unpopular stand. "Evidence-based" is a term he coined in the early 1980s, and it has since become a rallying cry among medical reformers. The goal of this movement is to pierce the fog that envelops the practice of medicine—a state of ignorance for which doctors cannot really be blamed. "The limitation is the human mind," Eddy says. Without extensive information on the outcomes of treatments, it's fiendishly difficult to know the best approach for care.

The human brain, Eddy explains, needs help to make sense of patients who have combinations of diseases, and of the complex probabilities involved in each. To provide that assistance, Eddy has spent the past 10 years leading a team to develop the computer model that helped him crack the diabetes puzzle. Dubbed Archimedes, this program seeks to mimic in equations the actual biology of the body, and make treatment recommendations as well as figure out what each approach costs. It is at least 10 times "better than the model we use now, which is called thinking," says Dr. Richard Kahn, chief scientific officer at the American Diabetes Assn.

Wasted Resources

Can one computer program offset all the ill-advised treatment options for a whole range of different diseases? The milestones in Eddy's long personal crusade highlight the looming challenges, and may offer a sliver of hope. Coming from a family of four generations of doctors, Eddy went to medical school "because I didn't know what else to do," he confesses. As a resident at Stanford Medical Center in the 1970s, he picked cardiac surgery because "it was the biggest hill—the glamour field."

But he soon became troubled. He began to ask if there was actual evidence to support what doctors were doing. The answer, he was surprised to hear, was no. Doctors

---

Leave Those Ears Alone

In the 1950s, kids routinely got their tonsils taken out. Then physicians such as Dr. Jack L. Paradise of the University of Pittsburgh School of Medicine showed that the procedure brought no benefits to most children. In a study published last August, Paradise took on another common treatment: Implanting tubes to drain the fluid in children's ears—thought to hamper hearing and slow language development. Children with fluid do tend to have more speech problems. But Paradise believes the two conditions have a common cause: poor living conditions. "Medicine is fraught with error when people assume correlation is causality," he says. So Paradise did a study of 6,000 babies. By age three, 429 had persistent fluid in their ears. Half got ear tubes, the other half didn't—and there was no difference in outcomes between the two groups. Paradise's advice to parents of such kids: "Don't just do something. Sit there." Many doctors still perform the surgery, however. "People are reluctant to believe our results," Paradise says. Why? "You get paid for operating and not paid for not operating."

Curing Without Cutting

Can you trust your doctor's recommendation to have surgery for an aching back? Make sure you have all the facts. Evidence says surgery does not fix the problem over the long term any better than time, physical therapy, and exercise. Indeed, says University of North Carolina's Dr. Nortin M. Hadler, pain clinics are full of people who have had back surgery and now are worse off. Geographic data suggest that such procedures may be a fad. In people with identical symptoms, operations like spinal fusion are performed 20 times as often in some parts of the U.S. as in others. "Spinal fusion is the most variable condition in all of medicine," says Dr. James N. Weinstein, editor of *Spine* magazine and chair of orthopedic surgery at Dartmouth.

---

decided whether or not to put a patient in intensive care or use a combination of drugs based on their best judgment and on rules and traditions handed down over the years, as opposed to real scientific proof. These rules and judgments weren't necessarily right. "I concluded that medicine was making decisions with an entirely different method from what we would call rational," says Eddy.

About the same time, the young resident discovered the beauty of mathematics, and its promise of answering medical questions. In just a couple of days, he devoured a calculus textbook (now framed on a shelf in his beautifully appointed home and office), then blasted through the books for a two-year math course in a couple of months. Next, he persuaded Stanford to accept him in a mathematically intense PhD program in the Engineering-Economics Systems Dept. "Dave came in—just this amazing guy," recalls Richard Smallwood, then a Stanford professor. "He had decided he wanted to spend the rest of his life bringing logic and rationality to the medical system, but said he didn't have the math. I said: 'Why not just take it?' So he went out and aced all those math courses."

To augment his wife's earnings while getting his PhD, Eddy landed a job at Xerox Corp.'s legendary Palo Alto Research Center. "They hired weird people," he says. "Here was a heart surgeon doing math. That was weird enough."

Treatments are based largely on rules and traditions, not scientific evidence

Eddy used his newfound math skills to model cancer screening. His Stanford PhD thesis made front-page news in 1980 by overturning the guidelines of the time.

It showed that annual chest X-rays and yearly Pap smears for women at low risk of cervical cancer were a waste of resources, and it won the most prestigious award in the field of operations research, the Frederick W. Lanchester prize. Based on his results, the American Cancer Society changed its guidelines. "He's smart as hell, with a towering clarity of thought," says Stanford health economist Allan Enthoven.

Dr. William H. Herman, director of the Michigan Diabetes Research & Training Center, has a competing computer model that clashes with Eddy's. Nonetheless, he says, "Dr. Eddy is one of my heroes. He's sort of the father of health economics—and he might be right."

Appointed a full professor at Stanford, then recruited as chairman of the Center for Health Policy Research & Education at Duke University, Eddy proved again and again that the emperor had no clothes. In one study, he ferreted out decades of research evaluating treatment of high pressure in the eyeball, a condition that can lead to glaucoma and blindness. He found about a dozen studies that looked at outcomes with pressure-lowering medications used on millions of people. The studies actually suggested that the 100-year-old treatment was harmful, causing more cases of blindness, not fewer.

Eddy submitted a paper to the *Journal of the American Medical Assn. (JAMA),* whose editors sent it out to specialists for review. "It was amazing," Eddy recalls. "The tom-toms sounded among all the ophthalmologists," who marshaled a counterattack. "I felt like Salman Rushdie." Stanford ophthalmologist Kuldev Singh says: "Dr. Eddy challenged the community to prove that we actually had evidence. He did a service by stimulating clinical trials," which showed that the treatment does slow the disease in a minority of patients.

By 1985, Eddy was "burned out" by the administrative side of academia, he says. Lured by a poster of the Tetons, he gave up his prestigious post. He moved to Jackson, Wyo., so he could climb in his spare time. He and a friend even made a first ascent of a new route on the Grand Teton, now named after them. Meanwhile, he carved out a niche showing doctors at specialty society meetings that their cherished beliefs were dubious. "At each meeting I would do the same exercise," he says. He would ask doctors to think of a typical patient and typical treatment, then write down the results of that treatment. For urologists, for instance, what were the chances that a man with an enlarged prostate could urinate normally after having corrective surgery? Eddy then asked the society's president to read the predictions.

The results were startling. The predictions of success invariably ranged from 0% to 100%, with no clear pattern. "All the doctors were trying to estimate the same thing—and they all gave different numbers," he says. "I've spent 25 years proving that what we lovingly call clinical judgment is woefully outmatched by the complexities of medicine." Think about the implications for helping patients make decisions, Eddy adds. "Go to one doctor, and get one answer. Go to another, and get a different one." Or think about expert testimony. "You don't have to hire an expert to lie. You can just find one who truly believes the number you want."

More important, the lack of evidence creates a costly clash. Americans and their doctors want access to any new treatment, and many doctors fervently believe such care is warranted. On the other hand, those beliefs can be flat wrong. As a consultant on Blue Cross's insurance coverage decisions, Eddy testified on the insurer's behalf in high-profile court cases, such as bone marrow transplants for breast cancer. Women and doctors demanded the treatment, even though there was no evidence it saved lives. Insurers who refused coverage usually lost in court. "I was the bad guy," Eddy recalls. When clinical trials were actually done, they showed that the treatment, costing from $50,000 to $150,000, didn't work. The doctors who pushed the painful, risky procedure on women "owe this country an apology," Eddy says.

"Go to one doctor, and get one answer. Go to another, and get a different one." —Dr. David Eddy, Heart Surgeon and Health-Care Economist

---

Is medicine doing any better today? In recognizing the problem, yes. But in solving it, unfortunately, no. Take prostate cancer. Doctors now routinely test for levels of prostate-specific antigen (PSA) to try to diagnose the disease. But there's no evidence that using the test improves survival. Some experts believe that as many cancers would be detected through random biopsies. Then, once cancer is spotted, there's no way to know who needs treatment and who doesn't. Plus, there is a plethora of treatment choices—four kinds of surgery, various types of implantable radioactive seeds, and competing external radiation regimens, notes Dr. Eric Klein, head of urologic oncology at the Cleveland Clinic. "How is a poor patient supposed to decide among those?" he asks. Most of the time, patients don't even know the options.

Vested Interests

"Because there are no definitive answers, you are at the whim of where you are and who you talk to," says

Bypass That Operation?

Each year doctors perform 400,000 bypass surgeries and 1 million angioplasties, where most tubes are placed in diseased arteries to hold them open. While most people believe that such surgery is life-saving, the available data say otherwise. Except for about 3% of people with severe heart disease, treatment with drugs alone works just as well to extend life and prevent heart attacks as surgery does. "Cardiologists like to open up arteries," says Dr. David D. Waters, chief of cardiology at San Francisco General Hospital. "But there is no evidence that opening up chronically narrowed arteries reduces the risk of heart attack." Harvard Medical School's Dr. Roger J. Laham figures that at least 400,000 angioplasties a year are unnecessary. "I'm sure we are way overtreating our patients," he says. Surgery carries big risks, such as mental declines after bypass operations. The overuse is exacting a big toll on individual patients and the health-care system, argue such experts as Dr. Nortin M. Hadler, professor of medicine at the University of North Carolina at Chapel Hill.

Dr. Gary M. Kirsh at the Urology Group in Cincinnati. Kirsh does many brachytherapies—implanting radioactive seeds. But "if you drive one and a half hours down the road to Indianapolis, there is almost no brachytherapy," he says. Head to Loma Linda, Calif., where the first proton-beam therapy machine was installed, in 1990, and the rates of proton-beam treatment are far higher than in most other parts of the country. Go to a surgeon, and he'll probably recommend surgery. Go to a radiologist, and the chances are high of getting radiation instead. "Doctors often assume that they know what a patient wants, leading them to recommend the treatment they know best," says Dr. David E. Wennberg, president of Health Dialog Analytic Solutions.

More troubling, many doctors hold not just a professional interest in which treatment to offer, but a financial one as well. "There is no question that the economic interests of the physician enter into the decision," says Kirsh. The bottom line: The conventional wisdom in prostate cancer—that surgery is the gold standard and the best chance for a cure—is unsustainable. Strangely enough, however, the choice may not matter very much. "There really isn't good evidence to suggest that one treatment is better than another," says Klein.

Compared with the skepticism Eddy faced in the 1990s, many physicians now concur that traditional treatments for serious illnesses often aren't best. Yet this message can be hard for Americans to believe. "When there is more than one medical option, people mistakenly think that the

more aggressive procedure is the best," says Annette M. Cormier O'Connor, senior scientist in clinical epidemiology at the Ottawa Health Research Institute. The message flies in the face of America's infatuation with the latest advances. "As a nation, we always want the best, the most recent technology," explains Dr. Joe Thompson, health adviser to Arkansas Governor Mike Huckabee. "We spend a huge amount developing it, and we get a big increase in supply." New radiation machines for cancer or operating rooms for heart surgery are profit centers for hospitals, for instance. Once a hospital installs a shiny new catheter lab, it has a powerful incentive to refer more patients for the procedure. It's a classic case of increased supply driving demand, instead of the other way around. "Combine that with Americans' demand to be treated immediately, and it is a cauldron for overuse and inappropriate use," says Thompson.

The consequences for the U.S. are disturbing. This nation spends 2 1/2 times as much as any other country per person on health care. Yet middle-aged Americans are in far worse health than their British counterparts, who spend less than half as much and practice less intensive medicine, according to a new study. "The investment in health care in the U.S. is just not paying off," argues Gerard Anderson, director of the Center for Hospital Finance & Management at Johns Hopkins' Bloomberg School of Public Health. Speaking not for attribution, the head of health care at one of America's largest corporations puts it more bluntly: "There is a massive amount of spending on things that really don't help patients, and even put them at greater risk. Everyone that's informed on the topic knows it, but it is such a scary thing to discuss that people are not willing to talk about it openly."

Of course, there are plenty of areas of medicine, from antibiotics and vaccines to early detection of certain tumors, where the benefits are huge and incontrovertible. But if these effective treatments are black and white, much of the rest of medicine is a dark shade of gray. "A lot of things we absolutely believe at the moment based on our intuition are ultimately absolutely wrong," says Dr. Paul Wallace, of the Care Management Institute.

The best way to go from intuition to evidence is the randomized clinical trial. Patients with a particular condition are randomly assigned to competing treatments or, if appropriate, to a placebo. By monitoring the patients for months or years, doctors learn the relative risks and benefits of the treatment being studied.

But such trials take years and cost many millions of dollars. By the time the results come in, science and medicine may have moved on, making the findings less relevant. Moreover, patients in a clinical trial usually aren't representative of real people, who tend to have complex

A Lumpectomy May Do It

For Jeanine Whitney, the diagnosis of breast cancer last June was bad enough. But when her doctor told her that her best chance was an immediate mastectomy, "I cried for 24 hours. I felt that part of my womanhood would have been taken," says Whitney, who works at an air conditioner factory in Rushville, Ind. Her employer, American Standard Cos., had a program to provide workers with unbiased information about the risks and benefits of potential treatments. Thanks to the program, Whitney learned that there was no evidence that a mastectomy would have a better outcome than a lumpectomy, provided the tissue around the lump was clear of cancer. Twenty years after treatment, the outcomes were the same, according to studies. "It was a total surprise," she recalls. She requested a lumpectomy, which was carried out in July, followed by seven weeks of radiation and six of recovery. Now, Whitney is grateful that she was able to get the information she needed to buck her doctor's recommendation. If Whitney had had to make a decision without that, she says she would have "ended up in the psychiatric ward."

combinations of diseases and medical problems. And patients often don't stick with the program.

Such difficulties are highlighted by an eight-year study of low-fat diets that cost upward of $400 million. Most subjects failed to stick to the low-fat regimen, making it tough to draw conclusions. In addition, the study failed to take stock of different kinds of fats, some of which are now known to have beneficial effects. Many trials fall into similar traps. So it's no surprise that up to one-third of clinical studies lead to conclusions that are later overturned, according to a recent paper in JAMA.

Even when common treatments are proved to be dubious, physicians don't rush to change their practice. They may still firmly believe in the treatment—or in the dollars it brings in. And doctors whose oxen get gored sometimes fight back. In 1993, the federal government's Agency for Health Care Policy & Research convened a panel to develop guidelines for back surgery. Fearing that the recommendations would cast doubt on what the doctors were doing, a prominent back surgeon protested to Congress, and lawmakers slashed funding for the agency. "Congress forced out the research," says Floyd J. Fowler Jr., president of the Foundation for Informed Medical Decision Making. "It was a national tragedy," he says—and not an isolated incident. The agency's budget is often targeted "by special interest groups who had their specialty threatened," says Arkansas' Dr. Thompson.

With proof about medical outcomes lacking, one possible solution is educating patients about the uncertainties.

"The popular version of evidence-based medicine is about proving things," says Kaiser's Wallace, "but it is really about transparency—being clear about what we know and don't know." The Foundation for Informed Medical Decision Making produces booklets, videotapes, and other material to put the full picture in the hands of patients. Health Dialog markets the information to providers and companies, addressing back pain, breast cancer, uterine fibroids and bleeding, coronary heart disease, depression, osteoarthritis, and other conditions.

In studies where one group of patients hears the full story while other patients simply receive their doctors' instructions, a key difference emerges. The well-informed patients opt for more invasive, aggressive approaches 23% less often, on average, than the other group. In some cases, the drop is much bigger—50% to 60%. "Patients typically don't understand that they have options, and even if they do, they often wildly exaggerate the benefits of surgery and wildly minimize the chances of harm," says Ottawa's O'Connor, a leader in this field of so-called decision aids.

Eddy's computer simulation could help more patients attain appropriate care. His approach is to create a SimCity-like world in silicon, where virtual doctors conduct trials of virtual patients and figure out what treatments work. After getting funding from Kaiser Permanente in 1991, Eddy hired a particle physicist, Len Schlessinger, who knew how to write equations describing the complex interactions in biology. The pair selected diabetes as a test case. In their virtual world, each simulated person has a heart, liver, kidneys, blood, and other organs. As in real people, cells in the pancreas make insulin, which regulates the uptake of glucose in other cells. And as in the real disease, key cells can fail to respond to the insulin, causing high blood-sugar levels and a cascade of biological effects. The virtual patients come down with high blood pressure, heart disease, and poor circulation, which can lead to foot ulcers and amputations, blindness, and other ills. The model also assesses the costs of treating the complications.

Eddy dubbed the model Archimedes and tested it by comparing it with two dozen real trials. One clinical study compared cholesterol-lowering statin drugs to a placebo in diabetics. After 4 1/2 years, the drugs reduced heart attacks by 35%. The exact same thing happened in Eddy's simulated patients. "The Archimedes model is just fabulous in the validation studies," says the University of Michigan's Herman.

Standard of Care

The team then put Archimedes to work on a tough, real problem: how best to treat diabetes in people who have additional aliments. "One thing not yet adequately embraced by evidence-based medicine is what to do for someone with diabetes, hypertension, heart disease, and depression," explains Kaiser's Wallace. Doctors now typically try to treat the most pressing problems. "But we fail to pick the right ones consistently, so we have misdirected utilization and a great deal of waste," he says. Kaiser Permanente's Dr. Jim Dudl had a counterintuitive suggestion. With diabetics, doctors assume that keeping blood sugar levels low and consistent is the best way to ward off problems such as heart disease. But Dudl wondered what would happen if he flipped it around, aiming treatment at the downstream problems. The idea is to give patients a trio of generic medicines: aspirin, a cholesterol-lowering statin, and drugs called ACE inhibitors.

Using Archimedes and thousands of virtual patients, Eddy and Schlessinger compared the traditional approach with the drug combination. The model took about a half-hour to simulate a 30-year trial, and showed that the three-drug combination was "cost- and life-saving," says Kaiser's Wallace. The benefits far surpassed "what can be achieved with aggressive glucose control." Kaiser Permanente docs switched their standard of care for diabetes, adding these drugs to other interventions. It is too early to declare a victory, but the experience with patients seems to be mimicking Eddy's computer model. "It goes against our mental picture of the disease," says Wallace. But it also makes sense, he adds. "Cardiovascular disease is the worst complication of diabetes—and what people die of."

Medicine's Industrial Revolution

BY HOWARD GLECKMAN

Sometimes medicine performs just as it should. Vaccines have banished smallpox. Surgery can cure early-stage colon cancer. But the disturbing truth is treatments that are proven to work reach only about half of the Americans who need them, according to a series of studies by RAND Corp. And in hospitals, simple measures that protect patients' lives are often hard to implement.

Hygiene is a good example. For 150 years we have known that doctors with unwashed hands pass infections from patient to patient. The Centers for Disease Control & Prevention figures that 80% of hospital-acquired infections are transmitted this way, costing billions of dollars annually to treat and killing thousands of people.

With this in mind, the University of Pittsburgh Medical Center's Presbyterian Hospital installed alcohol-wash dispensers in every room and allowed nurses to ban doctors who don't wash up from entering patients' rooms. Yet more than one-quarter of UPMC's doctors still haven't gotten the message, says Chief Medical Officer Loren H. Roth. Things have improved in recent years, "but a lot of physicians and residents are still not complying," he says.

One major cause for such huge gaps in care is that financial incentives can be skewed. Insurance companies, which have learned that high infection rates cost them money, are beginning to provide bonuses to encourage hospitals to make big improvements. Highmark Inc., which operates the Blue Cross/Blue Shield plans in Pittsburgh, will give UPMC $10 million this year for lowering infections.

But doctors don't have the same incentives. They are usually not hospital employees and are paid based on the number of patients they see and procedures they do. Repeatedly stopping to wash up may slow them down and cost them money. That has hospitals such as UPMC as well as private insurance companies and Medicare scrambling for new ideas. "How do we align incentives so we pay more for prevention than for solving the disaster after it happens?" asks Donald R. Fischer, chief medical officer at Highmark.

UPMC's Roth says that improving the quality of care may also mean challenging a bedrock belief: that each patient is unique and that doctors must bring individualized judgment to each case. This view "has a kind of appeal to it for both the profession and patients," says Roth, "but it is not so." Most illnesses and injuries can best be treated by standardizing care, he argues. The goal is to "industrialize every process we can."

This idea horrifies some doctors, but businesses and insurance companies, who pay many of the bills, are cheering Roth on. "We know if you take beta blockers, you are much less likely to have a heart attack," explains Helen Darling, president of the Washington-based National Business Group of Health, which represents major employers. "We can reward you for meeting those standards."

Independence Blue Cross has gone a step further. It gives physicians lists of members with chronic conditions such as diabetes and asthma. The list includes the recommended treatments and tells who has received them. "Then when a patient shows up, the missing services can be provided," explains Dr. I. Steven Udvarhelyi, senior vice-president at the insurer. Doctors, who were leery at first, have embraced the plan.

Of course, you have to get people into physicians' offices. To do this, several health plans and companies have learned up with Health Dialog Analytic Solutions, which identifies employees or plan members with the greatest needs and reaches out through phone calls and mailings. "The touch is very soft," says Joe Checkley, director of global benefits at American Standard Cos. "It's saying: 'Here are some tools for you, and what can I do to help?'"

The early results are good. At Independence Blue Cross, with about 2 million members, "we know that the program overall reduces medical costs by about 2%," says Udvarhelyi. "That's for the entire population, not just the people that we touch. For them the reduction is orders of magnitude larger." With efforts like these, treatments that do work are now getting to more of the people who need them.

—With John Carey

Eddy readily concedes that this example is a small beginning. In its current state of development, Archimedes is like "the Wright brothers' plane. We're off the sand and flying to Raleigh." But it won't be long, he says, "before we're offering transcontinental flights, with movies."

The modeling approach allows each of us, in essence, to have an imaginary twin. We can use our twin to predict what our lives and state of health are likely to be with different lifestyles and approaches to care. Companies could create virtual clones of each employee, predicting what will occur with current care or with added prevention or treatment programs. "They can see what happens to such things as the complications suffered by diabetics, the lost time from work, the amount of angina or the rate of heart attacks, the number of deaths, and the cost of new employees if one dies," Eddy explains. "Our mission is that in 10 years, no one will make an important decision in health care without first asking: 'What does Archimedes say?'"

Reprinted by special permission from *Business Week,* May 29, 2006, pp. 73–79. Copyright © 2006 by The McGraw-Hill Companies, Inc.

In Search of the Spiritual

Move over, politics. Americans are looking for personal, ecstatic experiences of God, and, according to our poll, they don't much care what the neighbors are doing.

JERRY ADLER

The 1960s did not penetrate very deeply into the small towns of the Quaboag Valley of central Massachusetts. Even so, Father Thomas Keating, the abbot of St. Joseph's Abbey, couldn't help noticing the attraction that the exotic religious practices of the East held for many young Roman Catholics. To him, as a Trappist monk, meditation was second nature. He invited the great Zen master Roshi Sasaki to lead retreats at the abbey. And surely, he thought, there must be a precedent within the church for making such simple but powerful spiritual techniques available to laypeople. His Trappist brother Father William Meninger found it in one day in 1974, in a dusty copy of a 14th-century guide to contemplative meditation, "The Cloud of Unknowing." Drawing on that work, as well as the writings of the contemplatives Saint John of the Cross and Saint Teresa of Avila, the two monks began teaching a form of Christian meditation that grew into the worldwide phenomenon known as centering prayer. Twice a day for 20 minutes, practitioners find a quiet place to sit with their eyes closed and surrender their minds to God. In more than a dozen books and in speeches and retreats that have attracted tens of thousands, Keating has spread the word to a world of "hungry people, looking for a deeper relationship with God."

For most of history, that's exactly what most people have been looking for. But only a generation ago it appeared from some vantage points, such as midtown Manhattan, that Americans were on their way to turning their backs on God. In sepulchral black and red, the cover of Time magazine dated April 8, 1966—Good Friday—introduced millions of readers to existential anguish with the question *Is God Dead?* If he was, the likely culprit was science, whose triumph was deemed so complete that "what cannot be known [by scientific methods] seems uninteresting, unreal." Nobody would write such an article now, in an era of round-the-clock televangelism and official presidential displays of Christian piety. Even more remarkable today is the article's obsession with the experience of a handful of the most prestigious Protestant denominations. No one looked for God in the Pentecostal churches of East Los Angeles or among the backwoods Baptists of Arkansas. Muslims earned no notice, nor did American Hindus or Buddhists, except for a passage that raised the alarming prospect of seekers' "desperately" turning to "psychiatry, Zen or drugs."

History records that the vanguard of angst-ridden intellectuals in Time, struggling to imagine God as a cloud of gas in the far reaches of the galaxy, never did sweep the nation. What was dying in 1966 was a well-meaning but arid theology born of rationalism: a wavering trumpet call for ethical behavior, a search for meaning in a letter to the editor in favor of civil rights. What would be born in its stead, in a cycle of renewal that has played itself out many times since the Temple of Solomon, was a passion for an immediate, transcendent experience of God. And a uniquely American acceptance of the amazingly diverse paths people have taken to find it. NEWSWEEK set out to map this new topography of faith, visiting storefront churches in Brooklyn and mosques in Los Angeles, an environmental Christian activist in West Virginia and a Catholic college in Ohio—talking to Americans of all creeds, and none, about their spiritual journeys. A major poll, commissioned jointly with Beliefnet.com, reveals a breadth of tolerance and curiosity virtually across the religious spectrum. And everywhere we looked, a flowering of spirituality: in the hollering, swooning, foot-stomping services of the new wave of Pentecostals; in Catholic churches where worshipers pass the small hours of the night alone contemplating the eucharist, and among Jews who are seeking God in the mystical thickets of Kabbalah. Also, in the rebirth of Pagan religions that look for God in the wonders of the natural world; in Zen and innumerable other threads of Buddhism, whose followers seek enlightenment through meditation and prayer, and in the efforts of American Muslims to achieve a more God-centered Islam. And, for that matter, at the Church of the Holy Communion, described by the Rev. Gary Jones as "a proper Episcopal church in one of the wealthiest parts of Memphis," where increasingly "personal experience is at the heart of much of what we do." A few years ago Jones added a Sunday-evening service that has evolved into a blend of Celtic evensong with communion. Congregants were invited to make a sign of the cross with holy water. Jones was relieved when this innovation quickly won acceptance. "We thought people would be embarrassed," he says.

Where We Stand on Faith

Forget Red States and Blue States. On matters of faith, the U.S. is still one nation, under God. In early August, NEWSWEEK and Beliefnet asked 1,004 Americans how they worship and what they believe. The results:

79% of those polled describe themselves as 'spiritual'; 64% say 'religious.'

Which best describes you?

Spiritual but not religious	24%
Religious but not spiritual	9
Religious and spiritual	55
Not spiritual/not religious	8
Don't know	4

How important is spirituality in your daily life?

Very important	57%
Somewhat important	27
Not too important	7
Not at all important	7
Don't know	2

How important is spirituality in your daily life?
THOSE RESPONDING "VERY"

Age 18–39	44%
40–59	63
60+	66

What is your current religion?

Evangelical Protestant	33%
Non-evangelical Protestant	25
Roman Catholic	22
Other Christian	5
Jewish	1
Muslim	1
Other non-Christian	3
Atheist/agnostic/no religion	6
Religion undesignated	4

What is your current religion?

	EVANGELICAL	ATHEIST*
Age 18–39	28%	9%
40–59	36	5
60+	36	3

Compare what you practice today with what you practiced growing up. Is your current religion the same?

The same	38%
Mostly the same	30
Mostly different	9
Completely different	11
Became an atheist/agnostic	4
Not raised in any religion	5
Don't know	5

20% have changed faiths since childhood; 4% have abandoned religion altogether.

How traditional are your religious practices?

Very traditional	27%
Somewhat traditional	44
Not traditional	19
On the cutting edge	6
Don't know	4

Why do you practice religion?†

To forge a personal relationship with God	39%
To help you be a better person and live a moral life	30
To find peace and happiness	17
To connect with something larger than yourself	10
To give your life meaning and structure	8
To be part of a community	3
Other	13

How often do you engage in these religious or spiritual activities?†
THOSE RESPONDING "EVERY DAY"

Pray	64%
Meditate	29
Participate in a spiritual activity not connected with church	21
Read the Bible, Qur'an, etc.	20
Attend church or services	2

When do you feel the strongest connection to God?

When you are praying alone	40%
When you are in nature	21
In a house of worship	21
When praying with others	6
When reading a sacred text	2
None of these/doesn't apply	6
Don't know	4

Do you believe that God created the universe?

Created by God	80%
Not created by God	10
Don't believe in God	1
Don't know	9

Which of the following is the most important purpose of prayer?

To seek God's guidance	27%
To thank God	23
To help others	13
To improve a person's life	9
None of these/other	4
Don't know	5

67% believe that when we die, our souls go to heaven or hell; 24% do not believe that heaven and hell exist.

What happens when we die?

The soul goes to heaven or hell	67%
There is no heaven or hell, but the soul lives on in some kind of spiritual realm	13
It's all over; there is no soul	6
The soul is reincarnated into another creature	5
Don't know	9

How often do you explore the spiritual ideas of other faiths?

RESPONDING "OFTEN" OR "SOMETIMES"

Evangelical Protestants	30%
Non-evangelical Protestants	31
Roman Catholics	35
Non-Christians	48

THOSE RESPONDING "NEVER"

Evangelical Protestants	35%
Non-evangelical Protestants	37
Roman Catholics	36
Non-Christians	12

Is your spouse's/partner's religion the same as yours?

The same	70%
Mostly the same	14
Mostly different	5
Completely different	10
Atheist/agnostic/no religion	1

Can a good person who doesn't share your religious beliefs attain salvation or go to heaven?

THOSE RESPONDING "YES"

Evangelical Protestants	68%
Non-evangelical Protestants	83
Roman Catholics	91
Non-Christians	73

79% believe someone of another faith can attain salvation or go to heaven.

Whatever is going on here, it's not an explosion of people going to church. The great public manifestations of religiosity in America today—the megachurches seating 8,000 worshipers at one service, the emergence of evangelical preachers as political power brokers—haven't been reflected in increased attendance at services. Of 1,004 respondents to the NEWSWEEK/Beliefnet Poll, 45 percent said they attend worship services weekly, virtually identical to the figure (44 percent) in a Gallup poll cited by Time in 1966. Then as now, however, there is probably a fair amount of wishful thinking in those figures; researchers who have done actual head counts in churches think the figure is probably more like 20 percent. There has been a particular falloff in attendance by African-Americans, for whom the church is no longer the only respectable avenue of social advancement, according to Darren Sherkat, a sociologist at Southern Illinois University. The fastest-growing category on surveys that ask people to give their religious affiliation, says Patricia O'Connell Killen of Pacific Lutheran University in Tacoma, Wash., is "none." But "spirituality," the impulse to seek communion with the Divine, is thriving. The NEWSWEEK/Beliefnet Poll found that more Americans, especially those younger than 60, described themselves as "spiritual" (79 percent) than "religious" (64 percent). Almost two thirds of Americans say they pray every day, and nearly a third meditate.

These figures tell you more about what Americans care about than a 10,000-foot-high monument to the Ten Commandments. "You can know all about God," says Tony Campolo, a prominent evangelist, "but the question is, do you *know* God? You can have solid theology and be orthodox to the core, but have you *experienced* God in your own life?" In the broadest sense, Campolo says, the Christian believer and the New Age acolyte are on the same mission: "We are looking for transcendence in the midst of the mundane." And what could be more mundane than politics? Seventy-five percent say that a "very important" reason for their faith is to "forge a personal relationship with God"—not fighting political battles.

Today, then, the real spiritual quest is not to put another conservative on the Supreme Court, or to get creation science into the schools. If you experience God directly, your faith is not going to hinge on whether natural selection could have produced the flagellum of a bacterium. If you feel God within you, then the important question is settled; the rest is details.

As diverse as America itself are the ways in which Americans seek spiritual enlightenment. One of the unexpected results of the immigration reform of 1965 was its effect on American religiosity. Even Christian immigrants brought with them unfamiliar practices and beliefs, planting on American soil branches of the True Jesus Church (from China) or the Zairean Kimbangu Church. Beliefnet, the religious Web site, sends out more than 8 million daily e-mails of spiritual wisdom in various flavors to more than 5 million subscribers. Generic "inspiration" is most popular (2.4 million), followed by the Bible (1.6 million), but there are 460,000 subscribers to the Buddhist thought of the day, 313,000 Torah devotees, 268,000 subscribers to Daily Muslim Wisdom (and 236,000 who get the Spiritual Weight Loss message). Even nature-worshiping Pagans are divided into a mind-boggling panoply of sects, including Wicca, Druidism, Pantheism, Animism, Teutonic Paganism, the God of Spirituality Folk and, in case you can't find one to suit you on that list, Eclectic Paganism.

Along with diversity has come a degree of inclusiveness that would have scandalized an earlier generation. According to the NEWSWEEK/Beliefnet Poll, eight in 10 Americans—including 68 percent of evangelicals—believe that more than one faith can be a path to salvation, which is most likely not what they were taught in Sunday school. One out of five respondents said he had switched religions as an adult.

This is not surprising in the United States, which for much of its history was a spiritual hothouse in which Methodism, Mormonism, Adventism, Christian Science, Jehovah's Witnesses and the Nation of Islam all took root and flourished. In America even *atheists* are spiritualists, searching for meaning in parapsychology and near-death experiences. There is a streak in the United States of relying on what Pacific Lutheran's Killen calls "individual visceral experience" to validate religious ideas. American faiths have long been characterized by creativity and individualism. "That's their secret to success," says Alan Wolfe, director of the Boisi Center for Religion and American Public Life at Boston College. "Rather than being about a god who commands you, it's about finding a religion that empowers you."

Empowerment is at the heart of Pentecostalism, which has burgeoned from a single Spirit-touched believer at a Kansas Bible school at the turn of the last century to 30 million adherents in America and more than half a billion worldwide. Marching under the Pentecostal banner is a host of denominations whose names roll off the tongue like a voice from heaven: Church of God, International Church of the Four-square Gospel, International Pentecostal Holiness Church, the Assemblies of God. Among them is a tiny Brooklyn storefront church whose sign grandly proclaims the Cathedral of Deliverance. This is where 43-year-old Ron Cox, who left his mother's large Southern Baptist church in his teens, now lives and works as an assistant to the bishop, Steven Wagnon. He tried Hinduism, but it failed to move him; looked into Buddhism, but lost interest when a Buddhist couldn't tell him the meaning of her chant. But one summer night recently, guided by the voice of God to a Pentecostal revival in full-throated swing, he was transfixed by the sight of worshipers so moved by the Holy Spirit that they were jumping, shouting and falling to the floor in a faint. Soon he, too, was experiencing the ecstasy of the Holy Spirit. Once, it seemed to lift him right out of his body:

"I felt the Spirit come upon me, and it was an overwhelming presence. It was bliss. I thought only 10 or 15 minutes had passed, but three hours had gone by. And I remember just shouting, 'Hallelujah, hallelujah, hallelujah!'"

The bliss Cox felt was mingled with awe—the Holy Spirit was inside his very own body. That helps explain Pentecostalism's historical appeal to the poor and marginalized: rural Southerners, African-Americans and, more recently, Hispanics and other immigrants. It is burgeoning in the developing world. "For people who feel overlooked, it provides a sense that you're a very important person," observes Harvey Cox of the Harvard Divinity School. By the same token, people with social aspirations preferred other churches, but nowadays Pentecostalism—the faith of former attorney general John Ashcroft—has lost its stigma as a religion of the poor. And elements of Pentecostal worship are invading other denominations, a change that coincided with the introduction of arena-style screens in churches, replacing hymnals and freeing up people's hands to clap and wave. Naturally, there is some attenuation as you move up the socioeconomic scale. Babbling in foreign-sounding "tongues" turns into discreet murmurs of affirmation. "An atmosphere that is joyous, ecstatic and emotionally expressive is appearing in all kinds of churches now," says Harvard's Cox, "even if it's not labeled Pentecostal."

Empowerment requires intensity of effort; Americans like the idea of taking responsibility for their own souls. This may be why Buddhism—a religion without a personal god and only a few broad ethical precepts—has made such inroads in the American imagination. "People are looking for transformative experience, not just a new creed or dogma," says Surya Das, a U.S.-born Tibetan lama whose spiritual journey began in 1970, when he was a student from New York's Long Island named Jeffrey Miller. "The Ten Commandments and Sermon on the Mount are already there." In most Buddhist countries, and among immigrants in America, the role of the layperson is to support the monks in their lives of contemplation. But American converts want to do their own contemplating. Stephen Cope, who attended Episcopal divinity school but later trained as a psychotherapist, dropped into a meditation center in Cambridge, Mass., one day and soon found himself spending six hours every Sunday sitting and walking in silent contemplation. Then he added yoga to his routine, which he happily describes as "like gasoline on fire" when it comes to igniting a meditative state. And the great thing is, he still attends his Episcopal church—a perfect example of the new American spirituality, with a thirst for transcendence too powerful to be met by just one religion.

People like that could become panentheists, too—a new term for people who believe in the divinity of the natural universe (like the better-known Pantheists), but also postulate an intelligent being or force behind it. To Bridgette O'Brien, a 32-year-old student in the recently created Ph.D. program in Religion and Nature at the University of Florida, "the divine is something significant in terms of the energy that pervades the natural world at large." Her worship consists of composting, recycling and daily five-mile runs; she describes herself as "the person that picks the earthworms off the sidewalk after the rain to make sure they don't get stepped on." Those seeking a more structured nature-based religion have many choices, including several branches of Druidism. "I talk to my ancestors, the spirits of nature and other deities on a regular basis," says Isaac Bonewits, a 55-year-old New Yorker who founded one of the best-known Druid orders. Wicca, the largest Pagan sect, with an elaborate calendar of seasonal holidays and rituals, is popular enough to demand its own military chaplains. Unfortunately from the political standpoint, Wiccans refer to themselves as "witches," although they do not, in fact, worship Satan. This confusion led President Bush, when he was Texas governor, to urge the Army to reconsider allowing Wiccan rites at a military base, with the comment "I don't think witchcraft is a religion."

Unlike Buddhists, Catholics cannot take sole responsibility for their souls; they need the sacraments of the church to be saved. But they, too, have experienced a flowering of spirituality, especially among the "John Paul II Catholics," who were energized by the late pope's call for a new outpouring of the Holy Spirit. Since it arrived in the United States in 1957, the "cursillo" movement has initiated more than a half-million American Catholics into the techniques for seeking a direct communion with God. Cursillo, which means "short course," involves a three-day retreat of silent contemplation and lectures that lean heavily on the spiritual vocabulary of evangelism. Also on the rise is the Adoration of the Eucharist: shifts of silent prayer, sometimes round the clock, before the consecrated host in an otherwise empty church. (You can do the same thing over the Internet; one site says it received 2.5 million hits in a year for its unchanging Webcam image of an altar and a monstrance.) "It's been surprisingly popular," says Robert Kloska, director of campus ministry at Holy Cross College in Indiana. "You

wouldn't think in modern society there's such a yearning for silence and mysticism, but there is."

Kloska is less enthusiastic about the other manifestation of spirituality he sees on campus, an affinity for "high-energy, almost charismatic prayer and worship." Catholic Charismatic Renewal, which got its start in 1967 when a Duquesne University group on a weekend retreat felt a visitation by the Holy Spirit, now runs thousands of prayer groups in the United States, where worshipers may speak in tongues or collapse in laughter or tears. "Young people got tired of hearing that once upon a time people experienced God directly," says historian Martin E. Marty of the University of Chicago. "They want it to happen for themselves. They don't want to hear that Joan of Arc had a vision. They want to have a vision." It's a little more problematic when the Holy Spirit visits during a regular mass. Clayton Ebsch, a retired technician, was enthusiastic when a charismatic priest took over Precious Blood Parish in Stephenson, Mich., even after some of his friends left for more-traditional parishes. Still, he found that speaking in tongues didn't come naturally. "It was just unfamiliar, speaking gibberish and jibber-jabbering," he says, although he sees one virtue in it: "It humbles you."

The Vatican seems ambivalent about these developments. On the one hand, the church wants to keep the allegiance of adherents who have been deserting to evangelical and Pentecostal churches. Three quarters of Hispanic immigrants to the United States are Catholic, but the figure drops to about half by the third generation in America. On the other hand, the raison d'etre of the church is to mediate between the faithful and God. The future Pope Benedict XVI summed up the Vatican's attitude back in 1983, when he wrote of the relationship between "personal experience and the common faith of the Church." Both are important, he said: "a dogmatic faith unsupported by personal experience remains empty; mere personal experience unrelated to the faith of the Church remains blind." In simpler terms: Let's not get carried away here. Emotions come and go, but the mass endures.

The quest for spiritual union with God is as old as mankind itself, uniting the ancient desert tribes of Mesopotamia with the Christian hermits on their mountaintops with American pop singers at the Kabbalah Centre in Los Angeles, poring over the esoteric wisdom encoded in early Jewish texts. And who can begrudge it to them? Well, David Blumenthal of Emory University's Institute for Jewish Studies, for one. His view of the aspiring scholar Madonna is that "anyone who claims to be a Kabbalist and then sings in public largely in the nude is hardly a Kabbalist." The mystical impulse in Judaism—kept alive for centuries by the tiny, fervent band of Hasidim, but long overshadowed in America by the dominance of the rational, decorous Conservative movement—is reasserting itself. The founding text of Kabbalah, the Zohar, conveys the message that God's power depends on humanity's actions. God needs our worship. "It's the same impulse behind Zen Buddhism, Tibetan masters, Hopi Indians," says Arthur Green, rector of the rabbinical school at Hebrew College in Boston. "The ancient esoteric traditions might have something to teach us about living in this age." Even at Hebrew Union College, a citadel of

Reform Judaism, provost Norman Cohen admits that "what the Kabbalah can teach us—how to have a relationship with God—has to be treated seriously."

The Hasidim pray ecstatically; they dance with the Torah; they fast to achieve a higher spiritual state, and they drink wine for the same reason. With their distinctive black frock coats and curly sideburns, they are a visible and growing presence in New York and some other cities. Orthodox Judaism, of which they are a branch, is on the rise among young Jews who trade Friday-night dances and shrimp egg foo yung for a more intense religious experience. Orthodox Rabbi Irving Greenberg calls the phenomenon "Jews by choice," reflecting the reality that Jewish practice is no longer a tribal imperative. In a world in which practically every religion has its own cable-TV channel, to step inside a synagogue becomes an existential choice. "To me, that is the revolution of our time, and I don't mean just Judaism," Greenberg says.

In fact, the same issue is very much on the minds of America's Muslims. Forced to define themselves in the face of an alien—and, in recent years, sometimes hostile—majority, the second generation especially has turned increasingly observant. Unlike their parents, they may attend mosque several times a week and pray five times a day, anywhere they can unroll a prayer mat. It has not been lost on them that the way to fit in in present-day America is to be religious. "When our parents came here in the 1960s or '70s there was a pro-secular culture," explains Yusuf Hussein, 22, who was born in Somalia but came to southern California as a teenager. "For us, being a Muslim is the way to forge our own identity, to move forward, to be modern."

Islam emphasizes the unity of all believers, so American-born Muslims are shedding the cultural accouterments of the many countries from which their parents came, or the political freight of African-American converts. They are intent on forging a purer and more spiritual religion. "It's easier being Muslim and African-American than just being African," says Imam Saadiq Saafir, 60, whose journey took him from Christianity to the Nation of Islam and then to orthodox Sunni Islam. Muslims pray to God without the intervention of a priest or a religious hierarchy; he is never farther away than the Qur'an, which is the direct and unmediated word of Allah. "There are many ways to be spiritual," says Megan Wyatt, a blond Ohioan who converted to Islam three years ago. "People find it in yoga. For me, becoming a Muslim gave me the ultimate connection to God."

So, a generation after the question was posed, we can certainly answer that God seems very much alive in the hearts of those who seek him. We have come a long way, it would appear, from that dark year when the young Catholic philosopher Michael Novak was quoted in Time, saying, "If, occasionally, I raise my heart in prayer, it is to no God I can see, or hear, or feel." To make the point, we gave Novak, who is now 72 and among the most distinguished theologians in America, the chance to correct the record on his youthful despair. And he replied that God is as far away as he's ever been. Religious revivals are always exuberant and filled with spirit, he says, but the true measure of faith is in adversity and despair, when God doesn't show up in every blade of grass or storefront church. "That's when the true nature of belief comes out," he says. "Joy is appropriate to the beginnings of your faith. But sooner or later somebody will get cancer, or your best friends will betray you. That's when you will be tested."

So let us say together: *Hallelujah! Praise the Lord! Sh'ma Yisrael. Allahu Akbar. Om.* And store up the light against the darkness.

With ANNE UNDERWOOD; BEN WHITFORD; JULIET CHUNG; VANESSA JUAREZ; DAN BERRETT and LORRAINE ALI

UNIT 6

Social Change and the Future

Unit Selections

Key Points to Consider

- What problems can be caused by an aging population?

- What dangers does mankind's overexploitation of the environment create?

- What are some of the major problems that technology is creating?

- Debate the issue of biotechnology on the farm.

- How should America handle the terrorist threat?

- What motivates terrorists?

- How bright is America's future? What are the main threats to it? What are some of its main challenges?

- What are the pros and cons of globalization?

- What major changes do you predict for the future?

Student Web Site

www.mhcls.com/online

Internet References

Further information regarding these Web sites may be found in this book's preface or online.

Human Rights and Humanitarian Affairs
http://www.etown.edu/vl/humrts.html
The Hunger Project
http://www.thp.org
Terrorism Research Center
http://www.terrorism.com/index.shtml
United Nations Environment Program (UNEP)
http://www.unep.ch
William Davidson Institute
http://www.wdi.bus.umich.edu

Fascination with the future is an enduring theme in literature, art, poetry, and religion. Human beings are anxious to know if tomorrow will be different from today, and in what ways it might differ. Coping with change has become a top priority in the lives of many. One result of change is stress. When the future is uncertain and the individual appears to have little control over what happens, stress can be a serious problem. On the other hand, stress can have positive effects on people's lives if they can perceive changes as challenges and opportunities.

Any discussion of the future must begin with a look at issues of population that are addressed in this unit's first subsection. In the first article, the authors warn us that too little population is the main demographic problem in the West today. As our population ages and the ratio of workers to retirees declines, economic problems mount. Health-care costs could conceivably become unmanageable, so the authors warn that health care will have to be rationed. The next selection deals with the population issue that is dividing America today: immigration. Washington is in a quandary about what to do about illegal aliens, and how to keep them out. One solution is to build a big fence on the Mexican border and increase the border guard, but most experts believe these steps will not solve the problem.

The next subsection addresses environmental problems. First, Lester Brown catalogs many of the environmental problems which are deteriorating the earth's life support systems. He also identifies potential future problems, such as the crisis in grain prices if much cropland becomes devoted to the production of ethanol for fuel. The world must make many changes to put it on a sustainable course, and Brown offers his suggestions. Jeffrey Kluger writes that the environment has many tipping points which, when crossed, can lead to more rapid and cataclysmic changes because of feedback loops. Kluger explores this problem with global warming.

The next subsection deals with the linkage between technological change and society. Both articles in this section raise concerns about the possible negative effects of supposedly beneficial technologies. One big technology story concerns genetic engineering, and one of its most important areas of application is agriculture. The crucial question is whether it will produce great agricultural advances or ecological nightmares. Next, Clifton Anderson evaluates the potential of genetic engineering in agriculture. It can have both very good and very bad impacts, so he recommends a Genetic Science Commission to guide the development of genetic research in order to maximize the gains and minimize the risks. Eduardo Goncalves evaluates another sophisticated technology, nuclear power. It can win wars and supply useful electrical energy, but it may have already killed 175 million people. Furthermore, the way scientists and governments have acted regarding nuclear energy shows that they cannot always be trusted to pursue the public good in their decisions regarding new technologies.

The following subsection focuses on the new crisis of terrorism. First, Robert S. Mueller III, director of the FBI, provides an update on the situation of terrorism concerning the United States. Al Qaeda has been weakened worldwide, failing to perpetrate a terrorist event in America since 9/11. The danger from home-grown terrorists, however, has increased. On the positive side, Mueller argues that the skill and capacity of the FBI in countering terrorism has increased. Then, Frank Gaffney describes the potential terrorist act against the U.S. that would cause the greatest damage, though not the greatest carnage. Detonating a nuclear bomb high above the U.S. would knock out almost all unhardened computers and badly damage our electricity infrastructure. This "could destroy America as a twenty-first century society and superpower."

The final subsection assesses the prospects for the future. Two prominent futurists provide a wide range of predictions based on analysis of many trends and current plans. They predict many improvements but also many problems, such as massive increases in inequality, frightening environmental problems, WMD terrorism, and worldwide plagues from drug resistant diseases. Pranab Bardhan focuses on globalization and examines whether it helps or hurts the world's poor. It does both, and Bardhan suggests ways to make it help the poor far more than it hurts them. In the final article, William Van Dusen Wishard, a leading world trends expert, asserts that the world is undergoing a great transition. Globalization, information technologies, urbanization, the explosion of knowledge and technologies, the quickening pace of change and a long-term spiritual and psychological reorientation are creating a future unlike the past.

The Challenge of an Aging Society

The future of U.S. health care must involve some form of rationing, argue a former governor and a medical-policy scholar. The problem is not simply how to control costs, but how to achieve social justice.

RICHARD D. LAMM AND ROBERT H. BLANK

One of the great challenges in America's future is to retire the baby boomers without bankrupting the country or unduly burdening future generations. This crisis could soon overwhelm American public policy, as yesterday's baby boom becomes tomorrow's grandparent boom.

This demographic revolution raises some awesome challenges:

- How can we continue to fund present programs for the elderly and also expand those programs for the aging baby boomers?
- How can we fund retirement as well as general health-care programs in an America with ever more older citizens and ever fewer children?
- How do we provide the social infrastructure for an aging society?
- And finally, how can we do politically what needs to be done while being fair to both the present generation and the future generations who will fund these programs?

If we act soon, we can answer these questions rationally, prepare for our future, and avoid steep economic decline. But if we wait, the decisions we will be forced to make will be truly draconian. Age could well be as divisive in the next 40 years as race and sex have been for the last.

There are basically two ways to provide health care and retirement benefits for the elderly: Society can prefund these programs, much as most private-sector retirement programs are funded today, or it can develop a social-insurance scheme. The United States chose social insurance, and it has worked well so far, but how long can it continue?

The U.S. retirement system is now actuarially unsustainable, and health-care expenditures in the nation have grown over the past 40 years at about two and one-half times the rate of inflation, now consuming more than 15% of GDP. Thoughtful people are coming to realize that, given science's seemingly endless production of new miracle treatments, the efforts expended to maintain our own aging bodies can bankrupt our children and our grandchildren.

Today's elderly account for approximately 13% of the U.S. population, yet they get more than 60% of all federal social spending. Americans spend about three times more taxpayer funds on the elderly than on children; the federal government's spending is even more disproportionate. It is not a workable nation-building strategy to spend significantly more on the last generation than we do on the next generation. We must rethink many of our basic public-policy assumptions, because the status quo in health care and retirement spending is no longer an option. The only question is how much and what type of reform we need.

The Next New Deal

To admit that the current system of funding health care is unsustainable requires us to give up a cherished dream: the dream of total, universal care for any ailment freely available on demand. Like the "take backs" some employers now demand from union members, many Americans find it unacceptable to even consider renouncing benefits they have enjoyed, or expected to enjoy, no matter what the reason.

Reform will thus require leadership—strong bipartisan leadership, which so far has been lacking. The public already distrusts the political process, and individual citizens are wrapped up in their own needs and lives. With the nation now politically split almost down the middle on many issues, it will be hard to prepare the public for the type and magnitude of change necessary.

The dominant issue in American medicine for the immediate future will be how we adjust to the demographic realities of an aging society. It will be politically and professionally painful. It will cause much agony in a medical profession trained to assume that there are virtually unlimited resources available and that cost is never a consideration. It will be a seminal issue, causing as much unsettling change as did the reform of medical education early in the twentieth century. It raises issues of limiting expectations in a society that has prided itself on setting no limits to potential in any area of life. Yet, it must be done.

We simply have invented and discovered more things to do to our bodies than our aging society can afford. We now are on the threshold of the bionic body, where medicine can have some positive impact on practically every organ. Modern medicine has outrun the ability of any nation, even a rich nation, to pay for everything beneficial to everyone within its borders. We have created a Faustian bargain, where our aging bodies can and will divert resources that our children and grandchildren need for their own families and that public policy needs for other important social goods.

Americans now spend an average of more than $6,000 a year per capita on health care. For most Americans today, the largest purchase in life is no longer a house but health care. Thoughtful people may worry that we are unbalancing our economy and that it's not wise national policy to spend $1 out of every $7 on health care, but polls show Americans believe health care to be a top priority. Most say they want to see more, not less, public spending on health care. This attitude is politically important, because in a democracy we generally get what we want. But do we truly realize how our wishes impact our society and its institutions, or how they may affect our nation's future?

Seeing the Big Picture: An Expanded Vision

Americans must look at today's new demographic realities with new eyes. We must look fully and honestly at what it means to run "a nation of 50 Floridas." British philosopher and novelist Iris Murdoch wrote, "Seeing is a moral art," noting that our "moral quality functions in what we see and remember and know." We have to morally open our eyes and gain a new moral vision for health care.

This new moral vision challenges long-held assumptions of unlimited resources and ever-rising standards of living. Especially disconcerting in America's individualistic culture is the vision's requirement that collective societal interests be placed above the perceived interests of individuals.

This new moral vision for health care must be built on the recognition that there are distinct moral duties at each of four levels of health care, and that at times these duties are in competition with each other. The four levels of moral duty are:

1. Personal responsibility of the patient.
2. The physician–patient relationship.
3. Insurance company or health plan.
4. The state and/or nation.

Each of these levels in health policy has a different moral radius—i.e., each has distinct yet overlapping moral roles.

In order to address the problems facing health policy, we must examine each level of health care and how they relate to one another. All levels owe a duty to the individual patient, but not the same duty. The moral radius of a physician is almost

solely to his or her patient. The moral radius of an insurance company or HMO is broader, and includes all its subscribers. The moral radius of the state or nation extends to all its citizens and must balance the good of one against the good of all. In effect, its geographic jurisdiction becomes its moral jurisdiction.

The physician's role will most likely stay substantially as it has been for 2,000 years, but neither the insurance company/ HMO nor the state/nation can issue a blank check to health-care providers. Insurance companies and governments owe a duty to the individual patient, but they also have much broader responsibilities toward a much larger group of stakeholders. It is therefore their duty to always consider costs as well as benefits—and sometimes refuse to pay—when a physician recommends a certain procedure for a specific patient.

The moral radius of the plan/group requires it to maximize the health of all its members. This means saying no to marginally effective medicine. Instead, there must be fair and understandable rules and regulations that clearly aim to maximize the health of the group. Further, these rules must be intellectually sound, procedurally valid, evidence based, and well publicized to physicians and subscribers alike. Similarly, the state or nation has a duty it cannot avoid: to provide basic health care for every citizen.

We must start by enlarging our concept of justice to embrace the interests of all generations, including those yet to come. One great step forward taken by the New Deal was to see clearly the plight of the elderly and poor. Today's challenge is to see what the solutions to past problems are doing to the future. Since World War II, many of the social policies Americans have consistently supported have encumbered the next generation. However successful and however popular our entitlement programs are, they have become unjust to our children who are paying into them. This applies with special urgency to our health-care programs.

Universal Coverage: Seeing the Forgotten Uninsured

One often-heard argument for not changing the present U.S. healthcare system is that change would require rationing health care. In fact, the United States already does ration health care, and probably denies more people more needed care than any other industrial country. We tell ourselves that, because we are not denying specific procedures to specific individuals, we are not rationing medicine, but a health-care system rations when it fails to deliver needed services to any citizen within its jurisdiction. The sad fact is, we don't mind people falling out of the lifeboat, so long as we don't personally have to throw them overboard or listen to them splash.

We lack the moral imagination to see the "forgotten men, women, and children" who don't have health coverage, and often, even if they are given charity treatment, receive only inadequate care. Studies show that the uninsured are less able to get adequate care, and their health statistics in virtually every category are below (often far below) those who have insurance. Those who must pay out of pocket often pay more than the same service would cost an insured patient, because third-party payers are able to negotiate discounted rates.

Oregon sailed into terra incognita in 1989, when it decided to limit state-funded health-care benefits rather than leave indigent Oregonians with no health coverage at all. If governments provide subsidized health care to some medically indigent citizens but not to others, they are rationing. A sustainable, publicly funded health-care system must look beyond what might be best for a single individual to ensure the justice of the system as a whole. Inevitably, this effort will require trade-offs, priority setting, and rationing—all three.

In health-care policy, "distributive justice" may be our most important ethic. You cannot build a modern health-care system one person at a time. Some institution must ask, "How do we keep a society healthy?" We need a method of assessing health needs that looks not at individuals, but at the broader health producing possibilities. Public policy must quantify "need" cumulatively and relate that need to the real world of affordable/sustainable resources. In short, we need a public policy that values universal health-care coverage.

Infinite Needs, Finite Resources

Setting limits may have a strange sound to American ears, but we must have the maturity to recognize that limits are necessary. A government cannot and should not allow health care to crowd out all other important social spending. The predominant characteristics of state and federal health programs, almost a unifying factor, is that they have ended up costing far more than was anticipated. We are a compassionate society and can afford a lot, but not everything. From the myriad of things medical science can do, governments must select only those services that limited budgets will allow them to guarantee for all, and provide these reliably. The price of modern medicine is honestly admitting that all health-care systems ration.

Once we admit that we must set limits, the whole nature of the health-care problem changes. Limited funds must be budgeted and prioritized because every individual in the system is entitled to his or her just share of the common resources, and not only for health care, but also with regard to other necessary social goods.

Today, nearly half of health care is funded by taxpayer money. Yet, just as no one person or family feels responsible for the air or water pollution of the community, people seldom consider the cumulative impact of their individual demands on public-service expenditures.

Reforming American health care is a two-front war. Just as we have to restrict, we must also broaden care to improve the total health and well-being of society. Total health for any segment of society, particularly among the elderly, involves much more than we now cover under Medicare. It is imperative that we spend some of the resources gained by setting limits to medical intervention to provide services aimed at improving quality of life for seniors, not just postponing death. Examples might include programs like Meals on Wheels,

health education, physician information and referral services, resource centers for elders, telephone reassurance providers, personal emergency response systems, homemaker services, transportation, and wellness programs.

The challenge of providing health care to an aging society is particularly difficult because it involves downsizing citizens' expectations; more importantly, it also involves moral and ethical issues about life and death on which there is no national agreement. In fact, even a preliminary discussion on these issues has hardly begun.

A New Framework: What It Means in Practice

The proliferation of expensive medical technology and treatments today is forcing us to adopt a new moral vision. The aging of America merely accelerates this problem. With that in mind, we would suggest the following moral visions to shape a new and vigorous debate over the future of health care in the United States.

A nation's health goal can never be, nor should it be, to fund the sum total of all its citizens' individual needs. Public policy should seek a healthy public and recognize that medical care is an important part of that search, but only a part. It must find policies that maximize the health of the public, not merely respond to the medical need of certain individuals.

No health-care-funding system can cover every possible treatment for every stakeholder's ailments and anxieties. Nor is it in the public interest to fund everything that might possibly benefit a patient. The question for health-care funders is not, "What do we want?" but "What do we need most and what can we reasonably afford?"

We do not maximize health by maximizing health care. Society must better analyze and study the factors that produce health. There is substantial evidence that medical technology is far down the list of determinants of health, behind socio-economic and lifestyle factors. It is also clear that a number of other countries do a considerably better job in health outcomes while spending considerably less than does the United States.

Public policy should concern itself more with extending the health-care floor (i.e., maximizing coverage) than raising the research ceiling. Public policy makers should be encouraged to care about the health of the total society as passionately as health-care providers care about the health of individual patients. When these conflict, it is the public health, not individual need, that must be maximized, so far as public expenditures are involved.

To some degree, a two-level health-care system is inevitable since individuals have the right to spend their own money as they see fit. Thus, whatever basic level of health care that government or health plans may provide, some patients may choose to supplement that benefit by spending their own funds. This fact should not negate efforts to ration collective resources. The right to health care, then, is what philosophers refer to as a negative right to do what you will with your own

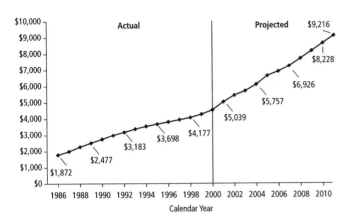

Figure 1   U.S. Health Expenditures Per Capita. Annual health spending per capita is projected to increase rapidly in the United States.

Source: Centers for Medicare and Medicaid Services.

resources—not a positive claim to unlimited expenditures by others.

Since more than 80% of health care is paid out of commonly collected funds, and not by individuals out of pocket, group funds—public or private—should be used to optimize the health of all those in the group. The doctor–patient relationship is thus not the only one to consider. Doctors are good patient advocates, but they are imperfect agents to maximize the health of a group of patients, let alone society as a whole.

Furthermore, when people pool funds, they cannot reasonably expect to generate unlimited benefits for every member of that pool, and cost-effectiveness must be considered when distributing those funds. To that end, the U.S. legal system must be amended to recognize these realities and limit grounds for claiming malpractice when tests or treatments judged not to be cost-effective are denied.

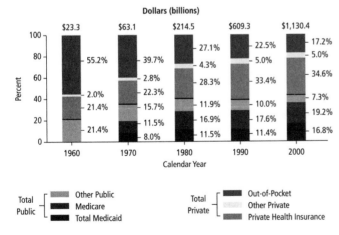

Figure 2   How Americans Pay for Personal Health Care. Over the last several decades, the public-sector share of health spending has increased in the United States, while the share people pay out of pocket has declined.

Source: Centers for Medicare and Medicaid Services.

Likewise, those in health plans who distribute pooled resources have an independent ethical duty to prioritize and budget funds to maximize the overall health of the group. As former Oregon Governor John Kitzhaber demands, we must pay attention to the "hydraulic relationship" among coverage, benefits, and cost. All are important; all are interrelated. An ethical public policy must find ways to prioritize benefits covered instead of patients covered. We must recognize that insuring the uninsured and containing costs are not separate problems, but inextricably intertwined and must be solved together.

What might ideally be considered unethical if infinite resources were available becomes ethical in the real world of finite resources. Many concepts must be reevaluated and debated anew, such as whether a society owes a greater moral duty to a 10-year-old than to a 90-year-old. To what degree must individuals bear responsibility for their own health, and when is it acceptable to deny public resources to people who cause or contribute to their own ill health? For instance, should not people's smoking and drinking habits over a lifetime be considered in deciding their eligibility for a high-cost rescue procedure in old age?

Life is always precious but it cannot be priceless. Death always involves loss, but that loss often includes extensive public subsidy. No matter how brilliant our medicine, there will always be "ten leading causes of death." The battle against death should not be permitted to hijack a disproportionate share of finite public resources needed elsewhere in society to raise or protect people's quality of life. Postponing death must take its place among other desirable social goals.

Rebuilding the House of Health

Goethe warned, "If you are going to live in your father's house, you must rebuild it." We have not adequately structured the house of health policy or ethics to prepare ourselves for our increasingly aging society. We have overbuilt and overfurnished the doctor/patient floor of health care and amassed an imposing economic configuration that has high stakes in maintaining it. But most of the rest of the structure remains not only unfinished but practically unframed. There are many levels of ethical analysis to consider as we frame a new health policy. Legislators, health-plan administrators, doctors, patients, and family members all have moral duties—different moral duties—and require different levels of ethical analysis that reflect their different obligations and priorities.

Health policy is only one element within a social landscape of many needs. Our aging society faces three overriding public policy issues if it is to have a just and adequate healthcare system. First, it must guarantee basic health care, income security, and long-term care. Second, it must balance spending for prioritized health needs, while also providing the full spectrum of other government-funded social services. Third, because rationing of some sort is inescapable, we need a rational, transparent, and workable framework within which to make our rationing decisions.

The United States is not the only Western nation facing this challenge, though we are very likely in the worst position to deal with it, due to our traditional individualistic medical culture and the high public expectations it has produced. Rather than despair, however, we should view the problems raised here as a challenge. We must use the same ingenuity that gave us the New Deal and fashion a fundamentally more equitable and sustainable health-care system—one that addresses the moral needs at all levels. If we fail to adopt a broadened vision along these lines, the outlook for health care in America's long-term future is ominous indeed.

Richard D. Lamm, former governor of Colorado and a 1996 U.S. presidential candidate (Reform Party), is director of the Center for Public Policy and Contemporary Issues at the University of Denver, 2199 South University Boulevard, #107, Denver, Colorado 80208. His most recent book is *The Brave New World of Health Care* (Fulcrum Publishing, 2003). **Robert H. Blank** is a political scientist and is currently a Research Scholar at New College of Florida. His most recent book is *End of Life Decision Making: A Comparative Study* (MIT Press, 2005). His address is 5218 Lake Arrowhead Trail, Sarasota, Florida 34231. E-mail rblank24601@hotmail.com.

Originally published in the July/August 2005, pp. 23–27 issue of *The Futurist*. Copyright © 2005 by World Future Society, 7910 Woodmont Avenue, Suite 450, Bethesda, MD 20814. Telephone: 301/656-8274; Fax: 301/951-0394; http://www.wfs.org. Used with permission from the World Future Society.

Alien Nation

With 12 million illegals in America, immigration policy is a shambles. Businesses want to hire more foreigners and can't because of antiterrorist laws. What's to be done?

MICHAEL MAIELLO AND NICOLE RIDGWAY

Where do you get your workers? We ask a certain highly successful roofing contractor in Washington, D.C. Technically speaking, he allows, his employees are all legal. They have papers, and it's not his responsibility to determine if the papers are forged. But he lives on the edge. That's why he recently declined to bid on a lucrative deal offered by the National Security Agency. The spy agency didn't want foreigners working on its premises and could be expected to do a much better job than Immigration & Customs Enforcement does of enforcing the law against employing illegals.

This entrepreneur won't admit that he has hired illegals. But, he concedes, "[If] I need five or ten additional men, I let it be known amongst a certain circle of guys. And I have access to those people immediately."

It's not easy finding American citizens willing to push shingles around on a hot roof during 100-degree weather. It's not easy finding engineers, either. James Goodnight, chief executive of sas, the world's largest privately held software company, recently went looking for Ph.D. engineers. He needed them for a project to help companies increase profits by getting a handle on their suppliers. Plenty of willing and able foreigners could have done the work but landing the H-1B visas, which allow foreigners with special skills to work in the U.S. for up to six years, would be next to impossible. As a result, Goodnight came close to opening an R&D center in Poland. "I wish I had done it," he laments.

America's immigration policy is a shambles. "The current situation can only be described as untenable," says Craig Barrett, chairman of Intel Corp., which has a voracious appetite for chip designers. The U.S. does a brilliant job educating foreigners in our engineering schools, and then, during the recruiting season, chases this human capital away. Australia and the U.K. have a much better system: They come pretty close to stapling a visa to an engineer's diploma. "If we had purposefully set out to design a system that would cripple our ability to be competitive, we could hardly do better than what we have today," says Barrett.

We've been here before. Twenty years ago Congress passed the Simpson-Rodino immigration reform, a bill four years in the making. The law was supposed to halt the flood of illegal immigrants swarming in to take low-paying jobs. It granted a one-year amnesty to aliens who had been living in the U.S. since before 1982 and let them apply for legal status; it also slapped businesses with criminal penalties for knowingly hiring illegals. But the government did not enforce the law. The public, it seems, does not have the appetite for chasing millions of workers back to Mexico. And so the government has settled on a half-hearted enforcement scheme that combines a game of tag played out in the Arizona desert with very few raids on employers. Every now and then some meatpacker or night cleaning firm is scolded and fined. The penalty for individuals caught employing an undocumented nanny is loss of a cabinet appointment.

Illegals keep cascading in, recently at the rate of 700,000 a year, and businesses and families keep hiring them. The Pew Hispanic Center estimates that in the last decade the number of undocumented aliens living in the U.S. has doubled to 12 million. This despite a growth in spending on domestic security averaging 13.4% a year. President Bush recently requested $42.7 billion for the Department of Homeland Security and $2.6 billion for guarding the border with Mexico, the source of no known terrorist.

Adding to this morass of ambivalence about foreigners doing our dirty work: the fear and xenophobia that grew out of Sept. 11. The resulting crackdown did nothing to stop the unskilled workers walking across the border, but it did choke off the engineers from India and China. Since 2001 Congress has whacked the number of H-1B visas from 195,000 to 65,000 a year. Separately, green cards—permanent resident visas that allow for work, among other things, and granted to noncitizens—are handed out at the rate of 140,000 a year. Rationing of these precious documents is done not by setting employment priorities but by trying applicants' patience and forcing them to spend money on lawyers. For employment visas the waiting period for an initial interview with the U.S. consulate in the home country can be up to 149 days. Homeland Security says it does 35 million security checks a year before issuing visas to workers, tourists, visiting lecturers and the like.

Chipmaker Texas Instruments was trying to secure 65 visas last summer when the federal limit ran out and was told it would have to wait for many of them until April, when applications for 2007 are accepted, to begin the process all over again. That means advertising the jobs for 30 days to find "minimally qualified" U.S. workers, sifting through résumés, submitting paperwork to the Labor Department and trying again to lure talented recruits from abroad, a process that can cost up to $30,000 for each employee—and increases the risk that a company will lose foreign candidates it has its eye on, as Texas Instruments did. "The more barriers we have in place and more process steps we have to take, the more we're going to see these things happen," says Steve W. Lyle, TI's director of worldwide staffing.

How to fix the mess? Herewith, a few proposals from the Beltway and the academic braintrust—and their chances of being adopted.

Compassionate Compromise.

President Bush has a plan that he claims "serves the American economy and reflects the American dream." Those illegals already in the U.S. would receive temporary worker cards that allow them to stay for up to three years and renew once for an unspecified period—then, vamoose. The same offer would apply to new aliens once a U.S. employer identifies a job and certifies that no American is qualified for or wants to take it. This isn't an amnesty program, the administration has been at pains to point out to avoid torpedoes from the hard right. (A bill introduced by John McCain and Edward Kennedy last May would let illegals apply for citizenship, once they pay a fine, clear up tax problems and learn English.) "I oppose amnesty—placing undocumented workers on the automatic path to citizenship," the President has said. Nor would he give them a leg up on foreigners who come legally and apply for a green card, which offers permanent resident status. He also supports lifting the ceiling on H-1Bs, but his plan doesn't say by how much.

If we had set out to design a system to cripple our competitiveness, we could hardly do better.

On the tough side, Bush's proposal would turn the screws on businesses that wittingly break the law but doesn't spell out the penalties. Enforcement would fall under the Department of Homeland Security, working with the Labor Department and other federal agencies. "Our homeland will be more secure when we can better account for those who enter our country," said Bush. Hard to disagree with that nostrum.

What's the likelihood we'll see some version of the plan? Not high, considering that no one in Congress has run with it—and the President introduced the idea on Jan. 7, 2004.

Build Up That Wall.

Last December, by 260–159, the House passed an amendment that would mandate the construction of a 700-mile fence along the 1,952-mile border with Mexico. Calling for a series of steel barriers armed with motion detectors, floodlights and surveillance equipment, the plan has been the pet project of Representative Duncan Hunter (R-Calif.) for the past 20 years. He finally got it on the radar as part of a get-tough immigration bill that would beef up security and tighten enforcement. Construction costs: $2.2 billion by Hunter's estimate; proponents of the idea, like Colin Hanna, president of Weneedafence.com, think it could easily reach $8 billion.

Good fences don't always make good neighbors, as Israel's recent attempt to wall itself off from the Palestinians most vividly illustrates. The House amendment drew immediate fire from Mexican President Vicente Fox, who complained that Congress had given into "xenophobic groups that impose the law at will." It would be hard for Mexico to swallow any reform plan that threatens the flow of dollars from Mexican expats to their families back home. Chance of success: iffy; there isn't much support in the Administration.

Caps Off.

Some people argue the best way to deal with illegals is to create so many opportunities for legal immigration that no rational migrant would risk a deadly trek through the desert. (Last year, 460 people died trying to get into the U.S., up from 61 in 1995.) Daniel Griswold, director of the Cato Institute's Center for Trade Policy Studies, suggests letting in at least 300,000 temporary workers on three-year, renewable visas each year. Undocumented workers here could receive the same visa. But unlike Bush's proposal, this one does not force illegal residents to go home; they could pursue citizenship, as long as they pay an unspecified fine ("not chump change," Griswold says) and have clean records. Douglas S. Massey, a Princeton University professor of sociology and public affairs and author of *Beyond Smoke and Mirrors: Mexican Immigration in an Era of Economic Integration* (Russell Sage, 2002), would also let in 300,000 temporary workers every year. Each of them would pay $400 or so, about one-third what a "coyote" charges to smuggle people across the border, giving immigrants a financial incentive to play by the rules. Griswold agrees, adding that such reform would "drain the swamp of human smuggling and document fraud that facilitates illegal immigration."

As for the illegals already in place, Massey would allow anyone who arrived as a minor to apply for permanent legal status right away. Their parents would have the option to apply for temporary status. But, in any event, Massey wants the U.S. to allow far more than the current 20,000 green cards for Mexicans each year. That would swell their contributions to the U.S. Treasury. Massey's surveys have shown that a surprising 62% of illegal workers have taxes withheld from their paychecks and 66% pay

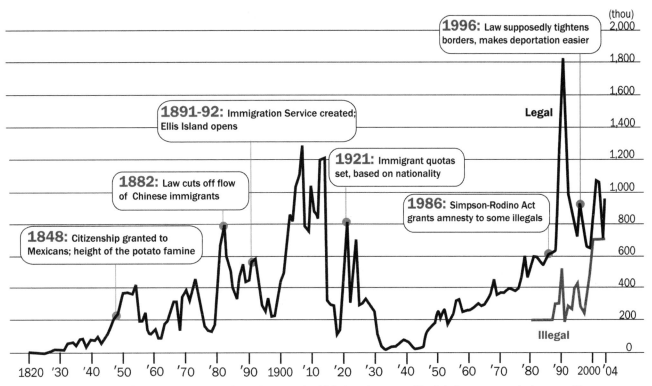

Figure 1   The Human Spigot.   A nation of immigrants, the U.S. has long used legislation to control who—and how many people—can enter the country legally.

Sources: U.S. Census; estimates by Department of Homeland Security; Pew Hispanic Center.

Social Security. In 2004, illegal workers contributed $7 billion to Social Security and $1.5 billion to Medicare. Yet these workers seldom use social services because they fear getting busted. Massey found that only 10% of illegal Mexicans have sent a child to a U.S. public school, and just 5% have received food stamps or unemployment.

Chances for any legislative action? Maybe some tidbit from the guest-worker program. So far, it hasn't caught fire with feds or Joe Six-Pack. A recent Zogby International poll says 56% of likely voters oppose giving illegals any chance at citizenship.

Selling the American Dream—for a Price.

Nobel laureate Gary Becker, who teaches economics at the University of Chicago, thinks the U.S. should welcome anyone who's not a criminal, a terrorist or a carrier of a communicable disease—for a fee of $50,000. That buys permanent status. Becker says the plan would lure skilled workers since they have more to gain. For those who can't afford a ticket, Becker would encourage commercial banks to make high-interest immigration loans.

$50,000 would buy permanent legal status for foreigners; it might help businesses lure more skilled workers.

Becker is tempted to push his own proposal a bit further. Why not auction off guest-worker visas—and the chance of citizenship—to the highest bidders? At a minimum, Becker thinks, such auctions could bring in $50 billion a year—enough to pay for the entire budget of the Department of Homeland Security.

Sound weird? There's a version already in place, known as the EB-5 visa, introduced in 1990. It's available to 10,000 foreigners a year who are willing to invest at least $500,000 (in some cases, $1 million) to create a new business or expand an existing one, creating ten or more jobs. But does the government really want to be in the business of marketing U.S. citizenship abroad?

Bring on Big Brother.

What if we could open our borders and safeguard the country? Technology is a ministep in that direction. Last summer Homeland Security began a $100 million pilot program that embedded radio-frequency identification on the entry documents of those coming in from Canada and Mexico, tracking their arrival and departure, as Wal-Mart does pallets of toothpaste. The test didn't sit well with civil liberties groups or with Senator Patrick Leahy (D.-Vt.), who pointed out that the so-called pass card used an RFID chip that was incompatible with the one the State Department was using in passports. Could bad guys jam the systems or hack into them? That would make our borders less secure.

More plausible is an extension of a new practice that already exists. All foreign applicants for visas must schedule an interview with the U.S. consulate in their host country, where they submit to biometric fingerprint scans of their left and right index fingers and a digital photo. Such high-tech ID is also in 105 U.S. airports, as well as in all American seaports and border crossings. Draft legislation by Arlen Specter (R.-Pa.), the chairman of the Senate Judiciary Committee, would require the same kind of whiz-bang identification on the visas of all immigrants already in the States by 2007 and, by that time, would force compatibility between systems used by the FBI and Homeland Security. To curtail fraud, Specter would require companies to enter a social security number on an online government database for each prospective employee—and if it's bounced, the employer is responsible for reporting the culprit to the Immigration & Customs Enforcement agency.

The Specter bill is a melting pot of competing proposals that draw from the right and the left. Illegals already in the States could stay here indefinitely, as long as they have been employed since January 2004 and passed a background investigation by Homeland Security; whether they could become American citizens is still murky. Newly arrived aliens don't get quite as good a deal. Citizenship is off the table. But as guest workers, they would receive visas and have a chance to stay in the U.S., as long as they had jobs, for up to six years, when they would have to leave. However, they could apply for green cards from their home country. (A competing proposal by Senators John Cornyn [R.-Tex.] and Jon Kyl [R.-Ariz.] would allow temporary workers six years of employment in U.S., so long as they go home for a year every two years, with little chance to gain citizenship.) Specter would also almost triple H-1Bs to 180,000 the first year and thereafter adjust the number to market demand. Anyone with an advanced degree in science, technology, engineering or math is exempt from a visa cap.

Business has warmed to his proposals. "We have talented people we want to hire, whom we've offered a job to—and we can't bring them into the country," says Pamela Passman, vice president of global corporate affairs for Microsoft. "We think Specter's bill does address the [H-1B] crisis."

So what are its chances? It's a complex, omnibus package with many wiggling parts. Nothing will be enacted quickly. The 1986 reform took four years, and that was before Sept. 11. Xenophobia and protectionism combined to defeat an honest airing about whether an Arab ally should operate U.S. ports. Immigration probably won't fare any better.

SOS: We Need a Plan B

A new book examines civilization in decline and calls for a rescue plan

LESTER R. BROWN

We recently entered a new century, but we are also entering a new world, one where the collisions between our demands and the earth's capacity to satisfy them are becoming daily events. It may be another crop-withering heat wave, another village abandoned because of invading sand dunes, or another aquifer pumped dry. If we do not act quickly to reverse the trends, these seemingly isolated events will come more and more frequently, accumulating and combining to determine our future.

Resources that accumulated over eons of geological time are being consumed in a single human lifespan. We are crossing natural thresholds that we cannot see and violating deadlines that we do not recognize. These deadlines, determined by nature, are not politically negotiable.

Nature has many thresholds that we discover only when it is too late. In our fast-forward world, we learn that we have crossed them only after the fact, leaving little time to adjust. For example, when we exceed the sustainable catch of a fishery, the stocks begin to shrink. Once this threshold is crossed, we have a limited time in which to back off and lighten the catch. If we fail to meet this deadline, breeding populations shrink to where the fishery is no longer viable, and it collapses.

We know from earlier civilizations that the lead indicators of economic decline were environmental, not economic. The trees went first, then the soil, and finally the civilization itself.

Our situation today is far more challenging because in addition to shrinking forests and eroding soils, we must deal with falling water tables, more frequent crop-withering heat waves, collapsing fisheries, expanding deserts, deteriorating rangelands, dying coral reefs, melting glaciers, rising seas, more-powerful storms, disappearing species, and, soon, shrinking oil supplies. Although these ecologically destructive trends have been evident for some time, and some have been reversed at the national level, not one has been reversed at the global level.

The bottom line is that the world is in what ecologists call an "overshoot-and-collapse" mode. Demand has exceeded the sustainable yield of natural systems at the local level countless times in the past. Now, for the first time, it is doing so at the global level. Forests are shrinking for the world as a whole. Fishery collapses are widespread. Grasslands are deteriorating on every continent. Water tables are falling in many countries. Carbon dioxide (CO_2) emissions exceed CO_2 fixation everywhere.

Overshoot leads sometimes to decline and sometimes to a complete collapse. It is not always clear which it will be. In the former, a remnant of the population or economic activity survives in a resource-depleted environment.

As of 2005, some 42 countries have populations that are stable or declining slightly in size as a result of falling birth rates. But now for the first time ever, demographers are projecting population declines in some countries because of rising death rates, among them Botswana, Lesotho, Namibia, and Swaziland. In the absence of an accelerated shift to smaller families, this list of countries is likely to grow much longer in the years immediately ahead.

The most recent mid-level U.N. demographic projections show world population increasing from 6.1 billion in 2000 to 9.1 billion in 2050. But such an increase seems highly unlikely, considering the deterioration in life-support systems now under way in much of the world. Will we not reach 9.1 billion because we quickly eradicate global poverty and also quickly lower birth rates? Or because we fail to do so and death rates begin to rise, as they are already doing in many African countries? We thus face two urgent major challenges: restructuring the global economy and stabilizing world population.

Oil and Biodiversity

Even as the economy's environmental support systems are deteriorating, the world is pumping oil with reckless abandon. Leading geologists now think oil production may soon peak and turn downward. This collision between the ever-growing demand for oil and the Earth's finite resources is but the latest in a long series of collisions. Although no one knows exactly when oil production will peak, supply is already lagging behind demand, driving prices upward.

In this new world, the price of oil begins to set the price of food, not so much because of rising fuel costs for farmers and food processors but more because almost everything we eat can be converted into fuel for cars. In this new world of high oil prices, supermarkets and service stations will compete in commodity markets for basic food commodities such as wheat, corn, soybeans, and sugarcane.

Wheat going into the market can be converted into bread for supermarkets or ethanol for service stations. Soybean oil can go onto supermarket shelves or it can go to service stations to be used as diesel fuel. In effect, owners of the world's 800 million cars will be competing for food resources with the 1.2 billion people living on less than $1 a day.

Faced with a seemingly insatiable demand for automotive fuel, farmers will want to clear more and more of the remaining tropical forests to produce sugarcane, oil palms, and other high-yielding fuel crops. Already, billions of dollars of private capital are moving into this effort. In effect, the rising price of oil is generating a massive new threat to the earth's biological diversity.

As the role of oil recedes, the process of globalization will be reversed in fundamental ways. As the world turned to oil during the last century, the energy economy became increasingly globalized, with the world depending heavily on a handful of countries in the Middle East for energy supplies. Now as the world turns to wind, solar cells, and geothermal energy in this century, we are witnessing the localization of the world energy economy.

The globalization of the world food economy will also be reversed, as the higher price of oil raises the cost of transporting food internationally. In response, food production and consumption will become much more localized, leading to diets based more on locally produced food and seasonal availability.

The world is facing the emergence of a geopolitics of scarcity, which is already highly visible in the efforts by China, India, and other developing countries to ensure their access to oil supplies. In the future, the issue will be who gets access to not only Middle Eastern oil but also Brazilian ethanol and North American grain. Pressures on land and water resources, already excessive in most of the world, will intensify further as the demand for biofuels climbs. This geopolitics of scarcity is an early manifestation of civilization in an overshoot-and-collapse mode, much like the one that emerged among the Mayan cities competing for food in that civilization's waning years.

Learning from China

For many years environmentalists have pointed to the United States as the world's leading consumer, noting that 5% of the world's people were consuming nearly a third of the earth's resources. Although that was true for some time, it no longer is. China has replaced the United States as the leading consumer of basic commodities.

Among the five basic food, energy, and industrial commodities—grain and meat, oil and coal, and steel—consumption in China has eclipsed that of the United States in all but oil. China has opened a wide lead with grain, consuming 380 million tons in 2005 versus 260 million tons in the United States. Among the big three grains, China leads in the consumption of both wheat and rice and trails the United States only in corn.

Although eating hamburgers is a defining element of the U.S. lifestyle, China's 2005 meat consumption of 67 million tons is far above the 38 million tons eaten in the United States. While U.S. meat intake is rather evenly distributed between beef, pork, and poultry, in China pork totally dominates. Indeed, half the world's pigs are now found in China.

With oil, the United States was still solidly in the lead in 2004, using more than three times as much as China—20.4 million barrels per day versus 6.5 million barrels. But U.S. oil use expanded by only 15% between 1994 and 2004, while use in China more than doubled. Having recently eclipsed Japan as an oil consumer, China now trails only the United States.

Energy use in China also obviously includes coal, which supplies nearly two-thirds of the country's energy. China's annual burning of 960 million tons easily exceeds the 560 million tons used in the United States. With this level of coal use and with oil and natural gas use also climbing fast, it is only a matter of time before China's carbon emissions match those of the United States. Then the world will have two major countries driving climate change.

China's consumption of steel, a basic indicator of industrial development, is now nearly two and a half times that of the United States: 258 million tons to 104 million tons in 2003. As China has moved into the construction phase of development, building hundreds of thousands of factories and high-rise apartment and office buildings, steel consumption has climbed to levels never seen before.

With consumer goods, China leads in the number of cell phones, television sets, and refrigerators. The United States still leads in the number of personal computers, though likely not for much longer, and in automobiles.

That China has overtaken the United States in consumption of basic resources gives us license to ask the next question. What if China catches up with the United States in consumption per person? If the Chinese economy continues to grow at 8% a year, by 2031 income per person will equal that in the United States in 2004. If we further assume that consumption patterns of China's affluent population in 2031, by then 1.45 billion, will be roughly similar to those of Americans in 2004, we have a startling answer to our question.

At the current annual U.S. grain consumption of 900 kilograms per person, including industrial use, China's grain consumption in 2031 would equal roughly two-thirds of the current world grain harvest. If paper use per person in China in 2031 reaches the current U.S. level, this translates into 305 million tons of paper—double existing world production of 161 million tons. There go the world's forests. And if oil consumption per person reaches the U.S. level by 2031, China will use 99 million barrels of oil a day. The world is currently producing 84 million barrels a day and may never produce much more. This helps explain why China's fast-expanding use of oil is already helping to create a politics of scarcity.

The inevitable conclusion is that there are not enough resources for China to reach U.S. consumption levels. The western economic model—the fossil-fuel-based, automobile-centered, throwaway economy—will not work for China's 1.45 billion in 2031. If it does not work for China, it will not work for India either, which by 2031 is projected to have even more people than China. Nor will it work for the other 3 billion people in developing countries who are also dreaming the

"American Dream." And in an increasingly integrated world economy, where countries everywhere are competing for the same resources—the same oil, grain, and iron ore—the existing economic model will not work for industrial countries either.

The Politics of Scarcity

The first big test of the international community's capacity to manage scarcity may come with oil or it could come with grain. If the latter is the case, this could occur when China—whose grain harvest fell by 34 million tons, or 9%, between 1998 and 2005—turns to the world market for massive imports of 30 million, 50 million, or possibly even 100 million tons of grain per year. Demand on this scale could quickly overwhelm world grain markets. When this happens, China will have to look to the United States, which controls the world's grain exports of over 40% of some 200 million tons.

This will pose a fascinating geopolitical situation. More than 1.3 billion Chinese consumers, who had an estimated $160 billion trade surplus with the United States in 2004—enough to buy the entire U.S. grain harvest twice—will be competing with Americans for U.S. grain, driving up U.S. food prices. In such a situation 30 years ago, the United States simply restricted exports. But China is now banker to the United States, underwriting much of the massive U.S. fiscal deficit with monthly purchases of U.S. Treasury bonds.

Within the next few years, the United States may be loading one or two ships a day with grain for China. This long line of ships stretching across the Pacific, like an umbilical cord providing nourishment, will intimately link the two economies. Managing this flow of grain so as to simultaneously satisfy the food needs of consumers in both countries, at a time when ethanol fuel distilleries are taking a growing share of the U.S. grain harvest, may become one of the leading foreign policy challenges of this new century.

The way the world accommodates the vast projected needs of China, India, and other developing countries for grain, oil, and other resources will help determine how the world addresses the stresses associated with outgrowing the Earth. The most imminent risk is that China's entry into the world market, combined with the growing diversion of farm commodities to biofuels, will drive grain prices so high that many low-income developing countries will not be able to import enough grain. This in turn could lead to escalating food prices and political instability on a scale that will disrupt global economic progress.

Failed States and Terrorism

The stresses in our early 21st-century civilization take many forms. Economically we see them in the widening income gap between the world's rich and poor. Socially they take the form of the widening gap in education and health care and a swelling flow of environmental refugees as productive land turns to desert and as wells go dry. Politically we see them manifest in conflict over basic resources such as cropland, grazing land, and water. And perhaps most fundamentally, we see the stresses

the world is facing in the growing number of failed and failing states.

The term "failed states" is now part of our working vocabulary, describing countries where there is no longer a central government. Recognizing this increasingly common phenomenon, various groups concerned with economic development and international affairs have begun to identify failing or failed states and the indicators associated with their failure. The World Bank, for example, has constructed a list of 30 "low-income countries under stress."

Motivated by a similar concern, the United Kingdom's Department for International Development has identified 46 "fragile" states. The U.S. Central Intelligence Agency has constructed a list of 20 failing states. Most recently, the Fund for Peace and the Carnegie Endowment for International Peace have worked together to identify a list of 60 states, ranking them according to "their vulnerability to violent internal conflict."

This analysis is based on 12 social, economic, political, and military indicators. It puts Côte d'Ivoire at the top of the list of failed states, followed by the Democratic Republic of the Congo, Sudan, Iraq, Somalia, Sierra Leone, Chad, Yemen, Liberia, and Haiti. Next in line are three countries that have been much in the news in recent years: Afghanistan, Rwanda, and North Korea.

Five oil-exporting countries make the top 60 list, including the two largest exporters and producers—Saudi Arabia (45 on the list) and Russia (59)—plus Venezuela (21), Indonesia (46), and Nigeria (54). Two countries with nuclear arsenals are also on the list: Pakistan and Russia.

The three top indicators used in constructing the scorecard are uneven development, the loss of governmental legitimacy, and demographic pressure. Uneven development typically means that a small segment of the population is accumulating wealth while much of the society may be suffering a decline in living conditions. This unevenness, often associated with political corruption, creates unrest and can lead to civil conflict.

Governments that fail to effectively manage emerging issues and provide basic services are seen as useless. This often causes segments of the population to shift their allegiance to warlords, tribal chieftains, or religious leaders. A loss of political legitimacy is an early sign of state decline.

Population Indicator of Failed States

The third top indicator is demographic pressure. All the countries in the top 20 have fast-growing populations. In many that have experienced rapid population growth for several decades, governments are suffering from demographic fatigue, unable to cope with the steady shrinkage in per capita cropland and fresh water supplies or to build schools fast enough for the swelling ranks of children.

Foreign investment drying up and a resultant rise in unemployment are also part of the decline syndrome. Another characteristic is a deterioration of the physical infrastructure—roads and power, water, and sewage systems. Care for natural systems is also neglected as people struggle to survive. Forests, grasslands, and croplands deteriorate, creating a downward economic spiral.

Among the most conspicuous indications of state failure is a breakdown in law and order and a related loss of personal security. In Haiti, armed gangs rule the streets. Kidnapping for ransom of local people who are lucky enough to be among the 30% of the labor force that is employed is commonplace. In Afghanistan it is the local warlords, not the central government, that control the country outside of Kabul. Somalia, which now exists only on maps, is ruled by tribal leaders, each claiming a piece of what was once a country.

Some of these countries are involved in long-standing civil conflicts. The Democratic Republic of the Congo, occupying a large part of the Congo River basin in the heart of Africa, has been the site of an ongoing civil conflict for six years, a conflict that has claimed 3.8 million lives and driven millions more from their homes. According to the International Rescue Committee, for each violent death in this conflict there are 62 nonviolent deaths related to it, including deaths from hunger, respiratory illnesses, diarrhea, and other diseases.

Some potential sources of instability are taking the world into uncharted territory. In sub-Saharan Africa, where HIV infection rates sometimes exceed 30% of all adults, there will be millions of orphans in the years ahead. With the number of orphans overwhelming society's capacity to care for them, many will become street children. Growing up without parental guidance and appropriate role models, and with their behavior shaped by the desperation of survival, these orphans will become a new threat to stability and progress.

Failing states are of growing international concern because they are a source of terrorists, drugs, weapons, and refugees. Not only was Afghanistan a training ground for terrorists, but it quickly became, under the Allied occupation, the world's leading supplier of heroin. Refugees from Rwanda, including thousands of armed soldiers, contributed to the destabilization of the Congo. As The Economist notes, "Like a severely disturbed individual, a failed state is a danger not just to itself, but to those around it and beyond."

In many countries, the United Nations or other internationally organized peacekeeping forces are trying to keep the peace, often unsuccessfully. Among the countries with UN peacekeeping forces are the Democratic Republic of the Congo, Sierra Leone, and Liberia. Other countries with multinational peacekeeping forces include Afghanistan, Haiti, and Sudan. All too often these are token forces, not nearly large enough to assure stability.

Countries like Haiti and Afghanistan are surviving today because they are on international life-support systems. Economic assistance—including, it is worth noting, food aid—is helping to sustain them. But there is not now enough assistance to overcome the reinforcing trends of deterioration and replace them with state stability and sustained economic progress.

LESTER R. BROWN is president of the Earth Policy Institute. This article is part one of an excerpt from his book. *Plan B 2.0: Rescuing a Planet Under Stress and a Civilization in Trouble.* In part two, Brown outlines his rescue plan and calls for a wartime mobilization.

As seen in *Pop!ulation Press,* Winter 2006, pp. 4–8; originally from *Plan B: 2.0 Rescuing a Planet Under Stress and a Civilization in Trouble,* by Lester R. Brown. Copyright© 2006 by Lester R. Brown. Reprinted by permission of Earth Policy Institute.

By Any Measure, Earth Is at . . .

The Tipping Point

The climate is crashing, and global warming is to blame. Why the crisis hit so soon—and what we can do about it

JEFFREY KLUGER

No one can say exactly what it looks like when a planet takes ill, but it probably looks a lot like Earth. Never mind what you've heard about global warming as a slow-motion emergency that would take decades to play out. Suddenly and unexpectedly, the crisis is upon us.

It certainly looked that way last week as the atmospheric bomb that was Cyclone Larry—a Category 5 storm with wind bursts that reached 180 m.p.h.—exploded through northeastern Australia. It certainly looked that way last year as curtains of fire and dust turned the skies of Indonesia orange, thanks to drought-fueled blazes sweeping the island nation. It certainly looks that way as sections of ice the size of small states calve from the disintegrating Arctic and Antarctic. And it certainly looks that way as the sodden wreckage of New Orleans continues to molder, while the waters of the Atlantic gather themselves for a new hurricane season just two months away. Disasters have always been with us and surely always will be. But when they hit this hard and come this fast—when the emergency becomes commonplace—something has gone grievously wrong. That something is global warming.

The image of Earth as organism—famously dubbed Gaia by environmentalist James Lovelock—has probably been overworked, but that's not to say the planet can't behave like a living thing, and these days, it's a living thing fighting a fever. From heat waves to storms to floods to fires to massive glacial melts, the global climate seems to be crashing around us. Scientists have been calling this shot for decades. This is precisely what they have been warning would happen if we continued pumping greenhouse gases into the atmosphere, trapping the heat that flows in from the sun and raising global temperatures.

Environmentalists and lawmakers spent years shouting at one another about whether the grim forecasts were true, but in the past five years or so, the serious debate has quietly ended. Global warming, even most skeptics have concluded, is the real deal, and human activity has been causing it. If there was any consolation, it was that the glacial pace of nature would give us decades or even centuries to sort out the problem.

But glaciers, it turns out, can move with surprising speed, and so can nature. What few people reckoned on was that global climate systems are booby-trapped with tipping points and feedback loops, thresholds past which the slow creep of environmental decay gives way to sudden and self-perpetuating collapse. Pump enough CO_2 into the sky, and that last part per million of greenhouse gas behaves like the 212th degree Fahrenheit that turns a pot of hot water into a plume of billowing steam. Melt enough Greenland ice, and you reach the point at which you're not simply dripping meltwater into the sea but dumping whole glaciers. By one recent measure, several Greenland ice sheets have doubled their rate of slide, and just last week the journal *Science* published a study suggesting that by the end of the century, the world could be locked in to an eventual rise in sea levels of as much as 20 ft. Nature, it seems, has finally got a bellyful of us.

"Things are happening a lot faster than anyone predicted," says Bill Chameides, chief scientist for the advocacy group Environmental Defense and a former professor of atmospheric chemistry. "The last 12 months have been alarming." Adds Ruth Curry of the Woods Hole Oceanographic Institution in Massachusetts: "The ripple through the scientific community is palpable."

And it's not just scientists who are taking notice. Even as nature crosses its tipping points, the public seems to have reached its own. For years, popular skepticism about climatological science stood in the way of addressing the problem, but the naysayers—many of whom were on the payroll of energy companies—have become an increasingly marginalized breed. In a new TIME/ABC News/Stanford University poll, 85% of respondents agree that global warming probably is happening. Moreover, most respondents say they want some action taken. Of those polled, 87% believe the government should either encourage or require lowering of power-plant emissions, and 85% think something should be done to get cars to use less gasoline. Even Evangelical Christians, once one of the most reliable columns in the conservative base, are demanding action, most notably in February, when 86 Christian leaders formed the Evangelical Climate Initiative, demanding that Congress regulate greenhouse gases.

A collection of new global-warming books is hitting the shelves in response to that awakening interest, followed closely by TV and theatrical documentaries. The most notable of them is *An Inconvenient Truth,* due out in May, a profile of former Vice President Al Gore and his climate-change work, which is generating a lot of prerelease buzz over an unlikely topic and an equally unlikely star. For all its lack of Hollywood flash, the film compensates by conveying both the hard science of global warming and Gore's particular passion.

Such public stirrings are at last getting the attention of politicians and business leaders, who may not always respond to science but have a keen nose for where votes and profits lie. State and local lawmakers have started taking action to curb emissions, and major corporations are doing the same. Wal-Mart has begun installing wind turbines on its stores to generate electricity and is talking about putting solar reflectors over its parking lots. HSBC, the world's second largest bank, has pledged to neutralize its carbon output by investing in wind farms and other green projects. Even President Bush, hardly a favorite of greens, now acknowledges climate change and boasts of the steps he is taking to fight it. Most of those steps, however, involve research and voluntary emissions controls, not exactly the laws with teeth scientists are calling for.

Is it too late to reverse the changes global warming has wrought? That's still not clear. Reducing our emissions output year to year is hard enough. Getting it low enough so that the atmosphere can heal is a multigenerational commitment. "Ecosystems are usually able to maintain themselves," says Terry Chapin, a biologist and professor of ecology at the University of Alaska, Fairbanks. "But eventually they get pushed to the limit of tolerance."

CO$_2$ and the Poles

As a tiny component of our atmosphere, carbon dioxide helped warm Earth to comfort levels we are all used to. But too much of it does an awful lot of damage. The gas represents just a few hundred parts per million (p.p.m.) in the overall air blanket, but they're powerful parts because they allow sunlight to stream in but prevent much of the heat from radiating back out. During the last ice age, the atmosphere's CO$_2$ concentration was just 180 p.p.m., putting Earth into a deep freeze. After the glaciers retreated but before the dawn of the modern era, the total had risen to a comfortable 280 p.p.m. In just the past century and a half, we have pushed the level to 381 p.p.m., and we're feeling the effects. Of the 20 hottest years on record, 19 occurred in the 1980s or later. According to NASA scientists, 2005 was one of the hottest years in more than a century.

It's at the North and South poles that those steambath conditions are felt particularly acutely, with glaciers and ice caps crumbling to slush. Once the thaw begins, a number of mechanisms kick in to keep it going. Greenland is a vivid example. Late last year, glaciologist Eric Rignot of the Jet Propulsion

Laboratory in Pasadena, Calif., and Pannir Kanagaratnam, a research assistant professor at the University of Kansas, analyzed data from Canadian and European satellites and found that Greenland ice is not just melting but doing so more than twice as fast, with 53 cu. mi. draining away into the sea last year alone, compared with 22 cu. mi. in 1996. A cubic mile of water is about five times the amount Los Angeles uses in a year.

Dumping that much water into the ocean is a very dangerous thing. Icebergs don't raise sea levels when they melt because they're floating, which means they have displaced all the water they're ever going to. But ice on land, like Greenland's, is a different matter. Pour that into oceans that are already rising (because warm water expands), and you deluge shorelines. By some estimates, the entire Greenland ice sheet would be enough to raise global sea levels 23 ft., swallowing up large parts of coastal Florida and most of Bangladesh. The Antarctic holds enough ice to raise sea levels more than 215 ft.

Feedback Loops

One of the reasons the loss of the planet's ice cover is accelerating is that as the poles' bright white surface shrinks, it changes the relationship of Earth and the sun. Polar ice is so reflective that 90% of the sunlight that strikes it simply bounces back into space, taking much of its energy with it. Ocean water does just the opposite, absorbing 90% of the energy it receives. The more energy it retains, the warmer it gets, with the result that each mile of ice that melts vanishes faster than the mile that preceded it.

That is what scientists call a feedback loop, and it's a nasty one, since once you uncap the Arctic Ocean, you unleash another beast: the comparatively warm layer of water about 600 ft. deep that circulates in and out of the Atlantic. "Remove the ice," says Woods Hole's Curry, "and the water starts talking to the atmosphere, releasing its heat. This is not a good thing."

A similar feedback loop is melting permafrost, usually defined as land that has been continuously frozen for two years or more. There's a lot of earthly real estate that qualifies, and much of it has been frozen much longer than two years—since the end of the last ice age, or at least 8,000 years ago. Sealed inside that cryonic time capsule are layers of partially decayed organic matter, rich in carbon. In high-altitude regions of Alaska, Canada and Siberia, the soil is warming and decomposing, releasing gases that will turn into methane and CO$_2$. That, in turn, could lead to more warming and permafrost thaw, says research scientist David Lawrence of the National Center for Atmospheric Research (NCAR) in Boulder, Colo. And how much carbon is socked away in Arctic soils? Lawrence puts the figure at 200 gigatons to 800 gigatons. The total human carbon output is only 7 gigatons a year.

One result of all that is warmer oceans, and a result of warmer oceans can be, paradoxically, colder continents within a hotter globe. Ocean currents running between warm and cold regions serve as natural thermoregulators, distributing heat from the equator toward the poles. The Gulf Stream, carrying warmth up from the tropics, is what keeps Europe's climate relatively mild. Whenever Europe is cut off from the Gulf Stream, temperatures plummet. At the end of the last ice age, the warm current was temporarily blocked, and temperatures in Europe fell as much as 10°F, locking the continent in glaciers.

What usually keeps the Gulf Stream running is that warm water is lighter than cold water, so it floats on the surface. As it reaches Europe and releases its heat, the current grows denser and sinks, flowing back to the south and crossing under the northbound Gulf Stream until it reaches the tropics and starts to warm again. The cycle works splendidly, provided the water remains salty enough. But if it becomes diluted by freshwater, the salt concentration drops, and the water gets lighter, idling on top and stalling the current. Last December, researchers associated with Britain's National Oceanography Center reported that one component of the system that drives the Gulf Stream has slowed about 30% since 1957. It's the increased release of Arctic and Greenland meltwater that appears to be causing the problem, introducing a gush of freshwater that's overwhelming the natural cycle. In a global-warming world, it's unlikely that any amount of cooling that resulted from this would be sufficient to support glaciers, but it could make things awfully uncomfortable.

"The big worry is that the whole climate of Europe will change," says Adrian Luckman, senior lecturer in geography at the University of Wales, Swansea. "We in the U.K. are on the same latitude as Alaska. The reason we can live here is the Gulf Stream."

Drought

As fast as global warming is transforming the oceans and the ice caps, it's having an even more immediate effect on land. People, animals and plants living in dry, mountainous regions like the western U.S. make it through summer thanks to snowpack that collects on peaks all winter and slowly melts off in warm months. Lately the early arrival of spring and the unusually blistering summers have caused the snowpack to melt too early, so that by the time it's needed, it's largely gone. Climatologist Philip Mote of the University of Washington has compared decades of snowpack levels in Washington, Oregon and California and found that they are a fraction of what they were in the 1940s, and some snowpacks have vanished entirely.

Global warming is tipping other regions of the world into drought in different ways. Higher temperatures bake moisture out of soil faster, causing dry regions that live at the margins to cross the line into full-blown crisis. Meanwhile, El Niño events—the warm pooling of Pacific waters that periodically drives worldwide climate patterns and has been occurring more frequently in global-warming years—further inhibit precipitation in dry areas of Africa and East Asia. According to a recent study by NCAR, the percentage of Earth's surface suffering drought has more than doubled since the 1970s.

Flora and Fauna

Hot, dry land can be murder on flora and fauna, and both are taking a bad hit. Wildfires in such regions as Indonesia, the western U.S. and even inland Alaska have been increasing as timberlands and forest floors grow more parched. The blazes create a feedback loop of their own, pouring more carbon into the atmosphere and reducing the number of trees, which inhale CO_2 and release oxygen.

Those forests that don't succumb to fire die in other, slower ways. Connie Millar, a paleoecologist for the U.S. Forest Service, studies the history of vegetation in the Sierra Nevada. Over the past 100 years, she has found, the forests have shifted their tree lines as much as 100 ft. upslope, trying to escape the heat and drought of the lowlands. Such slow-motion evacuation may seem like a sensible strategy, but when you're on a mountain, you can go only so far before you run out of room. "Sometimes we say the trees are going to heaven because they're walking off the mountaintops," Millar says.

Across North America, warming-related changes are mowing down other flora too. Manzanita bushes in the West are dying back; some prickly pear cacti have lost their signature green and are instead a sickly pink; pine beetles in western Canada and the U.S. are chewing their way through tens of millions of acres of forest, thanks to warmer winters. The beetles may even breach the once insurmountable Rocky Mountain divide, opening up a path into the rich timbering lands of the American Southeast.

With habitats crashing, animals that live there are succumbing too. Environmental groups can tick off scores of species that have been determined to be at risk as a result of global warming. Last year, researchers in Costa Rica announced that two-thirds of 110 species of colorful harlequin frogs have vanished in the past 30 years, with the severity of each season's die-off following in lockstep with the severity of that year's warming.

In Alaska, salmon populations are at risk as melting permafrost pours mud into rivers, burying the gravel the fish need for spawning. Small animals such as bushy-tailed wood rats, alpine chipmunks and piñon mice are being chased upslope by rising temperatures, following the path of the fleeing trees. And with sea ice vanishing, polar bears—prodigious swimmers but not inexhaustible ones—are starting to turn up drowned. "There will be no polar ice by 2060," says Larry Schweiger, president of the National Wildlife Federation. "Somewhere along that path, the polar bear drops out."

What about Us?

It is fitting, perhaps, that as the species causing all the problems, we're suffering the destruction of our habitat too, and we have experienced that loss in terrible ways. Ocean waters have warmed by a full degree Fahrenheit since 1970, and warmer water is like rocket fuel for typhoons and hurricanes. Two studies last year found that in the past 35 years the number of Category 4 and 5 hurricanes worldwide has doubled while the wind speed and duration of all hurricanes has jumped 50%. Since atmospheric heat is not choosy about the water it warms, tropical storms could start turning up in some decidedly nontropical places. "There's a school of thought that sea surface temperatures are warming up toward Canada," says Greg Holland, senior scientist for NCAR in Boulder. "If so, you're likely to get tropical cyclones there, but we honestly don't know."

What We Can Do

So much environmental collapse happening in so many places at once has at last awakened much of the world, particularly the 141 nations that have ratified the Kyoto treaty to reduce emissions—an imperfect accord, to be sure, but an accord all the same. The U.S., however, which is home to less than 5% of Earth's population but produces 25% of CO_2 emissions, remains intransigent. Many environmentalists declared the Bush Administration hopeless from the start, and while that may have been premature, it's undeniable that the White House's environmental record—from the abandonment of Kyoto to the President's broken campaign pledge to control carbon output to the relaxation of emission standards—has been dismal. George W. Bush's recent rhetorical nods to America's oil addiction and his praise of such alternative fuel sources as switchgrass have yet to be followed by real initiatives.

The anger surrounding all that exploded recently when NASA researcher Jim Hansen, director of the Goddard Institute for Space Studies and a longtime leader in climate-change research, complained that he had been harassed by White House appointees as he tried to sound the global-warming alarm. "The way democracy is supposed to work, the presumption is that the public is well informed," he told TIME. "They're trying to deny the science." Up against such resistance, many environmental groups have resolved simply to wait out this Administration and hope for something better in 2009.

The Republican-dominated Congress has not been much more encouraging. Senators John McCain and Joe Lieberman have twice been unable to get through the Senate even mild measures to limit carbon. Senators Pete Domenici and Jeff Bingaman, both of New Mexico and both ranking members of the chamber's Energy Committee, have made global warming a high-profile matter. A white paper issued in February will be the subject of an investigatory Senate conference next week. A House delegation recently traveled to Antarctica, Australia and New Zealand to visit researchers studying climate change. "Of the 10 of us, only three were believers," says Representative Sherwood Boehlert of New York. "Every one of the others said this opened their eyes."

Boehlert himself has long fought the environmental fight, but if the best that can be said for most lawmakers is that they are finally recognizing the global-warming problem, there's reason to wonder whether they will have the courage to reverse it. Increasingly, state and local governments are filling the void. The mayors of more than 200 cities have signed the U.S. Mayors Climate Protection Agreement, pledging, among other things, that they will meet the Kyoto goal of reducing greenhouse-gas emissions in their cities to 1990 levels by 2012. Nine eastern states have established the Regional Greenhouse Gas Initiative for the purpose of developing a cap-and-trade program that would set ceilings on industrial emissions and allow companies that overperform to sell pollution credits to those that underperform—the same smart, incentive-based strategy that got sulfur dioxide under control and reduced acid rain. And California passed the nation's toughest automobile-emissions law last summer.

"There are a whole series of things that demonstrate that people want to act and want their government to act," says Fred Krupp, president of Environmental Defense. Krupp and others believe that we should probably accept that it's too late to prevent CO_2 concentrations from climbing to 450 p.p.m. (or 70 p.p.m. higher than where they are now). From there, however, we should be able to stabilize them and start to dial them back down.

That goal should be attainable. Curbing global warming may be an order of magnitude harder than, say, eradicating smallpox or putting a man on the moon. But is it moral not to try? We did not so much march toward the environmental precipice as drunkenly reel there, snapping at the scientific scolds who told us we had a problem.

The scolds, however, knew what they were talking about. In a solar system crowded with sister worlds that either emerged stillborn like Mercury and Venus or died in infancy like Mars, we're finally coming to appreciate the knife-blade margins within which life can thrive. For more than a century we've been monkeying with those margins. It's long past time we set them right.

With reporting by **DAVID BJERKLIE** and **ANDREA DORFMAN**, New York; **DAN CRAY**, Los Angeles; **GREG FULTON**, Atlanta; **ANDREA GERLIN**, London; **RITA HEALY**, Denver and **ERIC ROSTON**, Washington

Biotech on the Farm

Realizing the Promise

Genetic engineering can help farmers feed future populations, but the public remains concerned about GM crops. To ensure safety and reassure the public, an agricultural expert calls for the creation of a Genetic Science Commission.

CLIFTON E. ANDERSON

The promise of genetic engineering to conquer world hunger has not yet been realized. Researchers have produced genetically modified (GM) crops that are useful and interesting, but where are the high-yielding new varieties that were supposed to feed the masses? An element of fear has also crept into public consideration of genetic engineering's future. In the public's mind, genetic engineering's risks still outweigh its benefits—at least so far.

In this time of environmental crisis, genetic engineering and other new technologies should be examined for possible flaws that indicate they might be environmentally hazardous or disruptive. On an ecological balance sheet, genetic engineering should be credited with both assets and liabilities. Consider these hits and misses in biotechnology's history:

- **Toxic-waste cleanup—a hit (potentially):** Genetic engineering is now addressing the problem of toxic waste site cleanups by, for instance, modifying the genes of chemical-eating bacteria in order to improve their ability to detoxify waste. With many GM bacteria at work, a toxic site might be cleaned up less expensively than by using conventional treatments. Of course, field tests must be monitored carefully to detect unforeseen problems. The GM bacteria may be shown to be excellent performers, but it is also possible that natural bacteria may have the edge over their modified brethren.

- **Nitrogen fixing—a miss:** Finding a way to use nitrogen-fixing bacteria more extensively has been a dream shared by many biologists. The bacteria colonize near the roots of alfalfa and other legume plants, and they provide their hosts with nitrogen obtained from the air. Corn, wheat, and other crops that do not have a symbiotic relationship with bacteria require applications of nitrogen fertilizer. Using genetic engineering, scientists tried to develop nitrogen-fixing bacteria that would live contentedly with non-legume host plants. Some experimental trials in the laboratory were somewhat promising, but field trials failed. The research was discontinued.

- **Safer pest control—hits and misses:** Insecticides used to protect field crops are expensive and environmentally hazardous. Geneticists have succeeded in helping plants produce their own insect-killing toxin. From the bacterium *Bacillus thuringiensis,* they obtained a toxic gene, which they cloned and then transferred to plants. Cotton and corn genetically engineered with the *Bt* toxin genes are able to produce their own insecticide.

On the negative side, there are still unanswered questions regarding the *Bt* experiment. Butterflies feeding on corn pollen have been killed by the *Bt* toxin, and other beneficial insects may be harmed. Also, if some target insects become resistant to the toxin, they will survive and breed new strains of hard-to-kill pests. Only time will tell if the *Bt* experiment was a success.

- **Higher-yield crops—raising concerns.** The GM crops most popular with growers—corn, soybeans, and cotton—are high-yielding and possess other good qualities. For peak performance, GM crops require heavy applications of synthetic fertilizers, insecticides, and weed killers—chemicals that can damage the environment.

But farmers who want to help save the environment are disappointed by present-day GM crops, because they believe the crops' dependence on chemical treatments is a serious deficiency. Also of concern to environmentalists is GM crops' limited genetic diversity. The spread of crop diseases is deterred in areas where farmers plant a number of different crops—and each crop is represented by many varieties with different genetic germlines. Today's monocropping—corn or soybeans as far as the eye can see—invites crop disease epidemics, and the problem is compounded by the widespread planting of genetically uniform GM crops. In the future, GM crops need to be tailored to the requirements of farmers who want to grow healthy, productive crops without incurring environmental damage.

Science and the Common Good

Scientific research in the public interest has long received support from the government. In 1861, when the U.S. Congress passed the Morrill Act, it seemed clear to legislators that the people should receive the benefits of government-aided research. This legislation created the landgrant educational system, with the objective of bringing to farmers, mechanics, and other working people valuable, practical information. Research projects supported by the Morrill Act were to be directed at aiding the common good. Agricultural research programs, for example, included breeding experiments that produced new varieties of corn, wheat, barley, and other crops. All work was for the public good, not tailored to the specifications of special interests.

Today, procedures for reviewing research proposals now vary considerably in federal agencies, and it is likely that review boards do not always carefully consider the proposed research's relevance to the common good. "Is this proposal in the public's interest?" is a pertinent question in any setting where proposed research is being evaluated. Wherever public funding of research is involved, decision-making groups definitely should consider how new discoveries might impact the common good. But money has a way of clouding decisions.

Universities now see an influx of dollars from corporations contracting for use of patent rights garnered from government-funded research. Among the many troublesome questions this issue raises in the research community is whether genetic engineering research could be compromised by catering to the interests of corporations rather than the public good.

Needed: A Genetic Science Commission

Unfortunately, even the scientific community has historically shown indifference to the social consequences of genetic engineering research—an indifference mirrored by policy makers. But the issues are too critical to ignore. Right now, there is no central planning and policy-framing agency overseeing genetic engineering in the United States, although other nations have such agencies. Recognizing the importance of atomic energy, the United States created the Atomic Energy Commission. It is past time to establish a Genetic Science Commission.

Currently, three U.S federal agencies share the responsibility for reviewing genetically modified organisms (GMOs). The U.S. Department of Agriculture is concerned with protecting the welfare of agriculture and forestry; it appraises environmental risks that GMOs may pose. The Environmental Protection Agency, as watchdog for the environment, looks for environmental risks. The Food and Drug Administration, regulator of food, food additives, cosmetics, and drugs, evaluates GMO products from a consumer-protection standpoint. What is missing is long-range planning, careful analysis of biotechnology's problems and opportunities, and also a system for prioritizing research programs on the basis of national and global needs.

The patent system now has a powerful influence on scientific research and development. Since 1980, the patentability of GM products issuing from federally funded research has helped the biotechnology industry grow to giant proportions. As long as the goal of research is to create profitable products rather than to solve agricultural problems, as some critics have charged, we may be developing GM products that sell well but that are not agriculture's most needed products.

Biotechnology research could be strengthened by a central agency that defined and prioritized genetic engineering research goals from the standpoint of the common interest. Researchers would be aware of these guidelines and would understand the rules that would be used in the awarding of federal research funds.

Biotech's Global Ramifications

When Monsanto Chemical, a biotech/chemical firm, announced plans to market seed of GM wheat, American wheat growers were upset. Economists had told them that world markets disliked GM food commodities, that a shift to GM wheat would cut U.S. wheat exports by half, and that this would cut crop prices by a third. The wheat growers protested loudly, and Monsanto suspended its GM wheat venture. When GM corn, soybeans, and canola finally won widespread adoption by U.S. farmers, export demand for these commodities declined. More than 35 countries now have restrictions on the importation of GM food.

Much of the opposition to GM food is linked to safety concerns. Consumers are not able to prove GM foods are hazardous, but they are suspicious. Biotech supporters insist GM food is safe, but they cannot prove their point, either. Our experience with GM food has been brief, and it is possible that some genetically modified foods may contain allergens or toxic compounds. At this point, we just don't know.

Instead of trying to convince the European Union and the rest of the world that they are wrong about GM food safety issues, the United States might end the present impasse by using a policy of accommodation. Expanded testing and analysis of GM foods would indicate the United States is serious about food safety. Also, it would be appropriate to pass a law requiring GM food labeling, which many countries have done. In the United States, food labels already carry a lot of information useful for the consumer's health and safety, so providing additional information on GM content of food would give consumers more choice. In opinion polls, a majority of Americans (up to 58%) say they would prefer to buy GM-free food if they had the choice. And, since international trading partners need to maintain good relations, GM labeling might help end today's global food fight.

On another front of the global GM food battle is the relationship between patent hunters from biotech companies in the industrialized North and farmers in the developing South.

"Today's GM crops do not correct agriculture's chemical dependency problems. Sustainable agriculture . . . offers constructive alternatives."

"Patenting plant varieties from Third World countries robs farmers of their livelihood, and can have widespread repercussions," notes Mae-Wan Ho, director of the London-based Institute of Science in Society. New GM-food crops introduced into developing countries represent a foreign technology—one that is highly mechanized and dependent on costly chemical inputs. Sustainable farming systems for the Third World would add better soil and crop management to the crop production practices traditionally used in an area. Biological control of insect pests and crop diseases could be achieved without use of chemicals. By helping Third World farmers construct practical, environment friendly farming systems, the Northern specialists could make an enduring contribution to the people of the South.

Tomorrow's Genetic Engineering

The newness of agricultural biotechnology is partly illusory. Gene manipulation, leading to the creation of new life-forms, is a brand-new technique, but the genetically modified crop varieties currently available were designed to meet the requirements of an outmoded agricultural production system—one that relies on large inputs of chemical fertilizers, insecticides, and weed killers. The system is ecologically flawed, and today's GM crops do not correct agriculture's chemical dependency problems. Sustainable agriculture, with its low input, environment-friendly programs, offers constructive alternatives.

We need to reappraise production systems and their components—judging them not by economic performance alone, but also on the basis of safety and sustainability. In such a reappraisal, some of genetic engineering's current products would fail to meet the mark. However, promising new developments are in prospect. For example:

- New genetically modified crops appear to thrive in saline soils and in stressful climates.
- GM bacteria may perform useful functions in waste disposal, in environmental monitoring, and in giving plants protection from frost damage.

- Scientists are trying to engineer disease resistance into American chestnut trees, which are highly susceptible to chestnut blight.
- Genetically modified plants may someday be an important energy source, supplementing our dwindling oil reserves.

"Genetic engineering—impressive though it is—cannot by itself cleanse and revitalize the global environment."

Continuing biotech research will bring new achievements. It is entirely possible that environmentalists and biotechnology specialists will learn to work together. The core problem of our time is how to make the world a more livable place—for ourselves and for future generations. Through their intensive searching for new GMOs, biotechnologists will contribute some answers. Additional answers will come from environmentalists who are intent on avoiding environmental damage and on minimizing depletion of natural resources. But cooperation between the two camps is complicated by unresolved issues, such as:

- **Genetic pollution.** Genes from GMOs may be transmitted to natural, unmodified organisms. This is a serious matter, say environmentalists, pointing out that the integrity of a gene pool infested by GMO genes has been compromised forever. But genetic change is inevitable, many researchers say, and genetic pollution may sometimes be beneficial, argues geneticist C. Neal Stewart Jr. A species that is under attack by a serious disease might get a new lease on life if it encountered genes from GMOs engineered for disease resistance, he points out.
- **The precautionary principle.** Genetic engineering development should proceed carefully under the close supervision of government regulators, environmentalists maintain. They cite the precautionary principle, which calls for careful consideration of all possible dangers before action is taken in a risky field filled with unknowns. Using this principle, Europeans are proceeding with a go-slow policy in regard to genetic engineering development. However, the American biotech industry wants to expedite development, not delay it. While some geneticists think today's regulatory system is adequate, others see the need for tightening regulations. How extensive the tightening should be is an open question.
- **Role of the public.** Genetics is a highly technical field of study, and many geneticists do not believe that ordinary citizens are competent to make intelligent decisions concerning genetic engineering. Environmentalists want to have the public involved in all decisions affecting public policy. To raise public awareness, they conduct teach-ins, forums, and other educational activities.

- **Labeling GM food.** Some advocates of genetic engineering say widespread demands for labeling GM food are nonscientists' emotional response to issues they do not understand. Others disagree. Paul F. Lurquin, a geneticist, says people should "be able to choose whether or not to consume food products containing foreign genes."
- **Isolating GM crops.** GM plants that produce pharmaceutically active proteins could be hazardous if grown in open fields. The place for them, it is generally agreed, is in secure greenhouses. If "pharm" plants must be prevented from crossing with other plants, why not restrict other GM crops? The idea of isolating GM crops has come up in political debates in many parts of the world. Bans on transgenic crops have been ordered for entire nations or merely for some lesser areas. Europe seems to be moving toward an area-by-area approach for segregating GM crops from regular crops, and the issue is alive in the United States.

Partnerships between biotechnology and sustainable agriculture could enrich rural development programs in Asia, Africa, and Latin America. The "godfather" of India's green revolution, M.S. Swaminathan, is establishing "biovillages" throughout the southern part of his country. In each biovillage, sustainable farming methods are taught to impoverished rural people. Putting their new knowledge into practice, the villagers are improving southern India's ecology. In a biovillage, genetic engineering has a place alongside organic farming. To clean up wastes or polluted soil, villagers use waste-eating GM bacteria. They develop young trees through micropropagation techniques and eventually plant them in [reforestation] groves.

Dealing with the difficulties and unique possibilities of genetic engineering will require foresight, innovation, and strategy—and a level of institutional support that a national or even global Genetic Science Commission could provide. In the years ahead, we will need to avoid trying to solve momentous problems with quick fixes. Genetic engineering—impressive though it is—cannot by itself cleanse and revitalize the global environment. Working in cooperation with conservationists, ecologists, and sustainable agriculture specialists, geneticists could help work out solutions to many of the world's most-pressing environmental problems.

CLIFTON E. ANDERSON is a University of Idaho professor emeritus in the field of agricultural communications. His last article for THE FUTURIST, "Genetic Engineering: Dangers and Opportunities," appeared in the March-April 2000 issue. His address is 234 North Washington Street, Moscow, Idaho 83843. E-mail clifa@uidaho.edu.

This article draws from his essay, "Looking beyond Today's Genetic Engineering," in Foresight, Innovation, and Strategy: Toward a Wiser Future (World Future Society, 2005).

The Secret Nuclear War

The equivalent of a nuclear war has already happened. Over the last half-century, millions have died as a result of accidents, experiments, lies and cover-ups by the nuclear industry. **Eduardo Goncalves** pulls together a number of examples, and counts the fearful total cost.

EDUARDO GONCALVES

H ugo Paulino was proud to be a fusilier. He was even prouder to be serving as a UN peacekeeper in Kosovo. It was his chance to help the innocent casualties of war. His parents did not expect him to become one.

Hugo, says his father Luis, died of leukaemia caused by radiation from depleted uranium (DU) shells fired by NATO during the Kosovo war. He was one of hundreds of Portuguese peacekeepers sent to Klina, an area heavily bombed with these munitions. Their patrol detail included the local lorry park, bombed because it had served as a Serb tank reserve, and the Valujak mines, which sheltered Serbian troops.

In their time off, the soldiers bathed in the river and gratefully supplemented their tasteless rations with local fruit and cheeses given to them by thankful nuns from the convent they guarded. Out of curiosity, they would climb inside the destroyed Serbian tanks littering the area.

Hugo arrived back in Portugal from his tour of duty on 12 February 2000, complaining of headaches, nausea and 'flu-like symptoms'. Ten days later, on 22 February, he suffered a major seizure. He was rushed to Lisbon's military hospital, where his condition rapidly deteriorated. On 9 March, he died. He was 21.

The military autopsy, which was kept secret for 10 months, claimed his death was due to septicaemia and 'herpes of the brain'. Not so, says Luis Paulino. 'When he was undergoing tests, a doctor called me over and said he thought it could be from radiation.'

It was only then that Luis learnt about the uranium shells—something his son had never been warned about or given protective clothing against. He contacted doctors and relatives of Belgian and Italian soldiers suspected of having succumbed to radiation poisoning.

'The similarities were extraordinary', he said. 'My son had died from leukemia. That is why the military classified the autopsy report and wanted me to sign over all rights to its release.'

Today, Kosovo is littered with destroyed tanks, and pieces of radioactive shrapnel. NATO forces fired 31,000 depleted uranium shells during the Kosovo campaign, and 10,800 into neighbouring Bosnia. The people NATO set out to protect—and the soldiers it sent out to protect them—are now dying. According to Bosnia's health minister, Boza Ljubic, cancer deaths among civilians have risen to 230 cases per 100,000 last year, up from 152 in 1999. Leukaemia cases, he added, had doubled.

Scientists predict that the use of DU in Serbia will lead to more than 10,000 deaths from cancer among local residents, aid workers, and peacekeepers. Belated confessions that plutonium was also used may prompt these estimates to be revised. But while NATO struggles to stave off accusations of a cover-up, the Balkans are merely the newest battlefield in a silent world war that has claimed millions of lives. Most of its victims have died not in war-zones, but in ordinary communities scattered across the globe.

The Hidden Deaths of Newbury

Far away from the war-torn Balkans is Newbury, a prosperous white-collar industrial town in London's commuter belt. On its outskirts is Greenham Common, the former US Air Force station that was one of America's most important strategic bases during the Cold War. The base was closed down after the signing of the INF (Intermediate Nuclear Forces) Treaty by Ronald Reagan and Mikhail Gorbachev. The nuclear threat was over. Or so people thought.

In August 1993, Ann Capewell—who lived just one mile away from the base's former runway—died of acute myeloid leukaemia. She was 16 when she passed away, just 40 days after diagnosis. As they were coming to terms with their sudden loss, her parents—Richard and Elizabeth—were surprised to find a number of other cases of leukaemia in their locality.

The more they looked, the more cases they found. 'Many were just a stone's throw from our front door,' says Richard, 'mainly cases of myeloid leukaemia in young people.' What none of them knew was that they were the victims of a nuclear accident at Greenham Common that had been carefully covered up by successive British and American administrations.

> '**It is believed that the estimated 1,900 nuclear tests conducted during the Cold War released fallout equivalent to 40,000 Hiroshimas in every corner of the globe.**'

On February 28 1958, a laden B-47 nuclear bomber was awaiting clearance for take-off when it was suddenly engulfed in a huge fireball. Another bomber flying overhead had dropped a full fuel tank just 65 feet away. The plane exploded and burnt uncontrollably for days. As did its deadly payload.

A secret study by scientists at Britain's nearby nuclear bomb laboratory at Aldermaston documented the fallout, but the findings were never disclosed. The report showed how radioactive particles had been 'glued' to the runway surface by fire-fighters attempting to extinguish the blazing bomber—and that these were now being slowly blown into Newbury and over other local communities by aircraft jet blast.

'Virtually all the cases of leukaemias and lymphomas are in a band stretching from Greenham Common into south Newbury,' says Elizabeth. However, the British government continues to deny the cluster's existence, whilst the Americans still insist there was no accident.

Yet this was just one of countless disasters, experiments and officially-sanctioned activities which the nuclear powers have kept a closely-guarded secret. Between them, they have caused a global human death toll which is utterly unprecedented and profoundly shocking.

Broken Arrows

In 1981, the Pentagon publicly released a list of 32 'Broken Arrows'—official military terminology for an accident involving a nuclear weapon. The report gave few details and did not divulge the location of some accidents. It was prepared in response to mounting media pressure about possible accident cover-ups.

But another US government document, this time secret, indicates that the official report may be seriously misleading. It states that 'a total of 1,250 nuclear weapons have been involved in accidents during handling, storage and transportation', a number of which 'resulted in, or had high potential for, plutonium dispersal.'[1]

Washington has never acknowledged the human consequences of even those few accidents it admits to, such as the Thule disaster in Greenland in 1968. When a B-52 bomber crashed at this secret nuclear base, all four bombs detonated, and a cloud of plutonium rose 800 metres in the air, blowing deadly radioactive particles hundreds of miles. The authorities downplayed the possibility of any health risks. But today, many local Eskimos, and their huskies, suffer from cancer, and over 300 people involved in the clean-up operation alone have since died of cancer and mysterious illnesses.

We may never know the true toll from all the bomb accidents, as the nuclear powers classify these disasters not as matters of public interest but of 'national security' instead. Indeed, it is only now that details are beginning to emerge of some accidents at bomb factories and nuclear plants that took place several decades ago.

Soviet Sins

In 1991, Polish film-maker Slawomir Grunberg was invited to a little-known town in Russia's Ural mountains that was once part of a top-secret Soviet nuclear bomb-making complex. What he found was a tragedy of extraordinary dimensions, largely unknown to the outside world, and ignored by post-Cold War leaders.

His film—*Chelyabinsk: The Most Contaminated Spot on the Planet*—tells the story of the disasters at the Soviet Union's first plutonium factory, and the poisoning of hundreds of thousands of people. For years, the complex dumped its nuclear waste—totalling 76 million cubic metres—into the Techa River, the sole water source for scores of local communities that line its banks. According to a local doctor, people received an average radiation dose 57 times higher than that of Chernobyl's inhabitants.

In 1957, there was an explosion at a waste storage facility that blew 2 million curies of radiation into the atmosphere. The kilometre-high cloud drifted over three Soviet provinces, contaminating over 250,000 people living in 217 towns and villages. Only a handful of local inhabitants were ever evacuated.

10 years later, Lake Karachay, also used as a waste dump, began to dry up. The sediment around its shores blew 5 million curies of radioactive dust over 25,000 square kilometres, irradiating 500,000 people. Even today, the lake is so 'hot' that standing on its shore will kill a person within one hour.

Grunberg's film tells of the terrible toll of these disasters on local families, such as that of Idris Sunrasin, whose grandmother, parents and three siblings have died of cancer. Leukaemia cases increased by 41 per cent after the plant began operations, and the average life span for women in 1993 was 47, compared to 72 nationally. For men it was just 45.

The Cancer Epidemic

Scientists at St Andrew's University recently found that cells exposed to a dose of just two alpha particles of radiation produced as many cancers as much higher doses of radiation. They concluded that a single alpha particle of radiation could be carcinogenic.

Herman Muller, who has received a Nobel Prize for his work, has shown how the human race's continuous exposure to so-called 'low-level' radiation is causing a gradual reduction in its ability to survive, as successive generations are genetically damaged. The spreading and accumulation of even tiny genetic mutations pass through family lines, provoking allergies, asthma, juvenile diabetes, hypertension, arthritis, high blood cholesterol conditions, and muscular and bone defects.

Dr Chris Busby, who has extensively researched the low-level radiation threat, has made a link between everyday radiation exposure and a range of modern ailments: 'There have been tremendous increases in diseases resulting from the breakdown of the immune system in the last 20 years: diabetes, asthma, AIDS and others which may have an immune-system link, such as MS and ME. A whole spectrum of neurological conditions of unknown origin has developed'.[10]

Around the world, a pattern is emerging. For the first time in modern history, mortality rates among adults between the ages of 15 and 54 are actually increasing, and have been since 1982. In July 1983, the US Center for Birth Defects in Atlanta, Georgia, reported that physical and mental disabilities in the under-17s had doubled—despite a reduction in diseases such as polio, and improved vaccines and medical care.

Defects in new-born babies doubled between the 1950s and 1980s, as did long-term debilitating diseases. The US Environmental Protection Agency adds that 23 per cent of US males were sterile in 1980, compared to 0.5 per cent in 1938.

Above all, cancer is now an epidemic. In 1900, cancer accounted for only 4 per cent of deaths in the US. Now it is the second leading cause of premature mortality. Worldwide, the World Health Organisation (WHO) estimates the number of cancers will double in most countries over the next 25 years.

Within a few years, the chances of getting cancer in Britain will be as high as 40 per cent—virtually the toss of a coin.

The Secret Nuclear War

Russia's nuclear industry is commonly regarded as cavalier in regard to health and safety. But the fact is that the nuclear military-industrial complex everywhere has been quite willing to deliberately endanger and sacrifice the lives of innocent civilians to further its ambitions.

The US government, for example, recently admitted its nuclear scientists carried out over 4,000 experiments on live humans between 1944 and 1974. They included feeding radioactive food to disabled children, irradiating prisoners' testicles, and trials on new-born babies and pregnant mothers. Scientists involved with the Manhattan Project injected people with plutonium without telling them. An autopsy of one of the victims reportedly showed that his bones 'looked like Swiss cheese'. At the University of Cincinnati, 88 mainly low-income, black women were subjected to huge doses of radiation in an experiment funded by the military. They suffered acute radiation sickness. Nineteen of them died.

'Scientists predict that millions will die in centuries to come from nuclear tests that happened in the 1950s and 1960s.'

Details of many experiments still remain shrouded in secrecy, whilst little is known of the more shocking ones to come to light—such as one when a man was injected with what a report described as 'about a lethal dose' of strontium-89.[2]

In Britain too, scientists have experimented with plutonium on new-born babies, ethnic minorities and the disabled. When American colleagues reviewed a British proposal for a joint experiment, they concluded: 'What is the worst thing that can happen to a human being as a result of being a subject? Death.'[3]

They also conducted experiments similar to America's 'Green Run' programme, in which 'dirty' radiation was released over populated areas in the western states of Washington and Oregon contaminating farmland, crops and water. The 'scrubber' filters in Hanford's nuclear stacks were deliberately switched off first. Scientists, posing as agriculture department officials, found radiation contamination levels on farms hundreds of times above 'safety' levels.

But America's farmers and consumers were not told this, and the British public has never been officially told about experiments on its own soil.

Forty Thousand Hiroshimas

It is believed that the estimated 1,900 nuclear tests conducted during the Cold War released fallout equivalent to 40,000 Hiroshimas in every corner of the globe. Fission products from the Nevada Test site can be detected in the ecosystems of countries as far apart as South Africa, Brazil, and Malaysia. Here, too, ordinary people were guinea pigs in a global nuclear experiment. The public health hazards were known right from the beginning, but concealed from the public. A 1957 US government study predicted that recent American tests had produced an extra 2,000 'genetically defective' babies in the US each year, and up to 35,000 every year around the globe. They continued regardless.

Ernest Sternglass's research shows how, in 1964, between 10,000 and 15,000 children were lost by miscarriage and still-birth in New York state alone—and that there were some 10 to 15 times this number of fetal deaths across America.[4]

'Over the years, the Harwell, Aldermaston and Amersham plants have pumped millions of gallons of liquid contaminated with radioactive waste into the River Thames.'

Those who lived closest to the test sites have seen their families decimated. Such as the 100,000 people who were directly downwind of Nevada's fallout. They included the Mormon community of St George in Utah, 100 miles away from 'Ground Zero'—the spot where the bombs were detonated. Cancer used to be virtually unheard of among its population. Mormons do not smoke or drink alcohol or coffee, and live largely off their own homegrown produce.

Mormons are also highly patriotic. They believe government to be 'God-given', and do not protest. The military could afford to wait until the wind was blowing from the test site towards St George before detonating a device. After all, President Eisenhower had said: 'We can afford to sacrifice a few thousand people out there in defence of national security.'[5]

When the leukaemia cases suddenly appeared, doctors—unused to the disease—literally had no idea what it was. A nine-year-old boy, misdiagnosed with diabetes, died after a single shot of insulin. Women who complained of radiation sickness symptoms were told they had 'housewife syndrome'. Many gave birth to terribly deformed babies that became known as 'the sacrifice babies'. Elmer Pickett, the local mortician, had to learn new embalming techniques for the small bodies of wasted children killed by leukaemia. He himself was to lose no fewer than 16 members of his immediate family to cancer.

By the mid-1950s, just a few years after the tests began, St George had a leukaemia rate 2.5 times the national average, whereas before it was virtually non-existent. The total number of radiation deaths are said to have totalled 1,600—in a town with a population of just 5,000.

The military simply lied about the radiation doses people were getting. Former army medic Van Brandon later revealed how his unit kept two sets of radiation readings for test fall-out in the area. 'One set was to show that no one received an [elevated] exposure' whilst 'the other set of books showed the actual reading. That set was brought in a locked briefcase every morning.'[6]

Continuous Fallout

The world's population is still being subjected to the continuous fallout of the 170 megatons of long-lived nuclear fission products blasted into the atmosphere and returned daily to earth by wind and rain—slowly poisoning our bodies via the air we breathe, the food we eat, and the water we drink. Scientists predict that millions will die in centuries to come from tests that happened in the 1950s and 1960s.

But whilst atmospheric testing is now banned, over 400 nuclear bomb factories and power plants around the world make 'routine discharges' of nuclear waste into the environment. Thousands of nuclear waste dumping grounds, many of them leaking, are contaminating soil and water every day. The production of America's nuclear weapons arsenal alone has produced 100 million cubic metres of long-lived radioactive waste.

The notorious Hanford plutonium factory—which produced the fissile materials for the Trinity test and Nagasaki bomb—has discharged over 440 billion gallons of contaminated liquid into the surrounding area, contaminating 200 square miles of groundwater, but concealed the dangers from the public. Officials knew as early as the late 1940s that the nearby Columbia River was becoming seriously contaminated and a hazard to local fishermen. They chose to keep information about discharges secret and not to issue warnings.

In Britain, there are 7,000 sites licensed to use nuclear materials, 1,000 of which are allowed to discharge wastes. Three of them, closely involved in Britain's nuclear bomb programme, are located near the River Thames. Over the years, the Harwell, Aldermaston and Amersham plants have pumped millions of gallons of liquid contaminated with radioactive waste into the river.

They did so in the face of opposition from government ministers and officials who said 'the 6 million inhabitants of London derive their drinking water from this source. Any increase in [radio-]activity of the water supply would increase the genetic load on this comparatively large group.'[7] One government minister even wrote of his fears that the dumping 'would produce between 10 and 300 severely abnormal individuals per generation'.

Public relations officers at Harwell themselves added: 'the potential sufferers are 8 million in number, including both Houses of Parliament, Fleet Street and Whitehall'. These discharges continue to this day.

Study after study has uncovered 'clusters' of cancers and high rates of other unusual illnesses near nuclear plants, including deformities and Down Syndrome. Exposure to radiation among Sellafield's workers, in northwest England, has been linked to a greater risk of fathering a stillborn child and leukaemia among off-spring. Reports also suggest a higher risk of babies developing spina bifida in the womb.

Although the plant denies any link, even official MAFF studies have shown high levels of contamination in locally-grown fruit and vegetables, as well as wild animals. The pollution from Sellafield alone is such that it has coated the shores of the whole of Britain—from Wales to Scotland, and even Hartlepool in north-eastern England. A nationwide study organised by Harwell found that Sellafield 'is a source of plutonium contamination in the wider population of the British Isles'.[8]

'Study after study has uncovered 'clusters' of cancers and high rates of other illnesses near nuclear plants, including deformities and Down Syndrome. Exposure to radiation among Sellafield's workers, in NW England, has been linked to a greater risk of fathering a stillborn child and leukaemia among off-spring.'

Those who live nearest the plant face the greatest threat. A study of autopsy tissue by the National Radiological Protection Board (NRPB) found high plutonium levels in the lungs of local Cumbrians—350 per cent higher than people in other parts of the country. 'Cancer clusters' have been found around nuclear plants across the globe—from France to Taiwan, Germany to Canada. A joint White House/US Department of Energy investigation recently found a high incidence of 22 different kinds of cancer at 14 different US nuclear weapons facilities around the country.

Meanwhile, a Greenpeace USA study of the toxicity of the Mississippi river showed that from 1968–83 there were 66,000 radiation deaths in the counties lining its banks—more than the number of Americans who died during the Vietnam war.

Don't Blame Us

Despite the growing catalogue of tragedy, the nuclear establishment has consistently tried to deny responsibility. It claims that only high doses of radiation—such as those experienced by the victims of the Hiroshima and Nagasaki bombs—are dangerous, though even here they have misrepresented the data. They say that the everyday doses from nuclear plant discharges, bomb factories and transportation of radioactive materials are 'insignificant', and that accidents are virtually impossible.

The truth, however, is that the real number and seriousness of accidents has never been disclosed, and that the damage from fallout has been covered up. The nuclear establishment now grudgingly (and belatedly) accepts that there is no such thing as a safe dose of radiation, however 'low', yet the poisonous discharges continue. When those within the nuclear establishment try to speak out, they are harassed, intimidated—and even threatened.

John Gofman, former head of Lawrence Livermore's biomedical unit, who helped produce the world's first plutonium for the bomb, was for years at the heart of the nuclear complex. He recalls painfully the time he was called to give evidence before a Congressional inquiry set up to defuse mounting concern over radiation's dangers.

'Chet Holifield and Craig Hosmer of the Joint Committee (on Atomic Energy) came in and turned to me and said: "Just what the hell do you think you two are doing, getting all those little old ladies in tennis shoes up in arms about our atomic energy program? There are people like you who have tried to hurt the Atomic Energy Commission program before. We got them, and we'll get you."'[9]

Gofman was eventually forced out of his job. But the facts of his research—and that of many other scientists—speak for themselves.

The Final Reckoning

But could radiation really be to blame for these deaths? Are the health costs really that great? The latest research suggests they are.

It is only very recently that clues have surfaced as to the massive destructive power of radiation in terms of human health. The accident at Chernobyl will kill an estimated half a million people worldwide from cancer, and perhaps more. 90 per cent of children in the neighbouring former Soviet republic of Belarus are contaminated for life—the poisoning of an entire country's gene pool.

Ernest Sternglass calculates that, at the height of nuclear testing, there were as many as 3 million foetal deaths, spontaneous abortions and stillbirths in the US alone. In addition, 375,000 babies died in their first year of life from radiation-linked diseases.[11]

Rosalie Bertell, author of the classic book *No Immediate Danger,* now revised and re-released, has attempted to piece together a global casualty list from the nuclear establishment's own data. The figures she has come up with are chilling—but entirely plausible.

Using the official 'radiation risk' estimates published in 1991 by the International Commission on Radiological Protection (ICRP), and the total radiation exposure data to the global population calculated by the UN Scientific Committee on the Effects of Atomic Radiation (UNSCEAR) in 1993, she has come up with a terrifying tally:

- 358 million cancers from nuclear bomb production and testing
- 9.7 million cancers from bomb and plant accidents
- 6.6 million cancers from the 'routine discharges' of nuclear power plants (5 million of them among populations living nearby).
- As many as 175 million of these cancers could be fatal.

Added to this number are no fewer than 235 million genetically damaged and diseased people, and a staggering 588 million children born with what are called 'teratogenic effects'—diseases such as brain damage, mental disabilities, spina bifida, genital deformities, and childhood cancers.

Furthermore, says Bertell, we should include the problem of nonfatal cancers and of other damage which is debilitating but not counted for insurance and liability purposes'[12]—such as the 500 million babies lost as stillbirths because they were exposed to radiation whilst still in the womb, but are not counted as 'official' radiation victims.

It is what the nuclear holocaust peace campaigners always warned of if war between the old superpowers broke out, yet it has already happened and with barely a shot being fired. Its toll

The Final Reckoning

How many deaths is the nuclear industry responsible for? The following calculations of numbers of cancers caused by radiation are the latest and most accurate:*
from nuclear bomb production and testing: 385 million
from bomb and plant accidents: 9.7 million
from the 'routine discharges' of nuclear power plants (5 million of them among populations living nearby): 6.6 million
likely number of total cancer fatalities worldwide:
175 million
[Added to this number are 235 million genetically damaged and diseased people, and 588 million children born with diseases such as brain damage, mental disabilities, spina bifida, genital deformities, and childhood cancers.]

*Calculated by Rosalie Bertell, using the official 'radiation risk' estimates published in 1991 by the International Commission on Radiological Protection (ICRP), and the total radiation exposure data to the global population calculated by the UN Scientific Committee on the Effects of Atomic Radiation (UNSCEAR) in 1993.

is greater than that of all the wars in history put together, yet no one is counted as among the war dead.

'It is the nuclear holocaust that peace campaigners always warned of if war between the old superpowers broke out, yet it has already happened and with barely a shot being fired.'

Its virtually infinite killing and maiming power leads Rosalie Bertell to demand that we learn a new language to express a terrifying possibility: 'The concept of species annihilation means a relatively swift, deliberately induced end to history, culture, science, biological reproduction and memory. It is the ultimate human rejection of the gift of life, an act which requires a new word to describe it: omnicide'.[13]

Notes

1. 'Report of the safety criteria for plutonium-bearing weapons—summary', US Department of Energy, February 14, 1973, document RS5640/1035.

2. Strontium metabolism meeting, Atomic Energy Division–Division of Biology and Medicine, January 17, 1954.

3. Memorandum to Bart Gledhill, chairman, Human Subjects Committee. LLNL, from Larry Anderson, LLNL, February 21, 1989.

4. See 'Secret Fallout, Low-Level Radiation from Hiroshima to Three-Mile Island'. Ernest Sternglass, McGraw-Hill, New York, 1981.

5. See 'American Ground Zero; The Secret Nuclear War', Carole Gallagher, MIT Press. Boston, 1993.

6. Washington Post, February 24, 1994.

7. See PRO files AB 6/1379 and AB 6/2453 and 3584.

8. 'Variations in the concentration of plutonium, strontium-90 and total alpha-emitters in human teeth', RG. O'Donnell et al, Sd. Tot. Env, 201 (1997) 235–243.

9. Interview with Gofman, DOE/OHRE Oral History Project, December 1994, pp 49–50 of official transcripts.

10. 'Wings of Death—nuclear pollution and human health', Dr. Chris Busby, Green Audit, Wales, 1995

11. See 'Secret Fallout, Low-Level Radiation from Hiroshima to Three-Mile Island', Ernest Sternglass, McGraw-Hill, New York, 1981.

12. From 'No Immediate Danger—Prognosis for a Radioactive Earth', Dr Rosalie Bertell. Women's Press. London 1985 (revised 2001)

13. Pers. Comm. 4 February 2001

Further Reading

'No Immediate Danger—Prognosis for a Radioactive Earth', Dr Rosalie Bertell, Women's Press, London (revised 2001)

'Deadly Deceit—low-level radiation, high-level cover-up', Dr. Jay Gould and Benjamin A. Goldman, Four Walls Eight Windows, New York, 1991

'Wings of Death—nuclear pollution and human health', Dr. Chris Busby, Green Audit, Wales, 1995

'American Ground Zero: The Secret Nuclear War', Carole Gallagher, MIT Press, Boston, 1993

'Radioactive Heaven and Earth—the health effects of nuclear weapons testing in, on, and above the earth', a report of the IPPNW International Commission, Zed Books, 1991 'Secret Fallout. Low-Level Radiation from Hiroshima to Three-Mile Island', Ernest Sternglass, McGraw-Hill, New York, 1981

'Clouds of Deceit—the deadly legacy of Britain's bomb tests', Joan Smith, Faber and Faber, London, 1985

'Nuclear Wastelands', Arjun Makhijani et al (eds), MIT Press, Boston, 1995 'Radiation and Human Health', Dr. John W. Gofman, Sierra Book Club, San Francisco, 1981

'The Greenpeace Book of the Nuclear Age—The Hidden History, the Human Cost', John May, Victor Gollancz, 1989

'The Unsinkable Aircraft Carrier—American military power in Britain', Duncan Campbell, Michael Joseph, London 1984

EDUARDO GONCALVES is a freelance journalist and environmental researcher. He is author of title reports *Broken Arrow—Greenham Common's Secret Nuclear Accident* and *Nuclear Guinea Pigs—British Human Radiation Experiments,* published by CND (UK), and was researcher to the film *The Dragon that Slew St George.* He is currently writing a book about the hidden history of the nuclear age.

Homegrown Terrorism and the Radicalization Process

The Emerging Threat

ROBERT S. MUELLER, III
Director, Federal Bureau of Investigation

Good afternoon. I am honored to join you today. My thanks to Jim Foster for inviting me to be a part of this well-respected series.

In recent weeks, we have watched the Toronto terrorism investigation unfold. To date, 17 suspects have been arrested in an alleged terrorist plot to bomb several prominent buildings in Toronto and Ottawa and to behead the prime minister.

These men did not merely talk of taking action; they tried to purchase three tons of ammonium nitrate fertilizer. That is three times the amount used in the Oklahoma City bombing.

Although the Canadian authorities uncovered this plot before these men harmed anyone, we face the sobering fact that yet another group of extremists planned a terrorist attack and took steps to execute that attack.

Like the terrorists responsible for both the London and the Madrid bombings, the Toronto suspects lived in the area they intended to attack. They were not sleeper operatives sent on suicide missions; they were students and business people and members of the community. They were persons who, for whatever reason, came to view their home country as the enemy.

I want to talk today about the changing shape of terrorism and, in particular, the threat of homegrown terrorism. I want to talk about the radicalization process—how an extremist becomes a terrorist—and what we in the FBI are doing to address this new threat.

For more than a decade, al Qaeda has been the driving force of terrorism—moving thousands of people through training camps in Afghanistan and providing the motivation, the money, and the management for worldwide attacks.

In the past five years, with our military, law enforcement and intelligence partners around the world, we have disrupted al Qaeda's central operations. We have captured or killed many key leaders, including the mastermind behind the 9/11 attacks, Khalid Sheikh Mohammed, as well as al-Zarqawi and many of his associates in Iraq.

We have destroyed their training camps, and disrupted both their funding and their means of communication. Through these efforts, we have transformed al Qaeda from a strong hierarchy that plans and executes attacks to being a decentralized and amorphous group.

Unfortunately, while al Qaeda may be weakened, it is not dead. We continue to face threats from al Qaeda and its offshoots in Saudi Arabia, Iraq, and East Africa. Their plots have included blowing up a Columbus area shopping mall in 2004, as well as the recently reported plot to release cyanide gas in the New York City subway system in 2003.

We also face threats from organizations affiliated with al Qaeda, like Ansar al-Sunnah in Africa and Jemmah Islamiya in southeast Asia. These groups continue to train, recruit, and plan attacks, but their chains of command are fractured and they are not as stable as they were five years ago.

While we have made great strides in disabling traditional terrorist models like al Qaeda, the convergence of globalization and technology has created a new brand of terrorism. Today, terrorist threats may come from smaller, more loosely-defined individuals and cells who are not affiliated with al Qaeda, but who are inspired by a violent jihadist message. These homegrown terrorists may prove to be as dangerous as groups like al Qaeda, if not more so.

We have already seen this new face of terrorism on a global scale in Madrid, London, and Toronto. We have also witnessed this so-called "self-radicalization" here at home.

In Torrance, California, for example, four men were indicted last year, charged with plotting to attack U.S. military recruiting facilities and synagogues in the Los Angeles area.

In Toledo, three men were recently charged with conspiring to provide money, training, communications equipment, and computers to extremists in the Middle East. As alleged in the indictment, these men taught themselves how to make and use explosives. They conducted their own training exercises. And they did it all here in Ohio.

Just this morning, the FBI and the Department of Justice announced the indictment of seven individuals involved in what appears to be another homegrown terrorist cell. The leader of this cell is a U.S. citizen living in Miami. He and six others are alleged to have plotted to attack the Sears Tower in Chicago and key federal buildings in Miami-Dade County.

These extremists are self-recruited, self-trained, and self-executing. They may not have any connection to al Qaeda or to other terrorist groups. They share ideas and information in the shadows of the Internet. They gain inspiration from radical websites that call for violence.

They raise money by committing low-level crimes that do not generate much attention. They answer not to a particular leader, but to an ideology. In short, they operate under the radar. And that makes their detection that much more difficult for all of us.

To detect homegrown terrorists, it helps to understand the radicalization process. How does an individual become a radical extremist? And how does an extremist then become a terrorist? We have found that radicalization is fluid; it does not follow a set formula or timetable.

Radicalization often starts with individuals who are frustrated with their lives or with the politics of their home governments. They may be U.S.-born, or, as we saw in London, second-generation citizens.

Some may be lonely or dissatisfied with their role in society. Others may have friends or mentors who encourage membership for social reasons.

Once a person has joined an extremist group, he or she may start to identify with an ideology—one that encourages violence against a government and its citizens. They may become increasingly isolated from their old lives, drift away from family and friends, and spend more time with other members of the extremist group.

As they become more and more involved in the group, they may decide to take action to support the cause—actions such as selecting targets, conducting surveillance, raising money, and procuring materials. As talk moves to action, an extremist can become a terrorist.

The evolution from extremism to terrorism can take place anywhere, from academic settings, mosques, prisons, and community centers to the Internet.

Schools and universities, for example, are both open as well as isolated. Many students are at an impressionable age, and are seeking ways to establish their own unique identities.

Prisons are also fertile ground for extremists. Inmates may be drawn to an extreme form of Islam because it may help justify their violent tendencies. These persons represent a heightened threat because of their criminal histories, their propensity for violence, and their contacts with fellow criminals.

The four suspected terrorists arrested last year in Torrance, California were recruited by one Kevin James, the founder of a radical group called J.I.S. James founded J.I.S from his cell in Folsom Prison in California. He recruited fellow inmates and radicals outside prison to join his mission, which was to kill those he saw as "infidels."

We are working with prison officials and academic leaders across the country to identify these potential recruiting venues. But we must also identify the recruiters themselves—who sometimes act as the leaders of these homegrown cells.

In recent cases, we have seen one key person, such as Kevin James, who brought the Torrance group together. These are not always spiritual leaders; they can be mentors or friends. Regardless of their role, they can transform their followers from radicals to terrorists.

Radical fundamentalists are particularly difficult to pinpoint in cyberspace. There are between 5,000 to 6,000 extremist websites on the Internet, encouraging extremists to initiate their own radicalization and to cultivate relationships with other like-minded persons.

Although we have destroyed many terrorist training camps in the past five years, extremists increasingly turn to the Internet for virtual instruction. Of course, not every extremist will become a terrorist. But the radicalization process has become more rapid, more widespread, and anonymous in this Internet age, making detection that much more difficult.

Whether we are talking about al Qaeda's operations overseas, sleeper operatives who have been in place for years, or the emergence of homegrown terrorists, our greatest challenge is in mapping these underground networks. This can be tedious, intricate work, but it is absolutely essential to the safety of this country. We need to see how certain individuals fit into the big picture. We need to know where to set the trip wires to identify the line between the extremist and the operational. To meet that mission, we are relying on three things: firstly, intelligence; secondly, technology; and thirdly, partnerships.

Intelligence is the key to preventing terrorist attacks. We must be able to transform bits and pieces of information into actionable intelligence and then disseminate that intelligence to the people who need it—all within an exceptionally tight time frame.

In the past five years, we have doubled the number of intelligence analysts in the FBI and placed Field Intelligence Groups in every one of our offices. Together, agents, analysts, linguists, and surveillance specialists collect and analyze vital intelligence and share it with our partners in the law enforcement and in the intelligence communities.

As part of this effort, agents and analysts in each of our field offices are taking a good, hard look at their communities. Here in Cleveland, for instance, we have learned more about the mass transit system, the ports on Lake Erie, and the many airports, airstrips, and heliports in the area. We have increased our knowledge of Ohio's agricultural base and its key industries, academic institutions, and people.

We call it "knowing your domain." We need to know the risk factors and the potential targets for criminal and terrorist activity. With this information, we can find and stop homegrown terrorists before they strike.

Intelligence provides the information we need, but technology enables us to find patterns and connections in that intelligence. Using searchable databases, we can track suspected terrorists through biographical information, travel histories, and criminal and financial records.

Using our Investigative Data Warehouse, agents, analysts, and law enforcement officers on Joint Terrorism Task Forces across the country can search more than 50 databases, with more than 500 million terrorism-related documents. In 2005 alone, users ran more than 10 million inquiries, with an average response time of under eight seconds.

Our Terrorist Screening Center provides federal, state, and local officials with real-time connectivity to the terrorist watch list. We maintain a database of more than 200,000 known or suspected terrorists. When a police officer encounters a suspicious person, the officer can access the screening center on the spot for further information and direction.

But we are not the only ones making ready use of emerging technology. Terrorists are doing it as well. To keep pace, we must be able to identify the links between extremists and their activities. Technology provides the means to make those connections.

While technology is indeed vital, the role of our partners in state and local law enforcement has become that much more important in our fight against homegrown terrorism. They are the feet on the street—the first to see new trends in crime and terrorism.

The FBI is a relatively small organization with but 12,000 agents, compared to 800,000 law enforcement officers across the United States. That is why partnerships like our Joint Terrorism Task Forces are so vital. Police officers and others from the federal government—including the CIA, the Secret Service, and the Department of Homeland Security, just to name a few—work side-by-side with FBI agents and analysts, cooperating on investigations and sharing information with their own departments and agencies.

In the Torrance investigation, the police officers who arrested two of the suspects in what looked like a routine gas station robbery discovered evidence that they were planning a terrorist attack. The officers passed that information on to the local Joint Terrorism Task Force. Together, they traced the steps of these terrorists and exposed the entire cell.

Without the initial information from the Torrance Police Department, and the work of the Los Angeles Sheriff's and Police departments, we might not have made the connection between the terrorists' criminal activities and their plans for attack.

These partnerships also extend overseas. The ongoing Toronto terrorism investigation is an outstanding example of high-level coordination—coordination between international law enforcement and intelligence agencies in Canada, America, Denmark, Britain, Bosnia, Bangladesh and other countries.

We have come together to share information and to address the terrorist threat. We are investigating possible ties between the Toronto suspects and terrorist cells around the world. We must continue to work together. We cannot stop global terrorism without global cooperation.

Our partnerships with those of you in the private sector are equally important. Countering the spread of global terrorism will take more than just the capture of terrorist leaders. We are doubling our efforts to reach out to communities across the country.

In recent months, we have hosted town meetings from Los Angeles to New York. We are also meeting with community leaders and minority groups to demystify the work we're doing. It's an important step in strengthening bonds between the FBI and the citizens we protect.

There are those who view the FBI with suspicion, and we must bridge that gap. We must build confidence in one another and forge lasting relationships. We want to improve our understanding of our communities by creating an open dialogue. We need to reach the point where you are willing to come forward and say, "I have seen or heard something that you need to know."

We must also build relationships within the Muslim community to counter the spread of extremist ideology. Increasingly, mainstream Muslim leaders are challenging the extremist message of hatred and violence. Just yesterday, representatives from the Muslim community met with FBI leaders at Headquarters and in the field to talk about sharing information and working together to prevent terrorism and fight crime. The radicalization cycle can only be broken if we stand together against terrorism.

It has been nearly five years since the last terrorist attack on America. Yet there is no room for complacency. As we have seen in recent months, our enemies are adaptive and evasive. They are taking full advantage of technology. They are combining their resources and their expertise to great effect. We must do the same.

Our greatest weapon against terrorism is unity. That unity is built on information sharing and coordination among our partners in the law enforcement and the intelligence communities. It is built on partnerships with the private sector and effective outreach to the public as our eyes and ears. It is built on the idea that, together, we are smarter and stronger than we are standing alone.

No one person, no one agency, no one police department, and no one country has all the answers. We may not always know where and when terrorists will attempt to strike. But we do know they will try again. And we must combine our intelligence, our technology, and our resources to stop them.

We face many challenges today, both from overseas and from those living in our midst. But we must not let terrorism change our way of life.

James Thurber, one of Ohio's native sons and one of the best-known writers and cartoonists of the 20th century, once wrote, "Let us not look back in anger, nor forward in fear, but around in awareness."

We cannot look back in anger. Nor should we look forward in fear. Terrorism is designed to incite both fear and anger. Its very purpose is to make us afraid—afraid of what may happen, afraid of each other.

Instead, let us look around in awareness . . . of our citizens and our communities, and of the dangers we face. Most importantly, let us look around in awareness of the strength of our democracy, the strength of our unity, and the strength of our resolve. Armed with these strengths, we cannot and we will not fail.

Thank you and God Bless.

From *Vital Speeches of the Day*, August 2006, pp. 562–565.

EMP: America's Achilles' Heel

FRANK J. GAFFNEY, JR.

President, Center for Security Policy

The following is adapted from a speech delivered on May 24, 2005, in Dallas, Texas, at a Hillsdale College National Leadership Seminar on the topic, "America's War Against Islamic Terrorism."

If Osama bin Laden—or the dictators of North Korea or Iran—could destroy America as a twenty-first century society and superpower, would they be tempted to try? Given their track records and stated hostility to the United States, we have to operate on the assumption that they would. That assumption would be especially frightening if this destruction could be accomplished with a *single attack* involving just one relatively small-yield nuclear weapon—and if the nature of the attack would mean that its perpetrator might not be immediately or easily identified.

Unfortunately, such a scenario is not far-fetched. According to a report issued last summer by a blue-ribbon, Congressionally-mandated commission, a single specialized nuclear weapon delivered to an altitude of a few hundred miles over the United States by a ballistic missile would be "capable of causing catastrophe for the nation." The source of such a cataclysm might be considered the ultimate "weapon of mass destruction" (WMD)—yet it is hardly ever mentioned in the litany of dangerous WMDs we face today. It is known as electromagnetic pulse (EMP).

How EMP Works

A nuclear weapon produces several different effects. The best known, of course, are the intense heat and overpressures associated with the fireball and accompanying blast. But a nuclear explosion also generates intense outputs of energy in the form of x- and gamma-rays. If the latter are unleashed outside the Earth's atmosphere, some portion of them will interact with the upper atmosphere's air molecules. This in turn will generate an enormous pulsed current of high-energy electrons that will interact with the Earth's magnetic field. The result is the instantaneous creation of an invisible radio-frequency wave of uniquely great intensity—roughly a million-fold greater than that of the most powerful radio station.

The energy of this pulse would reach everything in line-of-sight of the explosion's center point at the speed of light. The higher the altitude of the weapon's detonation, the larger the affected terrestrial area would be. For example, at a height of 300 miles, the entire continental United States, some of its offshore areas and parts of Canada and Mexico would be affected. What is more, as the nuclear explosion's fireball expands in space, it would generate additional electrical currents in the Earth below and in extended electrical conductors, such as electricity transmission lines. If the electrical wiring of things like computers, microchips and power grids is exposed to these effects, they may be temporarily or permanently disabled.

Estimates of the combined direct and indirect effects of an EMP attack prompted the Commission to Assess the Threat to the United States from Electromagnetic Pulse Attack to state the following in its report to Congress[1]:

> The electromagnetic fields produced by weapons designed and deployed with the intent to produce EMP have a high likelihood of damaging electrical power systems, electronics, and information systems upon which American society depends. Their effects on dependent systems and infrastructures could be sufficient to qualify as catastrophic to the nation.

If it seems incredible that a single weapon could have such an extraordinarily destructive effect, consider the nature and repercussions of the three distinct components of an electromagnetic pulse: fast, medium and slow. The "fast component" is essentially an "electromagnetic shock-wave" that can temporarily or permanently disrupt the functioning of electronic devices. In twenty-first century America, such devices are virtually everywhere, including in controls, sensors, communications equipment, protective systems, computers, cell phones, cars and airplanes. The extent of the damage induced by this component of EMP, which occurs virtually simultaneously over a very large area, is determined by the altitude of the explosion.

The "medium-speed component" of EMP covers roughly the same geographic area as the "fast" one, although the peak power level of its electrical shock would be far lower. Since it follows the "fast component" by a small fraction of a second, however, the medium-speed component has the potential to do extensive damage to systems whose protective and control features have been impaired or destroyed by the first onslaught.

If the first two EMP components were not bad enough, there is a third one—a "slow component" resulting from the expansion of the explosion's fireball in the Earth's magnetic field. It is this "slow component"—a pulse that lasts tens of seconds to minutes—which creates disruptive currents in electricity transmission lines, resulting in damage to electrical supply and distribution systems connected to such lines. Just as the second component compounds the destructive impact of the first, the fact that the third follows on the first two ensures significantly greater damage to power grids and related infrastructure.

The EMP Threat Commission estimates that, all other things being equal, it may take "months to years" to bring such systems fully back online. Here is how it depicts the horrifying ripple effect of the sustained loss of electricity on contemporary American society:

Depending on the specific characteristics of the attacks, unprecedented cascading failures of our major infrastructures could result. In that event, a regional or national recovery would be long and difficult and would seriously degrade the safety and overall viability of our nation. The primary avenues for catastrophic damage to the nation are through our electric power infrastructure and thence into our telecommunications, energy, and other infrastructures. These, in turn, can seriously impact other important aspects of our nation's life, including the financial system; means of getting food, water, and medical care to the citizenry; trade; and production of goods and services.

The recovery of any one of the key national infrastructures is dependent on the recovery of others. The longer the outage, the more problematic and uncertain the recovery will be. It is possible for the functional outages to become mutually reinforcing until at some point the degradation of infrastructure could have irreversible effects on the country's ability to support its population.

The EMP Threat Today

The destructive power of electromagnetic pulses has been recognized by the United States national security community for some time. The EMP Threat Commission noted that

EMP effects from nuclear bursts are not new threats to our nation. . . . Historically, [however,] this application of nuclear weaponry was mixed with a much larger population of nuclear devices that were the primary source of destruction, and thus EMP as a weapons effect was not the primary focus.

As long as the Cold War threat arose principally from the prospect of tens, hundreds or even thousands of nuclear weapons detonating on American soil, such attention as was given to protecting against EMP effects was confined to shielding critical components of our strategic forces. The military's conventional forces were generally not systematically "hardened" against such effects. And little, if any, effort was made even to assess—let alone to mitigate—the vulnerabilities of our civilian infrastructure. As the theory went, as long as our nuclear

deterrent worked, there was no need to worry about everything else. If, on the other hand, deterrence failed, the disruptions caused by EMP would be pretty far down the list of things about which we would have to worry.

Unfortunately, today's strategic environment has changed dramatically from that of the Cold War, when only the Soviet Union and Communist China could realistically threaten an EMP attack on the United States. In particular, as the EMP Threat Commission put it:

The emerging threat environment, characterized by a wide spectrum of actors that include near-peers, established nuclear powers, rogue nations, sub-national groups, and terrorist organizations that either now have access to nuclear weapons and ballistic missiles or may have such access over the next 15 years, have combined to raise the risk of EMP attack and adverse consequences on the U.S. to a level that is not acceptable.

Worse yet, the Commission observed that "some potential sources of EMP threats are difficult to deter." This is particularly true of "terrorist groups that have no state identity, have only one or a few weapons, and are motivated to attack the U.S. without regard for their own safety." The same might be said of rogue states, such as North Korea and Iran. They "may also be developing the capability to pose an EMP threat to the United States, and may also be unpredictable and difficult to deter." Indeed, professionals associated with the former Soviet nuclear weapons complex are said to have told the Commission that some of their ex-colleagues who worked on advanced nuclear weaponry programs for the USSR are now working in North Korea.

Even more troubling, the Iranian military has reportedly tested its Shahab-3 medium-range ballistic missile in a manner consistent with an EMP attack scenario. The launches are said to have taken place from aboard a ship—an approach that would enable even short-range missiles to be employed in a strike against "the Great Satan." Ship-launched ballistic missiles have another advantage: The "return address" of the attacker may not be confidently fixed, especially if the missile is a generic Scud-type weapon available in many arsenals around the world. As just one example, in December 2002, North Korea got away with delivering twelve such missiles to Osama bin Laden's native Yemen. And Al Qaeda is estimated to have a score or more of sea-going vessels, any of which could readily be fitted with a Scud launcher and could try to steam undetected within range of our shores.

The EMP Threat Commission found that even nations with whom the United States is supposed to have friendly relations, China and Russia, are said to have considered limited nuclear attack options that, unlike their Cold War plans, employ EMP as the primary or sole means of attack. Indeed, as recently as May 1999, during the NATO bombing of the former Yugoslavia, high-ranking members of the Russian Duma, meeting with a U.S. congressional delegation to discuss the Balkans conflict, raised the specter of a Russian EMP attack that would paralyze the United States.

America the Vulnerable

What makes the growing EMP attack capabilities of hostile (and potentially hostile) nations a particular problem for America is that, in the words of the EMP Threat Commission, "the U.S. has developed more than most other nations as a modern society heavily dependent on electronics, telecommunications, energy, information networks, and a rich set of financial and transportation systems that leverage modern technology." Given our acute national dependence on such technologies, it is astonishing—and alarming—to realize that:

- Very little redundancy has been built into America's critical infrastructure. There is, for example, no parallel "national security power grid" built to enjoy greater resiliency than the civilian grid.
- America's critical infrastructure has scarcely any capacity to spare in the event of disruption—even in one part of the country (recall the electrical blackout that crippled the northeastern U.S. for just a few days in 2003), let alone nationwide.
- America is generally ill-prepared to reconstitute damaged or destroyed electrical and electricity-dependent systems upon which we rely so heavily.

These conditions are not entirely surprising. America in peacetime has not traditionally given thought to military preparedness, given our highly efficient economy and its ability to respond quickly when a threat or attack arises. But EMP threatens to strip our economy of that ability, by rendering the infrastructure on which it relies impotent.

In short, the attributes that make us a military and economic superpower without peer are also our potential Achilles' heel. In today's world, wracked by terrorists and their state sponsors, it must be asked: Might not the opportunity to exploit the essence of America's strength—the managed flow of electrons and all they make possible—in order to undo that strength prove irresistible to our foes? This line of thinking seems especially likely among our Islamofascist enemies, who disdain such man-made sources of power and the sorts of democratic, humane and secular societies which they help make possible. These enemies believe it to be their God-given responsibility to wage jihad against Western societies in general and the United States in particular.

Calculations that might lead some to contemplate an EMP attack on the United States can only be further encouraged by the fact that our ability to retaliate could be severely degraded by such a strike. In all likelihood, so would our ability to assess against whom to retaliate. Even if forward-deployed U.S. forces were unaffected by the devastation wrought on the homeland by such an attack, many of the systems that transmit their orders and the industrial base necessary to sustain their operations would almost certainly be seriously disrupted.

The impact on the American military's offensive operations would be even further diminished should units based outside the continental United States also be subjected to EMP. Particularly with the end of the Cold War, the Pentagon has been reluctant to pay the costs associated with shielding much of its equipment from electromagnetic pulses. Even if it had been more willing to do so, the end of underground nuclear testing in 1992 denied our armed forces their most reliable means of assessing and correcting the EMP vulnerabilities of weapon systems, sensors, telecommunications gear and satellites.

The military should also be concerned that although the sorts of shielding it has done in the past may be sufficient to protect against the EMP effects of traditional nuclear weapons designs, weapons optimized for such effects may well be able to defeat those measures. Without a robust program for assessing and testing advanced designs, we are unlikely to be able to quantify such threats—let alone protect our military hardware and capabilities against them.

What Is to Be Done?

If the EMP Threat Commission is correct about the phenomenon of electromagnetic pulse attacks, the capabilities of our enemies to engage in these attacks and the effects of such attacks on our national security, cosmopolitan society and democratic way of life, we have no choice but to take urgent action to mitigate this danger. To do so, we must immediately engage in three focused efforts:

First, *we must do everything possible to deter EMP attacks against the United States.* The EMP Threat Commission described a comprehensive approach:

> We must make it difficult and dangerous to acquire the materials to make a nuclear weapon and the means to deliver them. We must hold at risk of capture or destruction anyone who has such weaponry, wherever they are in the world. Those who engage in or support these activities must be made to understand that they do so at the risk of everything they value. Those who harbor or help those who conspire to create these weapons must suffer serious consequences as well.

To be effective, these measures will require vastly improved intelligence, the capacity to perform clandestine operations the world over, and the assured means of retaliating with devastating effect. The latter, in turn, will require not only forces capable of carrying out such retaliation in the aftermath of an EMP attack, but also the certain ability to command and control those forces. It may also require the communication, at least through private if not public channels, of the targets that will be subjected to retaliation—irrespective of whether a definitive determination can be made of culpability.

Second, *we must protect to the best of our ability our critical military capabilities and civilian infrastructure from the effects of EMP attacks.* This will require a comprehensive assessment of our vulnerabilities and proof of the effectiveness of corrective measures. Both of these may require, among other things, periodic underground nuclear testing.

The EMP Threat Commission judged that, given the sorry state of EMP-preparedness on the part of the tactical forces of the United States and its coalition partners, "It is not possible to protect [all of them] from EMP in a regional conflict." But it recommended that priority be given to protecting "satellite navigation systems, satellite and airborne intelligence and targeting systems [and] an adequate communications infrastructure."

Particularly noteworthy was the Commission's recommendation that America build a ballistic missile defense system. Given that a catastrophic EMP attack can be mounted only by putting a nuclear weapon into space over the United States and that, as a practical matter, this can only be done via a ballistic missile, it is imperative that the United States deploy as quickly as possible a comprehensive defense against such delivery systems. In particular, every effort should be made to give the Navy's existing fleet of some 65 AEGIS air defense ships the capability to shoot down short- to medium-range missiles of the kind that might well be used to carry out ship-launched EMP strikes.

Third, *an aggressive and sustained effort must be made to plan and otherwise prepare for the consequences of an EMP attack in the event all else fails.* This will require close collaboration between government at all levels and the private sector, which owns, designs, builds, and operates most of the nation's critical infrastructure. Among other things, we will need to do a far better job of monitoring that infrastructure and remediating events that could ensue if EMP attacks are made on it. We must also ensure that we have on hand, and properly protected, the equipment and parts—especially those that are difficult or time-consuming to produce—needed to repair EMP-damaged systems. The EMP Threat Commission identified the latter as including "large turbines, generators, and high-voltage transformers in electrical power systems, and electronic switching systems in telecommunications systems."

Conclusion

We have been warned. The members of the EMP Threat Commission—who are among the nation's most eminent experts with respect to nuclear weapons designs and effects—have rendered a real and timely public service. In the aftermath of their report and in the face of the dire warnings they have issued, there is no excuse for our continued inaction. Yet this report and these warnings continue to receive inadequate attention from the executive branch, Congress and the media. If Americans remain ignorant of the EMP danger and the need for urgent and sustained effort to address it, the United States will continue to remain woefully unprepared for one of the most serious dangers we have ever faced. And by remaining unprepared for such an attack, we will invite it.

The good news is that steps can be taken to mitigate this danger—and perhaps to prevent an EMP attack altogether. The bad news is that there will be significant costs associated with those steps, in terms of controversial policy changes and considerable expenditures. We have no choice but to bear such costs, however. The price of continued inaction could be a disaster of infinitely greater cost and unimaginable hardship for our generation and generations of Americans to come.

FRANK J. GAFFNEY, JR., the founder and president of the Center for Security Policy, holds an M.A. from the Johns Hopkins University School of Advanced International Studies and a B.S. from the Georgetown University School of Foreign Service. He acted in the Reagan administration as assistant secretary of defense for international security policy, following four years of service as deputy assistant secretary of defense for nuclear forces and arms control policy. Prior to that he was a professional staff member on the Senate Foreign Relations Committee chaired by the late Senator John Tower (R-Texas) and an aide to the late Senator Henry M. "Scoop" Jackson (D-Washington). He is a columnist for the *Washington Times, Jewish World Review* and *TownHall.com,* a contributing editor to *National Review Online* and a featured weekly contributor to Hugh Hewitt's nationally syndicated radio program. He has written for the *Wall Street Journal, USA Today,* the *New Republic,* the *Washington Post,* the *New York Times,* the *Christian Science Monitor,* the *Los Angeles Times* and *Newsday.* Mr. Gaffney resides in Washington, D.C.

Update on the State of the Future

JEROME C. GLENN AND THEODORE J. GORDON

Is the future getting better or worse? According to the latest edition of State of the Future, global prospects for improving the overall health, wealth, and sustainability of humanity are improving, but slowly.

The picture painted by the report gives much cause for hope. The world has grown to 6.5 billion people, 1 billion of whom are connected by the Internet, and the annual economy is approaching $60 trillion. However, there is also much cause for concern. The great paradox of our age is that, while more and more people enjoy the benefits of technological and economic growth, increasing numbers of people are poor, unhealthy, and lack access to education. In the years ahead, globalization will present humanity with both challenges and opportunities as increased connectivity highlights our strengths and our shortcomings as a global community.

A race is under way between the increasing proliferation of threats and our growing ability to improve humanity's condition. Understanding the nature of this race entails looking at the contradictory forces at work in our world. Here is a brief assessment of those forces, along with possible strategies for positive resolution.

World Trade: Engine of Opportunity and Disparity

Explosive economic growth over the previous decades has led to dramatic increases in life expectancy, literacy, and access to safe drinking water and sanitation, as well as to decreases in infant mortality for the vast majority of the world. At the same time, the ratio of the total income of people in the top 5% to those in the bottom 5% has grown from 6 to 1 in 1980 to more than 200 to 1 now. That ratio is not sustainable.

Unfortunately, economic disparities could grow unless a global partnership emerges between the rich and the poor, using the strength of free markets with rules based on global ethics. That, in turn, could trigger increased migration of the poor to rich areas and result in a range of complex conflicts and humanitarian disasters.

With their high technology and low wages, China and India will become giants of world trade. This should force the developing world to rethink its trade-led economic growth strategies. China alone could produce 25% of all manufactured goods in the world by 2025.

Environmental Sustainability

The Millennium Ecosystem Assessment found that 60% of our life-support systems are gone or in danger of collapse. A collaboration of 1,360 experts from 95 countries produced a global inventory of the state of the Earth's ecosystems. According to their assessment, degradation could grow worse by 2050 as another 2.6 billion people are added to the Earth. Current absorption capacity of carbon by oceans and forests is about 3 to 3.5 billion tons per year. Yet, 7 billion tons are added to the atmosphere annually, which could increase to 14 billion tons per year if current trends continue—eventually leading to greenhouse effects beyond the ability of humans to control. Events like the 2004 Asian tsunami and the Millennium Ecosystem Assessment's pronouncement are helping the world to realize that environmental security deserves greater attention.

At the same time, economic growth (often achieved at the expense of environmental security) is also sorely needed. A measure of the degree to which developing nations need growth can be seen in the increase in development aid from wealthier nations to economically struggling ones over recent years. Official development assistance to cash-strapped nations increased to $78.6 billion in 2004, the highest level ever.

Until Africa shifts from being primarily an exporter of raw materials to a more scientifically oriented culture, it has no chance of closing its economic gap with the developed world.

Organizations like the World Bank and the United Nations Development Program (UNDP) have long relied on economic development indicators, but integrated sustainable development indicators (to measure world progress toward sustainability) are recent inventions. Our ability to measure sustainable economic development has improved. As part of the multilateral Environment and Security Initiative, international organizations such as UNDP and NATO have begun to offer expertise and resources to promote environmental security in addition to economic security.

The Central European Node of the Millennium Project has created a Sustainable Development Index composed of seven major subject areas, 14 indicators (two for each major area), and 64 variables (various numbers of variables for individual indicators). This index was calculated for 179 countries to express their state of development and progress toward sustainable development. It allows a mapping of sustainable development as well as comparison among different countries.

The countries rated as most sustainable were Sweden, Finland, and Switzerland, while those rated as least sustainable were Afghanistan, Somalia, and Burundi. Other sustainable development indicators include the Environmental Sustainability Index, the Dashboard of Sustainability, the Ecological Footprint Calculator, the Living Planet Index, and the Well-Being Index.

The concepts of environmental diplomacy and human security are gaining recognition in both military and diplomatic circles. Our research showed a noticeable increase in the number of articles, formal studies, and conferences related to environmental security during the past year. The environment is becoming recognized as being on a par with cultural and ethnic issues in security analysis. Advances in satellites, sensors, and the Internet are making it possible to monitor environmental situations more effectively.

Development Goals: Moving Ahead or Lagging Behind?

It seems that the UN Millennium Development Goal of cutting poverty in half between 2000 and 2015 may well be met on a global basis—but not in Africa and some parts of Asia. The dynamics of urbanization have facilitated many important improvements to the human condition. In other words, urbanization, once thought a problem, is now seen as part of the solution to poverty, ignorance, disease, and malnutrition.

Hunger and water scarcity will worsen unless more serious and intelligent investments are made. Water supply has to be increased, not simply redistributed. Despite improved access to safe drinking water and better sanitation during the last decade, 1.1 billion people still do not have access to safe drinking water and 2.6 billion people—half the population in developing countries—lack adequate sanitation.

Global Information Culture

Nearly 15% of the world is connected to the Internet, and the majority of the world's population may be connected within 15 years, making cyberspace an unprecedented medium for civilization. This new distribution of the means of production in the knowledge economy is cutting through old hierarchical controls in politics, economics, and finance. It is becoming a self-organizing mechanism that could lead to dramatic increases in humanity's ability to invent its future. Millions share ideas and feelings with strangers around the world, increasing global understanding. Google and other search engines have made the world's knowledge available to previously isolated populations. This will provide a more even playing field for the future knowledge economy.

The advent of the "24-7 always on" globalized world of ubiquitous computing implies that we will be making many more decisions per day and constantly changing our own and others' schedules and priorities. Information overload will make it increasingly difficult to separate the noise from the signal of what is important to know in order to make good decisions.

Civilization is also becoming increasingly vulnerable to cyberterrorism, power outages, information pollution (misinformation, pornography, junk e-mail, and media violence), and virus attacks.

As the integration of cell phones, video, and the Internet grows, prices for this technology will fall. This will accelerate globalization and allow swarms of people to quickly form and disband, coordinate actions, and share information ranging from stock market tips to bold new contagious ideas (meme epidemics).

In a sad and ironic twist, despite the expansion of communications technology and, as a result, the power of individuals to speak freely, in 2004 only 17% of the world's people lived in countries that enjoyed a free press.

Medicine Is Becoming Cheaper as Some Illnesses Spread

Many of the world's most devastating illnesses will become less expensive to treat. However, increasing threats from new and reemerging diseases and from drug-resistant microorganisms have attracted the concern of the World Health Organization. Malaria, tuberculosis, and AIDS were expected to kill more than 6 million people in 2005. There were 4.9 million new HIV/AIDS cases in 2004, while more than 3.1 million people died of AIDS—200,000 more than the previous year. The current spread of HIV in eastern Europe and Asia implies that the number of AIDS patients in these areas may eventually dwarf the AIDS population in Africa. As human encroachment on the natural environment continues, increased interspecies contacts could lead to the spread to humans of infectious diseases known previously only in wild animals.

Peace and Security

The United Nations has defined terrorism as "actions already proscribed by existing conventions; any action constitutes terrorism if it is intended to cause death or serious bodily harm to civilians or noncombatants with the purpose of intimidating a population or compelling a government or an international organization to do or abstain from doing any act." This agreement should lead to greater international cooperation.

While prospects for security in places like Kashmir have improved, the horrors in Sudan, the Congo, Iraq, and Israeli-Palestinian areas continue, as do nuclear uncertainties with Iran and North Korea. The world has yet to agree about when it is right to use force to intervene in the affairs of a country that is significantly endangering its own or other peoples. Conventional military force has little effect in combating the asymmetrical and intrastate warfare as the boundaries between war, civil unrest, terrorism, and crime become increasingly blurred. Although Yasser Arafat's death has restarted the Middle East peace process, internal Islamist political reforms have been evolving quietly for the past several years that could lead either to new negotiations or negotiation setbacks as ideological hard-liners insert themselves into the negotiation process.

Because weapons of mass destruction may be available to individuals over the next generation, the welfare of anyone should be the concern of everyone. Such platitudes are not new, but the consequences of their failure will be quite different in the future when one person can be massively destructive.

Technology Is Accelerating, Along with Demand for Energy

Most people still do not appreciate how fast science and technology will change over the next 25 years and would be surprised to learn about recent breakthroughs. For example, several years ago light was stopped by a yttrium-silica crystal and then released; it has also been slowed in gas and then accelerated. Adult stem cells have been regressed to embryo-like flexibility to grow replacement tissue. In experiments, humans with small computer chips implanted in their brains have been able to perform limited computer functions via thought. To help the world cope with the acceleration of change, it may be necessary to create an international science and technology organization to arrange the world's science and technology knowledge as well as to examine the potential consequences of various technological breakthroughs.

The factors that caused the acceleration of science and technology innovation are themselves accelerating, hence, the acceleration of scientific and technological accomplishments over the past 25 years will appear slow compared with the rate of change in the next 25. Since technology is growing so rapidly along several fronts, the possibility of it growing beyond human control must now be taken seriously.

In contrast, running this technology will require energy. World energy demand is forecast to increase by 60% from 2002 to 2030 and to require about $568 billion in new investments every year to meet that demand. Oil production is declining among the majority of producers. Meanwhile, in 2003 the Texas Transportation Institute found that U.S. traffic jams alone wasted 2.3 billion gallons of gasoline, adding greenhouse gases and hastening the day when the oil wells run dry.

Technology has the power to resolve this issue if governments and people develop the will to use it toward that end. The time has come for an Apollolike program to increase the world's supply of nonpolluting energy.

Nanotechnology: Growing Possibility and Peril

Nanotechnology will provide an extraordinary range of benefits for humanity, but as with any advance, it is wise to forecast problems in order to avoid them. Little is known about the environmental and health risks of manufactured nanomaterials. For example, artificial blood cells (respirocytes) that dramatically enhance human performance could cause overheating of the body and bio-breakdowns. Disposal of highly efficient batteries that use nanomaterials could affect ecosystem and human health.

Since the military is a major force in nanotechnology research and development, it can play a key role in understanding and managing nanotechnology risks. As a result, the Millennium Project put together an expert Delphi panel to identify and rate important forms of nanotechnology-related environmental pollution, to look at health hazards that could result from any military and/or terrorist activities, and to suggest military research that might reduce these problems.

Other Key Issue Areas

Military expenditures in 2005 were expected to reach $1 trillion. At the same time, annual income for organized crime has passed $2 trillion. It is time for an international campaign to develop a global consensus for action against transnational organized crime, which is increasingly interfering with governments' ability to act. Weapons of mass destruction are still stockpiled and form a threat that has yet to be addressed realistically.

The global population is expanding, retracting and aging. The world population has grown by 4 billion people since 1950 and may grow another 2.6 billion by 2050 before it begins to fall. According to the UN's lower forecasts (which have proven to be more accurate), world population could fall to 5.5 billion by 2100—an astonishing 1 billion fewer people than are alive today. This assumes that there will be no major life extension breakthroughs by then. In any case, civilization will have to adapt to a world in which older people form the majority.

The world is slowly beginning to realize that improving the political and economic status of women is one of the most cost-effective ways to address various global challenges. Despite this, women, on average, are still paid 18% less than are men. Male violence toward women results in more casualties than does war.

The Challenge for Tomorrow's Leaders and Managers

The combination of economic growth and technological innovation has made it possible for 3 to 4 billion people to have relatively good health and living conditions. However, unless our financial, economic, environmental, and social behavior are improved along with our industrial technologies, that could change very quickly.

Few leaders have been trained in the theory and practice of decision making, and few know how advanced decision-support software could help them. We know the world is increasingly complex and that the most serious challenges are global in nature, yet we are unpracticed at improving and deploying Internet-based management tools and concepts. Formalized training in ethics and decision making for policy makers could result in a significant improvement in the quality of global decisions.

The heartening news is that global ethical standards are emerging from a variety of sources, such as the International Organization for Standardization (ISO), corporate ethics indexes, interreligious dialogues, UN treaties, the Olympic Committee, the International Criminal Court, various NGOs, Internet blogs, and the international news media. Ethical decision making in a global context should be informed by an understanding of the key challenges facing our world, as well as of their interconnectedness. The establishment of the eight UN Millennium Development Goals was a giant step in this direction.

The next should be the creation of global transinstitutions for water, energy, AIDS, education, and so on. Current institutional structures are not getting the job done. In addition to the moral imperative and social benefits of addressing these goals and challenges, there is also great wealth to be made resolving these issues on behalf of grateful populations. However, making this a reality will require future-oriented politicians, which in turn will require a better educated public to elect more future-minded leaders globally.

Meeting the Future's Challenges

Although many people criticize globalization's potential cultural impacts, it is increasingly clear that cultural change is necessary to address global challenges. Simply put, the development of genuine democracy requires cultural change, as does preventing AIDS, promoting sustainable development, ending violence against women, ending ethnic violence, etc. The tools of globalization, such as the Internet and global trade, should be used to help cultures adapt in a way that preserves their unique contributions to humanity while improving the human condition. These tools can help policy makers, leaders, and educators who fight against hopeless despair, blind confidence, and ignorant indifference—attitudes that too often have blocked efforts to improve the prospects for humanity.

Future synergies among nanotechnology, biotechnology, information technology, and cognitive science could dramatically increase the availability of food, energy, and water.

Connecting people and information will increase collective intelligence and create value and efficiency while lowering costs. Yet a previous and troubling finding from the Millennium Project remains unresolved. It is increasingly clear that humanity has the resources to address global challenges, but how much wisdom, goodwill, and intelligence humanity will focus on these challenges is anyone's guess.

Just as it would be difficult for the human body to work if the neurons, muscles, bones, and so on were not properly connected, so, too, is it difficult for the world to work if people, ideas, resources, and challenges are not seen in a single context. The initial global infrastructure to manage globalization is being built through such mechanisms as the ISO, the World Trade Organization's rules of trade, and Internet protocols.

The moment-by-moment connectivity among ideas, people, resources, and challenges in order to create optimal solutions, however, is yet to be developed. A worldwide race to connect everything not yet connected is just beginning. Wise institutions and organizations will make great wealth by completing the links among systems by which civilizations function and flourish.

JEROME C. GLENN has been the executive director of the American Council for the United Nations University (AC/UNU) since 1988. E-mail: jglenn@igc.org.

THEODORE J. GORDON has served as a space scientist in the Apollo program. He is the founder of The Futures Group and was a co-founder of the Institute for the Future. E-mail: Tedjgordon@att.net.

Glenn and Gordon have been codirectors of the Millennium Project of the AC/UNU since 1996. This article draws from *2005 State of the Future* (AC/UNU, 2005) which is available from the Futurist Bookshelf, www.wfs.org/bkshelf.htm. The Millennium Project's address is The Millennium Project, American Council for the United Nations University, 4421 Garrison St., N.W., Washington, D.C. 20016. Fax 202-686-5170; Web site www.stateofthefuture.org.

Originally published in the Vol. 40, issue 21, January/February 2006, pp. 21–25 issue of *The Futurist*. Copyright © 2006 by World Future Society, 7910 Woodmont Avenue, Suite 450, Bethesda, MD 20814. Telephone: 301/656-8274; Fax: 301/951-0394; http://www.wfs.org. Used with permission from the World Future Society.

Does Globalization Help or Hurt the World's Poor?

The answer is: both. The real question is how to maximize the help and minimize the hurt.

PRANAB BARDHAN

Globalization and the attendant concerns about poverty and inequality have become a focus of discussion in a way that few other topics, except for international terrorism or global warming, have. Most people I know have a strong opinion on globalization, and all of them express an interest in the well-being of the world's poor. The financial press and influential international officials confidently assert that global free markets expand the horizons for the poor, whereas activist-protesters hold the opposite belief with equal intensity. Yet the strength of people's conviction is often in inverse proportion to the amount of robust factual evidence they have.

As is common in contentious public debates, different people mean different things by the same word. Some interpret "globalization" to mean the global reach of communications technology and capital movements, some think of the outsourcing by domestic companies in rich countries, and others see globalization as a byword for corporate capitalism or American cultural and economic hegemony. So it is best to be clear at the outset of this article that I shall primarily refer to economic globalization—the expansion of foreign trade and investment. How does this process affect the wages, incomes and access to resources for the poorest people in the world? This question is one of the most important in social science today.

For a quarter century after World War II, most developing countries in Africa, Asia and Latin America insulated their economies from the rest of the world. Since then, though, most have opened their markets. For instance, between 1980 and 2000, trade in goods and services expanded from 23 to 46 percent of gross domestic product (GDP) in China and from 19 to 30 percent in India. Such changes have caused many hardships for the poor in developing countries but have also created opportunities that some nations utilize and others do not, largely depending on their *domestic* political and economic institutions. (The same is true for low-wage workers in the U.S., although the effects of globalization on rich countries are beyond the scope of this article.) The net outcome is often quite complex and almost always context-dependent, belying the glib pronouncements for or against globalization made in the opposing camps. Understanding the complexities is essential to taking effective action.

Neither Plague nor Panacea

The case for free trade rests on the age-old principle of comparative advantage, the idea that countries are better off when they export the things they are best at producing, and import the rest. Most mainstream economists accept the principle, but even they have serious differences of opinion on the balance of potential benefits and actual costs from trade and on the importance of social protection for the poor. Free traders believe that the rising tide of international specialization and investment lifts all boats. Others point out that many poor people lack the capacity to adjust, retool and relocate with changing market conditions. These scholars argue that the benefits of specialization materialize in the long run, over which people and resources are assumed to be fully mobile, whereas the adjustments can cause pain in the short run.

The debate among economists is a paragon of civility compared with the one taking place in the streets. Antiglobalizers' central claim is that globalization is making the rich richer and the poor poorer; proglobalizers assert that it actually helps the poor. But if one looks at the factual evidence, the matter is rather more complicated. On the basis of household survey data collected by different agencies, the World Bank estimates the fraction of the population in developing countries that falls below the $1-a-day poverty line (at 1993 prices)—an admittedly crude but internationally comparable level. By this measure, extreme poverty is declining in the aggregate.

The trend is particularly pronounced in East, South and Southeast Asia. Poverty has declined sharply in China, India and Indonesia—countries that have long been characterized by massive rural poverty and that together account for about half the total population of developing countries. Between 1981 and 2001 the percentage of rural people living on less than $1 a day decreased from 79 to 27 percent in China, 63 to 42 percent in India, and 55 to 11 percent in Indonesia.

But although the poorest are not, on the whole, getting poorer, no one has yet convincingly demonstrated that improvements in their condition are mainly the result of globalization. In China the poverty trend could instead be attributed to internal factors such as the expansion of infrastructure, the massive 1978 land reforms (in which the Mao-era communes were disbanded), changes in grain procurement prices, and the relaxation of restrictions on rural-to-urban migration. In fact, a substantial part of the decline in poverty had already happened by the mid-1980s, before the big strides in foreign trade or investment. Of the more than 400 million Chinese lifted above the international poverty line between 1981 and 2001, three fourths got there by 1987.

The sharp DECLINE IN EXTREME POVERTY in China may have more to do with the 1978 land reforms and other internal factors than with foreign trade or investment.

Similarly, rural poverty reduction in India may be attributable to the spread of the Green Revolution in agriculture, government antipoverty programs and social movements—not the trade liberalization of the 1990s. In Indonesia the Green Revolution, macroeconomic policies, stabilization of rice prices and massive investment in rural infrastructure played a substantial role in the large reduction of rural poverty. Of course, globalization, by expanding employment in labor-intensive manufacturing, has helped to pull many Chinese and Indonesians out of poverty since the mid-1980s (though not yet as much in India, for various domestic institutional and policy reasons). But it is only one factor among many accounting for the economic advances of the past 25 years.

Overview/Globalization and Poverty

- The expansion of international trade and investment is one of the dominant trends of our time, but policymakers and advocates tend to discuss it without carefully examining the evidence available in social science.
- Because the modern era of globalization has coincided with a sustained reduction in the proportion of people living in extreme poverty, one may conclude that globalization, on the whole, is not making the poor poorer. Equally, however, it cannot take much credit for the decrease in poverty, which in many cases preceded trade liberalization.
- Countries that get the economic basics right—improving infrastructure, ensuring political stability, carrying out land reform, providing social safety nets, addressing market failures such as impeded access to credit—tend to succeed at reducing poverty. Although globalization can help, it is only one factor among many.

Those who are dubious of the benefits of globalization point out that poverty has remained stubbornly high in sub-Saharan Africa. Between 1981 and 2001 the fraction of Africans living below the international poverty line increased from 42 to 47 percent. But this deterioration appears to have less to do with globalization than with unstable or failed political regimes. If anything, such instability reduced their extent of globalization, as it scared off many foreign investors and traders. Volatile politics amplifies longer-term factors such as geographic isolation, disease, overdependence on a small number of export products, and the slow spread of the Green Revolution. [See "Can Extreme Poverty Be Eliminaed?" by Jeffrey D. Sachs; SCIENTIFIC AMERICAN, September 2005].

Sweatshops

Global market competition in general rewards people with initiative, skills, information and entrepreneurship in all countries. Poor people everywhere are handicapped by their lack of access to capital and opportunities to learn new skills. Workers in some developing countries—say, Mexico—are losing their jobs in labor-intensive manufacturing to their counterparts in Asia. At the same time, foreign investment has also brought new jobs. Overall, the effect appears to be a net improvement. In Mexico, low-wage poverty is declining in the regions that are more involved in the international economy than others—even controlling for the fact that skilled and enterprising people migrate to those regions, improving incomes there independently of what globalization accomplishes. A recent study by Gordon H. Hanson of the University of California, San Diego, which took into account only people born in a particular region (thus leaving out migrants), found that during the 1990s average incomes in the Mexican states most affected by globalization increased 10 percent more than those least affected.

In poor Asian economies, such as Bangladesh, Vietnam and Cambodia, large numbers of women now have work in garment export factories. Their wages are low by world standards but much higher than they would earn in alternative occupations. Advocates who worry about exploitative sweatshops have to appreciate the relative improvement in these women's conditions and status. An Oxfam report in 2002 quoted Rahana Chaudhuri, a 23-year-old mother working in the garment industry in Bangladesh:

> This job is hard—and we are not treated fairly. The managers do not respect us women. But life is much harder for those working outside. Back in my village, I would have less money. Outside of the factories, people selling things in the street or carrying bricks on building sites earn less than we do. There are few other options. Of course, I want better conditions. But for me this job means that my children will have enough to eat and that their lives can improve.

In 2001 Naila Kabeer of the University of Sussex in England and Simeen Mahmud of the Bangladesh Institute of Development Studies did a survey of 1,322 women workers in Dhaka. They discovered that the average monthly income of workers in garment-export factories was 86 percent above that of other wage workers living in the same slum neighborhoods.

Another indication of this relative improvement can be gauged by what happens when such opportunities disappear. In 1993, anticipating a U.S. ban on imports of products made using child labor, the garment industry in Bangladesh dismissed an estimated 50,000 children. UNICEF and local aid groups investigated what happened to them. About 10,000 children went back to school, but the rest ended up in much inferior occupations, including stone breaking and child prostitution. That does not excuse the appalling working conditions in the sweatshops, let alone the cases of forced or unsafe labor, but advocates must recognize the severely limited existing opportunities for the poor and the possible unintended consequences of "fair trade" policies.

The Local Roots of Poverty

Integration into the international economy brings not only opportunities but also problems. Even when new jobs are better than the old ones, the transition can be wrenching. Most poor countries provide very little effective social protection to help people who have lost their jobs and not yet found new ones. Moreover, vast numbers of the poor work on their own small farms or for household enterprises. The major constraints they usually face are domestic, such as lack of access to credit, poor infrastructure, venal government officials and insecure land rights. Weak states, unaccountable regimes, lopsided wealth distribution, and inept or corrupt politicians and bureaucrats often combine to block out the opportunities for the poor. Opening markets without relieving these domestic constraints forces people to compete with one hand tied behind their back. The result can be deepened poverty.

Conversely, opening the economy to trade and long-term capital flows need not make the poor worse off if appropriate domestic policies and institutions are in place—particularly to help shift production to more marketable goods and help workers enter new jobs.

Contrasting case studies of countries make this quite apparent. Although the island economies of Mauritius and Jamaica had similar per capita incomes in the early 1980s, their economic performance since then has diverged dramatically, with the former having better participatory institutions and rule of law and the latter mired in crime and violence. South Korea and the Philippines had similar per capita incomes in the early 1960s, but the Philippines languished in terms of political and economic institutions (especially because power and wealth were concentrated in a few hands), so it remains a developing country, while South Korea has joined the ranks of the developed. Botswana and Angola are two diamond-exporting countries in southern Africa, the former democratic and fast-growing, the latter ravaged by civil war and plunder.

The experiences of these and other countries demonstrate that antipoverty programs need not be blocked by the forces of globalization. There is no "race to the bottom" in which countries must abandon social programs to keep up economically; in fact, social and economic goals can be mutually supportive. Land reform, expansion of credit and services for small producers, retraining and income support for displaced workers, public-works programs for the unemployed, and provision of basic education and health can enhance the productivity of workers and farmers and thereby contribute to a country's global competitiveness. Such programs may require a rethinking of budget priorities in those nations and a more accountable political and administrative framework, but the obstacles are largely domestic. Conversely, closing the economy to international trade does not reduce the power of the relevant vested interests: landlords, politicians and bureaucrats, and the rich who enjoy government subsidies. Thus, globalization is not the main cause of developing countries' problems, contrary to the claim of critics of globalization—just as globalization is often not the main solution to these problems, contrary to the claim of overenthusiastic free traders.

What about the environment? Many conservationists argue that international integration encourages the overexploitation of fragile natural resources, such as forests and fisheries, damaging the livelihoods of the poor. A common charge against transnational companies is that they flock to poor countries with lax environmental standards. Anecdotes abound, but researchers have done very few statistical studies. One of the few, published in 2003 by Gunnar Eskeland of the World Bank and Ann Harrison of the University of California, Berkeley, considered Mexico, Morocco, Venezuela and Ivory Coast. It found very little evidence that companies chose to invest in these countries to shirk pollution-abatement costs in rich countries; the single most important factor in determining the amount of investment was the size of the local market. Within a given industry, foreign plants tended to pollute less than their local peers.

Wages and conditions in GARMENT FACTORIES are poor by world standards but better than those in alternative occupations such as domestic service or street prostitution.

Like persistent poverty, lax environmental standards are ultimately a domestic policy or institutional failure. A lack of well-defined or well-enforced property rights or regulation of common property resources often leads to their overuse. Responding to pressure from powerful political lobbies, governments have deliberately kept down the prices of precious environmental resources: irrigation water in India, energy in Russia, timber concessions in Indonesia and the Philippines.

The result, unsurprisingly, is resource depletion. To be sure, if a country opens its markets without dealing with these distortions, it can worsen the environmental problems.

When Talk Gives Way to Action

Fortunately, the two sides of the globalization debate are—slowly—developing some measure of agreement. In many areas, advocates in both camps see the potential for coordination among transnational companies, multilateral organizations, developing country governments and local aid groups on programs to help the poor. Going beyond the contentious debates and building on the areas of emerging consensus and cooperation, international partnerships may be able to make a dent in the poverty that continues to oppress the lives of billions of people in the world. Here are some measures under discussion.

Capital controls. The flow of international investment consists both of long-term capital (such as equipment) and of speculative short-term capital (such as shares, bonds and currency). The latter, shifted at the click of a mouse, can stampede around the globe in herdlike movements, causing massive damage to fragile economies. The Asian financial crisis of 1997 was an example. Following speculators' run on the Thai currency, the baht, the poverty rate in rural Thailand jumped 50 percent in just one year. In Indonesia, a mass withdrawal of short-term capital caused real wages in manufacturing to drop 44 percent. Many economists (including those who otherwise support free trade) now see a need for some form of control over short-term capital flows, particularly if domestic financial institutions and banking standards are weak. It is widely believed that China, India and Malaysia escaped the brunt of the Asian financial crisis because of their stringent controls on capital flight. Economists still disagree, though, on what form such control should take and what effect it has on the cost of capital.

Globalization does not explain the differing fates of Botswana and Angola, both diamond exporters, one democratic, the other RAVAGED BY CIVIL WAR.

Reduced protectionism. The major hurdle many poor countries face is not too much globalization but too little. It is hard for the poor of the world to climb out of poverty when rich countries (as well as the poor ones themselves) restrict imports and subsidize their own farmers and manufacturers. The annual loss to developing countries as a group from agricultural tariffs and subsidies in rich countries is estimated to be $45 billion; their annual loss from trade barriers on textile and clothing is estimated to be $24 billion. The toll exceeds rich countries' foreign aid to poor countries. Of course, the loss is not equally distributed among poor countries. Some would benefit more than others if these import restrictions and subsidies were lifted.

Trust-busting. Small exporters in poor nations often lack the marketing networks and brand names to make inroads into rich-country markets. Although transnational retail companies can help them, the margins and fees they charge are often very high. Restrictive business practices by these international middlemen are difficult to prove, but a great deal of circumstantial evidence exists. The international coffee market, for example, is dominated by four companies. In the early 1990s the coffee earnings of exporting countries were about $12 billion, and retail sales were $30 billion. By 2002 retail sales had more than doubled, yet coffee-producing countries received about half their earnings of a decade earlier. The problem is not global markets but impeded access to those markets or depressed prices received by producers, as a result of the near-monopoly power enjoyed by a few retail firms. In certain industries, companies may actively collude to fix prices. Some economists have proposed an international antitrust investigation agency. Even if such an agency did not have much enforcement power, it could mobilize public opinion and strengthen the hands of antitrust agencies in developing countries. In addition, internationally approved quality-certification programs can help poor-country products gain acceptance in global markets.

Social programs. Many economists argue that for trade to make a country better off, the government of that country may have to redistribute wealth and income to some extent, so that the winners from the policy of opening the economy share their gains with the losers. Of course, the phrase "to some extent" still leaves room for plenty of disagreement. Nevertheless, certain programs stir fairly little controversy, such as assistance programs to help workers cope with job losses and get retrained and redeployed. Scholarships allowing poor parents to send their children to school have proved to be more effective at reducing child labor than banning imports of products.

Research. The Green Revolution played a major role in reducing poverty in Asia. New international private-public partnerships could help develop other products suitable for the poor (such as medicines, vaccines and crops). Under the current international patent regime, global pharmaceutical companies do not have much incentive to do costly research on diseases such as malaria and tuberculosis that kill millions of people in poor countries every year. But research collaborations are emerging among donor agencies, the World Health Organization, groups such as Doctors Without Borders and private foundations such as the Bill & Melinda Gates Foundation.

Immigration reform in rich countries. A program to permit larger numbers of unskilled workers into rich countries as "guest workers" would do more to reduce world poverty than other forms of international integration, such as trade liberalization, can. The current climate, however, is not very hospitable to this idea.

Simplistic antiglobalization slogans or sermons on the unqualified benefits of free trade do not serve the cause of alleviating world poverty. An appreciation of the complexity of the issues and an active interweaving of domestic and international policies would be decidedly more fruitful.

Pranab Bardhan is an economics professor at the University of California, Berkeley. He has done theoretical research and field studies on rural institution in poor countries, on the political economy of development policies, and on international trade. He is perhaps best known for showing that economic efficiency and social justice are not antithetical goals; indeed, they are often complementary. Bardhan was editor in chief of the *Journal of Development Economics* from 1985 to 2003 and is currently co-chair of a MacArthur Foundation—funded international research network on inequality and economic performance.

Understanding Our Moment in History

Living Between Two Ages

VAN WISHARD

My work is trend analysis. My particular focus is looking at the dimension of global change taking place, and attempting to place that in some context of understanding.

It's clear something immense is happening. It's not just Iraq, or even terrorism. For some time now, it's been obvious the tectonic plates of life are shifting. We seem to be passing through one of those rare historic moments when a civilization progresses from a familiar worldview, to a new and broader outlook. That's what my book, Between Two Ages, is about, and what I'll discuss this morning.

How do we to make sense of how the global landscape is changing? Nukes in N. Korea. Jihad vs. MacWorld. Warnings of a nuclear incident in the U.S. within a decade. The merger of human and artificial intelligence creating what the scientists call the "post-human" era. We seem to have come to the end of the world, as we've known it. The next three decades increasingly loom as the most decisive 30-year period in history.

To consider how the global context is changing, I start by offering the comments of two people from the 1950s. Rollo May was one of America's foremost psychologists. In 1952, only seven years after the greatest military victory in history, May wrote, "The chief problem of people in the middle decade of the 20th century is emptiness." In May's view, "Our middle of the twentieth century is more anxiety-ridden than any period since the breakdown of the Middle Ages." Then he concluded, "We live at one of those points in history when one way of living is in its death throes, and another is being born."

A decade later I found myself in Palm Springs discussing the future of America with president Eisenhower. I had just returned from South America, and Ike was interested in knowing about certain developments there. After talking about South America, the conversation turned to the U.S. At one point Ike stood up, strode across the room, and decried with all the force of an Old Testament prophet, "We're living through the final stages of the Roman empire." He said it twice with all the conviction he could summon.

What both Rollo May and Eisenhower were suggesting is that the fundamentals of life that have anchored nations for centuries are shifting and forming some new configuration. We're living between two ages.

With these thoughts in mind, I want to be more specific, and briefly offer two trends that are helping shape the next two decades. After that, I'll focus more tightly on three more trends.

First, due to accelerating technology development, so much is happening so fast in every part of the world, leaders no longer have any familiar frame of reference within which to understand contemporary events. Life has become a passing blur. Yesterday's crisis has not been resolved, but we can't think about it any more because we've got to confront today's crisis. It's an ad hoc world. One result is that political leaders lack any larger order of purpose and significance, any pattern of meaning that could give collective human existence coherence and lasting relevance. Another result is there is no global center of stability and order such as Britain provided during the nineteenth century, and America supplied the second half of the twentieth century. And so the international climate is likely to continue to be characterized by instability and intermittent conflict.

Second, the information environment in which the individual lives has been radically altered. Throughout history, the transmission of information, ideas and images took place slowly, taking weeks, even months, to move around the world. Such a slow pace of information travel gave people time to adjust psychologically to a new information environment. Today, we zap information, ideas and images across the globe in nanoseconds. People have no time to adjust, no time to assimilate the new information and shape it into any coherent meaning. Taken together, the information technologies are eroding the primacy of place, which, ultimately, may be one of the greatest changes the human race has ever experienced.

These are only two of the trends shaping the coming decades. It's going to be a period of mounting complexity, dislocation and uncertainty. At the same time we shall realize creative possibilities beyond anything we've yet experienced.

Now, let's focus in more tightly on three other trends.

Globalization. We all have some idea of what globalization means. Most of the discussion about globalization focuses on trade, currency relationships, and the need for nations to adopt free markets and democratic political systems.

But globalization is far more than integration of economics and finance. The essence of globalization is the individual's expanding awareness of other peoples, cultures and religions as a result of technological advances in communications and travel. With the expansion of awareness has also come a broadening out of personal identity. For example, surveys show that in Europe, most of the people between the ages of 18 and 30 find their identity more in relationship to the concept of "Europe" than to the country in which they live. Across the globe, as people become more familiar with other modes of thought and belief, with other cultures and religions, their allegiance to earlier aspects of identity begins changing. Even evolving into an identity with, larger cultural and political expressions.

This process of a widening identity is not new to Americans. Before 1776, Americans didn't find their identity in relationship to the United States (there was no United States), but in relationship to the state in which they lived—Virginia, Massachusetts or Georgia. After the establishment of the United States, people slowly found their identity in a wider context. This widening process took time. Indeed, the historian Daniel Borstin tells us it wasn't until nearly ninety years later, at the end of the civil war, that a distinctly American identity had emerged.

The seeds of this process of expanding global awareness were planted in the 15th and 16th centuries with European exploration and colonialization of Africa, South America and Asia. It picked up speed in the 1840s with the invention of the telegraph, the first component of what has become the world's electronic information communication system. Clearly, in the 20th century globalization moved at an exponential pace. In its present phase, it means that western social, cultural and philosophical ideas are gradually seeping into the fabric of the rest of the world, and a reciprocal transfer of culture and lifestyles from non-western nations to the west.

Look what's happening. Nations are adopting such ideas as the sanctity of the individual, due process of law, universal education, the equality of women, human rights, private property, legal safeguards governing business and finance, concepts of civil society, and perhaps most importantly, the ability of people to take charge of their destiny and not simply accept the hand dealt them in life.

We take these ideas for granted. But for millions of people such concepts are completely new modes of thought and behavior. We must keep this in mind as we try to implant democracy in the Middle East. While we Americans believe what works for America will work for others, we're sometimes unaware that the cultural differences between the U.S. and the rest of the world represent significant psychological differences. Take some contrasts between America and Asia. America prizes individuality; Asia emphasizes relationships and community. Americans see humans dominating nature; Asians see humans as part of nature. In the U.S. there is a division between mind and heart; in Asia mind and heart are unified.

I mention this to illustrate the deep psychological trauma nations are experiencing as they confront the effects of globalization. We Americans, raised on the instinct of change, say, "Great. Let tradition go. Embrace the new." But much of the world says, "Wait a minute. Traditions are our connection to the past. If we jettison them, we'll endanger our social cohesion and psychic stability." Many thoughtful Muslims clearly fear that

the western model of globalization, based on secular, scientific rationalism and materialism, will eventually bring about the end of Islam.

When Muslims look to Europe and America, they see the de-Christianization that has taken place—over the past two centuries in Europe, and during the 20th century in America. They see the social, moral and psychological problems that have accompanied modernization and secularization. And while we may say, as some do in Washington, that we must "change the psychology of the Middle East and bring them into the modern world," even moderate Muslims are concerned as to what will happen to Islam if they go this route.

One aspect of globalization is the onslaught of the largest migration in world history. In China alone, there are one hundred million people—more than the population of either France or Germany—on the move from the countryside to the cities. This is causing urban problems of a magnitude never before experienced.

Another aspect of globalization is that in the west, migration is changing the face of Europe. The European Union needs 180 million immigrants in the next three decades simply to keep its population at 1995 levels, as well as to keep the current ratio of retirees to workers. In Brussels, over fifty percent of the babies born are Muslim. In Germany, the death rate has exceeded the birth rate for so long, that they now have to fly in plane loads of technicians from India just to maintain their high tech structure. In England, there are now more practicing Muslims than Anglicans. In Italy, the archbishop of Bologna recently warned that Italy is in danger of "losing its identity" due to the immigration from North Africa and central Europe. The Catholic Church is facing the distinct probability of Islam eventually becoming the largest European religion.

As migration increases in Europe, the historic legends that are the basis of national identities tend to wane. As one British historian put it, "A white majority that invented the national mythologies underpinning modern European culture lives in an almost perpetual state of fear that it and its way of life are about to disappear." This fear is the subtext for everything else happening in Europe today. It's far more traumatic than adjusting to increased economic integration or to the euro.

In the coming years, the face of nations will be very different from today. Traditional images of what it means to be French, German, Italian or English are going to change just as radically as the image of what it means to be American has changed in recent decades.

At the end of the day, for globalization to succeed, if we're going to build a global age, it's got to be built on more than free markets and the Internet. It's got to be built on some common view of life far more inclusive than "my nation," "my race" or "my religion". The challenge in the next decades is to see the world whole, as one entity, and to act in accord with that awareness. To be legitimate, globalization must validate itself in terms of equitable benefits for all nations, and sensitivity to other nations' need for social and political stability.

The second trend shaping the coming decades is a new stage of technology development that is without precedent in the history of science and technology. Science is in the process of redefining our understanding of terms first given us at the dawn of human consciousness: such terms as "nature," "human," and "life." Increasingly, scientists are subordinating humans to technology.

At least since Francis Bacon in the seventeenth century we have viewed the purpose of science and technology as being to improve the human condition. As Bacon put it, the "true and lawful end of the sciences is that human life be enriched by new discoveries and powers."

Indeed it has. Take America. During the last century, the real GDP, in constant dollars, increased by $48 trillion, much of this wealth built on the marvels of technology. A few years ago, I had a quadruple heart by-pass performed with the most modern medical technology. So believe me, I'm a fan of what technology can do.

But along with technological wonders, uncertainties arise. The question today is whether we're creating certain technologies not to improve the human condition, but for purposes that appear to be to replace human meaning and significance altogether. Let me explain.

For at least the past fifty years, psychologists have known that overwhelming people with more technological change than they can process clearly leads to various forms of emotional and mental instability. But what we're confronted with now is not simply acceleration in the pace of change; it's the acceleration of acceleration itself. In other words, technological change is growing not at a constant rate, but an exponential rate.

It's estimated that the rate of technological change doubles every decade—20% one decade, 40% the next decade, 80% the third decade, and so on; that at today's rate of change, we'll experience one hundred calendar years of technological change in the next twenty-five years; and that due to the nature of exponential growth, the 21st century as a whole will experience nearly one thousand times more technological change than did the 20th century.

But it's not only the rate of change that challenges us; it's also the character of change. British Telecom's fixtures research unit predicts that eventually "a combination of man and computer search will be able to identify the genes needed to produce a people of any chosen characteristics." Someone, somewhere, they say, "will produce an elite race of people, smart, agile and disease resistant." Ray Kurzweil, one of the world's foremost authorities on artificial intelligence, predicts, "when machines are derived from human intelligence but are a million times more capable, there won't be a clear distinction between human and machine intelligence—"there's going to be a merger." Or consider a remark by the cofounder of MIT's artificial intelligence labs and one of the world's leading authorities on artificial intelligence: "Suppose the robot had all the virtues of people and was smarter and understood things better. Then why would we want to prefer those grubby, old people? I don't see anything wrong with human life being devalued if we have something better." One of the world's leading scientists ready to "devalue human life" if we can create something he thinks is better. Thus arrives what some scientific intellectuals call the "post-human" or "post-species" age. For the tech visionaries, it's the next step in evolution.

If this sounds like science fiction, it's not. It's what some of America's most accomplished scientists are working to achieve, and it raises the question: is the speed of technology development exceeding humanity's moral and mental capacities to control it?

We seem to have dismissed the counsel of the scientific father of our age. Said Einstein in a speech at cal tech, "Concern for man himself and his fate must form the chief interest of all technical endeavors." If he were alive today, Einstein might feel we've created a secularized scientific culture that is an immense complex of technique and specialization without any guiding moral framework. It's a body without a soul. The highest standard is efficiency. The guiding ethic is, "if it can be done, it will be done."

Will all these technological visions come to pass? One wonders. Project forward the predicted million-fold increase in the speed of computers and the resulting ratcheting up of the pace of life over the next couple of decades, and one ends up asking, "How much more of this can human beings take?" As it is, multiplying social pathologies already indicate human resistance to such change. While stress is still a major issue, the deeper issue we now face is individual psychological integrity. Thirty years ago, major corporations didn't have to think much about the mental health of their employees. Now, mental and emotional health is the fastest growing component of health insurance for many companies. To help relieve the mounting pressures, some companies provide employees with special rooms for relaxing, meditation, prayer, taking naps or simply listening to music.

Other indicators tell of further psychic disturbances caused by too rapid a pace of change. Loneliness has reached epidemic proportions. ADD—attention deficit disorder—is skyrocketing for adults. The suicide rate among women has increased 200% in the past two decades. Books are now written for eight year-old children advising them how to recognize the symptoms of stress, and how to deal with it in their own lives. Character controlling drugs are now given to three year-olds. Thus the University of Louisville concludes in a study on health that our very mode of life has now become our principle cause of emotional and mental instability.

Some people are already searching for the wisest way to approach such potential challenges as the new technologies present. Bill Joy was cofounder and former chief scientist of Sun Microsystems, and he was described by the Economist magazine as "the Edison of the Internet." He suggests that we've reached the point where we must "limit development of technologies that are too dangerous, by limiting our pursuit of certain kinds of knowledge." His concerns are based on the unknown potential of genetics, nanotechnology and robotics, driven by computers capable of infinite speeds, and the possible uncontrollable self-replication of these technologies. Joy acknowledges the pursuit of knowledge as one of the primary human goals since earliest times. But, he says, "if open access to, and unlimited development of, knowledge henceforth puts us all in clear danger of extinction, then common sense demands that we reexamine even these basic, long-held beliefs." Joy well knows he's pushing against the wind, but he clearly thinks it's worth it.

But there's another question.

Ultimately, technology deals with extension of human capability. It does not address the question of the meaning and purpose of human society. Thus, in my view, the great need in the coming two decades is not so much for more mind-blowing technology, as it is to explore the depths of the human personality; to discover what deeper meaning can be given to human existence as we enter a radically changed environment of technological possibility.

To consider the third trend, I want to quote Adlai Stevenson, who had the unfortunate luck of twice being the democratic presidential candidate chosen to oppose Dwight Eisenhower. In a speech at Columbia university, Stevenson asked, "Are America's problems but surface symptoms of something even deeper, of a moral and human crisis in the western world which might even be compared to the fourth, fifth and sixth-century crisis where the Roman empire was transformed into feudalism and primitive Christianity? Are Americans," Stevenson queried, "passing through one of the great crises of history when man must make another mighty choice?"

A decade later, Joseph Campbell, perhaps the world's foremost authority on the symbolic and psychological meaning of myths, noted in a New York speech, "The world is passing through perhaps the greatest spiritual metamorphosis in the history of the human race."

Stevenson and Campbell—two of the most thoughtful Americans of the mid-20th century—comparing the condition of America and the western world to that of Rome during the end of the ancient world and the emergence of Christianity and feudal Europe. They were not alone in their concern. During the 20th century, such voices as Thomas Hardy, W.B. Yeats, Oswald Spengler, Arnold Toynbee, C.G. Jung, Rollo May, Peter Drucker, to name just a few, raised the same possibility in one way or another.

I want to explore the ramifications of their remarks a bit, for this issue has become a dominant driving force not only in America's spiritual life, but also in our culture, our politics, and international affairs.

What actually happened when the Greco-Roman world was transformed into early Christianity? The history books tell a certain amount—the corruption of Rome, the severe decline in population, the neglect and even collapse of the Roman aqueducts, roads and farms.

Those were the outer manifestations, but what happened to the inner life of the people? We get some sense from the Roman poet Lucretius who summed up the temper of the times when he wrote of "aching hearts in every home, racked incessantly by pangs the mind was powerless to assuage." Throughout Greece and Rome the cry "Great pan is dead" was heard. There was a loss of collective meaning; a disappearance of what had represented life's highest value. The God-image that had informed the inner life and culture of the Greco-Roman world for a thousand years lost its compelling force, especially for the leadership class. This led to a breakdown of the historic psychic structures that had been the source and container of Greco-Roman morals and beliefs. A collapse of the ethical and social guidelines underlying civilized order took place.

The history books speak of the "decline" of Rome. But at its heart, it was a long-term—at least four or five centuries—psychological shift of the prevailing God-image of the Greco-Roman period, to a new spiritual dispensation. A new God-image—the Christian expression—emerged for a new phase of psychological maturity and human experience. From Ireland to Italy, Europe went through a prolonged period of the transformation of underlying principles and symbols.

What Stevenson, Campbell and others have suggested is that America and the West have been experiencing a similar long-term spiritual and psychological reorientation. What they are suggesting is that America and Europe have come to the close of the Christian era, and the beginning of some fresh spiritual expression.

When we speak of the close of the Christian eon, what we're suggesting is that, while there will always be millions of Christians in America, the spiritual impulse that gave highest value and meaning to Western civilization is no longer the inner dynamic of the collective western psyche. It's no longer the informing force in the soul of America and Europe's "creative minority" who give us our literature, theater, science, technology, education, cinema and music. In this sense, the character of our postmodern culture is the best indication of what is bubbling up from the depths of the Western soul. For culture is to a nation what dreams are to an individual—an indication of what's going on in the depths of the inner life.

Thus America is in the midst of the greatest spiritual change and search in our history. To get an idea of this search, walk into any bookstore and look at the section on religion. As well as books on Christianity, you'll see books on New Age spirituality. Buddhism, Nostradamus, yoga, channeling, angels, miracles, Eastern philosophy, addiction, psychic health, mysticism, or finding meaning in life. All evidence of a massive search.

Let me summarize what we've been discussing. (1) Globalization—possibly the most far-reaching collective development in history; (2) A new stage of technology, one result of which would be to supplant human significance and meaning; (3) A long-term spiritual and psychological orientation, a change in worldview. These are only three of the basic trends moving us between two historic epochs.

The question remains, how do we respond to such a historic moment? In my view, we must respond on at least two levels. First is the level of our collective life, and here we're already undertaking the most sweeping redefinition of life in our history. All our institutions are being redefined and restructured. Corporations are redefining their mission, structure and modus operandi. In education, countless new experiments are underway, from vouchers to charter schools to home schooling. The legal system is assisted by the increasing use of alternative dispute resolution (ADR). Functions formerly executed by local governments are now undertaken by civic and charitable organizations. Numerous steps have been taken to redress the severe environmental imbalance we've created. It's estimated that well over fifty percent of all adult Americans donate a portion of their time to non-profit social efforts. Perhaps most importantly, we're gradually integrating a global perspective into the fabric of our education and culture. Take West Point, for example.

All the cadets at West Point learn a foreign language such as Chinese, Arabic or Russian, and they take a year's course in a foreign culture. So on one level, we're already at grips with some of the manifestations of the reorientation that engulfs us.

Against the background of the three trends I mentioned, perhaps this is a modest start, but at least it's a start. Clearly, there's another level of effort to move to. As Bill Joy suggests, such efforts must include a decision whether or not to continue research and development of technologies that could, in Joy's words, "bring the world to the edge of extinction." Obviously, such an examination must be done with global cooperation if it's to be valid.

But there's another question of how we respond. The psychological and spiritual change taking place in America and the world is not taking place out in the ether somewhere. It's taking place in all of us—in the depths of our collective soul, whether we're aware of it or not. So I suggest that understanding how these changes affect us both collectively and individually is essential.

Each person has to find his or her own way. There's no "one size fits all." But I'd like to offer four points that have helped me.

First, limit your information intake to what you absolutely need to know. We're all swamped by more information than we can process and integrate. There's much that is interesting and entertaining, but not essential. Cut back. The more information a person is exposed to, the more difficult context and meaning become. We live in two worlds—the world of abstract data and the world of human meaning. Meaning requires reflection and time-consuming thought.

Second, study the human-technology relationship. Technology is not passive. It actively changes us in ways we usually are totally unaware of. Too many of us are controlled by technology rather than our controlling technology. For a deeper understanding of the human-technical relationship, I suggest considering the whole discipline of Media Ecology. In recent years, Media Ecology has grown into a wide-ranging consideration how rapid change and technology affect both our social arrangements and us as individuals. "Google" Media Ecology and you'll gain indispensable insights. I especially recommend the books of Neil Postman.

Third, find some way to be part of building the future. Whether it's mentoring young people, or volunteering for some civic need, or contributing some way in preserving the environment, find a way to be actively engaged in building the future.

Fourth, deepen your inner life in whatever way is natural for you. Some may go to a church or synagogue. Others may want to reconnect with Nature in walks in the mountains or on the beach. Or listen to the great music and read some of the great literature and poetry of the past. The other day I was reading the 19th century poet John Greenleaf Whittier, and came across these lines that speak to the deepening of the inner life:

Drop Thy still dews of quietness till all our strivings cease. Take from our souls the strain and stress, and let our ordered lives confess the beauty of Thy peace.

For me, that experience is universal, and stands at the heart of eternal truth.

To sum up, as we look towards the coming decades, we cannot escape the fact that some great phase of the human experience is dying, while some new stage seeks to take shape. We daily watch and experience the trauma of this historic shift in world events, in our institutions, in our mounting emotional health issues, and in the ethos of destruction that has become such a cultural motif. At the deepest level, what we're experiencing is a sign of the collective soul passing through the throes of a reorientation, a death and rebirth. We shouldn't be surprised, as it's happened before in history. And now the whole world is experiencing such a critical moment. It's a process of some new hope, some new context of life coming to birth. Like all births it's painful.

We're living between two ages. There's a new epoch of broader and deeper meaning struggling to take shape for all humankind. Some Transcendent, infinite power is at work in each of us, as well as across the world. This power is the source of renewal of all man's most vital and creative energies. With all our problems and possibilities, the future depends on how we—each in his or her own unique way—lap into the eternal renewing dynamic that dwells in the deepest reaches of the human soul

These, I suggest, are some of the broader currents that we'll contend with over the next two decades.

Sometimes when I give a talk such as this, I'm asked what I expect people to do with such information. My response is simply: reflect, understand, assimilate and apply.

Thank you.

Address by **VAN WISHARD**, WorldTrends Research

Index

Index

Test Your Knowledge Form

We encourage you to photocopy and use this page as a tool to assess how the articles in *Annual Editions* expand on the information in your textbook. By reflecting on the articles you will gain enhanced text information. You can also access this useful form on a product's book support Web site at *http://www.mhcls.com/online/*.

NAME: DATE:

_____

TITLE AND NUMBER OF ARTICLE:

_____

BRIEFLY STATE THE MAIN IDEA OF THIS ARTICLE:

_____

LIST THREE IMPORTANT FACTS THAT THE AUTHOR USES TO SUPPORT THE MAIN IDEA:

_____

WHAT INFORMATION OR IDEAS DISCUSSED IN THIS ARTICLE ARE ALSO DISCUSSED IN YOUR TEXTBOOK OR OTHER READINGS THAT YOU HAVE DONE? LIST THE TEXTBOOK CHAPTERS AND PAGE NUMBERS:

_____

LIST ANY EXAMPLES OF BIAS OR FAULTY REASONING THAT YOU FOUND IN THE ARTICLE:

_____

LIST ANY NEW TERMS/CONCEPTS THAT WERE DISCUSSED IN THE ARTICLE, AND WRITE A SHORT DEFINITION: